Award for Endeavour
Level 2 Diploma in Countryside
Presented to Connor Doherty
June 2018.

C000199488

THE ONLY GUIDE TO SHOW BRITISH
BIRDS AT THEIR ACTUAL SIZE

COLLINS
LIFE-SIZE
BIRDS

WILLIAM
COLLINS

William Collins
An imprint of HarperCollins Publishers

1 London Bridge Street
London SE1 9GF

WilliamCollinsBooks.com

First published in 2016

Text © Rob Read and Paul Sterry 2016
Photographs © 2016 Paul Sterry and Rob Read/Nature Photographers Ltd except
where stated in the photo credits (p.448).

21 20 19 18 17
10 9 8 7 6 5 4 3 2

The authors assert their moral rights to be identified as the authors of this work.
All rights reserved. No parts of this publication may be reproduced, stored in a
retrieval system or transmitted, in any form or by any means, electronic, mechanical,
photocopying, recording or otherwise, without the prior permission of the publishers.

A catalogue record for this book is available from the British Library.

ISBN 978-0-00-818111-6

William Collins uses papers that are natural, renewable and recyclable products made
from wood grown in sustainable forests. The manufacturing processes conform to the
environmental regulations of the country of origin.

Edited and designed by D & N Publishing, Baydon, Wiltshire
Printed in China by RRD Asia Printing Solutions

Acknowledgements

The authors would like to thank the following people
who have helped with photography and the creation of
this book: Myles Archibald; Dominic Berridge of Wexford
Wildfowl Reserve; Sheldon Carey; Steve Castle; Andrew
Cleave; Mark and Susi Groves of Island Sea Safaris; Karl
Hughes; Chris Keep of Bentley Wildfowl Collection;
Chrissie Kelley of Pensthorpe Natural Park; Shane
O'Dwyer; David Price-Goodfellow of D & N Publishing;
and Graham Vick.

Contents

Introduction   4

What makes birds special?   4

Daily life   7

The aim and scope of this book   8

Bird topography and glossary   9

Species descriptions   12

Index   445

Photo credits and useful resources   448

Introduction

In Britain and northwest Europe, birds are the most diverse and numerous vertebrates (animals with backbones). You would be hard pushed to spend a day outdoors anywhere without seeing at least 20 species, and more than 250 species are seasonally or locally common in the region. By and large, most are colourful or well-marked and many are easy to see. Little wonder then that birdwatching is the most popular branch of natural history, and it lends itself to enthusiasts at all levels of knowledge and experience. For many it is simply enough to enjoy and cherish whatever they come across, while for others it becomes a thrilling and all-consuming passion.

For decades, bird photography has been used to capture and create images of these photogenic subjects. Recent advances in technology mean that digital imaging has come of age and, as a result, contemporary photographs of birds can reveal as much detail as can be seen with the naked eye and the bird in the hand. This has allowed the creation of a book that depicts birds in intricate detail at life-size, as well as larger than life in the case of many smaller species.

A flight feather has a rigid shaft and a zip-like arrangement that locks the barbs together.

Body feathers vary, but this one has downy, insulating properties towards its base while the outer barbs contribute to the contour of the bird.

What makes birds special?

Apart from bats, birds are the only vertebrates capable of flight. The ancestors of modern birds took to the air some 150 million years ago and since that time the ability to fly has allowed them to occupy almost every terrestrial habitat on earth, and many aquatic ones too.

For birds, flight would not be possible without feathers, but these lightweight, tough and resilient structures are also vital for thermal insulation. In addition, contours, shapes, patterns and colours confer species and gender identity on their owners, and camouflage is also

The feathers of waterbirds such as this Black Guillemot have water-repellent properties and provide extra thermal insulation.

Because feathers are so important, birds such as this immature Herring Gull spend a lot of time preening, to keep them clean and their structure intact.

A Song Thrush's nest is a beautifully woven cup of grasses, lined with a smooth coating of mud.

important for many species. Unsurprisingly, there are different feathers on a bird's body that fulfil a range of functions, those associated with flight being structurally different from those that insulate.

In common with their reptilian ancestors, birds lay eggs inside which their young develop. Eggs are laid in a nest, which varies from a rudimentary scrape in the ground to an intricately woven basket depending on the species. The eggs themselves are protected by a hard, chalky outer casing and the developing chick gains its nutrition from the egg's yolk.

Newly hatched birds are vulnerable, and not surprisingly chick mortality is high. The degree to which newly hatched birds can fend for themselves, and the effort invested by their parents in looking after them, varies considerably. With songbirds, and many other bird families too, adults brood and feed their young (which are essentially defenceless at first) until at

A Coal Tit's egg is small and rather rounded.

A Lapwing's egg is medium-sized and is pointed at one end.

A Grey Partridge chick can stand on its own two feet, literally and figuratively, a few minutes after hatching.

least the point where they fledge, and often for several weeks after they have left the nest. On the other hand, young gamebirds are active almost from the moment they hatch and leave the nest straight away, though they still depend on their parents to a degree for shelter and protection, and to be guided to good areas for feeding.

Although Buzzards are partial to the flesh of Rabbits, they will also eat the humble earthworm.

A Greenshank's long legs and bill provide clues to its diet and method of feeding.

Daily life

Not only are there birds in all terrestrial habitats in northwest Europe, but almost all sources of food are exploited by one species or another. Some birds are purely vegetarian, feeding perhaps on seeds, fruits or shoots, while many more include invertebrates – particularly insects – in their diet during the summer months. A few are strict predators, taking prey that includes other birds.

Although some birds lead rather solitary lives except during the breeding season, many species are gregarious and either breed in colonies or spend the winter months in sizeable groups. Complex behaviour patterns allow individuals to rub along with one another.

Rooks spend most of their lives in the company of others of the same species, nesting communally and feeding in flocks. Members of a breeding pair will sometimes forage together and maintain the bond between them with touchingly gentle interactions.

The aim and scope of this book

COLLINS LIFE-SIZE BIRDS is a photographic celebration of the region's richly varied birdlife. It is unique among books on the subject because for every species entry at least one image shows the bird in question, or the head and bill in the case of large species, depicted life-size. The images are gloriously detailed and the text that complements the photographs has been written as much with the beginner in mind as the experienced birdwatcher.

The photographs used throughout the book have been chosen carefully not only to show important identification features but also to depict a bird's typical posture, be that perched, standing, swimming or in flight. As many plumage variations as possible have been included. Annotations highlight key identification features that are discussed in the text.

For each species the main text contains descriptions of plumage and structural features that are useful for identification, plus further information about habits and behaviour. In addition a factfile section covers key details for each species: common name; scientific name; length (an average, measured from bill tip to the end of the tail; wingspan (an average, measured from wingtip to wingtip); habitat (or habitats, if these differ seasonally); food; status; and voice.

Layout of a typical species entry in *Collins Life-size Birds*.

Each species is introduced by its most commonly used English name followed by its scientific name. In the main these names are those recommended and used by the British Ornithologists' Union.

The main text for each species provides detailed information on appearance and plumage for all relevant ages and sexes. In addition, behavioural habits and background information are described where it helps the reader gain an insight into the bird in question.

The *Factfile* section provides an easy reference to important information about each species: Length; Wingspan; Habitat; Food; Status; and Voice.

The maps depict geographical ranges, a species' seasonal occurrence being represented by different colours:
indicates a species' presence year-round;
indicates a species' presence during spring and summer;
indicates a species' presence from late autumn and throughout winter;
indicates a species' presence on migration.
Note that the intensity of colour provides a very rough indication of the relative abundance of a given species; the colour intensities shown here are used when a species is common.

Where appropriate, images show birds in flight in addition to standing or perched individuals.

Captions provide additional information about the species in question, as depicted in particular photographs.

In addition to adult birds, a range of different ages and seasonal- and sex-related plumages are shown.

Where appropriate, a range of geographically distinct plumages are shown, including subspecies if relevant.

For each species, at least one image is reproduced at life-size.

Bird topography and glossary

Ornithologists give precise names to distinct parts of a bird's body, both to the bare parts (legs and bill, for example) and areas of feathering (wing coverts, primaries and the like). These terms have been used throughout the book to ensure precision and to avoid ambiguity about what is being described or discussed. As a reader, an understanding of this terminology helps with interpretation of the descriptive text in the book. It is also helps when talking about bird identification with other birdwatchers, and is useful in the process of identification in the field. On the following pages, a glossary of terms helps with the learning process, and annotated photographs show the important anatomical and topographical features for a range of common bird species.

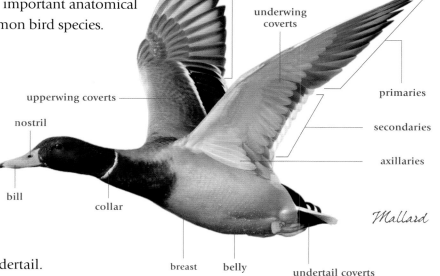

Adult A fully mature bird.
Axillaries The area of feathers that cover the 'armpit' of the bird; this is only visible on stretched wings or in flight.
Bill The beak.
Carpal The 'wrist' of a bird, formed at the bend of the wing.
Coverts Areas of contour feathers found on the upperwing, underwing, uppertail and undertail.
Culmen The upper ridge of the bill.
Eye-ring A ring of feathers, often colourful, that surrounds the eye.
First-winter A bird's plumage in its first winter after hatching.
Forewing The leading edge of the upperwing.
Immature A bird that is any age younger than an adult.
Juvenile A young bird with its first set of full feathers.
Lek A communal display.
Lores The area between the eye and the bill.
Malar A band or stripe of feathers on the side of the throat, in front of and below the submoustachial stripe.
Mandibles The two parts of a bird's bill: upper and lower.
Mantle Feathers covering the back.
Migrants Birds that have different geographically separate breeding grounds and winter quarters. Many birds of the region are breeding visitors, present here in spring and summer but wintering as far away as Africa. A few species use northwest Europe as their wintering grounds, and breed further north.

Moustachial stripe A stripe that runs from the bill to below the eye, fancifully resembling a moustache.

Nape The hind neck.

Orbital ring Ring of bare skin around the eye, often brightly coloured.

Pelagic Associated with or living in the open ocean.

Primaries The main flight feathers found on the outer half of the wing.

Primary projection The visible extent of the primary feathers beyond the tertials on the folded wing.

Scapulars A group of feathers that form the 'shoulder' of the bird between the back and folded wing.

Seabird A species that, outside the breeding season, spends its life at sea.

Redshank

Common Gull

Second-winter A bird's plumage in its second calendar winter after hatching.

Secondaries A group of relatively large flight feathers that form the inner part of the wing.

Species A taxonomic description relating to a population, members of which breed with one another but not with others. A species' scientific name is binomial, comprising the genus name first followed by the specific name; taken together the name is unique.

Speculum The coloured 'square' found on the inner wing of a duck.

Submoustachial stripe The contrasting line of feathers below the moustachial stripe.

Supercilium A stripe that runs above the eye.

Tarsus The obvious main section of a bird's leg, below the 'knee'.

Tertials The innermost flight feathers.

Third-winter A bird's plumage in its third calendar winter after hatching.

Tibia The area of the leg above the 'knee'.

Vent The area underneath the tail, covered by the undertail coverts.

Wingbar A bar or band on the wings, created by aligned pale feather tips, often those of the wing coverts.

Siskin

crown
lores
supercilium
ear coverts
nape
upper mandible
lower mandible
mantle
throat
breast
greater coverts (forming a wingbar)
belly
tertials
tarsus
feet
secondaries
upper tail coverts
primaries
tail

Common Gull

crown
eye
bill
nape
mantle
breast
tertials
belly
secondaries
primaries
feet
tarsus
undertail coverts

Mute Swan
Cygnus olor

An unmistakable large, elegant water bird with a characteristically long neck, commonly held in a graceful curve when standing or swimming. The sexes are similar but separable with care. Adults have uniformly clean white plumage, the head often tinged with an orange-buff colouration. The bill is bright orange-red with a large bulbous black knob at the base; males can often be distinguished from females by the brighter bill and larger basal knob. The legs are black and have large, powerful-looking webbed feet which are used to propel swimming birds in a seemingly effortless fashion. Juveniles have rather drab grey plumage and a dull-coloured bill that gradually give way to adult colouration.

juvenile
Juveniles, with grubby-looking plumage, are usually seen in the company of adult birds for much of the autumn and winter.

adult life-size
The bright orange-red bill is framed by black basal skin and a basal knob.

male
The S-shaped curve of the neck is typical of the species.

Mute Swans are extremely tolerant of human presence and are a common sight on a variety of waterways. Adults can be aggressive when encountered at the nest and with young, or at popular waterfowl feeding locations, issuing a threatening hiss if agitated. The species feeds primarily on aquatic plants which it grazes from the bottom by 'upending' and reaching with its long neck. It also consumes grit and gravel which aids digestion by grinding food material in the gizzard. Take-off requires great initial effort, with a long and laboured series of heavy wingbeats as the bird 'runs' across the water's surface before becoming airborne. The constant whooping noise made by the wings as it flies is often accompanied by a series of regular trumpeting honks. The nest is built on a mound of vegetation beside water.

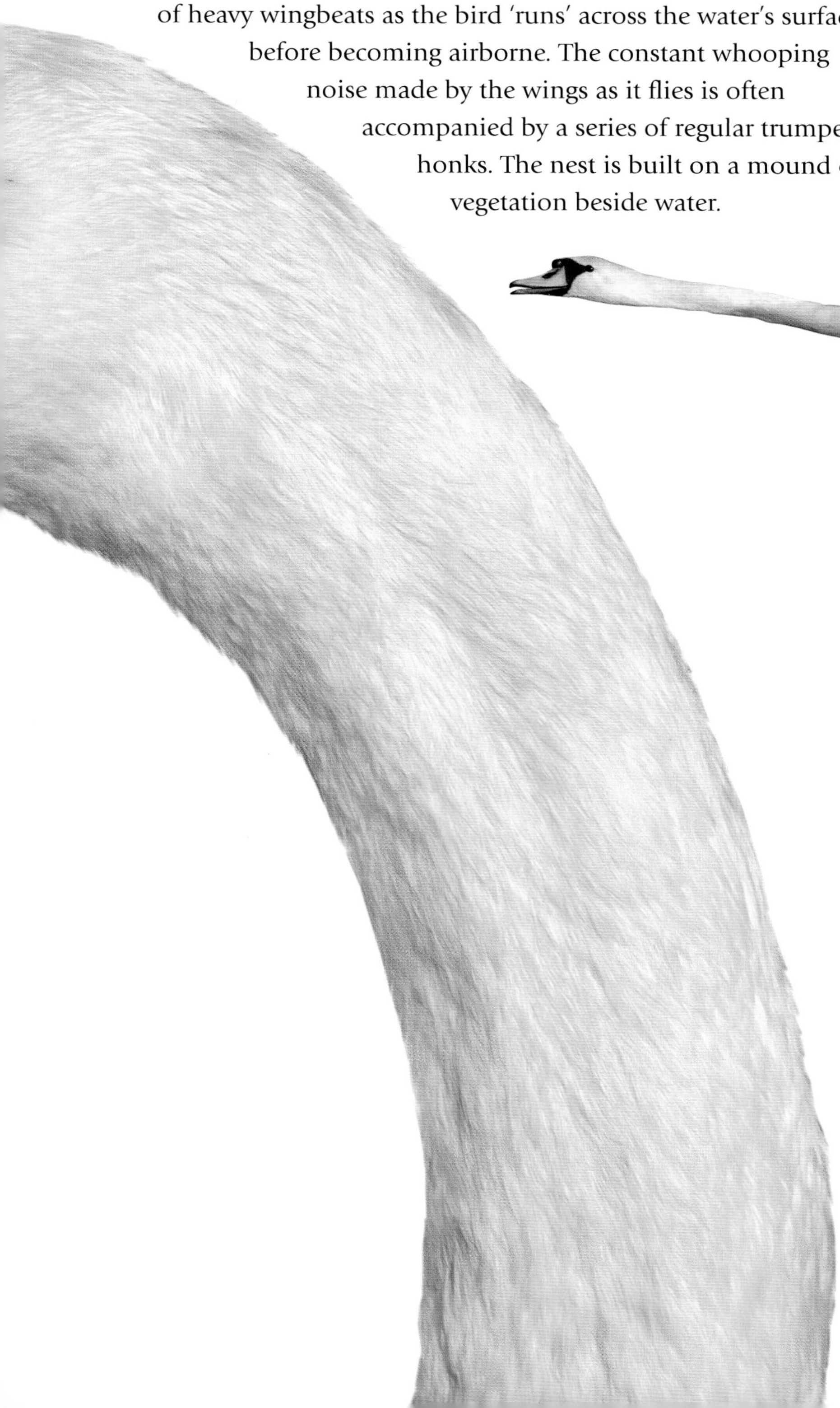

adult
In flight, the neck is held outstretched.

Factfile

LENGTH 150–160CM

WINGSPAN 200–240CM

HABITAT MAINLY FRESHWATER WETLANDS, ESTUARIES AND SHELTERED COASTAL AREAS.

FOOD AQUATIC AND WATERSIDE PLANTS AND GRASSES.

STATUS COMMON AND WIDESPREAD IN SUITABLE HABITATS, PARTICULARLY IN BRITAIN AND IRELAND; ABSENT FROM THE EXTREME NORTH. PRESENT YEAR-ROUND.

VOICE MAINLY SILENT BUT UTTERS OCCASIONAL GRUNTING NOISES AND SOMETIMES A TRUMPETING HONK IN FLIGHT.

Bewick's Swan
Cygnus columbianus

Factfile

LENGTH 115–125CM

WINGSPAN 170–210CM

HABITAT LOWLAND WETLANDS AND GRASSLAND, AND OCCASIONALLY ARABLE FARMLAND.

FOOD GRAZES ON A VARIETY OF GRASSES.

STATUS A VERY LOCAL WINTER VISITOR, PRESENT MAINLY OCTOBER TO MARCH. FAVOURS A SMALL NUMBER OF TRADITIONAL SITES, AND IT IS USUALLY SEEN IN LARGE FLOCKS.

VOICE UTTERS A VARIETY OF HONKING AND TRUMPETING CALLS.

Bewick's is similar in appearance to Whooper Swan but noticeably smaller, with a shorter neck and a different bill. The sexes are similar. The adult has predominantly pure white plumage with a long neck which is held in a slightly straighter posture than Mute Swan. The bill is shorter than that of the Whooper Swan, with a rounded (rather than triangular) yellow patch; this is proportionately smaller in area and rarely extends beyond the start of the nostrils (yellow extends past the nostrils in Whooper Swan). The stout legs and webbed feet are black. The juvenile has uniform drab buffish-grey plumage, and its dark-tipped bill is pink with a pale base.

This is the smallest swan encountered in the region. It is a migratory species that breeds in the Arctic tundra and a winter visitor that is encountered in sizeable flocks. The species is generally faithful to a number of traditional sites year on year, where it favours wet grassland and feeds by grazing on a variety of grasses. Family groups are easily distinguished (they stay together), and it is sometimes found with other swan species. Its flight appears more agile than that of other swans, with faster wingbeats and less laboured take-off and landing.

adult life-size

The yellow colouration on the bill is confined to an oval patch at the base; the precise pattern is unique to each individual. The white plumage sometimes becomes stained if the bird in question has been feeding in murky habitats.

adult

In flight and compared to a Whooper Swan, note the proportionately shorter neck and more compact appearance overall.

adult

In a feeding flock, a proportion of birds will always have their necks raised and be on the look-out for danger.

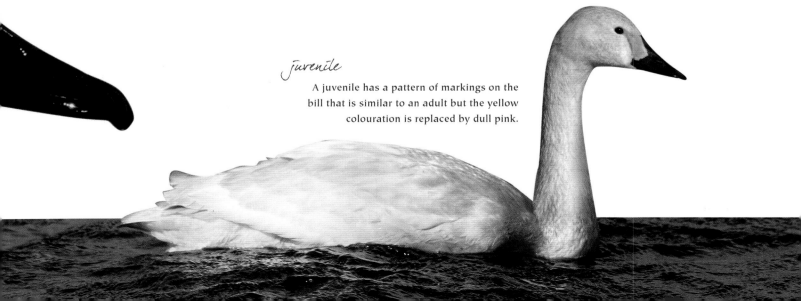

juvenile

A juvenile has a pattern of markings on the bill that is similar to an adult but the yellow colouration is replaced by dull pink.

Whooper Swan
Cygnus cygnus

This large swan is similar in size and general appearance to Mute Swan, but note the shorter tail and the long elegant neck, which is generally held in a straighter posture than that of its cousin. The sexes are similar. The adult has uniform pure white plumage. The bill is triangular and elongated, the colouration recalling that of Bewick's Swan, but the yellow commonly extends past the nostril. During the spring and summer months adults sometimes develop an orange tinge to the head and neck plumage. The legs and large webbed feet are black. The juvenile has uniform drab buffish-grey plumage, with a dark-tipped, pale pink bill.

The Whooper is a large migratory swan, and primarily a winter visitor to the region from breeding grounds in Iceland and Scandinavia; a handful of breeding pairs are recorded in northern Britain each year. The species is generally faithful to a number of traditional sites year on year, where it favours open areas of wet grassland, arable farmland and lakeside marshes. It feeds by grazing on a variety of grasses and it forms loose flocks within which family groups can be discerned. Flight is generally silent, the slow wingbeats lacking the whooshing sound of other species, and flocks typically fly in a 'V' formation. Take-off and landing appear ungainly and laboured. It nests on a down-lined mound of vegetation.

juvenile
Juvenile birds have an extensive pink patch on the base half of the bill.

adult
The Whooper Swan is a large bird, easily the size and stature of a Mute Swan.

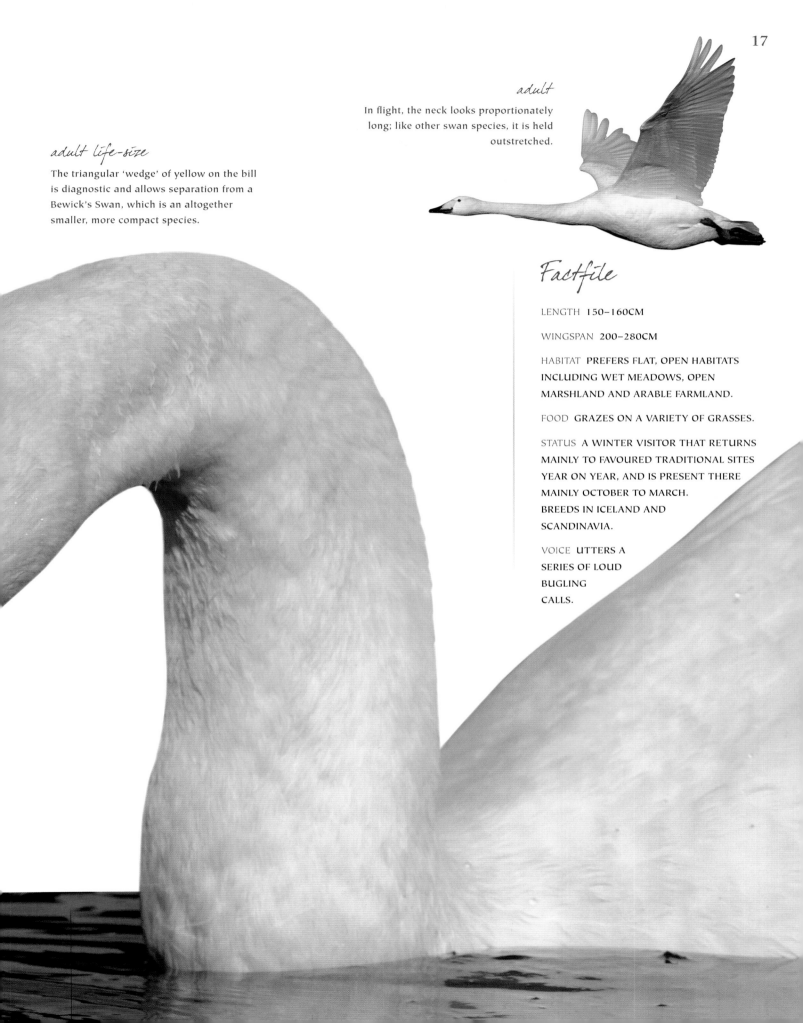

adult

In flight, the neck looks proportionately long; like other swan species, it is held outstretched.

adult life-size

The triangular 'wedge' of yellow on the bill is diagnostic and allows separation from a Bewick's Swan, which is an altogether smaller, more compact species.

Factfile

LENGTH 150–160CM

WINGSPAN 200–280CM

HABITAT PREFERS FLAT, OPEN HABITATS INCLUDING WET MEADOWS, OPEN MARSHLAND AND ARABLE FARMLAND.

FOOD GRAZES ON A VARIETY OF GRASSES.

STATUS A WINTER VISITOR THAT RETURNS MAINLY TO FAVOURED TRADITIONAL SITES YEAR ON YEAR, AND IS PRESENT THERE MAINLY OCTOBER TO MARCH. BREEDS IN ICELAND AND SCANDINAVIA.

VOICE UTTERS A SERIES OF LOUD BUGLING CALLS.

Bean Goose
Anser fabalis

A sturdy-looking, plump goose. The sexes are similar. The adult has a chocolate-brown head and neck, grading to lighter brown on the breast and underside, and eventually white at the stern. The upperwings have dark brown plumage, the feathers of which have pale margins that appear as faint bars when in flight. A narrow white band defines the tail base, contrasting with the dark rump and tail. The robust bill is orange with black at the base and tip, sometimes also displaying a hint of white at the base. The legs and large webbed feet are orange. Two distinct subspecies occur in the region: ssp. *fabalis* breeds in northern Europe and is large with a long neck and extensive orange on the bill; ssp. *rossicus* breeds in northern Siberia, and is proportionately smaller than *fabalis* with a shorter neck, and a smaller bill with less orange on it. Juveniles can be recognised by the subdued colour of the legs and feet.

adult, taiga race
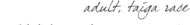
ssp. *fabalis* has much more orange on its bill than ssp. *rossicus*, and is the race that is typically seen in Britain.

Factfile

LENGTH 65–85CM

WINGSPAN 140–174CM

HABITAT FAVOURS WET GRASSLAND, MARSHES AND ARABLE FIELDS.

FOOD GRAZES ON A VARIETY OF GRASSES.

STATUS A MIGRATORY SPECIES THAT BREEDS IN THE NORTH OF THE REGION AND SIBERIA, MOVING SOUTH DURING THE WINTER MONTHS; FOUND IN TRADITIONAL SITES IN OUR REGION, MAINLY NOVEMBER TO MARCH.

VOICE UTTERS A LOUD, NASAL CACKLING HONK.

This is a migratory goose species that heads south from its breeding grounds for the winter, often forming single-species flocks. It is quick to take flight when threatened, rising almost vertically into the air. It favours open areas of wet grassland, marshes and arable land, grazing on a variety of grasses. It nests on a down-lined mound of vegetation.

adults

In flight, the upperwings look rather uniformly dark with only faint pale barring.

As is the case with other goose species, flocks are known as 'skeins'. In flight, they are often seen in 'V' formation and this orientation is thought to aid flight efficiency.

The two races of Bean Goose generally have separate wintering grounds; flocks that are encountered in northwest Europe typically comprise either ssp. *fabalis* or ssp. *rossicus*, but not both.

adult life-size, tundra race

ssp. *rossicus* has much less extensive orange on its bill than ssp. *fabalis*; it breeds in northern Scandinavia and winters mainly in mainland Europe.

Pink-footed Goose *Anser brachyrhynchus*

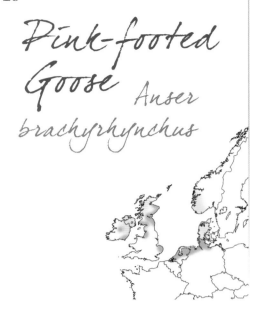

The Pink-foot is similar in overall appearance to a Bean Goose, but smaller and more compact-looking, and with a number of clear distinguishing features. The sexes are similar. The adult has a head and upper neck of dark chocolate-brown, grading to lighter buffish-brown on the breast and underside. The upperwings and back are dark bluish-grey with pale feather margins. In flight, the tail displays a considerable amount of white. The bill is smaller than that of Bean Goose and is recognisably pink, not orange, in colour. The legs and large webbed feet are also pink, giving the species its name. The juvenile recalls the adult but can be determined by the buffish plumage to the back, the less well-defined feather margins, and subdued leg and foot colour.

adult

This plump-looking goose has a relatively short-necked appearance, except when outstretched in nervous birds. The greyish look to the back contrasts with the browner neck and underparts.

Factfile

LENGTH **60–75CM**

WINGSPAN **135–170CM**

HABITAT **PERMANENT GRASSLAND, OPEN ARABLE FARMLAND AND FIELDS OF STUBBLE; FAVOURS LOCATIONS CLOSE TO ESTUARIES AND LARGE BODIES OF FRESHWATER TO ROOST.**

FOOD **GRAZES ON GRASSES AND ARABLE STUBBLE.**

STATUS **A MIGRATORY SPECIES AND WINTER VISITOR. THE ENTIRE WORLD POPULATION OVERWINTERS IN OUR REGION; LOCALLY ABUNDANT AT TRADITIONALLY FAVOURED SITES AT THIS TIME, AND PRESENT MAINLY OCTOBER TO MARCH. IT BREEDS IN THE ARCTIC.**

VOICE **UTTERS A NASAL, CACKLING HONK, SIMILAR TO BEAN GOOSE BUT HIGHER IN PITCH.**

This is a migratory species that breeds in Iceland, Greenland and Svalbard, moving south for the winter months. Birds from Iceland and Greenland make up the majority of the world's population and mainly winter in Great Britain; those from Svalbard tend to occur in Scandinavia and northern mainland Europe. Typically it forms large single-species flocks, favouring open grassland and arable stubble fields where it feeds on a variety of grasses and arable stubble. It prefers large open bodies of freshwater and coastal estuaries as roosting sites.

adults

In flight, the greyish wing coverts
contrast with the darker flight feathers.

In winter, feeding flocks sometimes mix
with other goose species – notably Greylag
and White-fronted Geese – in stubble
fields and grassland. But when they go to
roost the species separate and a flock of
Pink-feet will comprise just that species.

adult life-size

Compared to related species, the bill is proportionately
dainty-looking. The pink colouration helps distinguish the
species from a Bean Goose (which has orange on its bill).
However, be warned that the colours pink and orange can
be surprisingly hard to distinguish in the field in some
lighting conditions.

White-fronted Goose
Anser albifrons

Adults of this 'grey' goose species have a distinctive white patch on the forehead. The sexes are similar. Two subspecies occur in the region: Greenland White-front ssp. *flavirostris* and European White-front ssp. *albifrons*. Adults of both subspecies have a rather drab brown head that fades to a lighter brown on the neck and underside. The back and upperwing plumage is dark grey-brown with pale fringes to the feathers, resulting in light barring. The most distinctive features are the bold black patches on the breast and belly, the white stern and the large white blaze on the forehead. The two subspecies can be tricky to separate, especially in the field. European is paler overall and shorter-necked than Greenland, with a pale-tipped pink bill; Greenland has a pale-tipped orange bill. The legs and webbed feet are orange in both. The juvenile is similar to an adult but lacks the belly markings and forehead blaze.

This is a migratory goose that breeds in Greenland (ssp. *flavirostris*) and Russia (ssp. *albifrons*). The entire world population of Greenland White-fronted Geese winters in the British Isles, mainly in Ireland and Scotland; European White-fronts are more widespread in northern Europe in winter, including southern England and Wales. The species is typically site-faithful and forms large flocks, favouring open grassland and arable stubble fields.

European race adult life-size
The white forehead is diagnostic in adults but note that the orange bill can look pinkish in certain lights.

juvenile
Juveniles lack an adult's white forehead blaze, which is acquired with age from late winter onwards; they usually remain in loose family groups, within flocks, throughout winter.

European race adults
The dark barring on the underparts
is obvious in flight.

Greenland race adult
On average Greenland race birds are larger
than their European counterparts, and have
bolder dark markings on the belly and a
more robust bill.

Factfile

LENGTH 65–75CM

WINGSPAN 130–165CM

HABITAT OPEN GRASSLAND
AND ARABLE FARMLAND.

FOOD GRAZES ON VARIOUS GRASSES.

STATUS MIGRATORY SPECIES AND
WINTER VISITOR, PRESENT MAINLY
OCTOBER TO MARCH, AND MOSTLY
FAVOURING A HANDFUL OF TRADITIONAL
SITES IN THE BRITISH ISLES AND
NORTHERN FRANCE.

VOICE UTTERS A RATHER MUSICAL
BARKING HONK, TYPICALLY
WHEN IN FLIGHT.

Greylag Goose

Anser anser

This is the largest of the 'grey' geese, with a bulky body, long thick neck, large bill and a robust-looking head. The sexes are similar. The adult has mainly uniform grey-brown plumage, the sides of the neck being marked with dark lines. The upperwing and back feathers have pale margins, creating a barred pattern. In flight, the pale forewings, rump and tail contrast noticeably with the darker flight feathers. The bill is pinkish-orange with a pale tip, and the legs and webbed feet are pink. The juvenile is similar to the adult but has more uniformly brown plumage and lacks the pale bill tip.

adult

A Greylag has a stocky body, thick neck and proportionately large, robust bill.

adults
In flight, note the silvery grey upper forewings that contrast with the darker flight feathers.

The ancestor of domesticated farmyard geese, the Greylag is a common species that breeds in the region; numbers are boosted during the winter months by migratory birds, mainly from Iceland and Scandinavia. Seldom found far from water, this species forms small flocks in areas of damp grassland, farmland and lake and river margins, feeding on a variety of grasses and aquatic plants. It nests on the ground in a sheltered depression.

Factfile

LENGTH 75–90CM

WINGSPAN 147–180CM

HABITAT FAVOURS WET GRASSLAND, BOGGY LAKE MARGINS AND FARMLAND.

FOOD GRAZES ON VARIOUS GRASSES AND AQUATIC PLANTS.

STATUS WIDESPREAD AND COMMON IN SUITABLE HABITATS, AND PRESENT IN OUR REGION YEAR-ROUND. ITS NUMBERS ARE BOOSTED IN WINTER BY MIGRANTS FROM FURTHER AFIELD.

VOICE UTTERS A FAMILIAR LOUD HONKING CALL, RECALLING FARMYARD GEESE.

Depending on the light, the bill, which is proportionately larger than in other 'grey' geese, can look pinkish or tinged orange. Apart from the pale tip, it is always uniform in colour.

adult life-size
As with other grey geese, the serrated margin to the bill aids feeding, enabling the bird to 'shear' grass and other vegetation more easily.

Canada Goose
Branta canadensis

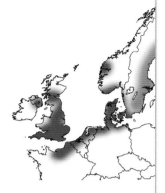

This is a large goose with a long, swan-like neck. The sexes are similar. The adult has mainly dark grey-brown body plumage and a distinctive black head and neck. A large white chin-strap marking extends from the cheeks underneath the head, behind the blackish bill. Its body plumage is darkest on its back and the feathers have pale margins, creating a barred effect. In flight, the white stern is clearly visible and is in stark contrast to the grey-brown wings and dark tail. The legs and webbed feet are dark. The juvenile recalls the adult but can be recognised by the more subdued barring on the back.

The Canada Goose was introduced to northern Europe in the mid-seventeenth century and is now well established and a common species. Thousands of pairs breed in the region. It can become extremely tame and is often found in urban parks and on ornamental ponds. Outside the breeding season it forms small- to medium-sized flocks and feeds primarily by grazing on grasses and aquatic plants. The nest is a pile of vegetation situated close to water.

Factfile

LENGTH 95–105CM

WINGSPAN 127–185CM

HABITAT FAVOURS AREAS OF LOWLAND, FREQUENTING OPEN GRASSLAND AND MARSHES; ALSO FARMLAND ADJACENT TO FRESHWATER LAKES, PONDS, GRAVEL PITS, RESERVOIRS, STREAMS AND RIVERS.

FOOD GRAZES ON VARIOUS GRASSES AND AQUATIC PLANTS.

STATUS INTRODUCED FROM NORTH AMERICA. NOW COMMON AND WIDESPREAD IN SUITABLE HABITATS, AND PRESENT YEAR-ROUND.

VOICE IN FLIGHT, UTTERS LOUD DISYLLABIC TRUMPETING HONKS.

adult

This large goose has a stocky body and diagnostic black neck and head, with a white chin patch. It is often seen in flocks feeding on grasslands in urban parks or farmland, usually in the vicinity of water.

adult life-size

Like other geese species, the neck is extended in
birds that are on the look-out for danger.

adult

In flight, Canada Geese form noisy flocks
whose bugling calls carry quite a distance;
the pale underparts contrast with the darker
wings and neck.

Genuinely wild birds, which have crossed the
Atlantic under their own steam, do occasionally turn
up in northwest Europe in late autumn and winter.
Typically they belong to subspecies that are much
smaller than our feral birds, and turn up amongst
flocks of migrant wildfowl, notably Barnacle Geese.

Barnacle Goose
Branta leucopsis

This is a medium-sized, well-marked goose with a striking and distinctive black head and neck. The sexes are similar. The adult has a white face contrasting with the black plumage on the head, the black extending to the breast where there is a sharp division between this and the greyish-white underside. The back is dark grey with obvious black-and-white barring; the flanks are lighter grey with dark barring. The stern is white and in stark contrast to the black tail. The bill, legs and webbed feet are also black. The juvenile is similar to the adult but can be separated by the less well-defined barring on the back, and the yellow tinge to the white plumage.

The Barnacle Goose is a migratory species with four distinct breeding populations in Greenland, Svalbard, the Siberian archipelago of Novaya Zemlya and (more recently) the Baltic Sea islands. These populations overwinter in large flocks at traditional sites; those from Greenland on the Hebrides and in coastal Scotland and Ireland, those from Svalbard on the Solway Firth between Scotland and England, and those from Novaya Zemlya and the Baltic in the Netherlands. The spectacle of large and noisy airborne flocks flying to and from roosting sites at dawn and dusk is worth seeing. Arctic-breeding Barnacle Geese nest on precipitous cliff ledges to avoid predation, the young having to undertake a perilous drop to the cliff base to feed only a few days after hatching.

Factfile

LENGTH 58–69CM

WINGSPAN 130–145CM

HABITAT AREAS OF COASTAL GRASSLAND, SALT MARSHES AND ARABLE FARMLAND CLOSE TO TIDAL MUDFLATS AND LAKES.

FOOD GRAZES ON VARIOUS GRASSES AND AQUATIC PLANTS.

STATUS A MIGRATORY SPECIES AND A WINTER VISITOR TO THE NORTHERN PART OF OUR REGION (MAINLY SCOTLAND, IRELAND, THE NETHERLANDS AND DENMARK); PRESENT MAINLY OCTOBER TO MARCH.

VOICE UTTERS A LOAD BARKING WHEN IN FLOCKS.

Compared to a Canada Goose, a Barnacle Goose is a smaller bird with a proportionately much shorter neck; the white face, which contrasts with the black cap and neck, is diagnostic.

adults

In flight, birds look strikingly black-and-white; the species is invariably seen in flocks.

adult life-size

adult

In good light, the black, white and grey markings on the back feathers create a scaly appearance, and the pale flanks show subtle vertical barring.

Brent Goose
Branta bernicla

This is the smallest goose to be encountered in the region. The sexes are similar. Two subspecies occur regularly in our region: Pale-bellied Brent ssp. *hrota* and Dark-bellied Brent ssp. *bernicla*. Adults of both subspecies have a dark (virtually black) head, neck and breast, with narrow white markings on the sides of the neck. The back is a uniform dark brownish-grey. In the Pale-bellied there is a clear separation between the dark breast and a much lighter, pale grey-buff belly. Dark-bellied is superficially similar and sometimes difficult to separate in the field, but the flanks appear paler beside the darker belly, and there is no clear contrast between belly and breast. The bill, legs and feet in all birds are black. The juvenile is similar but has pale feather margins on the back that appear as faint barring, and generally lacks the white neck markings until about midwinter.

This is a migratory species that winters in the north of our region, with a large proportion in the British Isles. Pale-bellied Brent breeds in Greenland and Svalbard, while Dark-bellied breeds in Russia. The species forms large flocks that favour mainly coastal areas, typically estuarine habitats and adjacent open grassland areas.

adult life-size

An adult bird has a uniformly dark head and neck except for the delicate white pattern on the throat.

Factfile

LENGTH 56–61CM

WINGSPAN 106–121CM

HABITAT A MAINLY COASTAL SPECIES, FAVOURING ESTUARIES, ARABLE FARMLAND, SALT MARSHES AND ADJACENT GRASSLAND.

FOOD FEEDS PRIMARILY ON EELGRASS, SALT-MARSH PLANTS, SEAWEEDS AND GRASSES.

STATUS A MIGRATORY SPECIES AND A WINTER VISITOR TO THE NORTHERN PART OF OUR REGION; PRESENT MAINLY SEPTEMBER TO MARCH.

VOICE A VOCAL GOOSE, UTTERING A FREQUENT NASAL *KRRRUT*.

dark- and pale-bellied adults

In flight, birds appear compact and relatively short-necked by goose standards. The difference between pale- and dark-bellied birds is strikingly obvious.

dark-bellied adult

As the name suggests, the belly and flanks of dark-bellied Brents are overall dark, the pale feather margins creating a subtle barred effect.

pale-bellied adult

In pale-bellied Brents, the pale belly and flanks are only marginally darker than the white stern and contrast markedly with the dark neck, back and wings.

Egyptian Goose
Alopochen aegyptiaca

This is a Shelduck-sized bird with distinctive markings. The sexes are similar. The adult has a head and neck with grubby white plumage, the pale eye surrounded by a diagnostic dark patch. The neck is clearly divided from the orange-buff breast, and the grey-buff belly is adorned with a small central dark blotch. The back is dark grey-brown, the sides displaying chestnut and white in standing birds. In flight, an obvious bold white patch on the inner wing is a good aid to identification. The juvenile can be distinguished by its duller colouration, and by the lack of eye-patch and dark breast blotch.

African in origin, the species was introduced to the region in the late eighteenth century. A modest breeding population has been established for some time now, generally in lowland areas with suitable habitat. It prefers lowland rivers, lakes and other areas of freshwater, requiring open grassland for grazing and trees for breeding. It forms small groups and constructs a mound of vegetation in a hole or bush on which to nest.

adult life-size

The markings on the head are unique amongst European wildfowl, in particular the dark 'highwayman's mask' that surrounds the pale eye, and which contrasts with the pale forecrown and lores. The bright pinkish-red bill is also a good identification feature.

adults

Egyptian Geese are sociable birds; solitary birds are seldom encountered and pairs or small groups are more typical.

In flight, large white patches on both upperwings and underwings are striking features, especially since they contrast with the dark flight feathers.

Factfile

LENGTH 65–72CM

WINGSPAN 135–155CM

HABITAT LOWLAND AREAS ADJACENT TO RIVERS, LAKES AND OTHER FRESHWATER SOURCES.

FOOD GRAZES ON VARIOUS GRASSES.

STATUS AN INTRODUCED SPECIES WITH A SCATTERED BUT ESTABLISHED SMALL BREEDING POPULATION IN SUITABLE HABITATS IN BRITAIN AND NORTHERN EUROPE. PRESENT YEAR-ROUND.

VOICE GENERALLY SILENT.

adult

A standing bird appears stocky and is the size and build of a Shelduck. The robust pink legs and unique plumage markings make identification straightforward.

In its natural range, the species is found in warm climates, around the margins of African lakes and rivers like the Nile. Nevertheless, it has adapted well to relatively chilly settings, such as urban parks on the banks of the River Thames, and flooded gravel pits.

Shelduck
Tadorna tadorna

This is a distinctively marked goose-sized duck. The sexes are similar but separable with experience. The adult has mainly white plumage with a dark green head and neck. The breast has a colourful band of chestnut that gives way to a black belly stripe; the undertail is orange-buff. The bill is a striking red colour with a conspicuous basal knob, the size of which can assist the separation of sexes (larger in the male and virtually absent in the female). When in flight, the wings show a diagnostic contrast between white coverts and black flight feathers. The juvenile is easily identifiable owing to its buffish-grey upperparts and white undersides.

The Shelduck is a partly migratory species, primarily found in coastal areas in the region and present in varying numbers at various times of the year. Preferring estuaries and expansive mudflats, it feeds by sifting small invertebrates from estuarine mud. It nests in abandoned rabbit burrows and hollow trees, and is sometimes encountered in suitable inland freshwater habitats such as large lakes and reservoirs. In the summer, many birds migrate to the Wadden Sea in the Netherlands, or Bridgwater Bay in Somerset, England, to moult.

adults
Birds look strikingly black-and-white in flight; in good light, the orange-chestnut breast band is obvious.

The rich orange-brown elements in an adult's plumage are offset by the otherwise white underparts, back and breast, and the dark neck and head.

adult

juvenile

Shelducks feed by sifting through the surface mud for invertebrates.

Factfile

LENGTH 55–65CM

WINGSPAN 100–120CM

HABITAT ESTUARIES AND COASTAL MUDFLATS, OCCASIONALLY INLAND FRESHWATER.

FOOD FEEDS ON MUD-DWELLING INVERTEBRATES.

STATUS RELATIVELY COMMON AND WIDESPREAD IN SUITABLE COASTAL HABITATS. PRESENT YEAR-ROUND.

VOICE VOCAL GENERALLY ONLY DURING THE BREEDING SEASON; MALE HAS A WHISTLING CALL, THE FEMALE A CACKLING *GAGAGA*.

adult life-size

Although the colour of the bright red bill is always obvious, the subtle green sheen to the head and neck can be hard to discern in some lights.

Mandarin Duck *Aix galericulata*

This is a striking and unmistakable medium-sized duck, the sexes of which are separable with ease. The adult male is colourfully marked with large white facial patches around the eyes and a mane of orange, greenish and brown feathers. The bright elongated orange facial plumes, together with the conspicuous orange sail-like feathers on its back, make this an attractive duck. The breast is dark with vertical white stripes, the flanks are brown and the stern is white. The pale-tipped bill is bright red. The female is dull by comparison, being grey-brown in colour, darkest on the back, and with pale buffish spots on the flanks. The eyes are surrounded by a white spectacle marking. The throat and belly are white and the pale-tipped bill is dull pink. The juvenile resembles the adult female, but with subdued colours and patterning.

male

In flight, the wings appear uniform and lack any distinctive markings or colours.

Mandarins originate from the Far East and were kept here originally as an ornamental species. Escapes and deliberate releases created feral populations throughout the region during the twentieth century. It is now a common sight in southern Britain in suitable freshwater habitats that offer a plentiful supply of food and mature trees. Its favoured nesting sites are tree holes. The diet is varied and changes seasonally, and includes seeds, plants, invertebrates, molluscs and even amphibians and small fish.

Factfile

LENGTH 41–49CM

WINGSPAN 65–75CM

HABITAT LARGE WELL-VEGETATED LAKES AND RIVERS WITH WOODED MARGINS.

FOOD DIET CHANGES SEASONALLY AND VARIES FROM SEEDS AND PLANTS TO MOLLUSCS, OTHER INVERTEBRATES AND SMALL FISH.

STATUS AN INTRODUCED SPECIES, LARGELY ABSENT IN MAINLAND EUROPE BUT NOW WIDESPREAD IN BRITAIN WITH A LARGE FERAL POPULATION IN SUITABLE HABITATS; PRESENT THERE YEAR-ROUND.

VOICE MAINLY SILENT.

female

The female's pale 'spectacles' and pale-spotted flanks are good features for identification of solitary individuals; typically though, they are seldom seen away from the company of males.

male life-size

The male has a truly exotic-looking appearance with extravagant, colourful feathering on the neck and unique sail-like feathers on the back. It is hard to confuse with any other regularly encountered wildfowl species.

Gadwall
Anas strepera

At first glance the Gadwall appears a rather drab dabbling duck, but, when seen well, it reveals surprisingly handsome plumage. The sexes are dissimilar. The adult male has a buff-coloured head and neck, clearly defined from the patterned grey breast and flanks. The centre of the belly is white and the black rear end is obvious. The back displays a subtle chestnut colour present in the wing plumage. The bill is dark and the legs are yellow. The adult female is a rich mottled brown with a greyish head, and recalls a female Mallard; note the orange-sided bill. A white speculum on the wings is conspicuous in flight, particularly in the male. The juvenile resembles the adult female.

female
Although superficially similar to a female Mallard, a female Gadwall has more richly-patterned markings and a less robust bill that is orange along its sides.

male life-size
Seen at close range, a male has fabulously intricate patterns on its body feathers. The black bill and stern are also aids to identification.

The Gadwall is a migratory dabbling duck that breeds in the region and is present all year. Numbers are boosted greatly in the winter months by migrating birds, and the species sometimes forms large flocks outside the breeding season. It is associated with a number of freshwater habitats with shallow margins, including lowland lakes, reservoirs, gravel pits, marshes and coastal wetlands. It feeds on aquatic plants and is often seen upended or 'dabbling' when feeding.

adults
In flight, a male's white speculum contrasts with adjacent black and chestnut feathering; the effect is altogether more subtle in the female.

male
Gadwalls swim relatively low in the water, and often upend to feed. The male's black stern is then an obvious feature, even at a considerable distance.

Factfile

LENGTH **46–55CM**

WINGSPAN **78–90CM**

HABITAT **OCCURS IN A VARIETY OF FRESHWATER HABITATS WITH SHALLOW MARGINS.**

FOOD **FEEDS ON AQUATIC PLANTS.**

STATUS **WIDESPREAD AND RELATIVELY COMMON IN SUITABLE HABITATS, ESPECIALLY IN WINTER; COMMONEST MAINLY OCTOBER TO MARCH.**

VOICE **GENERALLY A QUIET DUCK EXCEPT IN THE BREEDING SEASON, WHEN MALES UTTER A CROAKING GRUNT; THE FEMALE'S CALL IS A NASAL *QUACK*, SIMILAR TO MALLARD BUT HIGHER-PITCHED.**

Mallard
Anas platyrhynchos

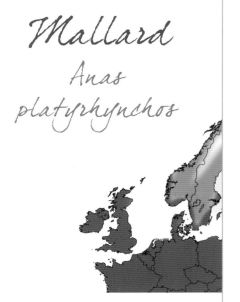

Factfile

LENGTH 50–65CM

WINGSPAN 81–98CM

HABITAT OCCURS IN A RANGE OF FRESHWATER HABITATS AND OCCASIONALLY SHELTERED COASTAL AREAS.

FOOD FEEDS ON AQUATIC PLANTS, ALTHOUGH TAME BIRDS WILL ACCEPT A WIDE RANGE OF FOODS.

STATUS COMMON AND WIDESPREAD IN SUITABLE HABITATS THROUGHOUT THE REGION. PRESENT YEAR-ROUND.

VOICE THE MALE MAKES A SERIES OF NASAL AND WHISTLING CALLS; THE FEMALE'S CALL IS A CLASSIC *QUACK*.

The Mallard is a familiar dabbling duck and the most common wildfowl species in the region. The sexes are dissimilar. The adult male has a shiny bottle-green head and neck, neatly separated from the chestnut breast by a delicate white collar. The upperparts are primarily grey-brown; the belly and underparts are light grey-brown with the exception of the obvious black rear end and white tail. The bill, legs and feet are yellow. The adult female has rich mottled brown

male

In flight, the male's underwings appear mainly pale while the upperwings show a blue speculum that is framed with white.

male life-size

The green sheen to the male's head is obvious only in good light but the reddish-brown breast and orange-yellow bill are always consistently good identification features.

plumage; the head is a buff colour with a subtle darker eye stripe and crown. The bill is a dull brown-orange colour, and the legs and feet are dull orange-yellow. Both sexes display a striking white-bordered blue speculum. The juvenile resembles an adult female. An eclipse (moulting) male resembles an adult female but retains its yellow bill.

The Mallard is the most commonly occurring dabbling duck in the region. It often becomes very tame and can be fed by hand. It is found in a wide variety of freshwater habitats from lakes, gravel pits, reservoirs, lowland rivers and estuaries, to ornamental ponds and urban lakes. An influx of migrating birds can boost numbers significantly during the winter months. It feeds primarily on aquatic plants upon which it grazes by upending or 'dabbling'. Where tame, it accepts a variety of foods, classically stale bread. It nests in a down-lined depression in the ground.

Mallards are often seen in grassland adjacent to water, walking with their characteristic 'waddling' gait. Note the bright orange feet of the male; the colour is less intense in females.

male

A female Mallard has attractive brown markings on the body plumage and a subtle stripy pattern on the face; the bill is grubby orange-yellow.

female

Wigeon
Anas penelope

male

In flight, the male's green speculum and adjacent contrasting white patch on the innerwing are striking features, along with the black stern.

The Wigeon is a distinctive dabbling duck and the classic species of winter estuaries and wetlands. The sexes are dissimilar. The adult male has a colourful orange-red head with a diagnostic pale yellow forehead and forecrown. The breast is pinkish; the flanks and back are grey, marked with a fine dark patterning. The belly is pale and the rear end is conspicuously black-and-white. The relatively short, dark-tipped bill is pale grey in colour. In flight, note the white wing patch, which is absent in the female. The adult female is reddish-brown, darkest on the head and back, the black tips of the folded wings forming a black tail-end when seen swimming or standing. The belly is contrastingly white and the bill is grey with a dark tip. The juvenile and eclipse male resemble the female.

The calls of Wigeon flocks are one of the iconic sounds of estuaries and wetlands in the winter months. Breeding pairs are present in the region in small numbers, but the species is best known as a winter visitor, when it forms large flocks on estuaries, mudflats and coastal grassland. It also frequents inland wetlands adjacent to open grassland and arable farmland. Wigeon are gregarious and feed on aquatic plants by 'dabbling'; they also graze on various grasses. They nest in cover on the ground.

male life-size

In swimming birds, the contrasting black-and-white stern and pale crown are good features; the intricate patterns on the body can only be appreciated at close range.

Factfile

LENGTH 45–47CM

WINGSPAN 71–80CM

HABITAT FAVOURS ESTUARIES, MUDFLATS AND COASTAL GRASSLAND; ALSO FOUND ON INLAND WETLANDS ADJACENT TO OPEN GRASSLAND AND FARMLAND.

FOOD VARIOUS GRASSES AND AQUATIC PLANTS.

STATUS THE REGION SUPPORTS A RELATIVELY SMALL BREEDING POPULATION, AND IT IS BEST KNOWN AS A WINTER VISITOR (MAINLY OCTOBER TO MARCH), OCCURRING IN LARGE NUMBERS IN SUITABLE HABITATS.

VOICE THE MALE UTTERS A WHISTLING *WHEEOO* CALL.

female

A female's white belly is obvious only in birds walking on land, and is lost to view in swimming birds.

Typically, Wigeon feed in shallow inundated grassland and on estuaries; when observed walking rather than swimming the subtle beauty of the male's plumage can be appreciated.

male

Teal
Anas
crecca

This is the region's smallest dabbling duck. The sexes are dissimilar. The adult male has a light chestnut head, with a large bottle-green eye-patch delicately bordered in yellow. The sides and back are light grey and finely patterned, with a distinctive horizontal white stripe along the flanks, leading to a black-bordered pale yellow undertail. The underside is paler with darker mottling. The bill is uniform dark grey, appearing almost black. The female has uniform mottled grey-brown plumage; the green speculum can sometimes be glimpsed along the flank. The bill is a lighter grey than in the male, with a hint of yellow at the base. In flight both sexes clearly display a white-bordered green speculum. The juvenile and eclipse male resemble the female.

female

In flight, Teal are fast, agile and difficult to follow, frequently twisting and turning, and adjusting their flight path.

male

male life-size

The male Teal has unique and beautiful markings on the face although the green sheen behind the eye is sometimes hard to discern in poor light.

male

The black-framed yellow stern is a good aid to identification of a male Teal and is visible even in poor light at considerable range.

Factfile

LENGTH 34–38CM

WINGSPAN 53–59CM

HABITAT ESTUARIES, MUDFLATS AND INLAND WETLANDS.

FOOD DIET VARIES WITH THE SEASON BUT INCLUDES GRASSES, SEEDS, AQUATIC VEGETATION, MOLLUSCS AND VARIOUS OTHER INVERTEBRATES.

STATUS A MODEST POPULATION IS PRESENT DURING THE BREEDING SEASON; BEST KNOWN AS A WINTER VISITOR (MAINLY OCTOBER TO MARCH), OCCURRING IN GOOD NUMBERS IN SUITABLE HABITATS.

VOICE AN EXTREMELY VOCAL SPECIES. THE MALE UTTERS A RINGING WHISTLE, *CRYEELYCC*; THE FEMALE A SOFT *QUACK*.

The Teal is a nimble and rather nervous bird, and takes flight easily, rising almost vertically. Northern areas accommodate breeding birds in habitats that provide dense waterside vegetation. However, the species is more commonly seen as a winter visitor to open lowland and coastal habitats, where it forms flocks; migrants arrive from breeding grounds further north. It nests in cover on the ground.

female

A female Teal is small and has rather uniformly brown body plumage that lacks distinctive features; fortunately, surprisingly often part of the diagnostic green speculum is revealed as the bird moves.

Garganey
Anas querquedula

The Garganey is medium-sized dabbling duck. The sexes differ. The adult male has a rich reddish-brown head with a distinctive bold white stripe that runs above and behind the eye, almost to the nape. The body plumage is mostly mottled greyish with a brown breast and mottled buffish-brown rear end. The bill is a uniform dark grey. In flight, the male has an obvious blue-grey forewing and a white-bordered greenish speculum. Resembling female Teal, the female has rather uniform mottled brown plumage with a darker crown and a subtle lighter buff-coloured eyebrow stripe. The pale edges to the back feathers are obvious. The bill is dark grey with a clear pale facial spot at the base. In flight, the female lacks the male's forewing colours and the speculum is brown. The juvenile and eclipse male resemble the adult female.

male

A male Garganey is instantly recognisable by the combination of the striking head pattern and grey flanks.

Factfile

LENGTH 37–41CM

WINGSPAN 59–67CM

HABITAT FAVOURS WELL-VEGETATED LAKE MARGINS AND GRASSLAND.

FOOD FEEDS ON A VARIETY OF SMALL INVERTEBRATES INCLUDING MOLLUSCS AND WORMS, AND ON PLANT MATTER.

STATUS EXCLUSIVELY A SUMMER BREEDER AND PASSAGE MIGRANT TO THE REGION (MAINLY APRIL TO AUGUST), AND PRESENT IN SMALL NUMBERS. OVERWINTERS IN AFRICA.

VOICE THE MALE HAS A DISTINCTIVE RATTLING CALL; THE FEMALE IS RATHER QUIET, UTTERING A SOFT *QUACK*.

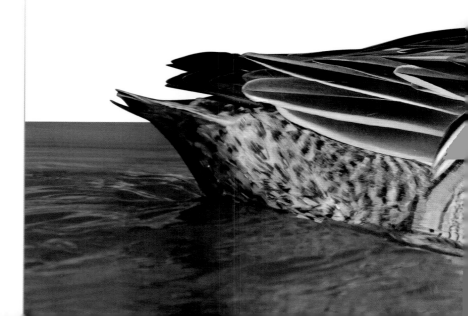

male

Garganey take to the wing at a steep angle, males revealing the diagnostic upperwing markings: a white-framed green speculum and blue forewing.

The Garganey is a rather secretive bird that seeks out well-vegetated lake margins, marshes and wetlands. It is easiest to see on migration, and the entire population returns to Africa for the winter months. It has an omnivorous diet consisting of plant material, invertebrates and even small amphibians and fish. It feeds by skimming rather than 'dabbling' and nests on the ground in cover.

A female Garganey is superficially similar to a female Teal but note the subtle different facial pattern and proportionately much longer bill.

female

male life-size

Generally speaking, the Garganey is a secretive bird that prefers to keep to the cover of marginal, emergent vegetation around freshwater pools.

Pintail
Anas acuta

female

The Pintail is an elegant dabbling duck. The sexes differ. The adult male has a chocolate-brown head and nape with a stark delineation from the white breast. A white stripe extends from the breast and up each side of the head. The plumage along the flanks and back is predominantly grey with a fine dark patterning; the back is a little darker with tinges of brown. The best distinguishing features are the cream and black rear end, and the long pointed tail. The bill is a light bluish-grey with a dark bridge-stripe. In flight, the wings appear grey and are marked with a green speculum with a white trailing edge. The female has a mottled brown appearance and a uniformly dark bill. In flight, the white trailing edge to the inner wing is a useful identification feature. The juvenile resembles the adult female, but the complex feather markings are more subdued.

Although a female Pintail lacks the male's distinctive markings and long tail plumes, she shares the same elongated body shape and proportionately long neck.

In swimming males, the striking head pattern, black-and-yellow stern, and long tail plumes make identification straightforward.

Frequently found in mixed flocks in sheltered coastal waters and estuaries over the winter period. It prefers marshland and open wetland for breeding. Its diet varies seasonally, feeding on small invertebrates and other animals during the breeding season, reverting to a plant-based diet in the winter months, grazing on aquatic plants by dabbling. It nests in a hollow on open ground.

male

adults

Outside the breeding season, Pintails are usually seen in single-species flocks. The elongated body shape is particularly obvious in flight.

male life-size

The male's chocolate-brown face is framed by a white line that extends up from the white breast and neck.

Factfile

LENGTH 51–66CM

WINGSPAN 80–95CM

HABITAT MARSHY WATERSIDE GROUND AND OPEN WETLAND DURING THE BREEDING SEASON; ESTUARIES AND SHELTERED COASTAL AREAS ARE PREFERRED IN THE WINTER.

FOOD AN OMNIVOROUS SPECIES, FEEDING ON A VARIETY OF AQUATIC PLANTS, GRASSES, SEEDS, AND VARIOUS INVERTEBRATES INCLUDING WORMS AND MOLLUSCS.

STATUS A SMALL BREEDING POPULATION IS PRESENT IN THE BREEDING SEASON, WITH NUMBERS BOOSTED SIGNIFICANTLY OUTSIDE THE BREEDING SEASON BY WINTER MIGRANTS; COMMONEST FROM OCTOBER TO MARCH.

VOICE THE MALE UTTERS A WHISTLING CALL; THE FEMALE CALL IS A RATHER LOW CROAK OR DESCENDING *QUACK*.

Shoveler
Anas clypeata

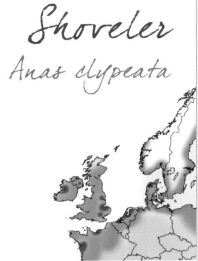

The long, flattened spatulate bill makes this species unmistakable. The sexes differ. The adult male has a shiny dark green head (which can look black at a distance), white breast and bright chestnut-orange flanks and belly. The back is dark, with striking white margins to some feathers. The rear end is black-and-white. The uniquely shaped bill is dark and the eye is yellow. In flight, note the distinctive large blue forewing panel and white-bordered green speculum. The female has mottled brown plumage and a yellowish bill. The wing pattern is similar to the male's in flight, the blue in the forewing panel replaced with blue-grey. The juvenile and eclipse male are similar to the female.

male life-size

The combination of plumage colours and markings, and unique bill shape make a male Shoveler an unmistakable bird.

Factfile

LENGTH 44–52CM

WINGSPAN 75–77CM

HABITAT SHALLOW, WELL-VEGETATED FRESHWATER LAKES AND MARSHES, ESTUARIES AND MUDFLATS.

FOOD AN OMNIVOROUS SPECIES, FEEDING ON AQUATIC PLANT MATERIAL AND SMALL INVERTEBRATES.

STATUS THE SMALL SUMMER BREEDING POPULATION IN OUR REGION IS BOOSTED DURING THE WINTER MONTHS BY MIGRATORY VISITORS; COMMONEST FROM OCTOBER TO MARCH.

VOICE THE MALE UTTERS A SHRILL *TUK-TUK*; THE FEMALE DELIVERS A SOFT *QUACK*.

A modest population is present during the breeding season, favouring well-vegetated, shallow marginal freshwater in lakes and marshes. Numbers in the region swell considerably during the winter months thanks to migratory visitors; at this time of year it can also be found on estuaries and mudflats. The Shoveler feeds on aquatic invertebrates and plants, swishing the bill from side to side and filtering material out of the water. It nests on the ground in a shallow depression.

adults

Outside the breeding season, Shovelers are seen in single-species flocks. In flight, the blue forewing panel on the upperwing is obvious in both sexes.

Although a female Shoveler may have body plumage whose colours and patterns are superficially similar to other female ducks, the unique size and shape of the bill mean identification is easy.

female

Pochard
Aythya ferina

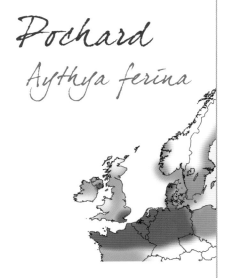

Factfile

LENGTH **42–49CM**

WINGSPAN **70–78CM**

HABITAT **FRESHWATER GRAVEL PITS, RESERVOIRS, LARGE LAKES AND LOCHS.**

FOOD **AN OMNIVOROUS SPECIES, FEEDING ON PLANTS AND INVERTEBRATES.**

STATUS **THE MODEST BREEDING POPULATION IS BOOSTED BY LARGE NUMBERS OF MIGRATING BIRDS DURING THE WINTER; COMMONEST FROM OCTOBER TO MARCH.**

VOICE **MOSTLY SILENT. THE MALES SOMETIMES UTTER A NASAL WHISTLE; THE FEMALE ISSUES A HOARSE GROWL.**

The Pochard is a robust-looking diving duck with a long bill, and a rounded, peaked and steeply curved, rich reddish-orange head. The sexes are separable. The adult male has a black breast; the flanks and back are a uniform light grey, and the rear end is black. The bill is dark and divided by a wide central light grey band. When in eclipse, black elements of the plumage take on a brown colouration. The female is more uniformly coloured with a brown head and breast. The flanks and back are a lighter drab grey-brown, darker at the rear end. Paler 'spectacle' markings usually surround the eyes. The bill is uniformly dark. In flight, both sexes display light grey-silver wings with a dark trailing edge to the primary feathers. The juvenile recalls the adult female, but the plumage detail is less pronounced.

A relatively small population is present in the region during the breeding season, favouring large expanses of still freshwater such as gravel pits, reservoirs and lakes. Numbers increase considerably during the winter months with migratory visitors forming flocks, sometimes in association with Tufted Ducks and Coots. The Pochard is a diving duck which feeds on aquatic invertebrates and plants around shallow water margins. It nests on open ground near water.

male life-size

The male's reddish-orange head, which contrasts with the dark bill and breast, and grey body, make identification straightforward.

male

Pochards swim rather low in the water and the black stern is obvious at a surprising distance.

male

In flight, the male's upperwings look silvery grey and lack a speculum, the feature seen in dabbling ducks.

male

In flight, the female shares the male's silver grey upperwings, the flight feathers being particularly pale.

females

female

The subtle pale 'spectacle' that surrounds a female Pochard's eye is not always striking. The bill always appears relatively large and long, with a pale central band.

Red-crested Pochard
Netta rufina

The Red-crested Pochard is a large and distinctive diving duck. The sexes differ. The adult male has a rounded head with an unmistakable bright orange colour. There is a clear separation of this from the black neck and breast. The underside and tail are also black, the flanks are white and the back is grey-buff. The rather narrow bill is red and slightly hook-tipped. In eclipse, the male resembles the female but retains the bill colouration. The female has a rounded head with striking pale grey cheeks and a darker, reddish crown. The remaining plumage is buffish-grey; the bill is dark with a pinkish tip. The juvenile recalls the adult female but with a uniformly dark bill. In flight, all birds display diagnostic white wingbars.

Factfile

LENGTH 54–57CM

WINGSPAN 84–90CM

HABITAT IT FAVOURS LARGE EXPANSES OF WELL-VEGETATED FRESHWATER INCLUDING RESERVOIRS, GRAVEL PITS AND LOWLAND LAKES.

FOOD ITS DIET CONSISTS PRIMARILY OF AQUATIC PLANTS.

STATUS A RELATIVELY COMMON SPECIES ON MAINLAND EUROPE IN SUITABLE HABITATS; A MUCH SMALLER FERAL POPULATION EXISTS IN THE BRITISH ISLES. PRESENT YEAR-ROUND.

VOICE A MOSTLY SILENT DUCK, BUT THE MALE SOMETIMES UTTERS A WHEEZING CALL.

male

A male Red-crested Pochard has a striking amount of white on the wing, both above and below.

male

A swimming male is easy to recognise. Even at a distance in poor light, the large white patch on the flanks is a striking feature.

male life-size

Seen head-on, a male is almost unmistakable with its large, rounded orange head, pinkish-red bill and contrasting black neck and breast.

With its white face and throat, and contrasting brown cap and body, a female is a distinctive bird, and unlike any other duck.

female

The species most commonly occurs on mainland Europe, with a small feral population and the occasional vagrant found in the British Isles. It prefers large expanses of well-vegetated freshwater such as reservoirs, gravel pits and lowland lakes, where it feeds on aquatic plants. In areas where it is common, it forms large, gregarious flocks in the winter months, often associating with other diving species. It seeks dense waterside vegetation in which to nest.

Tufted Duck
Aythya fuligula

This is a common species of diving duck with a large population of resident birds present year-round. An unmistakable tuft of feathers emanating from the crown gives the species its name. The sexes differ. The adult male has a black head, breast and body, with contrasting white flanks. The head has a purplish sheen in good light. The eyes are small and yellow, and the stout bill is blue-grey and tipped with black. The adult female has brown plumage, darkest on the head and breast. The eyes are yellow and the bill is similar to the adult male; there is a small pale facial patch at the base of the bill. Note the more subdued tufting to the head when compared to the male. The juvenile resembles the adult female, but with duller plumage and eye colour. In flight, all birds display a prominent white wingbar on the trailing edge of the wing.

In flying birds, the dark-edged white flight feathers are striking in both sexes.

adults

male life-size

The male's shaggy, tufted 'crest' and the contrasting pattern on the body make identification straightforward.

female

Most females have an obvious, shaggy 'tuft' of feathers on the rear of the crown, and many show a variable extent of white on the face, adjacent to the base of the bill.

male

In harsh light, a male's body can look all dark except for the extensive and contrasting white area on the flanks.

Factfile

LENGTH 40–47CM

WINGSPAN 70CM

HABITAT FAVOURS LAKES, GRAVEL PITS, RESERVOIRS AND OTHER BODIES OF STILL FRESHWATER WITH MARGINAL VEGETATION.

FOOD AN OMNIVOROUS SPECIES, IT FEEDS ON BOTH PLANTS AND INVERTEBRATES.

STATUS A COMMON AND WIDESPREAD DUCK IN SUITABLE HABITATS. WINTER NUMBERS ARE BOOSTED BY MIGRATING BIRDS FROM FURTHER NORTH AND EAST; COMMONEST FROM OCTOBER TO MARCH.

VOICE MOSTLY SILENT, BUT THE MALES UTTER A SOFT PEEPING CALL, MAINLY DURING THE BREEDING SEASON.

The Tufted Duck is a common species, and numbers are boosted in the winter months by migratory birds. It forms large flocks at this time, often with other species such as Coot. It shows a preference for large expanses of freshwater such as gravel pits, reservoirs and lakes with marginal vegetation. It feeds on a variety of small invertebrates and aquatic plants. It constructs a well-hidden nest on the ground and near water.

Scaup
Aythya marila

A male Scaup's grey back is an obvious way of separating it from a male Tufted Duck, which has a dark back; in addition, the head is more rounded in outline and lacks any tufted crest.

The Scaup is a plump, robust-looking diving duck. The sexes are dissimilar. The adult male has a dark (almost black) green-glossed head and dark breast. The flanks are contrastingly white, the back is pale grey and the rear is black. The eyes are yellow and the stout bill is light grey with a dark tip. At first glance, it recalls male Tufted Duck but it lacks the obvious head tuft and dark back. The male in eclipse plumage is similar, but dark elements of the plumage are buffish-brown. The adult female is brown, darkest on the head and neck, paler and greyish on the back and the flanks. The eyes are yellow and the bill is dark. Note the conspicuous white facial patch at the base of the bill. The juvenile resembles the adult female but the white facial patch is less prominent. When in flight, all birds display a striking white bar on the trailing edge of the wings.

male

Factfile

LENGTH 42–51CM

WINGSPAN 71–84CM

HABITAT FAVOURS ESTUARIES, FIRTHS AND SHELTERED COASTAL AREAS, BUT IT CAN SOMETIMES BE FOUND ON LARGE INLAND STILL WATERS.

FOOD IT FEEDS ON BOTTOM-DWELLING INVERTEBRATES, FAVOURING MOLLUSCS.

STATUS PRIMARILY A WINTER VISITOR (MAINLY OCTOBER TO MARCH), IN MODEST NUMBERS AND MAINLY TO THE NORTH OF THE REGION.

VOICE GENERALLY A SILENT SPECIES OUTSIDE THE BREEDING SEASON.

Although Scaup do occasionally turn up on inland bodies of freshwater outside the breeding season, they are more usually associated with coastal and marine habitats at this time of year.

59

female

A female Scaup recalls those female Tufted Ducks that have white on the face, but note the rounded head outline and complete lack of a tufted crest.

Generally associated with northern latitudes, a handful of breeding birds have been recorded in our region. However, it is more commonly encountered in winter when migratory birds arrive from further afield. Favoured habitats are estuaries, bays and sheltered coastal areas, although birds can be encountered occasionally on large inland bodies of water such as reservoirs and large lakes. Typically, it forms flocks outside the breeding season and feeds by diving for bottom-dwelling molluscs. It nests close to pools on Arctic tundra.

In flight, note the dark-edged white flight feathers and bold white patch on the face.

female

male life-size

In flight, the grey back allows separation from a male Tufted Duck, which has a black back.

male

Eider
Somateria mollissima

Although a female Eider lacks distinctive plumage patterns, the uniquely elongated head and long, triangular bill make her an unmistakable sea duck.

The Eider is a large sea duck with an unmistakable wedge-shaped bill and head. The sexes differ. The male has striking plumage. The head, breast and back are mainly white, the breast having a pink flush, and the nape has a lime-green tinge. The head has a bold black crown extending below the dark eye and meeting the base of the light-coloured bill. The flanks and tail are black. In eclipse, the male is predominantly brown and black with evidence of white on the back and a stripe above the eye. The adult female is a rich brown, marked with a subtle darker barring, appearing uniformly dark when seen at a distance in flight. The juvenile is similar to the adult female, but has a pale stripe above the eye.

female

male

A male may appear black-and-white at first glance, but a closer look will reveal subtle lime-green colouration on the nape. The bill colour varies according to the time of year and between individuals, but appears yellowish for much of the time.

The Eider is most commonly encountered around coastal areas in the north of the region. The resident breeding population is boosted by migrants from more northerly latitudes during the winter months, and the birds can be encountered further south at this time. The Eider prefers estuaries and sheltered rocky shores. It feeds in inshore waters, diving for invertebrates, particularly molluscs. When observed in flight, it often flies low over the water, flocks forming long lines. It nests in a down-lined depression on open ground.

In flight, an Eider appears thickset and relatively short-necked, with males often looking strikingly black-and-white at a distance. Typically, birds fly low over the water.

male

Factfile

LENGTH **50–70CM**   WINGSPAN **80–110CM**

HABITAT **A COASTAL SPECIES THAT FAVOURS ROCKY SHORES AND ESTUARIES.**

FOOD **IT FEEDS ON A VARIETY OF INVERTEBRATES, PARTICULARLY MOLLUSCS.**

STATUS **COMMON AND PRESENT YEAR-ROUND IN SUITABLE COASTAL HABITATS IN THE NORTH OF OUR REGION. ITS NUMBERS ARE BOOSTED BY WINTER MIGRANTS (PRESENT MAINLY OCTOBER TO MARCH), AND THE RANGE EXTENDS FURTHER SOUTH DURING THESE MONTHS.**

VOICE **THE MALE PRODUCES A COOING *AH-WHOO* WHILE THROWING ITS HEAD BACK; FEMALE UTTERS A VARIETY OF HOARSE QUACKS.**

male life-size

At the start of the breeding season, a subtle orange-pinkish flush often suffuses the male's breast and the bill can appear bluish.

Long-tailed Duck
Clangula hyemalis

This is a rather small and attractive sea duck. The sexes are separable. It is most commonly encountered in its winter plumage, when the male is a mixture of black, grey and white. The best distinguishing features are the white breast, the large buffish patch surrounding the eye, and the elongated black tail feathers that curve elegantly upwards. The bill is rather stubby and dark with an obvious lighter pinkish central band. The female lacks the male's showy tail plumage but is otherwise similar in appearance, with the exception of the face, which is mainly white with dark a crown and cheek patch. The bill is uniformly dark. The juvenile recalls the adult female, but has a brown head and is browner overall. In flight, the wings appear relatively long and narrow and the wingbeats are rapid.

winter male

A winter male is elegant and distinctive with long tail streamers and bold plumage patterns.

winter male life-size

In late winter, before they depart the shores of Northwest Europe for Arctic breeding grounds, males can sometimes be seen displaying.

The Long-tailed Duck is migratory species that breeds in Iceland and Norway. In our region it is most commonly encountered in the winter months when it can form small flocks around coastal areas in the north. It prefers gently shelving sandy beaches and is at home in rough seas and breaking waves, feeding by diving for invertebrates, particularly molluscs. It nests on the ground close to water.

Factfile

LENGTH 40–47CM

WINGSPAN 65–82CM

HABITAT A COASTAL SPECIES WHICH FAVOURS GENTLY SHELVING SANDY BEACHES.

FOOD IT FEEDS ON BOTTOM-DWELLING INVERTEBRATES.

STATUS A MIGRATORY DUCK, MOST IN EVIDENCE IN THE WINTER MONTHS (MAINLY OCTOBER TO MARCH) AND IN THE NORTH OF OUR REGION.

VOICE THE MALE'S CALL IS A DIAGNOSTIC NASAL OW-OWLEE.

female
In flight, a winter female has rather uniformly dark wings and white body plumage that emphasises the dark eye.

summer male
Males in full breeding plumage are sometimes seen in early spring; they can be recognised by the largely dark plumage, which contrasts with the white face.

winter female
A winter female is compact and recognised by the white face and flanks, and contrasting darker back and crown.

Common Scoter

Melanitta nigra

This is a large, thick-set diving sea duck. The sexes are dissimilar. The adult male is uniformly black, the head plumage displaying a slight oily sheen in good light. The dark eye is surrounded by a subtle yellow ring. The dark-coloured bill is large and robust-looking with a bulbous base and an obvious yellow patch on the bridge. Note the elongated tail, which is held in a slightly cocked position when swimming. The first-winter male is similar, but its plumage is browner and the yellow bill patch is absent. The adult female is mainly dark brown in appearance, with dark eyes and pale buff cheeks. The juvenile resembles the adult female. In flight most individuals look uniformly dark, although lighter flight feathers can be discerned in good light.

A male has uniformly black plumage that is relieved only by the patch of yellow on the dorsal surface of the bill.

male

In particularly good light, a sheen can be seen on the male's plumage; the tail is often held cocked-up.

male

In flight, Common Scoters look bulky and compact.

female

Even at a distance, a female's pale cheeks contrast with the dark brown body plumage.

Factfile

LENGTH 44–54CM

WINGSPAN 79–90CM

HABITAT FREQUENTS LARGE LAKES AND LOCHS WITH DENSE BANKSIDE VEGETATION DURING THE BREEDING SEASON. IT IS MORE COMMONLY SEEN IN THE WINTER, WHEN IT FAVOURS SANDY COASTAL AREAS.

FOOD IT FEEDS ON BOTTOM-DWELLING INVERTEBRATES.

STATUS A MIGRATORY SPECIES, WITH A SMALL NUMBER OF BREEDING BIRDS NESTING IN THE EXTREME NORTH OF OUR REGION. IT IS MORE COMMONLY ENCOUNTERED IN WINTER (MAINLY NOVEMBER TO MARCH), WHEN IT IS ALMOST EXCLUSIVELY COASTAL.

VOICE A MAINLY SILENT SPECIES, ALTHOUGH BREEDING MALES UTTER A PIPING CALL.

A small number of birds breed in the north of our region, mostly on inland lakes. The species is generally shy and secretive during the breeding season; it becomes more gregarious and showy in the winter months, when numbers increase dramatically, with flocks migrating southwards. Flocks are often encountered flying in long lines low over the water. The Common Scoter is almost exclusively coastal in winter, and prefers areas with sandy seabeds where it feed on invertebrates. It nests on the ground near water.

Winter flocks typically fly in long, snaking lines and keep low over the water.

male life-size

Velvet Scoter
Melanitta fusca

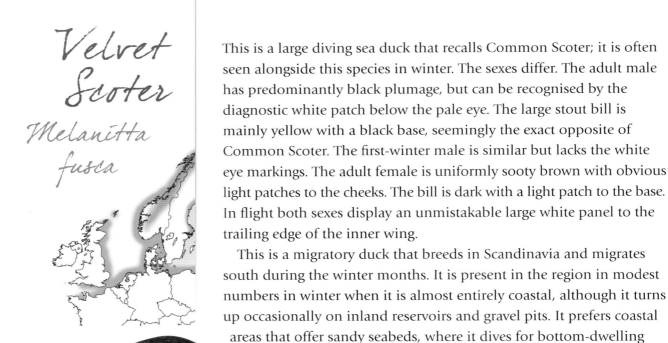

This is a large diving sea duck that recalls Common Scoter; it is often seen alongside this species in winter. The sexes differ. The adult male has predominantly black plumage, but can be recognised by the diagnostic white patch below the pale eye. The large stout bill is mainly yellow with a black base, seemingly the exact opposite of Common Scoter. The first-winter male is similar but lacks the white eye markings. The adult female is uniformly sooty brown with obvious light patches to the cheeks. The bill is dark with a light patch to the base. In flight both sexes display an unmistakable large white panel to the trailing edge of the inner wing.

This is a migratory duck that breeds in Scandinavia and migrates south during the winter months. It is present in the region in modest numbers in winter when it is almost entirely coastal, although it turns up occasionally on inland reservoirs and gravel pits. It prefers coastal areas that offer sandy seabeds, where it dives for bottom-dwelling invertebrates, and often associates with Common Scoter flocks. It nests on the ground adjacent to water.

male

A male has mostly jet-black plumage but even at a distance the white eye and white border below are easily discerned.

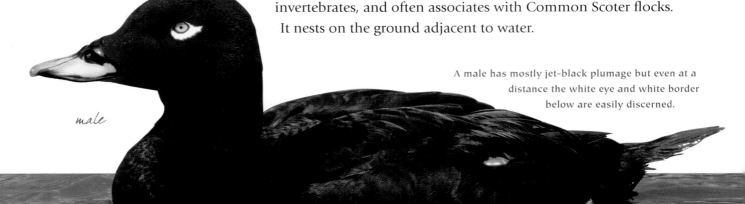

In flight, the large white panel on the wings contrasts with the otherwise uniformly dark plumage and makes identification straightforward.

adults

female

Factfile

LENGTH 51–58CM

WINGSPAN 86–99CM

HABITAT **FAVOURS COASTAL AREAS WITH SANDY SEABEDS.**

FOOD **FEEDS ON BOTTOM-DWELLING INVERTEBRATES.**

STATUS **A MIGRATORY DUCK THAT BREEDS IN SCANDINAVIA AND MIGRATES FURTHER SOUTH DURING THE WINTER MONTHS, WHERE IT IS PRESENT MAINLY FROM OCTOBER TO MARCH.**

VOICE **MOSTLY SILENT.**

The two pale patches on the female's face contrast with the otherwise dark brown plumage.

male life-size

A male's colourful bill shows up well, even in poor light, and part of the white wing panel is also usually visible in swimming birds.

Goldeneye
Bucephala clangula

The Goldeneye is a compact-looking diving duck with distinctive plumage. The sexes differ. The adult male has predominantly black-and-white plumage with a peaked, rounded black head, a conspicuous yellow eye and large rounded white cheek patch towards the base of the bill. The back and tail are black; the flanks, breast and underside are white. The stubby bill is black. Males in eclipse plumage resemble the adult female, but retain a more obvious wing pattern. The adult female has a dark brown rounded head with a yellow eye and pale neck. The remaining plumage is uniformly grey-brown with a white line adorning the top of the flanks. The juvenile resembles the adult female, but the eye is dark. In flight, both sexes display an obvious large white patch on the inner wing (less prominent in females than in males).

In flight and in both sexes, the white on the inner wing shows up well, as does the dark head, which contrasts with the white neck and underparts.

male

female

male life-size

In poor light, a male's head can look black but in sunshine a green gloss can be seen; the beady yellow eye and pale patch between the eye and bill are both good identification features.

male

Goldeneyes swim low in the water and dive frequently; the male's barred white flanks and white facial patches grab an observer's attention when a bird surfaces.

female

The female shares the same domed head shape as the male and has a pale eye; overall her plumage is less striking in other regards, being mainly grey and brown.

This species is primarily a winter visitor, the breeding population within our region restricted mainly to Scandinavia, although small numbers occur in Scotland and elsewhere. Migratory birds move south and numbers increase throughout the region significantly in the winter months, when they favour estuaries, sheltered coastal areas and inland freshwater habitats. They feed on invertebrates by diving frequently and for relatively lengthy periods of time. They nest in tree holes and also uses nest boxes.

Factfile

LENGTH 42–50CM

WINGSPAN 65–80CM

HABITAT IT FAVOURS ESTUARIES, SHELTERED COASTAL BAYS AND INLAND FRESHWATER.

FOOD IT FEEDS PRIMARILY ON INVERTEBRATES.

STATUS A MIGRATORY SPECIES THAT BREEDS IN SCANDINAVIA AND SCOTLAND, AND MIGRATES SOUTH FOR THE WINTER; IT IS WIDESPREAD BUT GENERALLY SCARCE IN SUITABLE HABITATS FROM OCTOBER TO MARCH.

VOICE MOSTLY VOCAL DURING THE BREEDING SEASON WHEN THE MALE UTTERS SQUEAKY CALLS AND A RATTLE SIMILAR TO THAT OF GARGANEY.

Smew
Mergellus albellus

The Smew is a small and elegant-looking diving duck. The sexes are dissimilar. The adult male is a striking, predominantly white bird, with a 'panda'-like black patch on the head that surrounds the dark eye and joins the base of the bill. Subtle black lines adorn the back of the neck, back and flanks. The hook-tipped and serrated bill is blue-grey. In flight, the male displays a large area of white on the inner wing. The adult female, first-winter and juvenile birds are all similar in appearance and are collectively referred to as 'redhead' Smew. The head has a dark orange cap with a rather tufted grebe-like appearance. The white cheek and throat plumage is striking in contrast. The remaining plumage is uniform grey-brown, and the wings generally show less white than in the adult male.

Adult female and immatures of both sexes are hard to separate and are referred to as 'redheads'; as the name suggests they have a reddish-brown head with a white chin.

The Smew is a migratory species that breeds north and east of our region. A relatively modest number of birds are present here during the winter months. It forms small flocks at this time and favours large, fish-rich inland freshwater habitats such as large gravel pits and reservoirs, although it can occur in sheltered coastal areas as well. It feeds by diving frequently and catching small fish, and it nests in tree holes.

female

male life-size

male

A male Smew looks strikingly black-and-white in flight, which is rapid with fast wingbeats.

The male is a striking waterbird with its mainly black-and-white plumage; at close range the bill looks bluish and the fine patterning on the flanks can be appreciated.

Factfile

LENGTH **38–44CM**

WINGSPAN **56–69CM**

HABITAT **LARGE EXPANSES OF INLAND FRESHWATER AND SHELTERED COASTAL AREAS.**

FOOD **IT FEEDS ON SMALL FISH.**

STATUS **A MIGRATORY SPECIES AND A WINTER VISITOR TO THE REGION IN SMALL NUMBERS, PRESENT MAINLY FROM OCTOBER TO MARCH.**

VOICE **SILENT.**

male

Birds dive frequently and for extended periods, in search of fish; however, well-fed birds may loaf around on the surface allowing good views to be obtained.

Red-breasted Merganser
Mergus serrator

This is a distinctive, slender-looking diving duck with a long, slim and serrated bill. The sexes are separable. The adult male has a dark green head, adorned with characteristic long unruly-looking feathers, giving it a rather straggly appearance. The neck is contrastingly white, and the breast is orange-red. The ridge of the back is black with a white stripe underneath, bordering the grey flanks. The small eyes and long serrated bill are bright red. The adult female has a rather grubby-orange head and nape, with similar straggly crown feathers to the male. The remaining plumage is mostly uniform greyish-buff, but with a pale throat. The eyes and bill are red. The juvenile recalls the adult female. In flight, both sexes display a prominent white patch on the upperwing, confined to the trailing half of the inner wing (larger in males than females).

male

In flight, note the extensive white patch on the wings, and white neck and underparts.

The shaggy crest and slender red bill are good identification features; the head can look black but in sunshine a green sheen can be discerned.

male life-size

female

Mergansers fly with necks extended; females have less white on the wings than males.

This is a migratory species with a modest breeding population in the region, mainly confined to Scandinavia and the north and west of the British Isles. Breeding birds show a preference for fish-rich large freshwater lakes, reservoirs and lochs, where they nest on the ground in waterside vegetation. During the winter months migratory birds increase numbers considerably in favoured coastal areas, particularly estuaries and other sheltered locations. It feeds by diving frequently and catching small fish and aquatic invertebrates.

Birds swim low in the water and dive frequently; Mergansers spend more time at the surface in spring, when display and courtship behaviours become apparent.

male

female

But for the shape and colour of the bill, a swimming female could be mistaken for a large grebe.

Factfile

LENGTH 52–58CM

WINGSPAN 70–86CM

HABITAT FISH-RICH FRESHWATER HABITATS DURING THE BREEDING SEASON. ALMOST ENTIRELY COASTAL DURING THE WINTER MONTHS, PREFERRING ESTUARIES AND SHELTERED AREAS.

FOOD IT FEEDS ON FISH AND AQUATIC INVERTEBRATES.

STATUS A SMALL POPULATION BREEDS IN THE BRITISH ISLES AND OTHER NORTHERLY PARTS OF OUR REGION. OUTSIDE THE BREEDING SEASON, MIGRATING BIRDS FROM FURTHER AFIELD SIGNIFICANTLY INCREASE NUMBERS IN FAVOURED COASTAL LOCATIONS; COMMONEST AND MOST WIDESPREAD FROM OCTOBER TO MARCH.

VOICE A MAINLY SILENT SPECIES. BREEDING MALES CAN UTTER A SOFT, GRUNTING CALL.

Goosander
Mergus merganser

Factfile

LENGTH 58–66CM

WINGSPAN 78–97CM

HABITAT FOUND IN FRESHWATER HABITATS, FAVOURING UPLAND RIVERS DURING THE BREEDING SEASON AND LARGE BODIES OF OPEN STILL WATER DURING THE WINTER MONTHS.

FOOD ITS DIET COMPRISES FISH, AMPHIBIANS AND LARGE AQUATIC INVERTEBRATES.

STATUS A MIGRATORY SPECIES THAT BREEDS IN THE NORTH. NUMBERS INCREASE AND ITS RANGE SPREADS SOUTHWARDS IN OUR REGION DURING THE WINTER MONTHS; COMMONEST FROM OCTOBER TO MARCH.

VOICE A MOSTLY SILENT SPECIES, BUT DISPLAYING MALES UTTER A RINGING CALL.

The Goosander is a rather regal-looking, elegant diving duck. The sexes are dissimilar. The adult male has a large, domed and rounded head; it is dark green and takes on a glossy sheen in good light. There is a clear separation between this and the white breast, flanks and underside; the back is black. In certain light, the white plumage can display a subtle pink tinge. The red bill is long, slender and serrated, with an obvious hook at the tip. In eclipse, the adult male resembles the female but retains the white wing pattern. The adult female has an orange-red head with a clear demarcation from the remaining uniformly grey plumage (unlike in the Red-breasted Merganser). The bill is long, slender and reddish in colour. The juvenile resembles the adult female but has duller plumage overall. In flight, all birds display an extensive area of white on the inner wing.

This is a migratory species that breeds in the north of the region, favouring upland river systems in wooded areas, where it nests in tree holes. It is far commoner in winter with numbers swelled by migrating birds, when it is encountered more widely and in more southerly locations. At this time of the year it has a preference for large open freshwater bodies such as gravel pits, reservoirs and lochs; it is often seen in small groups. It feeds by diving for fish, amphibians and large aquatic invertebrates.

female
A female has a reddish-orange head with a shaggy mane; both sexes dive frequently and cover considerable distances underwater in search of fish.

male
A swimming male Goosander is white at water level, with a dark back and glossy dark head.

male

In flight, the male's dark head contrasts well with the pale neck and underparts; note the extensive white patch on the upperwing.

female

Even outside the breeding season, females are usually seen in company of males.

Male has a steep forehead; a green gloss is evident in sunshine. As the breeding season approaches, a subtle pinkish-orange suffusion to the breast is acquired.

male life-size

Red Grouse/ Willow Ptarmigan

Lagopus lagopus

The Red Grouse is an iconic British gamebird and a subspecies of the Willow Ptarmigan, which occurs in northern mainland Europe. The sexes are separable; Willow Ptarmigan also shows seasonal plumage variation. The Red Grouse adult male has chestnut-brown plumage with a red wattle over the eye; the adult female is paler brown and more mottled, and lacks the red wattle. The juvenile resembles the adult female, but with less obvious plumage markings. In flight, all birds reveal uniformly dark wings and a blackish tail. In winter, adult Willow Ptarmigans have a black tail, but otherwise white plumage including the lores. In summer they recall their Red Grouse counterparts but have white underparts and white wings.

In flight, a Red Grouse has uniformly brown wings; depending on the sex, Willow Ptarmigan have a variable amount of white in their wings.

Red Grouse male

Red Grouse male
Male's plumage is uniformly reddish-brown throughout the year.

The Red Grouse is restricted to areas of upland heather moorland in the British Isles, where the land is often managed for commercial shooting; hundreds of thousands of birds are shot each year. Willow Ptarmigan is found in natural sub-Arctic and Arctic habitats. Both subspecies nest on the ground in a shallow cup beneath low vegetation.

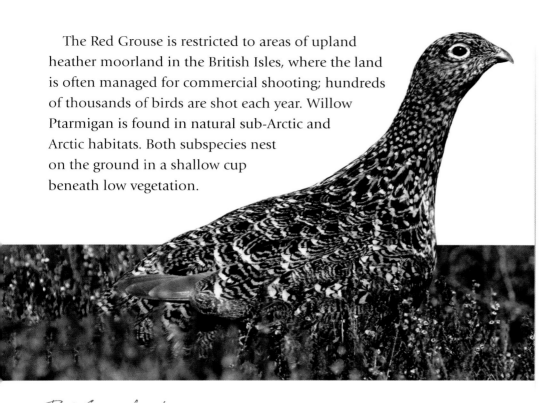

Factfile

LENGTH 37–42CM

WINGSPAN 55–66CM

HABITAT HEATHER MOORLAND IN THE NORTH OF THE BRITISH ISLES (RED GROUSE); TAIGA WOODLAND AND TUNDRA IN SCANDINAVIA (WILLOW PTARMIGAN).

FOOD FEEDS ON THE SHOOTS OF HEATHER AND RELATED PLANTS.

STATUS RED GROUSE SSP. *SCOTICA* IS RESIDENT ON MOORS IN BRITAIN; WILLOW PTARMIGAN SSP. *LAGOPUS* IS RESIDENT IN NORTHERN SCANDINAVIA.

VOICE UTTERS A NASAL CALL THAT IS SOMETIMES DESCRIBED AS '*GO BACK, GO BACK, GO BACK*'.

Red Grouse female

Female's plumage is intricately marked, and provides good camouflage among moorland vegetation.

Willow Ptarmigan summer male

Plumage varies throughout the year. In summer (seen here) the head and neck are reddish-brown but elsewhere extensively white; in winter, the plumage is almost entirely white.

Red Grouse male life-size

At close range, fine markings on the male's reddish-brown plumage can be appreciated; the red wattle is most evident in the breeding season.

Ptarmigan
Lagopus muta

The Ptarmigan is an iconic upland gamebird with different seasonal plumages. The sexes are separable at all times. The adult winter male has pure white plumage except for the dark bill, eye and lores (winter Willow Ptarmigan are similar but have white lores). A striking red wattle is situated above the eye. In summer the male takes on a marbled greyish-buff appearance to the upperparts, the white plumage gradually decreasing and the red wattle fading as the season progresses. The underside remains white. The winter female has uniform white plumage with a black bill and eye. As spring gives way to summer the plumage moults, the white on the upperparts gradually giving way to a buffish-grey, marked with a fine barred pattern. The juvenile is uniformly brown and resembles the summer female. In flight, all birds display white wings and a conspicuous black tail.

The Ptarmigan is a hardy gamebird of high mountains. Its changing seasonal plumage offers camouflage both in winter snow and against the leafy moorland scrub of summer, the degree of white in the plumage gradually decreasing as spring and summer progress. It is an unobtrusive bird that feeds on the shoots of a variety of plants, but with a preference for birch and willow. It nests in a feather-lined scrape on the ground.

winter male life-size

The plumage is mostly pure white in winter; the male has black lores and a red wattle that becomes more obvious later in the season.

summer male

The plumage is rather 'mottled' in appearance in spring and summer with variable amounts of white, particularly on the underparts.

Factfile

LENGTH 34–36CM   WINGSPAN 54–60CM

HABITAT INHABITS ROCKY TERRAIN, GENERALLY ABOVE 1,000M IN THE SOUTH OF ITS RANGE BUT OCCURS AT LOWER ALTITUDES FURTHER NORTH.

FOOD FEEDS ON VARIETY OF VEGETATION, WITH A PREFERENCE FOR WILLOW AND BIRCH BUDS AND CATKINS.

STATUS RESTRICTED TO NORTHERN SCANDINAVIA AND THE SCOTTISH HIGHLANDS, WHERE IT IS LOCALLY COMMON AND RESIDENT YEAR-ROUND.

VOICE UTTERS A RATTLING *KUR-KURR* CALL.

winter male

In winter, all birds have pure white plumage except for the black tail.

winter male

Pure white winter plumage is an adaptation to snowy conditions, providing good camouflage.

summer female

In summer, the female's plumage is intricate and a perfect match for moorland and mountain vegetation.

Black Grouse
Lyrurus tetrix

In flight, the plumage shows extensive patches of white on both the upperwing and underwing.

Factfile

LENGTH **40–55CM**

WINGSPAN **65–80CM**

HABITAT **OCCURS IN MOORLAND HABITATS WHERE A COMBINATION OF HEATHER, BILBERRY, GRASSLAND AND ADJACENT WOODLAND ARE PRESENT.**

FOOD **FEEDS ON THE SHOOTS AND BUDS OF A VARIETY OF PLANTS AND TREES.**

STATUS **OCCURS IN SMALL LOCALISED AND RESIDENT POPULATIONS IN SUITABLE HABITATS. NUMBERS ARE IN SEVERE DECLINE IN THE UK, AND THE SPECIES IS THE SUBJECT OF REINTRODUCTION PROGRAMMES; WIDESPREAD BUT ALSO VERY LOCAL IN MAINLAND EUROPE.**

VOICE **DISPLAYING MALES UTTER A PROLONGED BUBBLING, COOING CALL.**

The Black Grouse is a bulky gamebird. The sexes have different plumages, and males are larger than females. The adult male has mostly black plumage that has a bluish sheen in good light, and a large, bright red wattle above the eye. The white stern can often be discerned in displaying males as they fan their tails. In flight, the wings are white on the underside and display prominent white bars on the upperside; the tail is commonly fanned. The smaller female has fairly uniform orange-brown plumage, marked with a pattern of fine dark barring. The eye lacks the red wattle of the male, and

males

in flight a fine white bar is revealed on the wings. The juvenile resembles a small female but has more subdued markings.

This is a moorland gamebird whose numbers and range are in sharp decline. It is famous for its lekking behaviour: in spring, groups of males gather in the early morning at traditional sites to display and seek the attention of onlooking females. These displays can be quite a spectacle, with numbers of males jousting and squabbling with each other. It nests on the ground in a shallow, grass-lined scrape.

male life-size

In good light, the seemingly dark body plumage is revealed as having a beautiful bluish sheen.

female

A female's plumage is intricately patterned, which provides good camouflage when incubating eggs amongst moorland vegetation.

male

A displaying male calls loudly and spreads his lyre-shaped tail.

Capercaillie
Tetrao urogallus

The Capercaillie is a large and unmistakable northern and upland gamebird. The sexes differ. The adult male is an imposing bird that appears mainly dark at a distance. Closer inspection reveals a metallic green sheen to the breast, brownish wings and a red wattle above the eye. A distinctive round white spot is obvious on the base of the folded forewing. The large, dark tail is fanned out and held upright when the bird is displaying. In flight, the wings and tail are dark and appear proportionately long. The adult female is significantly smaller than the male and has grey-brown plumage, finely marked with dark barring. The breast displays a plain orange-brown patch. The juvenile resembles the adult female, but with duller plumage.

Male Capercaillies are known for their intimidating lekking displays during the winter and early spring months, and birds are sometimes aggressive towards people. When disturbed from cover it will sometimes 'explode' into flight. Capercaillies are restricted to a few derelict coniferous woodlands and mature coniferous plantations in Scotland; they were reintroduced during the nineteenth century, having been hunted to extinction. The species occurs in similar habitats in Scandinavia and the mountains of central Europe. It nests on the ground in a shallow depression.

male life-size

A displaying male is noisy and aggressive towards other males, and sometimes towards human intruders into his territory.

female

A female's plumage is orange-brown overall, darker above than below and marked with intricate patterning.

Factfile

LENGTH **60–90CM**

WINGSPAN **90–125CM**

HABITAT UPLAND AND MOUNTAINOUS MATURE CONIFEROUS WOODLAND, INCLUDING LONG-ESTABLISHED PLANTATIONS.

FOOD FEEDS ON PINE NEEDLES AND A VARIETY OF OTHER LEAVES, BUDS, GRASSES AND INSECTS.

STATUS WIDESPREAD RESIDENT IN SCANDINAVIA AND MOUNTAINS OF CENTRAL EUROPE. SMALL, LOCALISED RESIDENT POPULATIONS EXIST IN SCOTLAND.

VOICE THE MALE UTTERS A STRANGE CALL CONSISTING OF A SERIES OF CLICKING SOUNDS, FOLLOWED BY A NOISE SIMILAR TO THE REMOVAL OF THE CORK FROM A BOTTLE OF WINE.

male

A displaying male fans his tail. In good light his subtle colouration can be appreciated: the head and neck have a bluish sheen while the wings are brown.

Grey Partridge

Perdix perdix

The Grey Partridge is a small and rather rotund gamebird. Sexes are similar but separable with care. The adult male has finely marked grey plumage overall, with maroon stripes to the flanks, a distinctive orange-buff face and a large dark chestnut patch on the belly. The bill is small. The adult female recalls the male, but the chestnut belly patch is smaller and much less distinct. The juvenile is more uniformly grey-buff with a hint of the adult markings.

The Grey Partridge is a wary bird that lives in small groups outside the breeding season. It tends to run from the merest hint of danger; when taking to flight, it generally flies low to the ground. Once common and widespread, numbers are now in serious decline owing primarily

male

In alarm, birds take to the air on rapid wingbeats, then fly in level flight, gliding before dropping down again.

male

Factfile

LENGTH 29–31CM

WINGSPAN 45–48CM

HABITAT A SPECIES OF OPEN GRASSLAND AND ARABLE FARMLAND WITH MATURE HEDGEROWS.

FOOD FEEDS ON SEEDS, PLANTS AND INSECTS.

STATUS NATIVE RESIDENT. FORMERLY WIDESPREAD AND COMMON THROUGHOUT THE REGION, BUT NUMBERS ARE NOW IN SERIOUS DECLINE, WITH ONLY SMALL POPULATIONS IN LOCALISED AREAS REMAINING.

VOICE UTTERS A LOAD, HARSH *KIERR-IKK* CALL.

All birds have intricate patterning on the body feathers; the male has a more colourful orange face than the female and a dark belly patch.

to intensive farming practices and the use of pesticides and herbicides. The abundance of small invertebrates is crucial to successful breeding, as young birds rely almost entirely on this food source for the first few weeks of life. Small numbers still exist in sympathetically managed areas; the numbers are supported by the release each year of a small number of captive-bred birds. It nests in low cover on the ground in a shallow, grass-lined scrape.

female

A female's plumage is more subdued than a male, and overall less colourful.

male life-size

A male's territorial call is evocative of well-managed spring farmland, but an increasingly scarce sound in intensively farmed areas.

male

Seen head-on, the male's dark chestnut belly patch is distinctive and diagnostic.

Red-legged Partridge
Alectoris rufa

The facial pattern is distinctive with the red bill and eye-surround, and black-framed white throat.

Factfile

LENGTH 32–34CM

WINGSPAN 45–50CM

HABITAT TYPICALLY OCCURS ON ARABLE FARMLAND WITH MATURE HEDGEROWS AND PATCHY WOODLAND. ALSO INHABITS HEATHLAND AND COASTAL GRASSLAND.

FOOD FEEDS ON SEEDS, PLANTS AND INSECTS.

STATUS NATIVE RESIDENT OF MAINLAND EUROPE AND INTRODUCED TO BRITAIN, WHERE IT IS COMMONEST IN THE SOUTH AND EAST. A POPULAR GAMEBIRD WITH THE SHOOTING INDUSTRY, NUMBERS BOOSTED EACH AUTUMN BY THE RELEASE OF CAPTIVE-BRED BIRDS.

VOICE UTTERS A LOUD *KE CHE-CHE, KE CHE-CHE* CALL.

This is a small, plump and well-marked gamebird with a stubby-looking tail. The sexes are similar. The adult has mainly blue-grey and warm buff plumage, with distinctive black-and-white barring to the flanks. There is an obvious white throat patch surrounded by black spots. The eye is dark, the small bill is red, and the legs are also red. In flight, the wings appear rounded and the wingbeats are rapid.

The Red-legged Partridge is bred and released in large numbers by those involved in the shooting industry, keeping its numbers artificially high in many farmland areas. It is a shy, wary bird that often runs to avoid danger, in a rapid and rather comical motion. It flies low over the ground on stiffly held wings. The species is most commonly associated with arable farmland offering mature hedgerows and light woodland, but also occurs on heathland and areas of coastal grassland. It nests in low cover on the ground in a shallow, grass-lined scrape.

adult

The body is plump, marked with barring on the flanks and a 'necklace' of black spots on the breast. The species is usually seen in small groups known as 'covies' and prefers to run from danger rather than fly.

Quail
Coturnix coturnix

The Quail is a tiny, furtive gamebird that is heard more often than it is seen. The sexes are similar but separable with care. The adult male has mainly rich brown plumage overall, streaked with white on the head and flanks. The breast is lighter orange-brown, grading to pale buffish on the underside. Note the black-centred pale throat, defined by dark lines. The female is similar to the male, but lacks the black throat marking. The juvenile is similar to the adult female.

The Quail is a summer visitor to northwest Europe from its wintering grounds in Africa; it breeds throughout the region. It is heavily hunted on migration and numbers are relatively low, resulting in sparse, localised populations in suitable habitats. A reluctant flier, if flushed it flies low and direct with rapid beats from surprisingly narrow, bowed wings; it quickly drops down into cover. The Quail is an extremely shy bird that is rarely seen or flushed during daylight hours. It is most frequently located by its call, which it utters more commonly at dawn and dusk. It can sometimes be observed running low to the ground between rows of arable crops. The nest is a shallow scrape on the ground in dense grass.

adult

The body is rounded and compact, and legs are relatively short.

The plumage is subtly marked with brown, white and black streaking, with intricate barring on the back. A Quail prefers to run from danger rather than fly.

adult life-size

Factfile

LENGTH 16–18CM

WINGSPAN 32–35CM

HABITAT FAVOURS ARABLE FARMLAND.

FOOD ITS DIET CONSISTS OF VARIOUS SEEDS AND INVERTEBRATES.

STATUS A MIGRATORY SPECIES AND BREEDING SUMMER VISITOR FROM ITS WINTERING GROUNDS IN AFRICA. IT IS THE SUBJECT OF EXTREME HUNTING PRESSURE ON MIGRATION IN THE MEDITERRANEAN REGION. IT IS SPARSELY DISTRIBUTED, PARTICULARLY IN BRITAIN.

VOICE UTTERS A DISTINCTIVE, RATHER LIQUID TRISYLLABIC SONG, *WHIT-WE-WHIT*, SOMETIMES RENDERED AS '*WET MY LIPS*'.

Pheasant
Phasianus colchicus

The Pheasant is a large and colourful gamebird. The sexes are strikingly dissimilar. The adult male has rich orange-brown plumage and a dark blue-green head that can display a metallic sheen in good light. The eye is surrounded by an obvious rounded, bright red wattle. The neck is commonly adorned with a white neck ring, although some birds lack this feature. The long, showy tail is orange-brown with dark barring. The adult female is modest in comparison, being smaller than the male with finely mottled, buffish-brown plumage overall, and a shorter tail. The juvenile resembles a small adult female with a short tail. In flight, note the broad, rounded wings and long, finger-like primaries.

Factfile

LENGTH MALE 65–90CM; FEMALE 55–70CM

WINGSPAN 80–90CM

HABITAT OCCURS PRIMARILY IN FARMLAND AND WOODLAND HABITATS.

FOOD FEEDS ON A VARIETY OF SEEDS AND INVERTEBRATES.

STATUS INTRODUCED AND NOW COMMON AND WIDESPREAD. A VERY POPULAR HUNTING QUARRY, NUMBERS ARE BOOSTED SIGNIFICANTLY BY THE RELEASE OF CAPTIVE-BRED BIRDS BY THE SHOOTING INDUSTRY.

VOICE TERRITORIAL MALES UTTER A LOUD AND UNMISTAKABLE *COO-CUKK* SHRIEKING CALL, ACCOMPANIED BY VIGOROUS WING BEATING. WHEN ALARMED OR FLUSHED A LOUD *KE-TUK, KE-TUK, KE-TUK* IS UTTERED, ACCOMPANIED BY CONSPICUOUS AND RAPID WINGBEATS AS IT FLIES AWAY.

female

A female's plumage is overall brown with dark centres and white margins to the back feathers.

male

A male is colourful and unmistakable; many individuals have a white collar but some do not.

The Pheasant originates in Asia and has been introduced in the region over many centuries. Its breeding status is hard to determine owing to the millions of birds that are bred in captivity and released each year for shooting. It is a familiar sight in rural areas and commonly flushed from cover, taking flight with a series of rapid noisy wingbeats, accompanied by its distinctive alarm call. It roosts in trees and nests on the ground.

In flight, note the broad, rounded wings and very long tail, accompanied by loud calls.

male

female

In flight, the female appears uniformly brown; the tail is noticeably shorter than that of the male.

male life-size

At close range, note the male's bright red wattle, beady yellow eye and tufts of feathers at the back of the head; in good light a sheen can be seen on the neck feathers.

Red-throated Diver
Gavia stellata

This is a handsome diving bird that swims low in the water and typically holds its head pointing upwards. The sexes are similar. The summer adult has a uniform blue-grey colouration to the face and sides of the neck; the eye is bright red. The distinctive deep red throat patch present at this time of year can appear almost black in certain light. The back of the neck is marked with black-and-white lines that extend around the base of the neck and below the red throat. The back and sides are dark brownish-grey, and the underside is whitish. In contrast, the winter adult has a white throat and cheeks, with a grey neck and crown. Note the diagnostic white crescent around the front of the eye. The breast and underparts are white; the back and flanks are dark grey with a fine diamond patterning. The dagger-like bill is long and dark grey in summer but light grey, almost whitish, in winter. The juvenile recalls the winter adult, but the upperparts are browner, and the underparts are grubby-white. In flight, the head and neck are held outstretched with the legs and feet trailing behind.

adult summer life-size

The beady red eye, blue-grey neck colouration and black-and-white striped nape are obvious but the colour on the throat can be hard to discern.

adult winter

In flight, the head is held outstretched and birds typically fly low over the water.

The Red-throated Diver breeds on the margins of small freshwater pools, venturing to the sea to feed. During the winter the species is mainly coastal, favouring relatively shallow inshore waters. It feeds primarily on fish by diving frequently, which it does by slipping unobtrusively beneath the water rather than 'leaping' in the manner of a Cormorant or Shag. It nests in a shallow scrape on the ground among low vegetation.

adult winter

At a distance, a bird looks black-and-white but at close range an intricate pattern of white spots on the back can be appreciated.

Factfile

LENGTH **55–65CM**

WINGSPAN **106–116CM**

HABITAT **ALMOST EXCLUSIVELY COASTAL OUTSIDE THE BREEDING SEASON, WITH OCCASIONAL INDIVIDUALS ENCOUNTERED ON INLAND RESERVOIRS AND LARGE GRAVEL PITS. NESTS ON SMALL FRESHWATER POOLS WITHIN FLYING DISTANCE OF THE SEA, OR (IN SCANDINAVIA) LARGE FISH-RICH LAKES.**

FOOD **FEEDS PRIMARILY ON FISH.**

STATUS **DURING THE BREEDING SEASON IT OCCURS IN THE NORTH OF THE REGION, MAINLY IN SCANDINAVIA, WITH A RELATIVELY SMALL BREEDING POPULATION IN SCOTLAND. MORE WIDESPREAD DURING THE WINTER MONTHS, FAVOURING INSHORE WATERS.**

VOICE **MOSTLY SILENT. DURING THE BREEDING SEASON IT UTTERS WAILING AND CROAKING CALLS.**

adult summer

Birds swim with the bill tilted upwards; the red throat colouration is easiest to appreciate in swimming birds, in good light.

Black-throated Diver *Gavia arctica*

Factfile

LENGTH 60–70CM

WINGSPAN 100–120CM

HABITAT IN WINTER, ALMOST EXCLUSIVELY COASTAL, WITH OCCASIONAL INDIVIDUALS ENCOUNTERED ON LOCHS, RESERVOIRS AND LARGE GRAVEL PITS. DURING THE BREEDING SEASON IT FAVOURS LARGE LAKES.

FOOD FEEDS PRIMARILY ON FISH.

STATUS BREEDS PRIMARILY IN SCANDINAVIA, WITH A FEW PAIRS IN SCOTLAND. MORE COMMONLY SEEN DURING THE WINTER MONTHS WHEN THE POPULATION DISPERSES AROUND THE COAST, MAINTAINING A PREFERENCE FOR THE NORTH OF THE REGION.

VOICE MOSTLY SILENT. DURING THE BREEDING SEASON IT UTTERS WAILING AND CROAKING CALLS.

This is a robust diving bird that swims buoyantly in the water and holds its head and bill horizontally. The sexes are similar. The summer adult is a stunning bird with a uniform blue-grey head and nape, and a black throat. The sides of the neck are marked with contrasting black-and-white lines that continue below the black throat, grading to whitish on the breast and underside. The back and flanks are blackish and adorned with an attractive chequer-board pattern of white spots. In winter the adult takes on a more uniform dark grey colouration to the upperparts, with a whitish throat and underparts. Note the obvious white patch on the flanks close to the tail when swimming. The bill is relatively long and slender, black in the summer and grey during the winter months. The juvenile is similar to the winter adult, but the upperparts are browner and the underparts grubbier. In flight, the head and neck are held outstretched, the legs and feet trailing behind.

The Black-throated Diver is generally most widespread in our region in winter, when it spreads around the coast, although some individuals may be encountered on large bodies of freshwater such as reservoirs and gravel pits. It feeds primarily on fish by diving frequently, which it does by slipping beneath the water rather than 'leaping' like a Cormorant or Shag. It nests on the ground in a depression among low vegetation, often on small islands.

Could be confused with the (much larger) Great Northern Diver in winter plumage but note the more dainty bill and white flank patch seen at water level in swimming birds.

adult winter

adult summer

adult summer life-size

Patterns of black-and-white
stripes on the neck and breast are
obvious and striking even in poor light.

adult summer

Like other diver species, the
head and neck are held
outstretched in flight.

The head, neck and breast
patterns of breeding birds
are diagnostic.

Great Northern Diver

Gavia immer

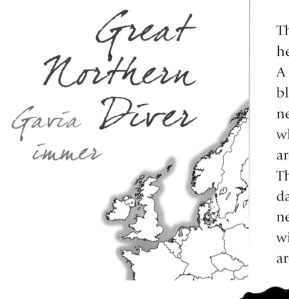

This is a large, solid-looking diving bird with a large bill that is held horizontally or pointed slightly upward. The sexes are similar. A summer adult (occasionally seen in the region) has a distinctive black head and neck that shows a slight sheen in good light. The neck is marked with two collar-like patches of vertical black-and-white lines. The breast and underparts are white; the flanks and back are blackish and marked with a chequer-board pattern of white spots. The bill is black. The more commonly seen winter adult is uniformly dark grey on the head, back and flanks, and whitish on the throat, neck, breast and underparts. The bill takes on a lighter grey colouration with a dark culmen. Juveniles recall a winter adult, but the upperparts are browner while the underparts are grubbier. In flight, the head and neck are held outstretched, the legs and feet trailing behind.

adult winter life-size

The bill is massive and the forehead has a rather angular profile when compared to the rounded profile of a Black-throated Diver.

Swimming birds spend lots of time preening and often have a good flap at the end of a session.

adult summer

Factfile

LENGTH 75–85CM

WINGSPAN 122–148CM

HABITAT FAVOURS INSHORE SEAS AND SHELTERED COASTAL AREAS, BUT IS ALSO THE DIVER MOST FREQUENTLY FOUND ON RESERVOIRS, LOCHS AND LARGE GRAVEL PITS.

FOOD FEEDS PRIMARILY ON FISH AND CRABS.

STATUS A MIGRATORY BIRD AND A WIDESPREAD WINTER VISITOR, SHOWING A PREFERENCE FOR THE NORTH OF THE REGION. A SMALL NUMBER OF BIRDS SOMETIMES LINGER INTO THE EARLY PART OF THE BREEDING SEASON.

VOICE SILENT DURING THE WINTER MONTHS. UTTERS A WAILING 'SONG' DURING THE BREEDING SEASON.

The Great Northern Diver is a migratory bird and most commonly seen as a winter visitor, favouring the coasts of the British Isles and the North Sea coast of mainland Europe. It occasionally lingers into the early part of the breeding season, but does not nest in our region. It is the most likely diver species to be encountered on large, inland expanses of freshwater. It is a buoyant swimmer that feeds by diving for fish and crabs, submerging in an elegant gliding motion rather than by 'leaping'.

It swims rather low in the water and submerges with a smooth 'gliding' action.

adult winter

adult summer

The breeding plumage is elegant and distinctive, the black neck emphasising the bands of white stripes, and large white spots adorning the black back.

Fulmar
Fulmarus glacialis

This is a superficially gull-like seabird with a stout head and neck. The sexes are similar. The adult typically has uniform blue-grey upperparts; the head and underparts are white, with a noticeable dark 'smudge' surrounding the dark eye. The heavy bill is blue-grey with a yellowish rounded and hooked tip and obvious tube nostrils at the base. In flight, the long slender wings are held characteristically rigid, the bird soaring and gliding on the air currents. The juvenile resembles the adult once the fluffy chick down has been lost.

The Fulmar breeds in good numbers (often in loose colonies) on steep cliffs and ledges, or in burrows, primarily around the British Isles. It is a buoyant swimmer and commonly seen swimming in groups surrounding boats in the hope of an easy meal. If threatened, it will discharge the oily contents of its crop in a projectile manner over an intruder.

adult life-size

Vocal when on breeding grounds and typically almost indifferent to the presence of human observers who keep a reasonable distance away. Note the large tube nostrils.

Factfile

LENGTH 43–52CM

WINGSPAN 105–110CM

HABITAT EXCLUSIVELY MARITIME. FAVOURS STEEP AND REMOTE SEA CLIFFS ON WHICH TO BREED; ENTIRELY PELAGIC AT OTHER TIMES.

FOOD FEEDS PRIMARILY ON FISH AND CRUSTACEANS.

STATUS WIDESPREAD AND RELATIVELY COMMON IN SUITABLE HABITATS ON THE COAST OF THE BRITISH ISLES; PRESENT IN SMALLER NUMBERS ON THE NORTH COASTS OF CONTINENTAL EUROPE.

VOICE UTTERS VARIOUS GRUNTS AND GURGLING CACKLES AT COLONIES.

Masterful flight means that birds can ride the up-currents alongside their breeding cliffs with ease.

adult

adult

At sea, a Fulmar typically employs a gliding flight and seldom has to flap its wings if conditions are windy.

adult

Swims buoyantly and, when visiting boats, not deterred by the presence of larger birds such as gulls.

Manx Shearwater
Puffinus puffinus

The Manx Shearwater is most commonly encountered in flight at sea. The sexes are similar. The adult has a blackish head and upperparts that can take on a reddish-brown appearance in evening light. In contrast, the underparts are predominantly white with dark wing margins. The dark bill is relatively long and slender, with a rounded and hooked tip, and the legs and feet are pinkish. The wings are long and slender and held stiffly when in flight, the bird most frequently seen swiftly banking, and gliding effortlessly low over the water.

adult life-size

Manxies (as they are known affectionately to birdwatchers) are vulnerable on land at breeding colonies. Their legs will only allow them to shuffle along; typically birds land within a few feet of their burrows, minimising the distance they need to cover.

Factfile

LENGTH 30–35CM

WINGSPAN 70–85CM

HABITAT A SEABIRD OF THE OPEN OCEAN.

FOOD FISH AND MARINE INVERTEBRATES.

STATUS A MIGRATORY SPECIES AND A SUMMER BREEDING VISITOR TO THE NORTH ATLANTIC AREA, NESTING ON REMOTE ISLANDS.

VOICE SILENT WHEN AT SEA, BUT NESTING BIRDS UTTER ODD, STRANGLED COUGHING CALLS AT NIGHT.

Typical flight is low over the sea on stiffly held wings, birds alternately revealing the dark upperwings then the contrastingly mainly white underparts.

adult

The upperwings appear mostly uniformly dark although the white throat and thigh patches are usually visible.

adult

This migratory species is only present in the North Atlantic region from April to September. During the breeding season the birds gather in huge numbers and nest in burrows on remote offshore islands, primarily off the coast of the British Isles. It visits land only after dark, and huge numbers can be seen flying low over the water, returning to their burrows at dusk. Their legs are incapable of fully supporting their weight, which results in a rather shuffled and laboured gait on land. Unsurprisingly they are vulnerable to terrestrial predators, and infestations of Brown Rats on breeding islands can cause rapid population declines. However, recent rat-eradication programmes have produced swift increases in breeding populations.

Storm Petrel
Hydrobates pelagicus

This is the smallest petrel encountered in the region, and it recalls a House Martin in size and colouration. The sexes are similar. At first glance, and at a distance, the adult plumage appears uniformly dark sooty-brown. Note the square-ended tail and the white rump-band, clearly visible when in flight. The underside of the wing displays a white bar situated towards the trailing edge. The bill is rather short and dark with a rounded, down-turned hook-tip. The juvenile recalls the adult, but the majority of first-winter birds have a pale white bar on the upperwing. Its flight is strong and direct, but also fluttering on occasions and commonly described as bat-like, with the legs dangling beneath the body. It generally stays low to the water.

The Storm Petrel occurs around the coasts of the region, especially in the west, with a population of breeding birds numbering in the hundreds of thousands. Observing the species is a challenge since it only visits land at night and during the breeding season, seeking remote islands off the coast of Ireland and the west coast of Britain; it nests in burrows and rock cavities. Otherwise, it is most commonly encountered on boat crossings, or on migration in the autumn when onshore gales blow birds close to land. It feeds by picking food items from the surface of the sea, and shallow diving.

Note the square-ended or slightly rounded tail

adult

adult life-size

In poor light, birds appear uniformly dark except for the white rump. At close range, a hint of a wingbar on the upperwing is visible in some individuals.

Factfile

LENGTH 15–16CM

WINGSPAN 37–41CM

HABITAT **ENTIRELY PELAGIC OUTSIDE THE BREEDING SEASON, IT BREEDS ON REMOTE ISLANDS.**

FOOD **FEEDS ON SMALL FISH AND VARIOUS MARINE INVERTEBRATES.**

STATUS **A SUMMER BREEDING VISITOR, REGULARLY ENCOUNTERED IN THE REGION, MOST COMMONLY ON THE WEST COAST OF THE BRITISH ISLES.**

VOICE **THEY ARE SILENT AT SEA, BUT UTTER STRANGE GURGLING AND PURRING NOISES FROM THEIR NESTING SITES.**

Leach's Petrel

Oceanodroma leucorhoa

This species recalls a Storm Petrel but is larger and more robust-looking, with longer wings. The sexes are similar. At first glance, the adult plumage has a uniform sooty-grey appearance, but note the central pale bar on the upperside of the wing. At the base of the forked tail the rump displays a clear white band with a faint dark central divide that is hard to discern, except at close range. The underwings are uniformly dark. The thick bill is dark with a rounded hooked tip. The juvenile resembles the adult. The flight is swift and erratic, with powerful wingbeats in between glides and constant changes of direction.

adult

Birds sometimes patter their feet on the water's surface when feeding.

The forked tail and pale upperwing panels are the best feature for separation from Storm Petrel.

adult

adult life-size

Exhausted birds sometimes rest on the water, swimming buoyantly.

Factfile

LENGTH 16–18CM

WINGSPAN 43–48CM

HABITAT MAINLY PELAGIC, AND RARELY SEEN CLOSE TO LAND. BREEDS ON REMOTE AND INACCESSIBLE ISLANDS.

FOOD FEEDS ON PLANKTON AND SMALL MARINE INVERTEBRATES.

STATUS A WIDESPREAD SPECIES WITH A LARGE BREEDING POPULATION IN THE REGION, BUT RARELY ENCOUNTERED CLOSE TO LAND.

VOICE SILENT WHEN AT SEA. BIRDS AT BREEDING COLONIES UTTER A STRANGE GURGLING RATTLE.

Leach's Petrel is a rarely encountered pelagic and migratory species, with a breeding population in the region that numbers many thousands. It breeds on remote and inaccessible islands, mainly off the coasts of the British Isles and Scandinavia, only visiting land at night; it nests in burrows and rock cavities. Otherwise, it is most commonly encountered on migration in the autumn when onshore gales blow birds close to land. It feeds by skimming low over the sea, picking plankton and small marine invertebrates from the surface.

Gannet
Morus bassanus

The Gannet is a large and easily identified seabird. The sexes are similar. The adult has a cigar-shaped body with long and rather slender wings. The plumage is mainly brilliant white with the exception of contrastingly black wingtips and a head that has a distinct yellow flush. The pale blue eyes are situated adjacent to the large, dagger-like bill. The adult plumage is acquired over a five-year period. The juvenile is uniformly grey-brown; a second-year bird is similar to the juvenile but with a white head and underparts; a third-year bird is mainly sooty black with scattered white feathers; a fourth-year recalls the adult but the white plumage is speckled with black feathers. In flight, note the deep, powerful wingbeats; it also glides and soars on stiffly held wings.

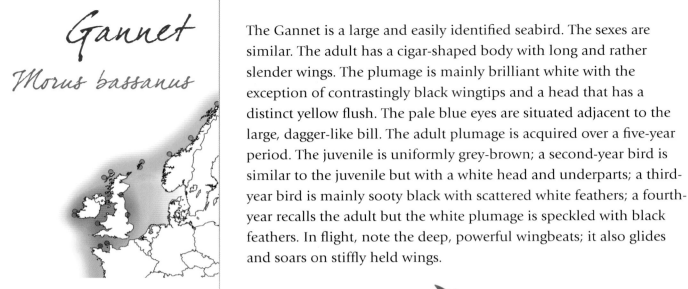

Immature's dark wings and back are retained into 2nd summer but head and neck have variably pale, adult-like feathering.

2nd summer

adult life-size
This is our largest seabird, with a massive pale bill, framed by dark edges. At close range (at a colony) note the pale eye with a blue surround, and orange-yellow flush to the back of the head and neck.

Factfile

LENGTH **85–97CM**   WINGSPAN **165–180CM**   HABITAT **SEEN EXCLUSIVELY AT SEA EXCEPT WHEN NESTING.**   FOOD **FEEDS ON FISH AND SQUID.**   STATUS **A LOCALLY COMMON AND WIDESPREAD COASTAL SPECIES DURING THE BREEDING SEASON, NESTING ON SUITABLE CLIFFS AND ISLANDS. THE MAJORITY MIGRATE SOUTH FOR THE WINTER WITH A FEW BIRDS REMAINING.** VOICE **SILENT WHEN AT SEA. NESTING BIRDS UTTER A HARSH, GRATING CALL.**

At close range, a juvenile's brown plumage is seen to be spangled with pale spots.

juvenile

adult

In flight, an adult's large size and mainly white plumage with contrasting black wingtips make it unmistakable.

adult

In breeding colonies, off-duty parents often stand watch on a rock adjacent to their nest.

The Gannet forms large breeding colonies at a number of traditional sites around the coast, favouring steep cliffs, headlands and uninhabited islands, especially in the north. The summer months see hundreds of thousands of birds in suitable coastal locations in the region. Southerly migration sees numbers dramatically decline over the winter months, but some birds do remain and may be encountered at sea. It feeds in groups on fish close to the surface, diving dramatically from great heights and rapidly entering the water in an arrow-like posture.

Cormorant
Phalacrocorax carbo

The Cormorant is a large, sleek-looking and dark-coloured waterbird with a long, slim neck and long hook-tipped bill. The sexes are similar. At first glance the adult appears mostly dark. On close inspection, and in good light, its plumage displays an oily sheen with a noticeably 'scaly' back of black-bordered brown upperwing coverts. The green eye is situated within a patch of pale bare skin with a yellow tinge closest to the bill. In breeding plumage, the adult has white 'thigh' patches

adult summer

In good light, summer birds show a sheen to their dark feathers, and dark-edged brown feathers on the back; in poor light, birds can look almost uniformly dark.

adult summer

Flies with its head and neck outstretched; the white 'thigh' patches are easiest to observe in flying birds.

Factfile

LENGTH 80–100CM

WINGSPAN 121–149CM

HABITAT TRADITIONALLY A BIRD OF COASTAL AREAS BUT INCREASINGLY COMMON IN FRESHWATER HABITATS SUCH AS RESERVOIRS, GRAVEL PITS AND LARGE RIVERS.

FOOD FEEDS ON FISH.

STATUS A WATERBIRD WITH A LARGE RESIDENT POPULATION, COMMON IN SUITABLE HABITATS. IT IS MORE WIDESPREAD IN THE WINTER MONTHS, WITH NUMBERS BOOSTED BY MIGRANT BIRDS.

VOICE IT IS SILENT OUTSIDE THE BREEDING SEASON, BUT UTTERS GUTTURAL AND NASAL CALLS AT BREEDING COLONIES.

(noticeable in flight) and white speckling to the head and neck. The juvenile is brown above, white underneath and takes two years to reach maturity. Cormorants swim low in the water with the bill tilted slightly upwards; they dive frequently with a distinct 'leap'. The head and neck are held extended when the bird is in flight.

The Cormorant forms large colonies during the breeding season, building nests of twigs and seaweed, most commonly on steep coastal cliffs, but also in trees. It is often seen perching in trees and on rocks with its wings outstretched, and it feeds by diving frequently for fish, propelling itself underwater with its large webbed feet. The resident population is more widespread during the winter months when numbers are also boosted in the region by birds that have migrated from elsewhere in Europe.

adult summer life-size

For a brief period in the breeding season, the head and upper neck of adult birds are adorned with white feather flecks and the bare skin surrounding the eye and bill base becomes colourful.

All birds swim low in the water. In winter, the plumage is more uniformly dark than in summer; the throat is contrastingly pale.

adult winter

Shag
Phalacrocorax aristotelis

The Shag is similar to the Cormorant, but smaller and separable with experience. The sexes are similar. The adult has a uniformly dark appearance, the plumage taking on an oily green sheen when seen in good light. The sleek head and long neck are slimmer than that of the Cormorant, and the bill is more slender and cleaner-looking with a less pronounced hook to the tip. The Shag's crown, unlike the Cormorant's, peaks at the forehead. Note also the feathering that surrounds the emerald-green eye, and the yellow at the base of the bill. A prominent crest is present during the early part of the breeding season. The winter adult lacks the conspicuous crest, and the colour to the bill base is subdued. The juvenile is dark brown above with lighter, buffish-brown underparts and a pale throat. The Shag swims low in the water with the bill tilted slightly upwards, and it dives frequently with a distinct 'leap'. It flies with the head and neck extended.

The tufted crown is most obvious during the breeding season. At close range the green eye and yellow skin at the base of the bill are obvious.

Factfile

LENGTH 65–80CM

WINGSPAN 95–110CM

HABITAT OCCURS EXCLUSIVELY AT SEA, FAVOURING EXPOSED ROCKY COASTLINES.

FOOD FEEDS ON FISH.

STATUS A MAINLY RESIDENT BIRD, COMMON AND WIDESPREAD IN SUITABLE COASTAL LOCATIONS AND MOST FREQUENTLY ENCOUNTERED DURING THE BREEDING SEASON.

VOICE GENERALLY SILENT, BUT UTTERS HARSH GRUNTS AND HISSES AT BREEDING COLONIES.

adult summer life-size

The Shag forms colonies during the breeding season on exposed steep coastal cliffs, nesting on ledges and in crevices. Birds are often seen standing with their wings outstretched at this time. It favours the north and west coasts of the region. Most birds remain close to breeding sites during the winter months but spend the majority of their time out to sea, rarely being encountered inland.

adult winter

All birds swim low in the water. Winter birds lose the tufted crown but retain a peaked forehead.

immature

All birds fly with the head and neck outstretched. An immature is browner overall than an adult.

summer adults

At close range, summer adults in particular show a green, oily-looking gloss to their feathers. The tufted crown is often raised when birds are present at breeding colonies.

Bittern
Botaurus stellaris

The Bittern is a large and unmistakable waterbird. The sexes are similar. The adult has brown plumage marked with fine and intricate patterns of dark and light streaks and barring. Its plumage affords the bird superb camouflage, making it very difficult to spot among the reeds. The neck is long and thick, but generally only extended when the bird is threatened or nervous. Note the long, dagger-like bill and dark moustache and cap markings on the head. The legs and feet are long and powerful. The juvenile is similar to the adult but lacks the obvious moustache and crown markings. It flies infrequently, but when it does so its large broad wings and slow deliberate beats recall those of an owl or large raptor.

adult

adult

The colour and patterning on the body plumage are an excellent match for wetland vegetation and provide good camouflage.

In flight, the head and neck are held hunched-up not outstretched; the wings are broad and rounded, reminiscent perhaps of a giant Short-eared Owl.

Factfile

LENGTH 70–80CM

WINGSPAN 100–130CM

HABITAT A WETLAND BIRD THAT IS ALMOST ENTIRELY RESTRICTED TO AREAS OF MARSHLAND AND SHALLOW WATER WITH EXTENSIVE REED BEDS.

FOOD FEEDS ON FISH AND AMPHIBIANS.

STATUS A RARELY SEEN BIRD WITH A SMALL RESIDENT POPULATION CONFINED TO A LIMITED NUMBER OF SUITABLE HABITATS AND TRADITIONAL BREEDING SITES.

VOICE MOST VOCAL DURING THE BREEDING SEASON, WHEN TERRITORIAL MALES UTTER A BOOMING *WHUMMP*, MOSTLY AT NIGHT.

The Bittern is a challenging bird to observe. There is a relatively small breeding population in our region, with birds favouring a number of traditional sites with extensive reed beds and shallow water; it builds a nests of flattened reeds at water level. It feeds by patiently stalking fish and amphibians in shallow water. Outside the breeding season birds tend to disperse, and resident numbers are boosted slightly in winter by small numbers of migrating birds from further afield in Europe.

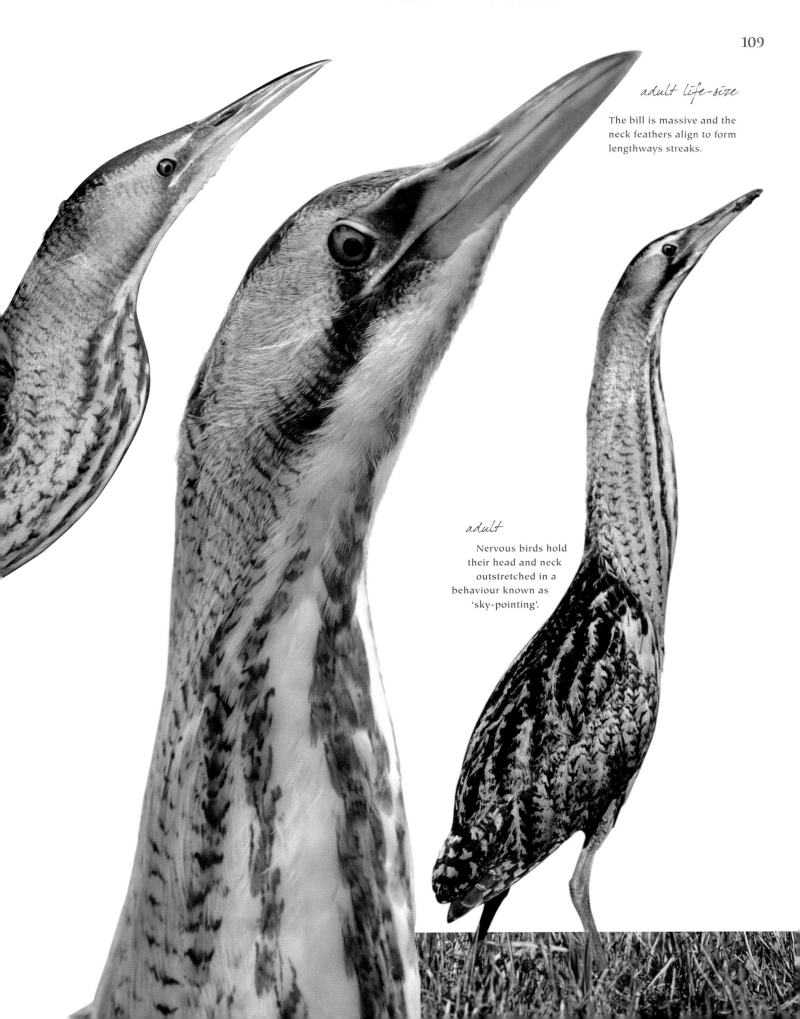

adult life-size

The bill is massive and the neck feathers align to form lengthways streaks.

adult

Nervous birds hold their head and neck outstretched in a behaviour known as 'sky-pointing'.

Little Egret
Egretta garzetta

The Little Egret is a handsome pure white bird with a long, dark, dagger-like bill. The sexes are similar. The adult has primarily brilliant white plumage with a yellow eye and blue-grey lores. The legs are black, and the yellow feet are a diagnostic guide to identification when they are visible. During the breeding season, long white plumes adorn the nape and the lores takes on a reddish flush. The juvenile is similar to the adult. When in flight, the large, broad wings deliver slow, powerful, lolloping wingbeats, the neck held in an 'S' shape with the legs trailing behind.

The species is encountered in a number of shallow-water habitats, in both coastal and freshwater locations. It feeds primarily on fish and amphibians which it catches in its bill with busy, stabbing movements. The Little Egret is often seen at rest, standing hunched motionless with its bill hidden from view. The range of this species has changed dramatically in recent years. Once a species primarily of North Africa and southern Europe, it is now commonly encountered throughout the region, except the far north. It nests colonially, constructing a twig platform among reeds or in a tree.

adult

A combination of size, shape and pure white plumage make this species unmistakable.

adult

Little Egrets hunt actively in shallow water and sometimes run at speed if they spot a shoal of fish.

adult

The bright yellow feet are most obvious in flying birds.

Factfile

LENGTH 55–65CM WINGSPAN 88–106CM

HABITAT FAVOURS ESTUARIES AND COASTAL RIVERS; INCREASINGLY COMMON ON INLAND FRESHWATER.

FOOD FEEDS ON FISH, AMPHIBIANS AND INVERTEBRATES.

STATUS RECENT NORTHWARD EXPANSION OF ITS BREEDING RANGE HAS RESULTED IN THIS SPECIES BECOMING INCREASINGLY COMMON THROUGHOUT THE REGION IN SUITABLE HABITATS.

VOICE MOSTLY SILENT. OCCASIONAL COARSE, GRATING CALLS ARE UTTERED BETWEEN RIVALS.

adult life-size

The dark bill and bright yellow eyes are striking, even at a distance. The neck is usually held in a gentle curve.

Grey Heron
Ardea cinerea

Factfile

LENGTH 90–98CM

WINGSPAN 155–175CM

HABITAT OCCURS IN A WIDE VARIETY OF FRESHWATER AND COASTAL HABITATS INCLUDING LAKES, RIVERS, MARSHES, ESTUARIES AND SHELTERED COASTLINES.

FOOD FEEDS PRIMARILY ON FISH AND AMPHIBIANS, BUT WILL CONSUME MOST THINGS INCLUDING SMALL MAMMALS AND BIRDS.

STATUS COMMON AND WIDESPREAD RESIDENT THROUGHOUT THE REGION IN SUITABLE HABITATS.

VOICE UTTERS A DISTINCTIVE HARSH *KRRARNK*, TYPICALLY IN FLIGHT.

Similar to adult but crown and forehead are dark grey and bill is duller.

juvenile

This large and imposing heron is a familiar sight in wetland areas throughout the region. The sexes are similar. The adult has a grey appearance with blue-grey back and flanks. The head is whitish-grey with a pure white forecrown and bold black sides leading to black nape plumage. The front of the neck and breast are marked with black streaks. The eyes are yellow, as is the large and distinctive dagger-like bill. The legs are long and gangly-looking, and yellowish-grey. The juvenile is similar to the adult but the head markings are less well defined, with less white and more grey plumage. In flight, the long neck is held close to the body in an 'S' shape with the feet trailing conspicuously behind. The wingbeats are slow, powerful and deliberate.

Note pure white forecrown and black sides to crown leading to black nape feathers.

Whitish-grey head, neck and underparts with dark streaks on the front of the neck and breast.

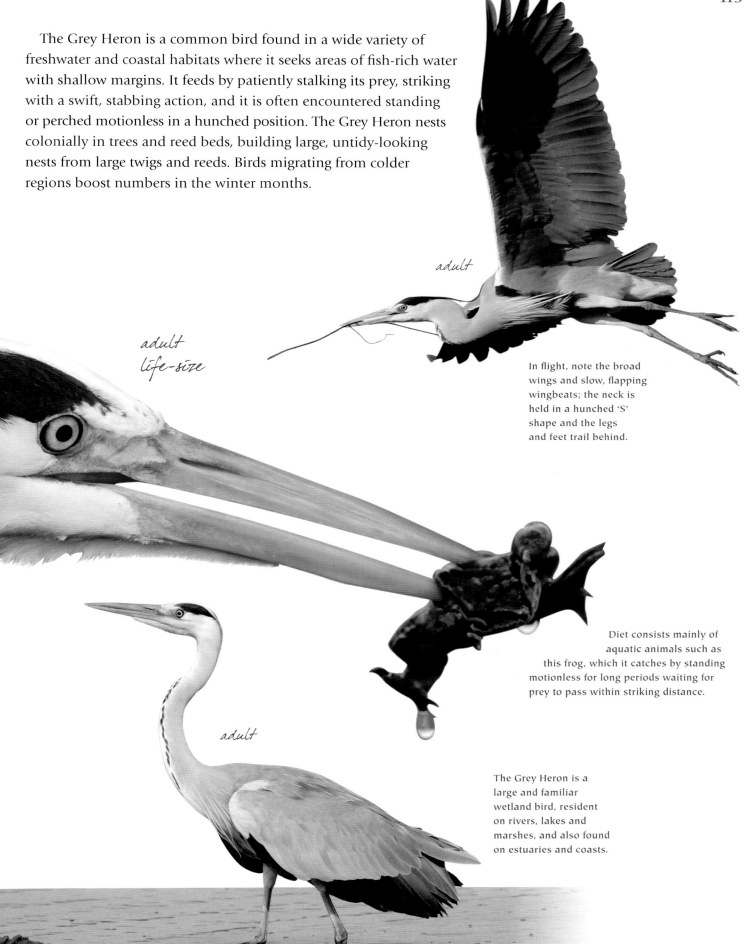

The Grey Heron is a common bird found in a wide variety of freshwater and coastal habitats where it seeks areas of fish-rich water with shallow margins. It feeds by patiently stalking its prey, striking with a swift, stabbing action, and it is often encountered standing or perched motionless in a hunched position. The Grey Heron nests colonially in trees and reed beds, building large, untidy-looking nests from large twigs and reeds. Birds migrating from colder regions boost numbers in the winter months.

adult

In flight, note the broad wings and slow, flapping wingbeats; the neck is held in a hunched 'S' shape and the legs and feet trail behind.

adult life-size

Diet consists mainly of aquatic animals such as this frog, which it catches by standing motionless for long periods waiting for prey to pass within striking distance.

adult

The Grey Heron is a large and familiar wetland bird, resident on rivers, lakes and marshes, and also found on estuaries and coasts.

White
Ciconia Stork
ciconia

The White Stork is a large and imposing white and black bird with a long neck and legs. The sexes are similar. The adult is unmistakable, being primarily grubby white in colour with contrasting black primary flight feathers. The robust dagger-like bill is long and red, and the legs are bright pinkish-red. The black-and-white wings are large and broad with long finger-like primary feathers at the wingtips. The juvenile is similar to the adult, but the bill and leg colours are more subdued.

White Storks nest sparingly in northwest Europe, where they are on the edge of the breeding range. Vagrants turn up in spring and autumn elsewhere, blown off course on migration to and from wintering grounds in Africa. It nests in small colonies on untidy platforms of sticks and twigs, often on chimney pots, telegraph poles and the roofs of houses. For such a large bird it is a consummate flier, soaring on thermals and updrafts, sometimes to a great height.

adult

In flight, the black flight feathers contrast with the otherwise white plumage.

adult

Walks in a stately manner and its long legs allow it to wade in wetland areas, in search of food.

Factfile

LENGTH 95–110CM   WINGSPAN 180–218CM

HABITAT MARSHLAND, LOWLAND WETLANDS, RIVER BASINS AND ADJACENT OPEN FARMLAND.

FOOD AMPHIBIANS, REPTILES AND INVERTEBRATES.

STATUS PRIMARILY A BREEDING BIRD OF CENTRAL EUROPE, ITS RANGE ENCOMPASSES PART OF THE REGION BUT IT IS MOSTLY ABSENT FROM SCANDINAVIA AND BRITAIN. IT MIGRATES TO AFRICA FOR THE WINTER.

VOICE MOSTLY SILENT. IN CONTRAST, NESTING BIRDS ENGAGE IN REGULAR, LOUD BILL SNAPPING.

adult

The head, neck and legs are held outstretched in flying birds; the wings are long and broad, ideal for soaring and long-distance migration.

adult life-size

At close range, white elements of the plumage appear subtly tinged yellow-buff. The massive bright red bill is a diagnostic feature of the species.

Glossy Ibis
Plegadis falcinellus

The Glossy Ibis is a distinctive and elegant waterbird with heron-like proportions and body shape, and a long, Curlew-like downward-curving bill. The sexes are similar. The adult has uniformly dark plumage, deep maroon in colour and often displaying a metallic sheen in good light. It can appear black at a distance or in poor light. The eye is dark, the slender bill is pinkish-brown and the legs are dull red. In summer, the adult has a narrow white line running from the base of the bill and framing the eye. The winter adult has duller plumage with paler yellowish-red legs and light streaks to the head and neck. The juvenile recalls a winter adult but with duller plumage. In flight, the head appears slightly bulbous, with the neck straight and extended and the legs trailing behind.

In flight, the head, neck and legs are held outstretched.

immature

adult

All birds are adept at 'perching' in trees. In good light, an adult's colourful plumage, and the oily sheen to the back and wing feathers can be appreciated.

This wetland bird of shallow water margins feeds on a variety of mud-dwelling invertebrates which it catches with its long, probing bill. It is a recent breeding colonist in northwest Europe. The long curved bill, heron-like profile and intense colouration make this an easy species to identify correctly when encountered.

Factfile

LENGTH 55–65CM

WINGSPAN 80–95CM

HABITAT A WETLAND BIRD THAT OCCURS IN A VARIETY OF FRESHWATER AND BRACKISH ENVIRONMENTS WITH SHALLOW, WELL VEGETATED MARGINS.

FOOD FEEDS ON AQUATIC INVERTEBRATES.

STATUS UNTIL RECENTLY, ITS STATUS WAS THAT OF A VAGRANT TO OUR REGION, SEEN MAINLY IN AUTUMN AND WINTER. RECENTLY ITS RANGE HAS EXPANDED, AND IT NOW BREEDS IN SMALL NUMBERS AND OCCURS OUTSIDE THE BREEDING SEASON MORE REGULARLY THAN IN THE PAST.

VOICE MOSTLY SILENT.

immature life-size

The long, downcurved bill is used to probe the ground for food, and often appears grubby.

immature

A Glossy Ibis walks in a stately manner, its long legs allowing it to wade in water, typically around the margins of pools and wetlands.

Spoonbill
Platalea leucorodia

Factfile

LENGTH 70–80CM

WINGSPAN 120–135CM

HABITAT FAVOURS ESTUARIES, MUDFLATS, LAGOONS AND OTHER SHALLOW, SHELTERED COASTAL AREAS. SOMETIMES ENCOUNTERED ON SHALLOW, LOWLAND LAKES.

FOOD FEEDS ON FISH, CRUSTACEANS AND OTHER MARINE INVERTEBRATES.

STATUS PRESENT YEAR-ROUND IN THE REGION WITH LOCALISED SMALL BREEDING POPULATIONS. NUMBERS FLUCTUATE THROUGHOUT THE YEAR DUE TO SEASONAL MIGRATION.

VOICE MOSTLY SILENT BUT OCCASIONALLY UTTERS GRUNTING SOUNDS WHEN AT THE NEST.

With its pure white plumage and overall body shape, the Spoonbill recalls a Little Egret at first glance. Its larger size and unique bill shape aid identification. The sexes are similar. The breeding adult displays a crest of bushy nape feathers, together with a yellow flush to the base of the bill and breast. The non-breeding adult lacks these features. In all adults, the black bill is long and broad with a diagnostic yellow-tipped, spoon-shaped end, giving the species its name. The neck is long and mostly held in a hunched 'S' shape, with the bill tucked away when at rest. The legs are long and black.

The combination of white plumage and a uniquely-shaped bill makes this species unmistakable.

adult life-size

adult

A Spoonbill uses its bill to sift fish and other food items from the water, deftly manoeuvring them to be swallowed.

immature

The head, neck and legs are held outstretched in flight. Only immature birds have black in the wingtips; adults have pure white plumage.

adult

Head plumes are more evident during the breeding season, and the colours around the eye and on the throat are most striking at this time.

The juvenile recalls the non-breeding adult, but the bill and legs are dull pinkish and it displays black wingtips when in flight. All birds extend their head and neck in flight, with their legs trailing.

The Spoonbill is an uncommon species in the region, with a sparse breeding population restricted to a handful of sites in suitable habitat. It breeds in small colonies, constructing twig pile nests in scrub and reed beds. It feeds in shallow water by sweeping its bill from side to side and catching fish and invertebrates.

Great Crested Grebe
Podiceps cristatus

This is a graceful and regal waterbird with a longish, slender neck. It is the largest grebe in the region; the sexes are similar but summer and winter plumages are different. The summer adult has uniform grey-brown upperparts; the underparts, breast and neck front are mainly whitish. The flanks are flushed with buffish-orange. The head has a distinctive black cap and crest, and the pale cheeks are bordered with an obvious orange-buff ruff. The winter adult loses the bright head colouration and ruff, retaining the dark cap and a hint of the crest. The plumage is primarily drab grey-brown on the upperparts, and white on the neck and flanks. In all birds the long dagger-like bill is pink and the eye is red; in flight, the neck is held straight and outstretched, and the inner wing shows extensive patches of white. The juvenile recalls the winter adult, but the cheeks are marked with diagnostic black streaks.

adult with chick

When they are young, chicks often ride on the backs of their parents.

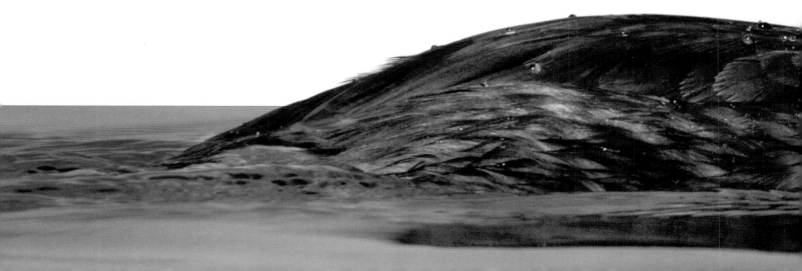

adult winter

Outside the breeding season, the elaborate head feathers are lost. The wings show a striking white panel in all birds, at all times.

pair displaying

Courting birds perform a range of displays that often involve the head 'ruff' being splayed and shaken.

This is a common species in lowland Britain and mainland Europe, breeding on large expanses of water such as reservoirs and gravel pits, where it builds floating nests of matted vegetation. It engages in a mesmerising courtship ritual involving elaborate headshaking displays. During the winter months some birds move to coastal areas, particularly in harsh weather. It swims relatively buoyantly, diving frequently for fish.

adult summer life-size

A Great Crested Grebe swims buoyantly but low in the water. The striking head plumage makes for easy identification during the spring and summer months.

Factfile

LENGTH 46–51CM

WINGSPAN 59–73CM

HABITAT FAVOURS LARGE EXPANSES OF FISH-RICH FRESHWATER INCLUDING RESERVOIRS, GRAVEL PITS, LARGE LAKES AND RIVERS. ALSO ENCOUNTERED ON THE COAST DURING THE WINTER MONTHS.

FOOD FEEDS ON SMALL FISH.

STATUS A WIDESPREAD AND LOCALLY COMMON SPECIES FOUND IN SUITABLE FRESHWATER HABITATS. PRESENT YEAR-ROUND IN MOST AREAS, ALTHOUGH A SUMMER BREEDING VISITOR TO MUCH OF SCANDINAVIA; ABSENT FROM THE FAR NORTH.

VOICE UTTERS A LOUD BARKING *RAH, RAH, RAH* AND A CLICKING *KEK*, PARTICULARLY DURING THE BREEDING SEASON.

Red-necked Grebe

Podiceps grisegena

This species is most commonly confused with Great Crested Grebe, but is smaller and stockier with a distinctive yellow base to the bill in all plumages. The sexes are similar but summer and winter plumages differ. The summer adult has uniform greyish-brown upperparts and nape, with a brick-red neck and upper breast. The underparts are whitish with grey streaking to the flanks. The head has white-bordered light grey cheeks and a well-defined dark cap showing the hint of a

adult summer life-size

An orange-red neck and white-edged grey cheeks are good identification features for summer birds.

adult winter

The yellow bill is a diagnostic feature in winter birds; the contrast between the grubby neck and the pale throat and breast also aids identification of swimming birds at this time.

adult summer

Red-necked Grebes dive frequently and for extended periods in search of fish.

Factfile

LENGTH **40–50CM**

WINGSPAN **80–85CM**

HABITAT **SHELTERED COASTAL AREAS, OCCASIONALLY OCCURRING INLAND ON RESERVOIRS AND LARGE LAKES.**

FOOD **FEEDS ON SMALL FISH AND AQUATIC INVERTEBRATES.**

STATUS **BREEDS IN SCATTERED LOOSE COLONIES IN THE EAST OF OUR REGION. ELSEWHERE IT IS MAINLY A WINTER VISITOR, FOUND IN SHELTERED COASTAL LOCATIONS FROM SEPTEMBER TO MARCH.**

VOICE **MOSTLY SILENT. DURING THE BREEDING SEASON, IT UTTERS VARIOUS WAILING AND GRUNTING CALLS.**

crest. The stout, dagger-like bill is dark with a yellow base. The winter adult loses the distinctive colouration to the head and neck, becoming duller and more grubby looking, but retaining a subtle red collar. The bill is yellow. In flight, the head and neck are held straight and outstretched with the legs trailing behind; note the white wing panels (the white less extensive than in Great Crested Grebe). The juvenile recalls the winter adult, but has more extensive red on the neck and diagnostic dark stripes on the cheeks.

The Red-necked Grebe is a buoyant bird that swims low in the water and dives frequently and for long periods, feeding on fish and aquatic invertebrates. It breeds in well-vegetated lakes in eastern Europe, where it nests on floating mats of aquatic vegetation. Most birds migrate to the coastal areas in the region during the winter months, when the population is sparse and well spread.

adult summer

The species is colourful and distinctive in breeding plumage. All birds swim low in the water but feather waterproofing makes them buoyant.

Slavonian Grebe

Podiceps auritus

This is a small, elegant grebe with different seasonal plumages. The sexes are similar. The summer adult has a black back and reddish flanks and neck. The head is rather striking, being predominantly black with contrasting golden yellow plumes above the cheek and behind the beady red eye. The bill is dark and stout with a diagnostic white tip which is present throughout the year. The winter adult is much duller, the bright head and neck colours being replaced with white cheeks and neck, and a black cap. The back is a dark greyish-black, and the underparts are white. The bill is also lighter in colour. The juvenile recalls the winter adult. In flight, note the white patches to both the leading and trailing edges of the wings.

adult winter
In flight, winter birds look very black-and-white, with notably contrasting patterns on the wings in particular.

adult summer life-size
Stunning in breeding plumage, the beady red eye complements the golden-yellow plumes that are framed by the dark crown and throat.

Factfile

LENGTH 31–38CM

WINGSPAN 60–65CM

HABITAT SHELTERED COASTAL AREAS DURING THE WINTER MONTHS, OCCASIONALLY OCCURRING INLAND ON RESERVOIRS AND LARGE LAKES. IT BREEDS ON SHALLOW, WELL-VEGETATED FRESHWATER LAKES.

FOOD FEEDS ON SMALL FISH AND AQUATIC INVERTEBRATES.

STATUS BEST KNOWN AS A WINTER VISITOR TO THE SHELTERED COASTAL AREAS OF THE REGION. A SMALL POPULATION OF BREEDING BIRDS OCCURS ON A FEW SUITABLE FRESHWATER SITES IN THE NORTH.

VOICE UTTERS VARIOUS CRIES AND RATTLING CALLS DURING THE BREEDING SEASON. MOSTLY SILENT AT OTHER TIMES.

adult summer

Slavonian Grebes swim buoyantly and dive frequently. On breeding pools, they often pop up amongst emergent vegetation, making their progress hard to follow.

The Slavonian Grebe is a buoyant swimmer that dives frequently, sometimes for long periods, in search of fish and aquatic invertebrates. It breeds on shallow, reed-fringed freshwater lakes, constructing floating nests of aquatic vegetation. It could be confused with the similar Black-necked Grebe, but note the slightly curved upper and lower mandibles, the pale tip to the bill and the flattish crown.

adult winter

The plumage can appear strikingly black-and-white outside the breeding season; bill shape and head profile offer good clues to separation from similar Black-necked Grebe in winter plumage.

Black-necked Grebe

Podiceps nigricollis

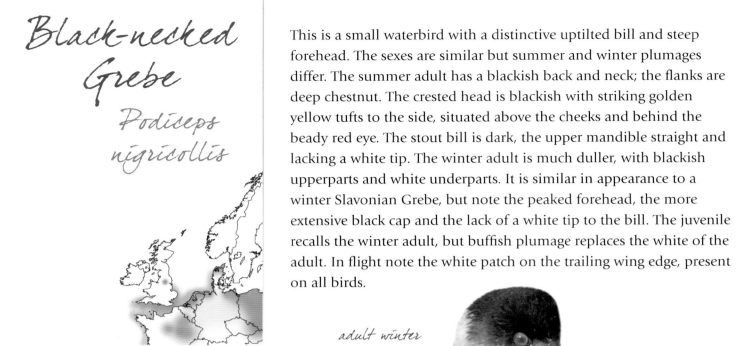

This is a small waterbird with a distinctive uptilted bill and steep forehead. The sexes are similar but summer and winter plumages differ. The summer adult has a blackish back and neck; the flanks are deep chestnut. The crested head is blackish with striking golden yellow tufts to the side, situated above the cheeks and behind the beady red eye. The stout bill is dark, the upper mandible straight and lacking a white tip. The winter adult is much duller, with blackish upperparts and white underparts. It is similar in appearance to a winter Slavonian Grebe, but note the peaked forehead, the more extensive black cap and the lack of a white tip to the bill. The juvenile recalls the winter adult, but buffish plumage replaces the white of the adult. In flight note the white patch on the trailing wing edge, present on all birds.

adult winter

Outside the breeding season, the plumage looks strikingly black-and-white; the bill lacks the white tip seen in similar Slavonian Grebe.

adult winter

Bill shape aids separation from similar Slavonian Grebe in winter plumage, but note that the black cap embraces the eye (the cut-off line runs through eye in Slavonian).

The Black-necked Grebe is a buoyant swimmer that dives frequently, feeding on fish and aquatic invertebrates. It requires a very specific breeding habitat and is a sparse breeding bird in the region. It favours shallow, well-vegetated freshwater lakes and ponds, constructing floating nests of vegetation. A secretive species during the breeding season with a sparse population, it is easiest to observe during the winter months.

adult summer

The steep forehead and peaked crown are particularly apparent when a bird turns sideways-on.

Factfile

LENGTH 28–34CM

WINGSPAN 55–60CM

HABITAT SHELTERED COASTAL AREAS DURING THE WINTER MONTHS, OCCASIONALLY OCCURRING INLAND ON RESERVOIRS AND LARGE LAKES. IT BREEDS ON SHALLOW, WELL-VEGETATED FRESHWATER LAKES.

FOOD SMALL FISH AND AQUATIC INVERTEBRATES.

STATUS BEST KNOWN AS A WINTER VISITOR TO THE SHELTERED COASTAL AREAS OF THE REGION, THE POPULATION BEING SPARSE AND WELL SPREAD. A SMALL POPULATION OF BREEDING BIRDS OCCURS ON A FEW SUITABLE FRESHWATER SITES.

VOICE MOSTLY SILENT OUTSIDE THE BREEDING SEASON, WHEN IT UTTERS VARIOUS WHISTLES AND SQUEAKS.

adult summer life-size

A Black-necked Grebe is stunning in the breeding season, with the mainly black plumage showing off the golden-yellow head plumes, beady red eye and orange flanks. In profile, the bird's upper mandible is rather straight while the lower one is obviously curved.

Little Grebe

Tachybaptus ruficollis

The Little Grebe is a small, dumpy and robust-looking bird with a rather squat head and neck. The sexes are similar but summer and winter plumages differ. The summer adult is predominantly dark brown with a bright chestnut neck and cheeks. Note the fluffy whitish tail-end visible on swimming birds. The pale-tipped, stout bill is dark with a diagnostic lime-green patch at the base. The winter adult is

adult summer

Birds fly low over the water so the pale underwings are only evident when birds flap and wing-stretch after preening.

Factfile

LENGTH 25–29CM

WINGSPAN 40–44CM

HABITAT FAVOURS SHALLOW-EDGED AND WELL-VEGETATED LAKES, PONDS, RIVERS AND CANALS.

FOOD FEEDS ON SMALL FISH AND AQUATIC INVERTEBRATES.

STATUS A WIDESPREAD RESIDENT BIRD, COMMON THROUGHOUT THE REGION IN SUITABLE HABITATS. NUMBERS ARE BOOSTED BY MIGRANTS FROM FURTHER EAST IN EUROPE DURING THE WINTER MONTHS.

VOICE UTTERS A HIGH-PITCHED WHINNYING TRILL.

adult summer life-size

Little Grebes swim buoyantly and waterproofing means that the plumage is often covered in water droplets after diving.

duller in comparison, generally dark above and lighter underneath, losing the bright chestnut colouration to the neck and cheeks. The bill is lighter in colour. The juvenile recalls the winter adult but has a paler throat and black streaks to the face. It is rarely seen in flight, but note the rounded wings with white undersides, and extended neck and trailing legs.

This is a buoyant waterbird that sits high in the water and is an accomplished swimmer, diving frequently for small fish and aquatic invertebrates. It breeds in the shallow, vegetated margins of lakes, ponds and rivers, constructing floating nests of tangled vegetation which it attaches to bankside plants. It often moves to larger expanses of freshwater during the winter months, with numbers boosted by migrants from further east in Europe.

adult summer

The plumage is rather dark overall but this emphasises the chestnut colouration on the head and lime-green patch at the base of the bill.

adult winter

In winter, the plumage looks brown overall, palest on the face, neck and flanks. It is much smaller and more dumpy than other grebe species.

Red Kite
Milvus milvus

adult

The Red Kite is a large and graceful raptor with a diagnostic 'V'-shaped tail. The sexes are similar. The adult has an overall reddish appearance when perched, but the distinctive grey head is obvious even at a distance. At close quarters, note the yellow base to the strongly hook-tipped bill, the yellow eye and yellow legs. Commonly seen from below in flight, the large broad wings are tipped with long, finger-like primary feathers, the underside showing a conspicuous silver-grey patch. On the upperparts, the reddish-brown back and red tail and wing coverts contrast noticeably with the dark brown flight feathers. The juvenile resembles the adult but has subdued colouration overall, and pale tips to the wing coverts.

When perched, a Red Kite adopts an upright posture. A seemingly effortless flyer, it is often seen gliding on thermals and breezes, flexing its deeply forked tail to assist direction control. It is rarely seen on the ground except when it is hunting for earthworms or feeding on road kill. In Britain the species was restricted to localised populations numbering only a handful of birds until a reintroduction programme expanded its numbers and range dramatically. It nests in trees, constructing a platform of sticks and mud.

Typically, a Red Kite adopts an upright posture when perched in a tree. In perching birds, it is not always obvious that the tail is forked.

adult

Factfile

LENGTH 60–65CM

WINGSPAN 145–165CM

HABITAT FAVOURS WOODED VALLEYS AND SCATTERED DECIDUOUS WOODLAND, TYPICALLY ADJACENT TO OPEN FARMLAND.

FOOD FEEDS ON CARRION, SMALL MAMMALS, BIRDS AND EARTHWORMS.

STATUS LARGELY SEDENTARY WITH RESIDENT POPULATIONS PRESENT YEAR-ROUND THROUGHOUT THE REGION AS FAR NORTH AS SWEDEN. REINTRODUCTION IN BRITAIN IN RECENT YEARS HAS SEEN A DRAMATIC INCREASE IN NUMBERS THERE. SOME DISPERSAL AND SOUTHWARD MIGRATION IN WINTER.

VOICE CALL IS A SHRILL *WEOO-WEOO-WEOO*, UTTERED MOST COMMONLY IN FLIGHT.

In flight, sometimes soars for extended periods but also extremely aerobatic and manoeuvrable, twisting and turning as it descends to pick up food from the ground.

adults

adult life-size

The grey head plumage contrasts with the reddish neck and underparts, and darker brown back. The hook-tipped bill is bright yellow at the base.

White-tailed Eagle

Haliaeetus albicilla

This is a huge and impressive bird that is difficult to mistake. The sexes are similar. The adult has overall brown plumage which is palest on the head and neck. The diagnostic white tail feathers are obvious in flight, but often difficult to discern when it is perched or standing. The legs and large feet are yellow, as is the powerful hook-tipped bill. In flight, note the long, broad parallel-sided wings and short wedge-shaped tail. The primary flight feathers are long and finger-like at the wingtips. The juvenile is similar to the adult but has subtly darker plumage and lacks the white tail feathers.

adult life-size
The proportionately large head and massive yellow bill are diagnostic.

immature
The plumage, including the tail, is rather uniformly dark brown. The wings are broad and huge, allowing birds to soar with ease.

For such an immense and impressive bird the White-tailed Eagle is surprisingly agile in flight. It is often seen flying low over the water hunting fish and birds, and it commonly takes species as large as ducks and geese. It nests in trees and on inaccessible cliff ledges, constructing a bulky mass of twigs and sticks.

adult

The white tail is most obvious in flying birds; despite their massive size, White-tailed Eagles are surprisingly manoeuvrable in low-level flight.

adult

The huge body appears rather stocky in standing birds; the white tail is sometimes partly hidden by the folded wings and not always obvious.

Factfile

LENGTH **70–90CM**

WINGSPAN **190–240CM**

HABITAT **ASSOCIATED WITH COASTS AND EXTENSIVE WETLANDS.**

FOOD **FEEDS ON CARRION, FISH, MAMMALS AND BIRDS.**

STATUS **RESIDENT BREEDING SPECIES PRESENT YEAR-ROUND IN THE NORTH OF THE REGION; MOST COMMONLY FOUND ALONG THE COAST OF SCANDINAVIA. A RECENT REINTRODUCTION PROGRAMME HAS SEEN NUMBERS INCREASE IN SUITABLE HABITATS IN SCOTLAND. MIGRATORY BIRDS ARRIVE FROM FURTHER EAST IN EUROPE IN WINTER, BOOSTING NUMBERS AT THIS TIME.**

VOICE **UTTERS LOUD, MOURNFUL WHISTLING CALLS.**

Golden Eagle
Aquila chrysaetos

A large, majestic raptor, recalling an outsized Buzzard, most often seen distantly soaring on thermals and updrafts. The sexes are similar but various ages are separable. The adult appears uniformly dark brown with paler brown margins to the feathers along the back, and the head and neck are a rich golden brown. The long barred tail displays a broad dark margin at the tip, which is sometimes difficult to discern at long range or in poor light. Its wings are large and broad with long, finger-like primary feathers at the tips. Note the slight narrowing of the wings as they join the body. The juvenile is similar to the adult but has conspicuous white patches at the base of the outer flight feathers, and a mainly white tail with a broad dark tip. The white elements of its plumage are gradually lost in successive moults over a period of years.

adult life-size
At close range, the beautiful golden mane of feathers can be appreciated; the large bill is yellow at the base.

Factfile

LENGTH 76–89CM

WINGSPAN 190–225CM

HABITAT FAVOURS REMOTE UPLANDS AND UNINHABITED LOWLAND WOODLAND AND MARSHES.

FOOD FEEDS ON SMALL MAMMALS, BIRDS AND CARRION.

STATUS PRIMARILY A SEDENTARY BREEDING SPECIES, PRESENT YEAR-ROUND. POPULATION IS WIDESPREAD BUT SPARSE, AND RESTRICTED TO SCANDINAVIA AND THE UPLANDS OF SCOTLAND.

VOICE MOSTLY SILENT, BUT VERY OCCASIONALLY UTTERS A YELPING CALL.

adult

When coming in to land, wing and tail feathers are splayed to allow greater control over speed and direction.

immature

The pale base to the tail is an obvious indication that the bird in question is not an adult. Full adult plumage is acquired gradually over several years.

adult

Typically, birds on the ground are wary and alert, on the look-out for danger. If undisturbed, prey items are generally dismembered and consumed where they were caught.

A consummate flyer, the Golden Eagle is often seen soaring effortlessly at height; the males are sometimes seen performing spectacular aerial displays in the spring. Golden Eagles stoop at speed to catch live prey such as mammals and birds. The adults are mostly sedentary, but the juveniles are often more mobile and disperse as they seek to establish new territories.

Marsh Harrier
Circus aeruginosus

The Marsh Harrier is a graceful raptor of wetland habitats. The sexes differ. The adult male has uniformly reddish-brown plumage, with the exception of the blue-grey head and clean grey tail. In flight, the broad wings are held in a characteristic shallow 'V' shape and display diagnostic grey and reddish-brown patches and black tips. The adult female has primarily uniform dark brown plumage. It can be distinguished from the adult male by the pale leading edges to the wings, the pale cream cap and chin markings, and the reddish-brown tail. The juvenile recalls the adult female but has a dark brown tail.

This is the classic wetland raptor, inhabiting areas of extensive reed beds during the breeding season, when it can be observed at traditional sites. Its flight is effortless and agile, and it hunts by flying low and dropping down suddenly on its prey. It nests on bulky collections of reeds within dense reed beds. Marsh Harriers are more widely dispersed outside the breeding season, and may be encountered on migration to their wintering grounds around the Mediterranean.

immature male

On the ground, a Marsh Harrier looks long-legged and slim-bodied.

Factfile

LENGTH **50–55CM** WINGSPAN **110–125CM**

HABITAT **WETLAND HABITATS WITH EXTENSIVE REED BEDS, AND OCCASIONALLY SEEN IN FARMLAND LOCATIONS.**

FOOD **FEEDS ON BIRDS, SMALL MAMMALS AND AMPHIBIANS.**

STATUS **EXTREMELY LOCAL AND MAINLY A VERY LOCAL SUMMER BREEDING SPECIES IN SUITABLE HABITATS THROUGHOUT THE REGION, EXCEPT THE NORTH. MOST MIGRATE TO THE MEDITERRANEAN FOR WINTER, ALTHOUGH SOME BIRDS REMAIN AND ARE RESIDENT YEAR-ROUND.**

VOICE **MOSTLY SILENT, BUT DISPLAYING BIRDS CAN UTTER THIN WHISTLING CALLS.**

male

A male shows more contrast in the wings than a female, with pale panels contrasting with the black primaries.

In flight, a female looks overall brown although pale markings on head show up clearly; immature birds can look superficially very similar.

female

female life-size

A female's plumage looks overall dark except for the whitish crown and throat.

Hen Harrier
Circus cyaneus

The Hen Harrier is a characteristic raptor of upland moorland, typically seen slowly gliding low over open ground. The sexes are separable. The adult male appears uniformly pale blue-grey with a paler underside, white rump and black wingtips. The eyes and legs are yellow, and the stout bill is dark and heavily hook-tipped. The adult female is light brown with dark barring on the wing and tail, with streaking to the underside of the body and a diagnostic white rump. The juvenile recalls the adult female, but note the more reddish appearance of the breast and underwing coverts; the upperwing coverts are brighter and more contrasting.

female

In flight, the long wings and tail create a distinctive profile and allow graceful flight.

In close up, a female looks superficially owl-like with her large eyes and rounded head.

female life-size

male

In flight, a male can look extremely pale but with black wingtips providing diagnostic contrast.

Hen Harriers are most frequently seen flying low, quartering over broken ground, when they use a combination of effortless gliding and leisurely wingbeats. During the breeding season, it seeks upland moorland areas and is highly territorial, constructing nests of heather and grasses on the ground. In the winter months it moves to lower ground and coastal areas. The Hen Harrier is famously the subject of illegal persecution, particularly in Britain, where numbers are in sharp decline.

Factfile

LENGTH 40–50CM WINGSPAN 100–120CM

HABITAT UPLAND HEATHER AND GRASS MOORLAND DURING THE BREEDING SEASON, MOVING TO LOWLAND HEATHLAND AND COASTAL GRASSLAND IN THE WINTER MONTHS.

FOOD FEEDS ON SMALL MAMMALS, BIRDS AND INSECTS.

STATUS RESIDENT BREEDING SPECIES. DURING THE BREEDING SEASON IT IS RESTRICTED TO SUITABLE HABITAT IN SCANDINAVIA AND THE NORTH AND WEST OF THE BRITISH ISLES. IT BECOMES MORE WIDESPREAD THROUGHOUT THE REGION IN WINTER WITH AN INFLUX OF MIGRATING BIRDS FROM FURTHER EAST IN EUROPE.

VOICE MOSTLY SILENT, BUT UTTERS A RAPID CHATTERING CALL DURING THE BREEDING SEASON.

Territorial males sometimes perch on low trees, on the look-out for rivals and danger. The long yellow legs are useful for catching agile prey.

male

female

A female is larger than a male, her plumage barred brown except for the striking white rump.

Montagu's Harrier
Circus pygargus

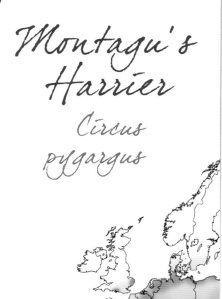

Montagu's Harrier is an elegant raptor similar in appearance to the Hen Harrier. The sexes differ. The adult male has mainly blue-grey plumage overall, but note the white rump, which is less extensive than in Hen Harrier. When in flight, note also the more extensive black wingtips, single dark bar to the upperwing and two dark bars on the underwing. Streaking on the belly and chestnut barring on the underwing coverts are also visible when it is observed at close range. The eyes and legs are yellow, and the stout bill is dark and heavily hook-tipped. The adult female is uniformly pale brown in colour with a narrow white rump, dark barring to the wings and tail and streaking to the underside of the body. Pale crescents above and below the eye are obvious and

male life-size
The male's plumage is mainly soft grey; at close range the forward-facing yellow eyes and yellow base to the bill are striking.

female

The plumage is strongly barred brown except for the white rump, which is narrower than in similar female Hen Harrier.

male

In flight, barring on both the underwing and upperwing help with separation from superficially similar male Hen Harrier, which has unmarked wings.

diagnostic features. The juvenile is similar to the adult female, but the underwing and the underparts are orange-red in colour and unstreaked.

Montagu's Harrier is an accomplished and agile flyer most commonly encountered quartering low to the ground, dropping down suddenly on unsuspecting prey, talons extended. A ground-nesting species, it constructs a nest lined with grasses.

Factfile

LENGTH 40–45CM

WINGSPAN 105–120CM

HABITAT A VARIETY OF OPEN HABITATS INCLUDING ARABLE FARMLAND, WETLANDS, HEATHS AND MOORLAND.

FOOD FEEDS ON SMALL MAMMALS, BIRDS, REPTILES AND LARGE INSECTS.

STATUS MIGRATORY SUMMER VISITOR (PRESENT MAINLY MAY TO AUGUST) THAT BREEDS IN SMALL NUMBERS IN THE SOUTHERN PARTS OF THE REGION. ALSO SEEN IN SPRING AND AUTUMN ON MIGRATION TO AND FROM ITS AFRICAN WINTERING GROUNDS.

VOICE MOSTLY SILENT, BUT UTTERS A HIGH-PITCHED CALL DURING THE BREEDING SEASON.

female

A female's brown plumage varies in intensity and some individuals are quite dark; this only serves to further emphasise the pale eye-surrounds.

male

The wings and tail appear strikingly long, even in standing birds. The barring on the upperwings is not always visible when the wings are folded.

Goshawk
Accipiter gentilis

The Goshawk is a shy and typically solitary raptor that is associated with dense woodland. The sexes are similar, but females are larger than males. The adult has primarily grey-brown upperparts; the underparts are pale and marked with a distinctive fine pattern of dark bars. The tail displays a broader barred pattern, most obvious when the bird is in flight. At close range, note the orange-yellow eyes, yellow feet and legs, and the striking pale supercilium. The powerful bill is dark and strongly hook-tipped. The juvenile has brown upperparts; the underside is buffish and adorned with a heavy pattern of teardrop-shaped marks. It could be confused with Sparrowhawk, but it is appreciably bigger, appearing slightly heavier-bodied and with a larger head. When in flight, note the comparatively long, more pointed wings, and longer inner 'forearm' of the wing. Also note the longer, slightly rounded tail.

immature

Despite its size and stature, a Goshawk is an extremely agile and manoeuvrable predator. A juvenile's plumage is warmer brown than an adult's, with streaked (not barred) underparts.

adult

Goshawks perch for long periods, scanning for prey. In general, they are more likely to be seen sitting in the open during the winter months when most trees are bare.

Factfile

LENGTH 50–60CM

WINGSPAN 100–115CM

HABITAT **WOODLAND AND FORESTS.**

FOOD **FEEDS ON BIRDS AND SMALL MAMMALS.**

STATUS **RESIDENT BREEDING SPECIES, PRESENT YEAR-ROUND IN SUITABLE HABITATS THROUGHOUT THE REGION. A RECOVERY OF NUMBERS HAS BEEN WITNESSED IN RECENT DECADES, PARTICULARLY IN BRITAIN.**

VOICE **MAINLY SILENT, BUT UTTERS A HARSH** *KIE-KIE-KIE* **CALL DURING THE BREEDING SEASON.**

The Goshawk is a secretive and elusive bird that spends the majority of its time sitting in tree cover, making it difficult to spot. It is most commonly encountered during the spring months when males can be seen performing soaring aerial displays, and fanning their rounded tails. It nests in trees, constructing a substantial platform of twigs.

adult

The long legs and powerful feet and talons are essential for catching fast-moving prey such as birds and medium-sized mammals.

adult life-size

Perched birds watch for movement, the large eyes affording them excellent vision.

Sparrowhawk
Accipiter nisus

The Sparrowhawk is a common but unobtrusive raptor, most often seen only fleetingly. The sexes are separable. The adult male is considerably smaller than the female and has uniformly blue-grey upperparts and head. The underparts, including the underwing coverts, are a warm reddish-brown and strongly marked with a pattern of fine dark barring. The eye is orange-yellow and the heavily hook-tipped bill is dark. The larger adult female has grey-brown upperparts and head; the underparts are pale and display fine dark barring. The eye is yellow. The first-winter bird recalls the adult female, but has browner upperparts and paler underparts marked with strong brown barring. The legs in all birds are yellow, and note the long toes, designed to pluck

A male has proportionately longer toes than a female, useful because generally he specialises in catching smaller, more agile bird species.

female

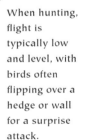

male

When hunting, flight is typically low and level, with birds often flipping over a hedge or wall for a surprise attack.

1st-winter male life-size

The eyes are proportionately very large, even by bird of prey standards.

1st-winter

prey from the air. In flight, the short rounded wings and barred square-cut tail are diagnostic.

Traditionally a bird of woodland habitats, the Sparrowhawk is an increasingly common sight in urban areas, particularly gardens, where it is usually glimpsed briefly. It feeds by catching small birds on the wing and is readily attracted to garden feeding stations owing to the concentration of suitable prey. Displaying males can be observed during the spring soaring overhead, but otherwise the flight is low and rapid. It nests in trees, constructing a platform of twigs.

In flight, note the broad, rounded wings and long tail; immature birds tend to have heavily barred underparts.

Factfile

LENGTH 30–40CM   WINGSPAN 60–75CM

HABITAT FAVOURS WOODED HABITATS IN BOTH RURAL AND (INCREASINGLY) URBAN AREAS.

FOOD FEEDS ON SMALL BIRDS, WHICH IT CATCHES ON THE WING.

STATUS COMMON AND WIDESPREAD RESIDENT BREEDER PRESENT YEAR-ROUND THROUGHOUT THE REGION. BIRDS IN THE EXTREME NORTH MIGRATE SOUTH FOR WINTER.

VOICE WHEN ALARMED, UTTERS A SHRILL *KEW, KEW, KEW.*

1st winter

Immature birds in particular are often attracted to areas of 'easy pickings' such as garden bird tables and feeders.

146

Honey-buzzard
Pernis apivorus

male

Although the overall outline in flight is similar to a Buzzard, patterning on the underwing and the proportionately small head help with identification.

male life-size

By bird of prey standards, the bill is relatively dainty; the nostril plates are designed to minimise the danger of getting stung internally by aggressive and protective bees and wasps.

Factfile

LENGTH **50–60CM**

WINGSPAN **135–140CM**

HABITAT **FAVOURS LARGE EXPANSES OF UNDISTURBED WOODLAND IN WHICH TO BREED.**

FOOD **WASP AND BEE LARVAE, ALSO INSECTS.**

STATUS **A SUMMER VISITOR (PRESENT MAINLY MAY TO SEPTEMBER) THAT BREEDS LOCALLY THROUGHOUT THE REGION. WINTERS IN AFRICA AND IS MOST COMMONLY SEEN ON MIGRATION.**

VOICE **MOSTLY SILENT.**

Females tend to be browner overall than males and strongly barred.

female

immature

Juvenile plumage is extremely variable but many individuals appear rather pale, particularly on the head.

This is a Buzzard-like raptor, typically seen in flight when on migration. The sexes are similar but separable with care. The adult is variable, but the upperparts are most commonly brownish, and the underparts are pale. The neck is relatively long, and the head is rather cuckoo-like and grey in colour. The eyes are yellow and the bill is elongated and heavily hook-tipped. The female can generally be discerned by the overall warmer brown colour, and the dark barring pattern on the underside. In flight, seen from below, all birds have a long grey tail that is diagnostically marked with three even bars. Note also the obvious barring to the underwing, the dark carpal patch and 'pinched-in' wing shape. The legs are yellow and the toes are relatively long. The juvenile is similar to the adult, but is browner overall with more subdued markings.

The Honey-buzzard is a rather secretive bird that is seldom seen other than when in flight. It feeds by raiding the nests of bees and wasps, digging out the nest with its long toes and consuming the larvae. A migratory species, it breeds throughout the region in suitable habitats, wintering in Africa. It is most commonly seen on migration, when it can be encountered in large numbers.

male

Long toes and claws are adapted to digging out the nests of bees and wasps from the ground.

Buzzard
Buteo buteo

The Buzzard is a medium-sized, broad-winged and robust-looking raptor. The sexes are similar, but females are larger than males. The species displays a high degree of plumage variability (in extreme cases from virtually white to uniformly dark), but a typical adult has brown plumage overall. Perched birds typically show fine barring to the breast, which is generally paler than the lower throat and belly. Seen in flight and from below, note the large broad wings and finger-like primary feathers. The flight feathers and tail are grey and marked with a fine pattern of dark bars, with a dark trailing edge to the wings and a dark band to the tip of the tail. Note also the dark carpal patch. The body and underwing coverts are commonly dark, although the extent is variable and pale bands and patches can occur.

Although it was previously persecuted, recent years have witnessed a resurgence in the population, and the Buzzard is now a common sight in suitable habitats. Often heard before it is seen, the cat-like mewing call is uttered regularly by soaring birds, and small groups are sometimes observed circling and calling together. It nests in woodland, typically adjacent to open countryside and farmland.

dark phase

adult

Plumage is variable. While a few birds are rather dark, occasionally almost white individuals are noted.

Buzzards often perch on fence posts, scanning the surrounding land for prey. Size varies considerably but on average females are larger than males.

Factfile

LENGTH 50–55CM

WINGSPAN 115–130CM

HABITAT OPEN COUNTRYSIDE AND FARMLAND WITH SCATTERED WOODLAND.

FOOD FEEDS ON SMALL MAMMALS, EARTHWORMS AND CARRION.

STATUS WIDESPREAD AND LOCALLY COMMON RESIDENT BREEDING SPECIES, PRESENT YEAR-ROUND THROUGHOUT THE REGION. SOME SOUTHWARD MIGRATION OCCURS FROM SCANDINAVIA IN AUTUMN. ITS NUMBERS HAVE INCREASED DRAMATICALLY OVER RECENT DECADES, PARTICULARLY IN BRITAIN.

VOICE UTTERS A DISTINCTIVE MEWING CALL, PARTICULARLY IN FLIGHT.

Soars on broad wings, with the tail often fanned. In most birds, contrast between the dark breast and pale chest band is striking.

adult

adult life-size

Despite their size, Buzzards will feed on prey as small as earthworms. Although primarily active predators, they will also scavenge at the carcasses of dead animals.

Rough-legged Buzzard

Buteo lagopus

This is a medium-sized, Buzzard-like raptor with proportionately longer wings and tail. The sexes are similar but are separable with care. The adult male has brown upperparts with the exception of the diagnostic white on the tail, which terminates with a dark bar and smaller secondary bar (also obvious on the underside). The underparts appear pale overall when seen from below, but note the dark head, dark carpal patches and dark trailing edge to the broad wings. The adult female is similar to the male but the tail is marked with a single terminal band and the belly is dark. The juvenile recalls the adult female but the dark markings are less well defined, particularly on the tail.

When in flight this species tends to keep relatively low to the ground and has a distinctive habit of hovering. It feeds primarily on small mammals,

adult life-size

Female and immature birds could be confused with a pale Buzzard but note the overall pale head, neck and breast, and contrasting dark belly.

Factfile

LENGTH 50–60CM

WINGSPAN 120–150CM

HABITAT FAVOURS MARSHES, MOORLAND, DOWNS AND COASTAL GRASSLAND.

FOOD FEEDS ON SMALL MAMMALS AND BIRDS.

STATUS BREEDS ON ARCTIC TUNDRA AND PRESENT IN NORTHERN SCANDINAVIA IN THE SUMMER MONTHS (MAINLY MAY TO AUGUST). ELSEWHERE IT IS PRIMARILY A PASSAGE MIGRANT AND A WINTER VISITOR.

VOICE MOSTLY SILENT, BUT SOMETIMES UTTERS A LOW-PITCHED, BUZZARD-LIKE MEW.

and lemmings form a large part of its diet on its Arctic breeding grounds. It nests on rocky ledges, constructing twig platforms. It is most commonly seen as a passage migrant in the autumn months in the eastern parts of the region. Numbers vary from year to year depending on weather conditions.

In flight, the wings are broad and the outline is very Buzzard-like. A habit of low-level hovering is a good clue to a Rough-legged's identity.

male

Birds that reach the west of this book's range, including Britain, are often juveniles, recognised by their overall pale underparts except for the dark belly, and white rump.

juvenile

Long periods are spent perched on fence posts and low bushes, scanning the surroundings for prey.

juvenile

Osprey
Pandion haliaetus

The Osprey is a large, pale-looking raptor with long, rather narrow wings. The sexes are similar. The adult has mainly brown upperparts with a distinctive pale crown. The underside is whitish and marked with a subtle dark chest band. When in flight and viewed from below, it appears rather pale with contrasting dark markings that include carpal patches, wingtips, a terminal tail-band and edges to the flight feathers. The head is slender-looking with orange-yellow eyes and a large and powerful dark, heavily hook-tipped bill. The legs are long and terminate in large feet with long talons. The juvenile resembles the adult but the pattern of dark markings is more subdued, and the upperparts appear 'scaly' due to pale feather margins. In flight, note the slender body and wings, which give the bird a rather gull-like appearance.

The Osprey is an iconic fish-eating raptor that seeks large expanses of water such as reservoirs and lakes on which to breed, constructing twig platforms in elevated positions. It catches fish by plunge-diving with its large talons outstretched, snatching its prey from the water spectacularly; on occasions, birds become

adult life-size

The combination of head shape and markings, bright yellow eyes, and a long bill are unique among birds of prey.

adult

completely immersed. It can be seen during the summer months at traditional breeding locations, mainly in the north of the region. However, it is more commonly encountered across northwest Europe when on migration.

In gliding flight and at a distance, an Osprey could be mistaken for a Lesser Black-backed Gull.

adult

adult

At the start of the breeding season, Ospreys are diligent nest-builders and repairers, often seen carrying bunches of twigs aloft in their talons.

Captured fish are often dismembered and eaten while perched in a tree, but sometimes on the ground around the margins of lakes.

Factfile

LENGTH 55–69CM   WINGSPAN 145–160CM

HABITAT FAVOURS LARGE BODIES OF FISH-RICH FRESHWATER SUCH AS RESERVOIRS AND LOCHS, ALSO COASTAL AREAS.

FOOD FEEDS EXCLUSIVELY ON FISH.

STATUS SUMMER BREEDING VISITOR (PRESENT MAINLY MAY TO SEPTEMBER) TO THE NORTH OF THE REGION; FAITHFUL TO TRADITIONAL SITES, ALTHOUGH ITS RANGE IS EXPANDING. IT WINTERS IN AFRICA AND IS MOST COMMONLY SEEN ELSEWHERE IN OUR REGION ON SPRING AND AUTUMN MIGRATION.

VOICE UTTERS VARIOUS MOURNFUL, PIPING CALLS.

Kestrel
Falco tinnunculus

Factfile

LENGTH 33–39CM

WINGSPAN 65–80CM

HABITAT **OPEN GRASSY HABITATS FROM LOWLAND GRASSLAND TO MOORLAND.**

FOOD **FEEDS ON SMALL MAMMALS, BIRDS AND INSECTS.**

STATUS – **WIDESPREAD AND COMMON RESIDENT BREEDING SPECIES, PRESENT YEAR-ROUND IN SUITABLE HABITAT THROUGHOUT THE REGION.**

VOICE – **UTTERS A PIERCING AND INSISTENT** *KEE-KEE-KEE.*

Female's plumage is rather uniform brown, but the head shows a suggestion of a dark 'moustache' contrasting with a paler throat.

The Kestrel is a common small raptor, often seen hovering by roadside verges. The sexes are separable. The adult male has an orange-brown back, adorned with a series of dark spots; the underparts are lighter, being creamy-buff with bold black spots. The head is blue-grey, as is the tail, which is also marked with a dark terminal band. When seen in flight and from above, the lighter back and inner wing contrasts noticeably with the dark outer wing. The adult female overall appears more uniformly brown in comparison, having a brown head and upperparts marked with a pattern of fine dark barring. The underside is creamy buff with dark spots. When seen in flight, the upperwing shows less contrast than that of the male, and the tail is brown and barred. The legs are yellow and the small bill stout and hook-tipped in both sexes. The juvenile recalls the adult female but the underside is more reddish-brown.

This is the commonest small raptor in the region and occurs throughout. Some Scandinavian birds migrate southwards in the autumn to avoid harsh winter weather. The Kestrel is a consummate flyer and is frequently seen hovering over grassland and roadside verges, dropping down suddenly on prey. It nests in tree holes and on cliff ledges and buildings.

male

female life-size

female

In flight, note the relatively long, narrow wings and long tail; the flight pattern tends to be relatively slow and leisurely.

male

Its habit of hovering, while scanning the ground for prey, is almost unique to a Kestrel-sized bird of prey in our region.

On calm days in particular, Kestrels spend long periods perched on branches, wires or fence posts, scanning the ground for potential quarry.

A male's plumage is rather colourful, the bluish head contrasting with the dark-spotted reddish-brown back.

female

Merlin
Falco columbarius

Factfile

LENGTH **25–30CM**

WINGSPAN **60–65CM**

HABITAT **MOORLAND AND UPLAND BOGS DURING THE SUMMER MONTHS, GENERALLY MOVING TO LOWLAND HEATHS AND COASTAL MARSHES FOR THE WINTER.**

FOOD **FEEDS PRIMARILY ON SMALL BIRDS.**

STATUS **PRESENT YEAR-ROUND IN THE REGION AS A WHOLE. BREEDS IN THE NORTH BUT MIGRATES SOUTHWARDS FOR THE WINTER, WITH NUMBERS BOOSTED BY MIGRANTS FROM FURTHER AFIELD.**

VOICE **MOSTLY SILENT, BUT CAN UTTER A SHRILL *KEK-KEK-KEK* IN ALARM.**

The Merlin is the smallest bird of prey in Europe and sleek in outline. The sexes are separable. The adult male has a head and upperparts of bluish-grey; the underparts are reddish-buff and heavily streaked and spotted. When the bird is seen in flight and from above, note the contrast between the blue-grey back, inner wings and tail, and the dark wingtips and terminal band on the square-cut tail. The adult female is noticeably larger than the male, with uniform brown upperparts; the underparts are pale and heavily patterned with large brown spots. The strong stout bill is heavily hook-tipped and the legs are yellow. The juvenile is similar to the adult female.

The combination of small size, a well-marked head and relatively colourful plumage make identification of a male straightforward.

male life-size

In spring and summer, look for birds perched on moorland fence posts; typically they adopt an upright posture, except on windy days.

The Merlin is most commonly seen in flight, sweeping low in search of small birds such as Meadow Pipits which it seeks to flush, surprising them with its rapid flight. It habitually sits on low perches such as fence posts, where it has a good view over open ground, its upright and slender profile obvious. It nests on the ground in moorland heather and bracken.

female
Flight is typically low-level and small birds are captured in surprise attacks.

juvenile

female
A female is appreciably larger than a male with more uniform grey-brown upperparts and barring on the underwings.

Hobby
Falco subbuteo

Factfile

LENGTH 28–35CM

WINGSPAN 75–90CM

HABITAT HEATHLAND AND FARMLAND WITH SCATTERED WOODLAND.

FOOD FEEDS ON INSECTS, SMALL BIRDS AND BATS.

STATUS MIGRANT SUMMER BREEDING VISITOR (PRESENT MAINLY MAY TO SEPTEMBER) FOUND THROUGHOUT THE REGION, EXCEPT FOR THE EXTREME NORTH. WINTERS IN AFRICA AND IS SOMETIMES SEEN ON MIGRATION IN COASTAL REGIONS IN SPRING AND AUTUMN.

VOICE UTTERS A SHRILL KIU-KIU-KIU IN ALARM.

The Hobby is a Kestrel-sized raptor and an expert aeronaut. The sexes are similar. The adult has a blue-grey head and upperparts, with pale underparts marked with heavy dark streaking. Note the white cheeks and dark moustachial markings which are obvious at close range. The diagnostic reddish-brown plumage around the vent and 'undercarriage' is often described as resembling trousers. The powerful, hook-tipped bill is dark with a yellow patch at the base. The legs are yellow. The juvenile resembles the adult but the underside is more buffish and the reddish 'trousers' are absent. The fine pale edging to the feathers of the upperparts and the pale crown are also diagnostic. When seen in flight, in all birds note the narrow, sharply tipped wings and long tail.

The Hobby is an agile flyer that soars but also employs rapid wingbeats interspersed with short glides. Typically a high flyer, it is capable of snatching small airborne birds (particularly hirundines and Swifts), large insects and even bats. It consumes small prey items in flight, seeking suitable perches on which to pluck and eat larger items. It nests in scattered woodland close to farmland and heaths, high up in treetops, and can often be seen circling and calling above its nesting site. The Hobby generally breeds later in the season than other raptors, to take advantage of small fledgling birds.

A Hobby is manoeuvrable and aerobatic, with its flight pattern quickly switching from soaring and gliding to rapid dives, then twists and turns as prey is captured.

Seen head-on, the head pattern is striking, most notably the dark 'moustache'.

adult

adult life-size

adult

adult

Flight is very speedy when in active
pursuit of prey such as dragonflies or
Swallows and martins.

adult

A close look at the plumage reveals dark
upperparts contrasting with well-marked
pale underparts overall, and colourful red
'trousers' and vent.

Peregrine
Falco peregrinus

The Peregrine is a classic, robust-looking falcon, the sexes of which are similar. The adult has dark blue-grey plumage to its head and upperparts. Note the diagnostic dark mask-like moustachial markings on the face. The underparts are whitish, variably flushed with peachy-buff, and adorned with a fine pattern of dark bars. The large dark eye is finely circled with yellow and the stout bill is heavily hook-tipped

adult

In active, level pursuit of prey, the flight is fast on powerful, deep wingbeats.

adult

Peregrines look bulky and imperious when perched; they often favour a rock or ledge that gives them a good vantage point overlooking areas where potential prey may be spotted.

adult

The thickset body is obvious even in flight, particularly in the case of large females.

with a yellow basal patch (cere). The powerful legs and feet are also yellow. When viewed from above in flight, the bird appears uniform in colour, but the rump may appear paler. When viewed from below the profile typically appears anchor-shaped, with the barred underside obvious and the dark facial mask striking against the pale cheeks and throat. The juvenile is similar to the adult but with brownish upperparts, a buffish-orange flush to the underparts, which are streaked rather than barred, and less distinct facial markings.

With its rather broad wings the Peregrine is an accomplished flier, often seen soaring on updrafts with grace and ease. It is well known for the rapid, stooping dives it makes to ambush its prey (typically a pigeon or duck), often from great heights. Recent years have witnessed a rapid recovery in the population, with birds now breeding in suitable locations in urban areas as well as the more traditional coastal and upland sites. It seeks cliff ledges and high buildings on which to nest.

Factfile

LENGTH 39–50CM

WINGSPAN 95–115CM

HABITAT COASTAL CLIFFS, QUARRIES, RIVER GORGES AND MOUNTAIN REGIONS, BUT ALSO INCREASINGLY COMMON IN URBAN AREAS IN RECENT YEARS.

FOOD FEEDS ON BIRDS TAKEN ON THE WING.

STATUS WIDESPREAD BREEDING RESIDENT PRESENT YEAR-ROUND THROUGHOUT THE REGION IN SUITABLE HABITATS. SOME SOUTHWARD WINTER MIGRATION OCCURS IN NORTHERN POPULATIONS.

VOICE CALL IS A SHRILL AND DISTINCTIVE *KEK-KEK-KEK*.

adult life-size

The black-and-white head markings are striking, even at a distance; the underparts are dark-barred, the background colour varying among individuals from pure white to buffish-yellow.

Water Rail
Rallus aquaticus

The Water Rail is a rather furtive wetland bird that is more often heard than seen. The sexes are similar. The adult is rather dumpy-looking with long, delicate dull-red legs and toes, and a long, red wader-like bill which is slightly downcurved. Its plumage is mainly reddish-brown on the crown and upperside, and blue-grey on the cheeks, neck and underside. The flanks are strikingly marked with black-and-white-barring. The tail is often held cocked upwards, revealing unmarked white plumage. The juvenile is similar to the adult but with more subdued colours. Water Rails are rarely seen in flight, but when witnessed note the rounded wings and trailing legs.

This is a secretive bird that is generally very hard to see, rarely emerging from heavy cover; its distinctive call most commonly betrays its presence. An agile bird on the ground, it often runs swiftly from one patch of cover to another and can sometimes be observed feeding busily in the water margins or sunning itself on the edge of cover. It nests on the ground in thick waterside vegetation.

adult

A Water Rail's body is rather flattened laterally, an adaption that allows birds to squeeze through dense wetland vegetation.

adult

Although the plumage is relatively colourful, it is a good match for many wetland habitats and allows birds to blend in well.

adult life-size

When seen well, the colourful red bill, reminiscent of a Redshank, is a good identification feature in a wetland bird of this size. This secretive but vocal species is easy to hear but more tricky to observe.

Factfile

LENGTH 22–28CM

WINGSPAN 38–45CM

HABITAT REED BEDS, MARSHES AND WELL-VEGETATED LAKE AND RIVER MARGINS.

FOOD FEEDS ON AQUATIC INVERTEBRATES, INSECTS AND PLANTS.

STATUS A MAINLY SEDENTARY POPULATION IS PRESENT YEAR-ROUND IN SUITABLE HABITATS. WINTER MIGRATION OCCURS FROM THE EAST, BOOSTING NUMBERS AT THIS TIME.

VOICE UTTERS LOUD PIG-LIKE SQUEALS, CHOKING CALLS AND A DISTINCTIVE *KIP-KIP-KIP*, TYPICALLY FROM COVER.

Spotted Crake

Porzana porzana

The Spotted Crake is a small, dumpy-looking and rather secretive wetland bird. The sexes are similar. The adult has primarily brown upperparts and blue-grey underparts; its entire body is marked with an array of white spots. Also striking is the barring on the flanks and dark central feathers on the back, making this a hard species to confuse when seen in good light. The face and throat have a sooty appearance and the undertail coverts are pale buff. The bill is short and stout, bright yellow with a red base and tipped reddish-orange. The legs are slender with long toes and greenish in colour. The juvenile recalls the adult but the spotting is more subdued, the underparts are buffish, and it lacks the dark face and throat.

The species is present in the region only during the breeding season and most commonly encountered on migration when solitary birds – typically juveniles in autumn – turn up on smaller wetland habitats than are favoured for nesting. It nests in thick waterside vegetation.

Juvenile
Motionless birds blend in well with the tangled vegetation of their favoured wetland habitats.

Juvenile
A juvenile Spotted Crake's plumage is heavily adorned with white spots.

adult

Adult is more strikingly marked than juvenile, with stronger black patterning on the head, back and wings in particular.

juvenile life-size

Long toes allow a Spotted Crake to walk across squelchy wetland vegetation with ease; it is adept at finding small aquatic invertebrates and sometimes turns leaves as it goes.

Factfile

LENGTH 22–24CM

WINGSPAN 37–42CM

HABITAT WETLANDS AND MARSHES WITH EXTENSIVE SEDGE BEDS AND BANKSIDE VEGETATION.

FOOD PLANTS AND AQUATIC INVERTEBRATES.

STATUS A SUMMER VISITOR TO THE MORE TEMPERATE AREAS OF THE REGION, PRESENT MAINLY FROM MAY TO AUGUST. MIGRATES TO AFRICA FOR THE WINTER MONTHS.

VOICE TERRITORIAL MALES UTTER A REPETITIVE WHIPLASH-LIKE *WHIT*, MAINLY HEARD AFTER DARK.

Corncrake
Crex crex

Factfile

LENGTH 27–30CM

WINGSPAN 46–53CM

HABITAT HAY MEADOWS
AND DAMP GRASSLAND.

FOOD FEEDS ON INVERTEBRATES
AND PLANT MATERIAL.

STATUS A SCARCE LOCAL SUMMER
BREEDING SPECIES, PRESENT MAINLY
FROM MAY TO AUGUST; WINTERS IN
AFRICA. THE POPULATION HAS SEEN A
CATASTROPHIC DECLINE IN RECENT
YEARS AND IS NOW RESTRICTED TO A
SMALL NUMBER OF TRADITIONAL SITES.

VOICE TERRITORIAL MALES UTTER AN
INSISTENT *CREK-CREK, CREK-CREK* (GIVING
RISE TO ITS SCIENTIFIC NAME) MAINLY
DURING THE HOURS OF DARKNESS.

The Corncrake is an elusive bird that is more easily heard than seen. The sexes are similar. The adult has sandy-brown upperparts with dark centres to the feathers, giving it a rather scaly appearance. The face and underparts are blue-grey, and the flanks are chestnut marked with a pattern of white barring. The neck is rather slender, and the adult often calls with its neck extended and head pointing upwards in the air. The pink bill is short and stout and the legs are slender and flesh-coloured. The juvenile is similar to the adult, but browner overall and less strongly marked. In flight, all birds reveal a chestnut panel on the inner wing, and fly with trailing legs.

adult
Calling birds throw their heads back. Note the plump body and well-marked reddish-brown upperparts, contrasting with the blue-grey on the throat and breast.

This is a scarce and elusive bird that is confined to a few traditional breeding sites. It is a real challenge to see a Corncrake: birds tend to remain in the safety of deep cover, although calling males do extend their necks and heads above cover at times. It nests on the ground, constructing a shallow cup of leaves. It is rarely seen in flight, as migration takes place during darkness.

adult life-size

Alert birds adopt an upright posture although when walking through vegetation the body is typically almost horizontal.

Moorhen
Gallinula chloropus

Factfile

LENGTH 32–35CM

WINGSPAN 50–55CM

HABITAT WELL-VEGETATED WETLAND HABITATS INCLUDING LAKES, PONDS, RIVERS, RESERVOIRS AND MARSHES.

FOOD PLANT MATERIAL AND INVERTEBRATES.

STATUS A COMMON AND WIDESPREAD RESIDENT BREEDING SPECIES PRESENT YEAR-ROUND THROUGHOUT THE REGION IN SUITABLE HABITATS. NUMBERS ARE BOOSTED IN THE WINTER MONTHS BY MIGRATING BIRDS FROM EASTERN EUROPE.

VOICE UTTERS A LOUD, HARSH *KURRRK*.

adult

adult life-size

The distinctive plump-bodied appearance, colourful bill and proportionately large feet and legs make identification of adult birds straightforward.

adult

In good light, a bluish sheen can sometimes be discerned on the neck and breast. In most circumstances, however, these plumage areas look dark and contrast with the brown back and wings.

Long toes allow birds to walk across soft wetland vegetation without sinking. The white undertail is a striking feature.

The Moorhen is a familiar wetland bird. The sexes are similar. At long range or in poor light, the adult can appear uniformly dark. Closer inspection in good light reveals a subtle contrast between the brownish back, wings and tail, and the dark blue-grey head, neck, breast and belly. In some lights, purplish-blue and yellowish-green hues can be discerned. Striking white flashes can be seen along the flanks and sides of the undertail of standing and swimming birds. The stout bill is extremely colourful, being bright red with a red frontal shield and an obvious yellow tip. The legs and toes are long and yellow. When swimming, note the jerky movements and the constant flicking of the tail. In flight, the wings appear uniformly dark and the legs dangle beneath. The juvenile is uniformly greyish-brown with a white throat patch and dull bill.

This widespread species is a common sight in a wide variety of wetland habitats, from large lakes to the smallest of ponds. It is a cautious bird in its natural surroundings, but where it occurs in urban environments it can become quite tame. Flight is a laboured affair, and it is often seen 'running' across the surface of the water, wings beating rapidly. It nests on an untidy floating platform of vegetation on or near water.

Juveniles are brown at first but begin to acquire adult-like plumage in late winter. At all ages, Moorhens are perfectly at home on water and swim well.

juvenile

Coot
Fulica atra

The Coot is a dumpy and aggressive waterbird and a common sight across a wide range of freshwater habitats. The sexes are similar. The adult is mainly sooty-black, darkest on the head and neck when seen in good light. The most diagnostic feature is its stout white bill and large white facial shield, in stark contrast to the dark plumage. Note also the beady red eye and, when seen on land, the large pale yellow lobed toes; these aid strong swimming. In flight, the wings appear rounded with a white trailing edge. The juvenile has grey-brown plumage on the upperparts, with white on the throat and front of the neck, somewhat recalling a small grebe in winter plumage.

This is a common and bold waterbird often seen in small groups. It is frequently observed in brief bouts of animated squabbling, particularly when defending a territory in the spring: two or more birds rear up out of the water and repeatedly kick each other with their lobed feet. The Coot feeds by upending or making a series of shallow dives, and nests on a platform of plant matter hidden in vegetation along shallow water margins.

The white frontal shield and bill contrast markedly with the otherwise dark plumage. Displaying birds typically raise their wings and puff themselves up to look intimidating.

adult

Typically, Coots are reluctant to fly but when they do, note the outstretched head, neck and legs, and overall dark plumage except for the pale trailing margin to the wings.

Factfile

LENGTH **36–38CM**

WINGSPAN **70–80CM**

HABITAT **A RANGE OF FRESHWATER WETLAND HABITATS INCLUDING LAKES, RIVERS, RESERVOIRS, PONDS AND CANALS.**

FOOD **AQUATIC PLANTS AND INVERTEBRATES.**

STATUS **COMMON AND WIDESPREAD BREEDING RESIDENT, PRESENT YEAR-ROUND, EXCEPT IN THE EXTREME NORTH OF THE REGION. WINTER POPULATIONS ARE BOOSTED BY AN INFLUX OF BIRDS FROM FURTHER EAST IN EUROPE.**

VOICE **UTTERS A LOUD AND REPETITIVE *KWOOT* CALL.**

adults fighting

Adults seem to spend much of the spring fighting one another, using their large, lobed feet to battle with opponents in an attempt to submerge them.

adult

The broadly-lobed feet are a great aid for swimming, but also allow birds to walk across mud without sinking.

adult life-size, displaying

Crane
Grus grus

The Crane is a large and unmistakable bird with a long neck and legs, and a 'bushy' tail-end. The sexes are similar. The adult is primarily blue-grey; the crown, face and neck are black with a contrasting white patch extending from the eye to the nape. The hindcrown is adorned with a small red patch. The back sometimes appears brownish, and the long, bushy plumes at the tail-end are black. It stands in a very upright posture on long, delicate-looking black legs, walking with very steady and deliberate movements. In flight, note the shallow

adult

Cranes fly with the legs, head and neck outstretched, the broad wings ensuring powerful flight.

adult

A Crane's tall and stately appearance, and its distinctive plumage, make it an species easy to identify even at a distance.

adult

Bushy plumes at the tail end are 'fluffed up' in courting birds.

Factfile

LENGTH **95–115CM**

WINGSPAN **200–230CM**

HABITAT **FAVOURS MARSHLAND, OPEN FARMLAND, GRASSLAND AND BOGGY FOREST CLEARINGS.**

FOOD **VARIED DIET INCLUDES SMALL MAMMALS, NESTLING BIRDS, INVERTEBRATES, FRUITS AND SEEDS.**

STATUS **SUMMER VISITOR TO THE NORTH, PRIMARILY SCANDINAVIA, WITH A FEW SMALL SCATTERED POPULATIONS OCCURRING ELSEWHERE. WINTERS IN SOUTHERN EUROPE AND NORTH AFRICA, ALTHOUGH SMALL NUMBERS OVERWINTER IN OUR REGION. MOST COMMONLY OBSERVED IN OUR REGION ON MIGRATION.**

VOICE **UTTERS A LOUD, BUGLING *KRRUU* CALL.**

wingbeats, the outstretched neck and trailing legs. The juvenile recalls the adult but lacks the distinctive black-and-white markings.

The Crane is encountered mainly as a passage migrant in northwest Europe, its numbers varying according to weather conditions elsewhere. It forms large flocks outside the breeding season that fly in a classic 'V' formation. During the spring, birds perform elaborate, jumping and wing-flapping displays in courtship. A solitary breeder, it nests in shallow water or on the ground, on a large pile of plant material.

adult life-size

The extent of red on the crown increases with maturity and its intensity varies throughout the year.

Oystercatcher
Haematopus ostralegus

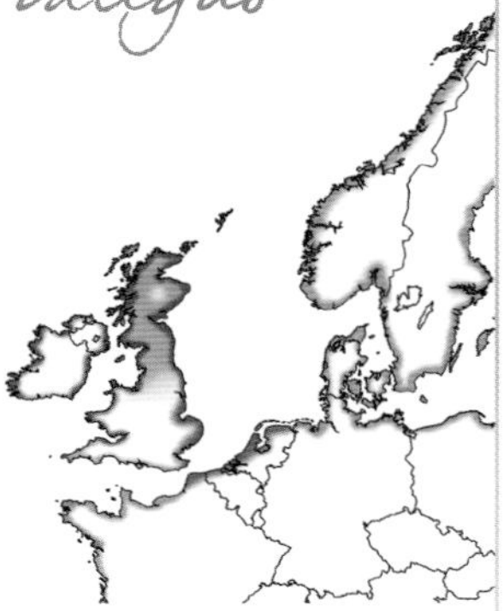

adult winter

The white half-collar is not always obvious in flight, when the neck is hunched up.

adult summer

Oystercatchers call loudly when alarmed or displaying over their breeding territory.

adult winter

Bill and leg colours are less intense in winter than in the summer months.

adult winter

The Oystercatcher is a common and distinctive wader. The sexes are similar but summer and winter plumages are subtly different. The summer adult has contrasting black-and-white plumage, essentially black on the head and upperparts and white on the underside, with a clear demarcation between the two occurring on the breast. The orange-red bill is long and slender, the beady eye is red and the legs are pinkish. The winter adult is similar but displays a white half-collar. The juvenile recalls the adult, but black elements of the plumage are more brownish and the bill and leg colours are subdued. In flight, note the obvious broad white wingbar to the trailing edge.

The Oystercatcher is generally widely dispersed during the breeding season, when it seeks stony and shingle beaches, nesting in the open in a shallow pebble-lined depression. During the winter months it can form large flocks, especially at high-tide roosts. It feeds by using its powerful bill to open the shells of molluscs and to probe the mud for marine worms.

adult summer life-size

The black-and-white plumage and bright red bill and eye make this species unmistakable.

Factfile

LENGTH **40–45CM**

WINGSPAN **80–86CM**

HABITAT **PRIMARILY A COASTAL BIRD OF ROCKY SHORES, ESTUARIES, MUDFLATS AND SHINGLE BEACHES, BUT SOMETIMES FOUND INLAND.**

FOOD **FEEDS ON MOLLUSCS AND MARINE WORMS.**

STATUS **COMMON AND WIDESPREAD RESIDENT BREEDING SPECIES PRESENT THROUGHOUT MOST OF THE REGION. BIRDS FROM SCANDINAVIA MIGRATE SOUTH FOR THE WINTER MONTHS, WHEN IT FORMS MORE CONCENTRATED GROUPS, WITH THE GREATEST DENSITY AROUND THE BRITISH ISLES AND THE NORTH COAST OF FRANCE.**

VOICE **UTTERS A DISTINCTIVE LOUD AND PIPING *KLEEP* CALL.**

Avocet
Recurvirostra avosetta

The Avocet is an unmistakable large black-and-white wader with a distinctive upturned bill. The sexes are similar but separable with care. The adult is predominantly white with a black cap and nape, and black patches to the wings. The long slender bill is black and diagnostically strongly upturned, and the pale blue legs are long and delicate-looking. The male has more contrasting plumage than that of the female and the bill is marginally longer. In flight, note the black wingtips and large black wing patches. The juvenile is similar to the adult, but the black elements of the plumage are less well defined and appear brownish.

The long bill and long trailing legs give a flying Avocet a distinctive, elongated appearance.

adult

adult life-size

The long, upcurved bill is unique among the region's birds and the iconic black-and-white plumage makes identification straightforward.

The Avocet generally breeds on shallow, brackish coastal lagoons, where it nests in a shallow pebble-lined scrape close to water, typically on small islands. Outside the breeding season it congregates in large flocks, favouring mudflats and estuaries. It is often seen wading in shallow water sweeping its long, upcurved bill from side to side in search of small mud-dwelling invertebrates.

adults

Avocets look strikingly black-and-white in flight; they are typically seen in flocks outside the breeding season.

Factfile

LENGTH 42–46CM

WINGSPAN 77–80CM

HABITAT COASTAL LAGOONS AND ESTUARIES.

FOOD FEEDS ON SMALL INVERTEBRATES IN ESTUARINE MUD.

STATUS BEST KNOWN AS A SUMMER BREEDING VISITOR (PRESENT MAINLY APRIL TO SEPTEMBER) TO SUITABLE COASTAL LOCATIONS IN THE REGION. AN INCREASING POPULATION NOW OVERWINTERS ON THE COASTS OF SOUTHERN BRITAIN.

VOICE UTTERS A RINGING *KLUEET-KLUEET* CALL.

adult

The long blue legs often get stained with mud as a bird feeds in the shallows, sweeping its bill from side to side.

Stone-curlew
Burhinus oedicnemus

The Stone-curlew is a secretive and unobtrusive dry-country wader, mainly active at night, making observation a challenge. The sexes are similar. The adult has streaked sandy-brown upperparts, buffish-white underparts, and subtle dark and whitish bars on the flanks. The large yellow eye is a distinctive feature, giving the bird a somewhat stern-looking appearance. The yellow, black-tipped bill is rather gull-like in proportion, and the legs are long, slender and yellow. In flight, the

The yellow colouration of the proportionately large yellow eyes matches that of the legs and base of the bill.

adult life-size

adult

In flight, note the bold patterning on the wings; birds typically fly rather low to the ground.

adult

The horizontal white bar on the wings, framed above and below by brown, is a striking feature.

bird recalls a gull in shape and pattern; note the obvious, strong black-and-white colouration to the outer wings, and the relatively long tail. The juvenile resembles the adult but with more subdued plumage markings.

Viewed in isolation, the Stone-curlew's plumage is very distinctive, but it provides superb camouflage in its chosen habitat. A timid bird that commonly hides by crouching and remaining still at the slightest hint of danger, it is a tricky species to observe in the field and is more commonly heard than seen. It seeks undisturbed dry ground such as heathland and chalk downland on which to breed, constructing a shallow scrape on the ground.

Factfile

LENGTH 40–44CM

WINGSPAN 75–85CM

HABITAT LARGE OPEN AREAS OF DRY GRASSLAND, HEATHLAND AND ARABLE FARMLAND.

FOOD FEEDS ON GROUND-DWELLING INVERTEBRATES, SMALL MAMMALS, BIRDS AND AMPHIBIANS.

STATUS SUMMER BREEDING VISITOR (PRESENT MAINLY APRIL TO SEPTEMBER) IN RELATIVELY SMALL NUMBERS, FAVOURING A FEW TRADITIONAL AND SCATTERED BREEDING SITES IN THE SOUTH OF THE REGION. OVERWINTERS IN COUNTRIES BORDERING THE MEDITERRANEAN.

VOICE MOST VOCAL AT DUSK AND AT NIGHT WHEN IT UTTERS AN EERIE, CURLEW-LIKE *CURLEE* WAILING CALL.

adult

In a sandy or stony environment, birds can be amazingly hard to spot, especially when crouched, which they sometimes do when alarmed.

Little Ringed Plover

Charadrius dubius

This is a small, slim-bodied plover. The sexes are similar. The summer adult has sandy-brown upperparts and crown. The underparts are white with an obvious wide black collar and breast-band. The black-and-white markings to the face, and bold yellow ring surrounding the dark eye, are obvious and diagnostic when observed at close range. The bill is rather stubby and black, the slender legs pinkish-brown. In flight, note the lack of a wingbar on the upperwing, allowing separation from Ringed Plover. The juvenile is more uniformly sandy-brown, lacking the black elements of plumage. Note also the unmarked face, lacking the yellow eye-ring of the adult and the pale supercilium that is present in juvenile Ringed Plover.

The Little Ringed Plover seeks slopes of sand and gravel, typically next to freshwater, on which to breed. The extraction of sand and gravel has created ideal habitat, and the species has adapted well to these man-made features. It is rather secretive when nesting, and is heard more often than seen at this time. It constructs a shallow scrape on the ground and is sometimes observed performing an elaborate distraction display to lure potential predators away from the nest.

adult

Feeds in a typical plover manner, running then pausing to pick an item of food from the surface of the mud in a deliberate manner.

Factfile

LENGTH 14–15CM

WINGSPAN 42–48CM

HABITAT FAVOURS INLAND FRESHWATER, TYPICALLY ON THE SHORES OF LARGE GRAVEL PITS AND OTHER MAN-MADE SITES.

FOOD INSECTS AND OTHER TERRESTRIAL AND AQUATIC INVERTEBRATES.

STATUS SUMMER BREEDING VISITOR (PRESENT MAINLY APRIL TO SEPTEMBER) THAT IS WIDESPREAD IN SUITABLE HABITATS THROUGHOUT THE REGION, EXCEPT THE FAR NORTH. IT OVERWINTERS IN NORTH AFRICA.

VOICE UTTERS A SHORT, LOUD *PEW* CALL.

adult

In flight, note the uniformly brown upperwings that lack the bold white wingbar seen in Ringed Plover.

juvenile

Pale feather margins can give the back a scaly appearance; the lack of a pale supercilium is another feature that aids separation from a juvenile Ringed Plover.

adult life-size

The bold black-and-white markings on the head and neck are distinctive but the yellow eye-ring is the most useful diagnostic feature.

Ringed Plover

Charadrius hiaticula

The Ringed Plover is a dumpy-looking little wader mainly found on the coast. The sexes are similar, but separable with care, and summer and winter plumages differ subtly. The summer adult male has predominantly sandy-brown upperparts and crown, and a white underside with a black breast and neck collar. The face is marked with contrasting black-and-white markings; note the white nape and throat and lack of an eye-ring. The short bill is orange with a dark tip, and the slender legs are orange-yellow. The summer adult female is similar but with duller head markings. During the winter months adult plumage becomes more subdued overall, the black elements to the head replaced with sandy-brown and the leg and bill colours becoming duller. Note the pale supercilium. The juvenile recalls the winter adult, but the breast-band is smaller and usually incomplete; the pale supercilium separates it from juvenile Little Ringed Plover. In flight, all birds display a striking wingbar on the upperwing.

Primarily a species that seeks sandy and shingle beaches on which to breed, the Ringed Plover also occurs in smaller numbers on the banks of gravel pits and rivers and other inland freshwater locations offering suitable breeding habitat. It nests in a shallow, pebble-lined scrape close to water. In the winter months, it congregates almost exclusively on the coast, and numbers in the south are boosted by migratory birds from further afield. It is often seen in large mixed wader flocks at this time.

Factfile

LENGTH 18–20CM

WINGSPAN 48–57CM

HABITAT MAINLY ASSOCIATED WITH COASTAL HABITATS, BUT ALSO OCCURS ON INLAND FRESHWATER HABITATS SUCH AS GRAVEL PITS AND RIVERS.

FOOD FEEDS ON INVERTEBRATES INCLUDING MOLLUSCS, WORMS AND SMALL CRUSTACEANS.

STATUS WIDESPREAD BREEDING SPECIES IN SUITABLE HABITATS THROUGHOUT THE REGION. ALMOST ENTIRELY COASTAL OUTSIDE THE BREEDING SEASON, THE MAJORITY WINTERING IN THE SOUTHERN PART OF OUR REGION.

VOICE THE CALL IS A SOFT, RISING, DISYLLABIC *TUU-EEP*.

adult life-size

A Ringed Plover's body is usually held in a horizontal stance. The lack of a yellow eye-ring and striking orange-yellow base to the bill help with separation from Little Ringed Plover.

adult

juvenile

The white wingbar is striking in birds of all ages.

Typically associated with coastal habitats, whereas Little Ringed Plover tends to favour inland, freshwater locations; in winter (when Little Ringed Plovers have migrated south) this is the most likely small plover species to be encountered.

juvenile

At close range, pale feather margins give a juvenile's back a subtle scaly appearance. The bill usually appears uniformly dark and the leg colour is subdued compared to an adult.

Dotterel
Charadrius morinellus

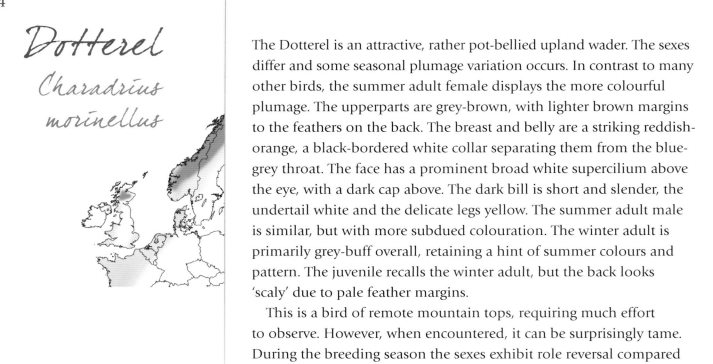

The Dotterel is an attractive, rather pot-bellied upland wader. The sexes differ and some seasonal plumage variation occurs. In contrast to many other birds, the summer adult female displays the more colourful plumage. The upperparts are grey-brown, with lighter brown margins to the feathers on the back. The breast and belly are a striking reddish-orange, a black-bordered white collar separating them from the blue-grey throat. The face has a prominent broad white supercilium above the eye, with a dark cap above. The dark bill is short and slender, the undertail white and the delicate legs yellow. The summer adult male is similar, but with more subdued colouration. The winter adult is primarily grey-buff overall, retaining a hint of summer colours and pattern. The juvenile recalls the winter adult, but the back looks 'scaly' due to pale feather margins.

This is a bird of remote mountain tops, requiring much effort to observe. However, when encountered, it can be surprisingly tame. During the breeding season the sexes exhibit role reversal compared to most other birds, the female undertaking territorial displays, and the male being responsible for incubation. It nests in a shallow, moss-lined scrape in the ground, often positioned close to a large boulder. It rarely takes to flight, most often running from danger.

juvenile
The pattern on a juvenile's head and breast suggest that seen in more boldly marked adult birds.

female

No other wader of this size and shape has the same amount of white on the face and such distinctively marked underparts.

female life-size

On average, females are more richly marked and colourful than males. The white supercilium and breast-band show up at a considerable distance in all birds.

Factfile

LENGTH 20–22CM

WINGSPAN 57–64CM

HABITAT DRY, OPEN MOUNTAIN PLATEAUX, GENERALLY ABOVE 1,000 METRES IN THE SOUTH OF ITS RANGE; OCCURS AT LOWER ALTITUDES FURTHER NORTH.

FOOD INSECTS AND SMALL INVERTEBRATES.

STATUS SUMMER VISITOR (PRESENT MAINLY MAY TO AUGUST), ITS BREEDING RANGE RESTRICTED TO SUITABLE HIGH GROUND IN SCANDINAVIA AND SCOTLAND. WINTERS IN SOUTHERN EUROPE AND NORTH AFRICA, AND OCCASIONALLY SEEN ON MIGRATION.

VOICE UTTERS A SOFT, TRILLING *PIERRR* CALL.

Golden Plover
Pluvialis apricaria

The Golden Plover is a handsomely marked wader and an iconic summer species of remote upland areas. The sexes are separable in the summer; wide plumage variations occur in individual birds and across its breeding range. The summer adult has finely patterned, spangled golden-brown upperparts, separated from the underparts by a band of white. The summer male displays bold, black plumage on the breast and belly, the extent differing with race. Males that breed in Britain have a black

adult summer life-size

juvenile

During breeding seasons, the plaintive song is evocative of moorland and mountain-slope habitats.

A juvenile's plumage is similar to that of a winter adult, but more colourful and cleaner-looking.

winter flock

Outside the breeding season, Golden Plovers are invariably seen in tight-formation flocks, with birds uttering their distinctive calls.

Factfile

LENGTH 26–29CM   WINGSPAN 67–76CM

HABITAT BREEDS ON REMOTE UPLAND MOORLAND, MOVING TO LOWLAND GRASSLAND AND ARABLE FARMLAND DURING THE WINTER MONTHS.

FOOD FEEDS ON INVERTEBRATES, FRUITS AND SEEDS.

STATUS A SUMMER BREEDING SPECIES IN UPLAND AREAS OF SCANDINAVIA AND NORTHERN BRITAIN (PRESENT MAINLY APRIL TO AUGUST), IT MIGRATES SOUTHWARDS TO LOWER GROUND OUTSIDE THE BREEDING SEASON AND WINTERS IN THE SOUTHERN PART OF OUR REGION. INFLUXES FROM FURTHER NORTH SWELL WINTER NUMBERS.

VOICE UTTERS A MELANCHOLIC PU-*PEEOO* SONG AND A *PEEOO* CALL WHEN IN FLIGHT.

belly that fades to grey on the neck. Males that breed further north are black on the belly, neck and face. The summer female is similar but with less distinctive black markings, easily separable in the case of birds that breed in Britain. Confusingly, females from further north are more heavily marked and can resemble British breeding males. The winter adult loses black markings on the underparts, and becomes streaked golden-buff on the neck and head, and white on the belly. The juvenile recalls the winter adult. All birds display pure white underwings in flight.

The Golden Plover nests in a shallow scrape on the ground, favouring areas of short vegetation. During the winter months it forms large flocks on lower ground, often mixing with Lapwings. It occasionally occurs on the coast during extreme weather.

adult summer

The extent of black on the underparts in the breeding season varies according to sex and race.

Grey Plover
Pluvialis squatarola

The Grey Plover is a coastal wader with a plump body. It is mostly encountered in winter plumage, when the sexes are similar, but the sexes in summer plumage are separable. The winter adult appears uniform grey at a distance but closer inspection reveals spangled black-and-white upperparts with whitish underparts. The bill and legs are blackish. The summer adult male has bold black underparts, separated from the upperparts by a broad white band. The summer adult female displays more mottled underparts. The juvenile is similar

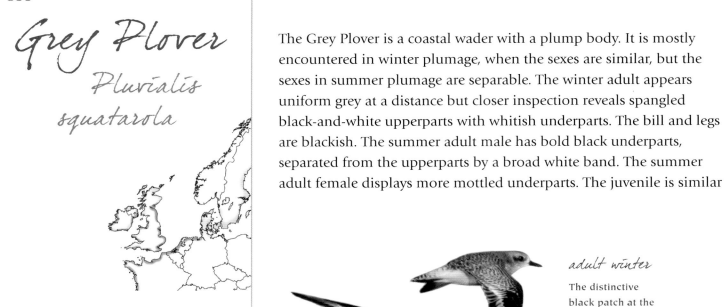

adult winter

The distinctive black patch at the base of the underwing, seen in flying birds, is a diagnostic feature.

adult winter

In the dead of winter, birds can appear distinctly black-and-white.

to the winter adult but with a subtle buffish tinge to the plumage. In flight, all birds reveal white underwings with contrasting black 'armpits'.

The Grey Plover is a species usually only encountered in our region during the winter months, when birds tend to be solitary. Typically seen feeding in estuaries and mudflats with a busy 'stop-go' running action, they can be territorial and defend prime feeding areas. Evidence also suggests that they are site-faithful over several years. They breed on Arctic tundra well beyond our region, nesting on the ground in shallow scrapes.

Factfile

LENGTH 27–30CM

WINGSPAN 71–83CM

HABITAT ALMOST ENTIRELY COASTAL, FAVOURING ESTUARIES AND MUDFLATS.

FOOD SMALL MOLLUSCS, CRUSTACEANS AND WORMS.

STATUS WIDESPREAD WINTER VISITOR (PRESENT MAINLY SEPTEMBER TO APRIL), COMMON IN SUITABLE COASTAL HABITAT, PARTICULARLY THE BRITISH ISLES AND THE NORTHERN COAST OF FRANCE. BREEDS IN THE HIGH ARCTIC DURING THE SUMMER MONTHS AND RARELY SEEN IN THE REGION AT THIS TIME.

VOICE UTTERS A DISTINCTIVE *PEE-OO-EE* CALL.

adult winter life-size

The head and bill are proportionately large by plover standards; in good light and at close range the back appears spangled grey-brown.

adult summer

Although Grey Plovers do not breed in our region, birds in summer plumage are often seen in spring and autumn, before and after migration.

Lapwing
Vanellus vanellus

The Lapwing is a familiar wader with a distinctive crest. The sexes are similar but separable in the summer. The summer adult has dark upperparts that, when seen in good light, display a green and purple sheen at certain angles. The underparts are predominantly white, but note the orange undertail coverts and the striking solid black throat and chin patch. The crown and plumes of the crest are black, and the face is black-and-white. The short slender bill is dark and the long, delicate legs are pink. The summer adult female is similar, but the crest feathers are shorter and patches of white are visible on the black throat patch. The winter adult recalls the summer female, but the feathers on the back have pale fringes, the nape is flushed buff and the throat is white. The juvenile is similar to the winter adult, but the crest is shorter and the pale fringing to the feathers on the back gives it a scaly appearance. In flight, the broad wings, rounded wingtips and black-and-white colouration make identification of all birds straightforward.

adult summer life-size

In good light, a beautiful sheen can be seen on the back feathers; the crest is a diagnostic feature amongst wader species.

adult winter

Outside the breeding season, the back feathers have subtle pale margins and white elements of the face pattern are rather grubby-looking.

adult summer displaying

When displaying, the flight pattern is 'floppy-looking' and exaggeratedly slow; the outer half of the wings appears proportionately large and rounded.

In areas where it is present in the breeding season, the Lapwing is often seen performing agile aerial displays over the nest, commonly accompanied by its distinctive call. It nests in a scrape in the ground, often lined with vegetation. Birds from the north migrate south and west to avoid harsh weather during the winter months, and they form large flocks.

Lapwings are seen in flocks in winter; in flight, birds often twist and turn in unison, alternately revealing the gleaming white underparts then the dark upperparts.

winter flock

Factfile

LENGTH **28–31CM**

WINGSPAN **75–85CM**

HABITAT **FAVOURS UNDISTURBED GRAZED GRASSLAND, MOORS AND SPRING-PLANTED ARABLE FARMLAND DURING THE BREEDING SEASON. MOVES TO LOWLANDS IN THE WINTER.**

FOOD **FEEDS ON WORMS, BEETLES AND OTHER INVERTEBRATES.**

STATUS **BREEDING SPECIES, PRESENT YEAR-ROUND AND WIDESPREAD IN THE WEST OF OUR REGION IN SUITABLE HABITATS. SUMMER BREEDING VISITOR TO UPLANDS, AND TO THE NORTH AND EAST OF OUR REGION, MIGRATING TO MORE TEMPERATE AREAS FOR WINTER. NUMBERS ARE IN DECLINE.**

VOICE **UTTERS A SHRILL *PEE-WIT* CALL.**

Knot
Calidris canutus

The Knot is a plump wader with a relatively short bill and legs. The sexes are similar, but seasonal plumage variation occurs. The winter adult has mostly uniformly grey upperparts, with a dark tip to the tail; the underparts are white. The dark bill is short and robust-looking, and the legs are dull yellowish-green. The summer adult is sometimes encountered in the region in late spring and early autumn, and has a colourful orange-red face, neck and underparts. A fair proportion of the feathers to the

adult summer

Although Knot do not breed in our region, birds in summer plumage are often seen in spring and autumn, before and after migration.

juvenile

Knot have a proportionately short bill; the yellow legs and scaly-looking back are useful identification features for juveniles.

upperparts are fringed grey, with black and red centres. The legs are black. The juvenile recalls the winter adult but has a buffish tinge, and the feathers on the back have a scaly appearance owing to the pale fringes and dark submarginal bands. In flight, all birds display a white wingbar and grey terminal band to the tail when seen from above.

The Knot is a classic wader of estuaries and mudflats and present very locally in large numbers during the winter months. It forms large flocks, which can be seen flying in tight formation when they take to the air and come in to roost.

In flight, birds look compact and medium-sized by wader standards; the pale wingbar is subtle at best, and not especially striking.

adult winter

adult winter

adult winter life-size

The yellow legs are a good identification feature amongst medium-sized waders; the plumage lacks any really distinctive features, being grey-brown above and pale below.

Factfile

LENGTH **23–25CM**

WINGSPAN **50–60CM**

HABITAT **COASTAL WADER OF ESTUARIES AND EXTENSIVE MUDFLATS.**

FOOD **MUD-DWELLING MARINE INVERTEBRATES.**

STATUS **WINTER VISITOR (PRESENT MAINLY SEPTEMBER TO APRIL) TO COASTAL REGIONS, TYPICALLY IN LARGE FLOCKS IN SUITABLE HABITATS. BREEDS ON TUNDRA IN THE HIGH ARCTIC DURING THE SUMMER MONTHS.**

VOICE **UTTERS A SHARP *KNUT* CALL.**

Sanderling
Calidris alba

The Sanderling is an endearing small wading bird associated with sandy beaches and breaking waves. The sexes are similar, but seasonal plumage variation occurs. The winter adult is a relatively pale bird with whitish-grey upperparts and white underparts; the upperparts are marked with a dark shoulder patch. The robust bill and rather short legs are black in contrast, and note the absence of a hind toe. Birds displaying summer plumage can sometimes be encountered in the

1st-winter life-size

Feeding birds seldom keep still, and spend most of the time running at speed, pausing only to pick items of food from the water's edge.

adult winter

A winter Sanderling looks strikingly white at a distance with contrastingly black legs and bill; at close range, the upperparts are seen to be subtly darker than the underparts.

region in the late spring or early autumn. The underparts remain white, but the upperparts are darker, showing a scattering of dark-centred feathers on the back, and the head and neck are flushed orange-red. The juvenile recalls the winter adult, but with a high proportion of dark-centred feathers on its back. In flight and from above, all birds display a striking white wingbar. When seen from below, they are pure white.

Sanderlings are associated with sandy beaches where they are never far from the breaking surf. They are commonly seen in small flocks feeding on the water's edge making swift, darting runs in and out of the surf. Evidence suggests that birds are site-faithful on their wintering grounds.

Factfile

LENGTH 20–21CM

WINGSPAN 36–42CM

HABITAT COASTAL WADER THAT FAVOURS SANDY BEACHES AND ESTUARY MUDFLATS.

FOOD FEEDS ON INVERTEBRATES.

STATUS LOCALLY COMMON WINTER VISITOR (USUALLY PRESENT SEPTEMBER TO APRIL), MAINLY TO THE COASTS OF BRITAIN AND NORTHERN FRANCE. BREEDS IN THE HIGH ARCTIC.

VOICE UTTERS A TRILLING *PLIT* CALL.

adult winter

The white wingbar on the upperwing is a striking feature in flight; the body and underwings are bright white.

adult summer

Sanderlings do not breed in our region but birds in summer plumage (with variably reddish-brown upperparts) are seen in spring and autumn, before and after migration.

Purple Sandpiper

Calidris maritima

The Purple Sandpiper is a plump-bodied wader. The sexes are similar but seasonal plumage variation occurs. The winter adult is the most widely seen plumage in the region and has a head, breast and upperparts of blue-grey, being darkest on the back. A purple sheen is only obvious in good light. The belly is white and the flanks are streaked with dark markings. The longish bill is slightly downcurved with an orange or yellow base, and the legs are yellowish. The summer adult has reddish-brown and black back feathers, and the head is streaked grey-brown with a contrasting rufous crown and ear coverts. The juvenile is similar to the winter adult, but the back has a rufous tinge

Outside the breeding season, small flocks can be found on rocky promontories; generally they are faithful to these sites throughout the winter months. In flight, note the dumpy body and pale wingbar.

winter flock

adult winter life-size

In good light, and with a bit of imagination, sometimes a purple sheen can be seen on the back feathers.

and the pale-edged feathers give it a scaly appearance. The neck, breast and flanks are streaked. In flight, note the subtle white wingbar.

The Purple Sandpiper overwinters further north than any other wading species, and has breeding populations in Scandinavia and the north of the British Isles. It is most commonly seen across the region during the winter months when overall the population moves southwards. It is a trusting species of rocky shorelines that can be easy to approach. It nests in a shallow scrape in the ground.

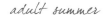
adult summer
In the breeding season, the back feathers are edged with reddish-brown and the cap also acquires this colouration.

Factfile

LENGTH 20–22CM

WINGSPAN 40–44CM

HABITAT TUNDRA BREEDER, ASSOCIATED WITH ROCKY SHORES OUTSIDE THE BREEDING SEASON.

FOOD FEEDS ON INVERTEBRATES.

STATUS SUMMER BREEDING VISITOR TO UPLAND CENTRAL SCANDINAVIA, PRESENT THERE MAINLY MAY TO AUGUST. AT OTHER TIMES, ALMOST EXCLUSIVELY COASTAL AND WIDESPREAD BUT RESTRICTED TO EXPOSED ROCKY SHORES.

VOICE UTTERS A SHARP *KWIT* CALL IN FLIGHT.

adult winter
The yellow legs and base to the bill are good identification features during the winter months.

Little Stint
Calidris minuta

adult summer
Breeding plumage is variable, but the head and upperparts are well-marked reddish-brown, while the underparts are white.

Factfile

LENGTH 13–14CM

WINGSPAN 28–35CM

HABITAT FAVOURS ESTUARIES AND SHELTERED COASTAL POOLS. OCCASIONALLY ENCOUNTERED ON INLAND FRESHWATER SUCH AS LAKES AND RESERVOIRS.

FOOD FEEDS ON SMALL INVERTEBRATES.

STATUS REGULAR PASSAGE MIGRANT, MOST COMMONLY SEEN ON AUTUMN MIGRATION THROUGHOUT THE REGION.

VOICE UTTERS A SHARP *STIP* CALL.

The Little Stint is a diminutive wader recalling a small Dunlin. The sexes are similar but summer and winter plumages differ. The summer adult has reddish-brown upperparts with a flush of reddish-orange on the head and neck; the underparts are white. The winter adult has uniform grey upperparts and white underparts. It is most commonly seen in the region in juvenile plumage, having pale-fringed reddish-brown and black feathers to the upperparts forming obvious 'V' patterns. The underparts are white with a distinctive buffish-orange flush to the side of the breast. The head is marked with a pale supercilium that forks above the eye, a dark centre to the crown and a pale forecrown. Birds in all plumages have black bills and legs.

The Little Stint has a very distinctive feeding pattern, busily picking up food items from the surface of the mud, rather than probing like so many other wading birds. It also is less likely to enter the water than other species, generally keeping to the water's edge. It breeds on Arctic tundra and winters in southern Europe and North Africa; it is seen in our region on migration.

juvenile
In flight, the underwings are pale and the upperwings show a pale wingbar.

juvenile life-size
A subtly divided supercilium frames the darker crown.

Temminck's Stint *Calidris temminckii*

Temminck's Stint is a rather slim-bodied little wader with short legs and a long tail. The sexes are similar but summer and winter plumages differ. The summer adult has grey-brown upperparts, many of the feathers along the back having dark centres. The head, neck and breast are streaked dark grey; the underparts are pure white. The winter adult is unlikely to be seen in the region, but has subdued grey-brown upperparts and white underparts. The juvenile has brown upperparts and white underparts; the back has a scaly appearance, the feathers being pale-fringed. All birds have a short and slightly downcurved bill, rather short yellowish legs, and a clear demarcation between the breast patch and the white underside. In flight, note the striking white outer tail feathers.

adult summer
On breeding grounds, displaying birds are vocal in flight.

adult summer life-size

Seen mainly in the spring, birds in breeding plumage recall a miniature Common Sandpiper; however, feeding behaviour is very different and birds creep along and do not bob up and down as they walk like the sandpiper.

Factfile

LENGTH 13–15CM

WINGSPAN 30–35CM

HABITAT TUNDRA AND MOUNTAINOUS AREAS DURING THE BREEDING SEASON, FAVOURING THE MARGINS OF SHALLOW FRESHWATER POOLS DURING MIGRATION.

FOOD FEEDS ON SMALL INSECTS AND WORMS.

STATUS SUMMER BREEDING SPECIES FOUND IN SUITABLE HABITAT IN SCANDINAVIA, PRESENT THERE MAINLY MAY TO AUGUST; PASSAGE MIGRANT ELSEWHERE IN THE REGION.

VOICE UTTERS A SHORT TRILLING CALL.

Temminck's Stint has a rather creeping movement when walking and feeding, holding its body horizontally. It nests on the ground in a shallow plant-lined cup. It overwinters in southern Europe and north Africa, and is occasionally encountered on migration.

Juvenile
The scaly-looking back, yellow legs and yellow base to the bill are good features for the identification of juveniles.

Curlew Sandpiper
Calidris ferruginea

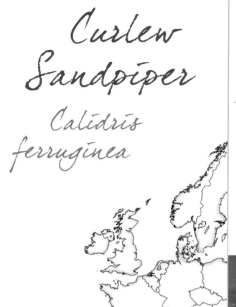

juvenile

In all birds, the bill is appreciably longer and more elegantly downcurved than in a superficially similar Dunlin. The peachy-orange flush and scaly-looking back are good identification features for juvenile birds.

adult spring

The plumage is well-marked in summer but the extent and intensity of the orange-red colour varies between individuals.

Factfile

LENGTH 18–20CM

WINGSPAN 38–45CM

HABITAT MAINLY COASTAL, FAVOURING ESTUARIES, MUDFLATS AND LAGOONS. OCCASIONALLY OCCURS INLAND ON LARGE EXPANSES OF FRESHWATER SUCH AS GRAVEL PITS AND RESERVOIRS.

FOOD MUD-DWELLING INVERTEBRATES.

STATUS SCARCE PASSAGE MIGRANT MOST COMMONLY SEEN IN AUGUST AND SEPTEMBER. BREEDS IN THE HIGH ARCTIC AND WINTERS IN TROPICAL AFRICA.

VOICE UTTERS A SOFT *PRRRP* CALL.

The Curlew Sandpiper is a small Dunlin-like wader with a relatively long downcurved bill. The sexes are similar but summer and winter plumages differ. The summer adult briefly has rich red underparts and face (quickly mottling and often seen in moulting migrants); the upperparts are a spangled pattern of reddish-brown, black-and-white. The female is less colourful, but individual variation can make separation tricky. Although seldom encountered here, the winter adult has uniformly grey upperparts with white underparts. The juvenile is the most commonly seen plumage in the region, having buff-orange upperparts with pale-edged feathers giving a scaly

Juveniles

Amongst *Calidris* waders, this is the only commonly encountered species in northwest Europe to have a white rump.

Juvenile life-size

Feeds in a deliberate and elegant manner; the proportionately long legs often become coated with mud when birds feed around the margins of drying pools.

Juvenile

appearance. The underparts are white; the breast is flushed warm buffish-peach. A pale supercilium is also present. The black downcurved bill is significantly longer than that of the similar Dunlin. The black legs are long and elegant. In flight, note the diagnostic white rump.

The Curlew Sandpiper breeds in the high Arctic, nesting close to water in a shallow scrape in the ground. It migrates to Africa to overwinter and is seen in the region as a scarce passage migrant, mainly in suitable coastal regions. It is often encountered in small groups in mixed wader flocks.

Dunlin
Calidris alpina

The Dunlin is the most commonly encountered wader in the region and regularly used as an identification yardstick by which to judge other species. The sexes are similar but subtle differences appear in the summer plumage. Several races also occur in the region, separable by bill length and size. The summer adult typically has reddish-brown upperparts, including the cap. The underparts are whitish and marked with a conspicuous black belly patch and streaking to the neck. The intensity of these markings differs with race, the brightest markings seen in males that breed in Siberia and northeast Europe. The male is often more intensely marked than the female. The winter

Factfile

LENGTH 17–21CM WINGSPAN 35–40CM

HABITAT FAVOURS UPLAND MOORLAND AND MOUNTAINS DURING THE BREEDING SEASON, MOVING TO COASTAL ESTUARIES AND MUDFLATS AT OTHER TIMES.

FOOD FEEDS ON INSECTS AND OTHER INVERTEBRATES IN SUMMER, AND MARINE INVERTEBRATES AT OTHER TIMES.

STATUS BREEDS IN SCANDINAVIA AND NORTHERN BRITAIN, AND PRESENT THERE MAINLY MAY TO AUGUST. MOVES TO COASTAL AREAS FOR THE WINTER, WHEN NUMBERS ARE BOOSTED BY MIGRANTS FROM FURTHER AFIELD. ALSO SEEN ON PASSAGE.

VOICE DISPLAYING BIRDS UTTER A SERIES OF WHISTLING CALLS. CALL IS A *PREEIT* AT OTHER TIMES.

adult summer

In flight, note the white wingbar and white outer feathers to the otherwise dark tail.

adult winter life-size
The plumage is unremarkable and lacks any obvious features for identification. The black legs and proportionately long, dark bill are useful indicators.

adult has uniform grey upperparts and white underparts. The juvenile is marked with reddish-brown and black on the upperparts, the feathers having pale fringes and aligning to form pale 'V' markings; the head and neck are brown and marked with darker streaking; the underparts are whitish and adorned with black spot-like streaking on the breast and flanks. All birds have a long dark bill and dark legs.

The Dunlin is a familiar small wader that forms large flocks during the winter months. They can be a spectacular sight, often taking flight briefly before settling again to feed. They nest on the ground in a lined scrape concealed by vegetation.

juvenile

Subtle dark spots on the flanks aid identification and ageing; the bill length varies considerably according to race and location of breeding grounds.

adult summer

Birds in summer plumage are sometimes noted away from breeding grounds in spring and autumn, before and after migration.

Ruff
Calidris pugnax

The Ruff varies considerably both in size and appearance. The sexes are separable and summer and winter plumages differ. The male is larger than the female and in summer plumage has brownish upperparts, the feathers marked with dark tips and bars producing a fine dark patterning overall. Distinctive ruff and crest feathers are briefly acquired, varying widely from male to male, but generally uniform black, white or chestnut coloured. Facial warts are also observed at this time. The summer adult female has grey-brown upperparts with black tips and bars to the feathers; the underparts are pale. Both male and female winter adults have uniform grey-brown upperparts and are pale underneath. The juvenile

juvenile

Note the pale margin to the rump, seen in flying birds.

summer male

A male's ruff feathers are used in display, and are present for a few weeks at most; the colour and pattern varies between individuals.

recalls the winter adult, but is uniformly buff, the pale fringing to the back feathers giving it a scaly appearance. The relatively small head, slightly downcurved bill and orange-yellow legs are consistent features in all birds. In flight, note the narrow white wingbar and obvious white-edged rump.

During the breeding season, males display their colourful plumage in groups or 'leks', performing elaborate dances and leaping around. It nests in a shallow scrape in the ground.

adult winter

In all birds, the head looks proportionately small by wader standards; the winter plumage lacks any striking features.

Factfile

LENGTH **23–29CM**

WINGSPAN **45–56CM**

HABITAT **FOUND MAINLY ON MARSHLAND AND FLOODED MEADOWS DURING THE BREEDING SEASON. MORE COMMONLY ENCOUNTERED ON MIGRATION, WHEN IT FAVOURS COASTAL POOLS.**

FOOD **FEEDS ON A VARIETY OF INVERTEBRATES.**

STATUS **SUMMER BREEDING POPULATION EXISTS TO THE EXTREME NORTH OF THE REGION, BUT BEST KNOWN AS A PASSAGE MIGRANT ELSEWHERE.**

VOICE **MOSTLY SILENT.**

juvenile life-size

Plumage colour varies between individuals but the scaly-looking back is common to all juveniles.

Jack Snipe
Lymnocryptes minimus

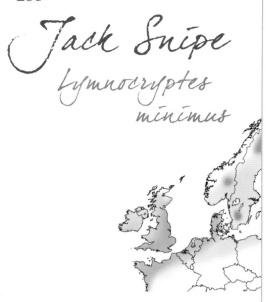

Factfile

LENGTH 17–19CM

WINGSPAN 36–40CM

HABITAT WELL-VEGETATED MARGINS OF MARSHES AND SHALLOW POOLS.

FOOD FEEDS ON A VARIETY OF MUD-DWELLING INVERTEBRATES.

STATUS SUMMER BREEDING RANGE ENCOMPASSES THE EXTREME NORTH OF OUR REGION, BUT MORE USUALLY KNOWN AS A PASSAGE MIGRANT AND SCARCE WINTER VISITOR.

VOICE MOSTLY SILENT.

The Jack Snipe is a furtive wader, and considerably smaller than the similar Snipe. The sexes are similar. Both the adult and juvenile have brown upperparts with conspicuous yellow stripes. On close inspection, the feathers are exquisitely patterned with detailed dark markings, and a greenish sheen can sometimes be seen in good light. The head is boldly marked with dark and pale-buff stripes; note particularly the pale forked supercilium and the lack of a central stripe to the crown. The underparts are pure white, with streaking to the neck and breast. The long and slender bill is yellowish with a dark tip, but noticeably shorter than that of Snipe. The legs and feet are light green.

adult

Jack Snipe bob up and down as they walk, a behaviour that is not seen in Snipe.

adult life-size

Body is small and dumpy; the divided pale supercilium is an identification pointer.

This is a rather secretive wader that seldom leaves the sanctuary of marginal cover, seeking dense areas of matted grass and reeds within which to conceal itself. It is less sociable than the Snipe, generally solitary, and easily overlooked. It is usually encountered wading at the edge of marginal cover, pumping its body up and down as it walks. It rarely takes to flight, preferring to remain still and crouch low at the sign of danger.
It breeds on tundra bogs, nesting on the ground in a grass-lined cup close to water.

adult
Although striking when seen in isolation, the streaking on the upperparts provides good camouflage amongst marginal wetland vegetation.

Snipe
Gallinago gallinago

The Snipe is an easily recognised wader with a plump, rounded body and long slender bill. The sexes are similar, and the juvenile is hard to separate from the adult. Both adult and juvenile birds have primarily buffish-brown upperparts that are attractively marked with a series of intricate black-and-white bars and lines. Note the distinctive yellow

adult life-size
The long bill is used to probe mud for invertebrates; the stripy-looking head pattern is distinctive.

adult
The upperparts are rich orange-brown and beautifully patterned.

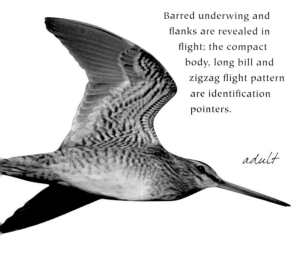

Barred underwing and flanks are revealed in flight; the compact body, long bill and zigzag flight pattern are identification pointers.

adult

stripes along the back and the head. The flanks and breast are variably streaked and barred; the underparts are white. The bill is pale reddish-brown with a dark tip; the legs are dull green. In flight the short, barred tail displays a buff margin.

The Snipe has a very characteristic feeding pattern, rapidly probing the mud for suitable food items in a manner reminiscent of the needle on a sewing machine. Breeding males perform elaborate flying displays, fanning and vibrating their tail feathers to make a rhythmic drumming sound. The Snipe nests on damp ground in a cup hidden by vegetation. Outside the breeding season the species is widespread, and birds are encountered in small groups in a variety of mainly freshwater habitats.

adult

On breeding grounds, birds often stand sentinel on fence posts, looking out for danger and rival birds.

Factfile

LENGTH 25–27CM

WINGSPAN 40–50CM

HABITAT DURING THE BREEDING SEASON, MOSTLY ASSOCIATED WITH MARSHLAND, BOGS AND MEADOWS. MORE WIDESPREAD IN MAINLY FRESHWATER HABITATS IN WINTER.

FOOD FEEDS ON A VARIETY OF INVERTEBRATES.

STATUS PRESENT YEAR-ROUND IN THE REGION, AND A WIDESPREAD BREEDING SPECIES. NORTHERN POPULATIONS MIGRATE SOUTH TO AVOID HARSH WEATHER IN WINTER, BOOSTING POPULATIONS IN THESE AREAS.

VOICE WHEN FLUSHED, UTTERS A SNEEZE LIKE *KREECH*.

Woodcock
Scolopax rusticola

The Woodcock is a rarely seen, secretive and rotund woodland wader with a long slender bill and relatively short legs. The sexes are similar, and the juvenile is difficult to separate from the adult. The adult and juvenile are brown overall with fine, marbled black, chestnut and white plumage that affords the bird superb camouflage against leaf litter on the woodland floor. The underside is paler overall with a more extensive pattern of barring. The large dark eyes are situated close to the top of the head, providing an extensive field of vision. The bill is flesh-coloured with a dark tip. It is most commonly seen in flight, when its distinguishing features include the broad rounded wings, long bill and white tips to the tail feathers.

Factfile

LENGTH 33–35CM   WINGSPAN 55–65CM

HABITAT DAMP, DECIDUOUS AND MIXED WOODLANDS.

FOOD A VARIETY OF GROUND-DWELLING INVERTEBRATES.

STATUS WIDESPREAD BREEDING RESIDENT THROUGHOUT MUCH OF THE REGION. NUMBERS ARE BOOSTED IN THE SOUTH IN WINTER BY MIGRATION FROM MORE NORTHERLY LATITUDES AND AN INFLUX FROM FURTHER EAST IN EUROPE.

VOICE IN FLIGHT, UTTERS SOFT DUCK-LIKE CALLS AND DISTINCTIVE HIGH-PITCHED SQUEAKS.

adult
Territorial males are vocal in flight; seen mainly at dusk, birds can look superficially owl-like if the long bill is not noticed.

adult
The plumage on the upperparts is a good match for fallen leaves; the underparts are strongly barred.

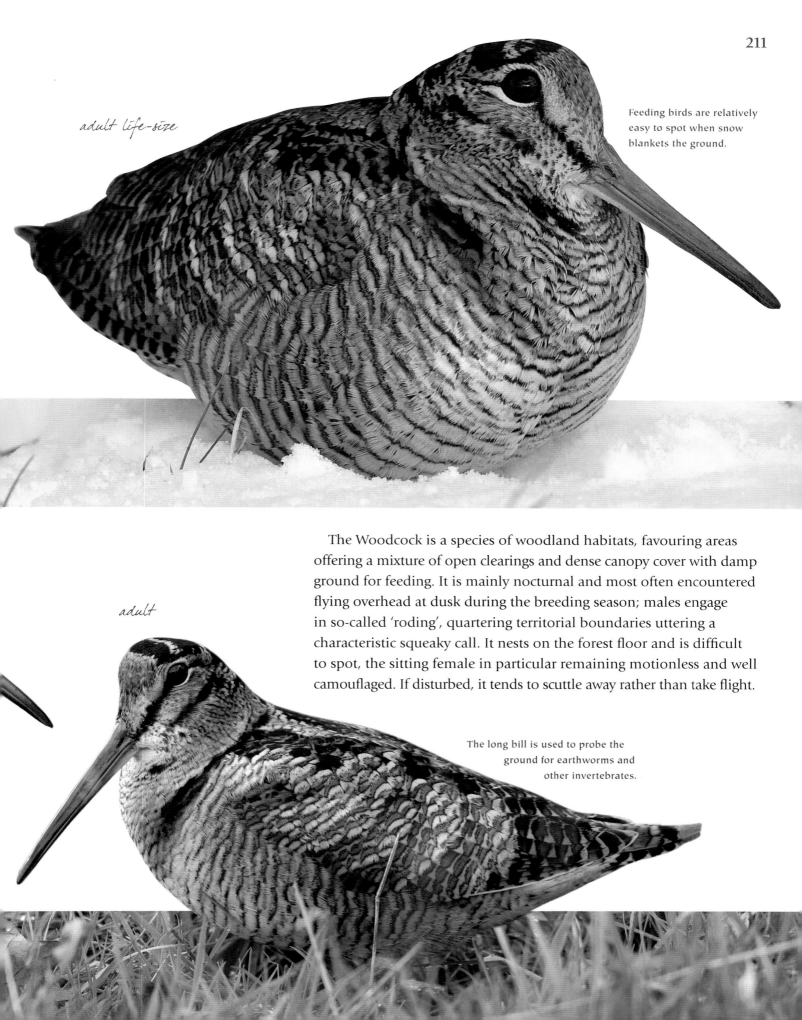

adult life-size

Feeding birds are relatively easy to spot when snow blankets the ground.

The Woodcock is a species of woodland habitats, favouring areas offering a mixture of open clearings and dense canopy cover with damp ground for feeding. It is mainly nocturnal and most often encountered flying overhead at dusk during the breeding season; males engage in so-called 'roding', quartering territorial boundaries uttering a characteristic squeaky call. It nests on the forest floor and is difficult to spot, the sitting female in particular remaining motionless and well camouflaged. If disturbed, it tends to scuttle away rather than take flight.

adult

The long bill is used to probe the ground for earthworms and other invertebrates.

Black-tailed Godwit
Limosa limosa

The Black-tailed Godwit is a large wader with distinctive long legs and a long slender and straight bill. The sexes differ in summer plumage and two distinct subspecies occur. The summer adult male has greyish upperparts that are spangled with reddish-brown. The face, neck and breast are bright reddish-orange with a darker crown. The belly is whitish and the flanks display a pattern of barring. The bill is orange with a dark tip. Birds that breed in Iceland (ssp. *islandica*) display darker red body plumage than birds that breed in northern Europe (ssp. *limosa*). The summer adult female recalls the male but has more subdued colouration overall. The winter adult loses all its bright summer colouration, becoming primarily grey-buff, darkest above and paler on the belly.

adult summer

Like other long-billed waders, it sometimes flexes the bill in a behaviour known as 'rhynchokinesis'; flexibility in the tip is useful when feeding.

Factfile

LENGTH **36–44CM**   WINGSPAN **70–80CM**

HABITAT **BREEDS ON DAMP MEADOWS AND BOGS. FAVOURS COASTAL MARSHES AND ESTUARIES DURING THE WINTER MONTHS.**

FOOD **FEEDS ON MUD-DWELLING INVERTEBRATES.**

STATUS **SCARCE SUMMER BREEDING SPECIES, PRESENT ON BREEDING GROUNDS MAINLY MAY TO AUGUST. PRIMARILY A PASSAGE MIGRANT AND WINTER VISITOR, WITH A SIGNIFICANT NUMBER OF BREEDING BIRDS FROM ICELAND AND EASTERN EUROPE OVERWINTERING IN OUR REGION.**

VOICE **IN FLIGHT, UTTERS A *KWE-WE-WE* CALL.**

In flight, note the contrasting white wingbar and dark flight feathers, and white rump and black tail.

adult winter

The undertail coverts are white and the base of the bill is pink. The juvenile is similar to the winter adult, but pale fringing and dark centres to the back feathers give it a scaly appearance. Note also the orange flush to the neck and breast. All birds display a dark terminal tail-band in flight, which contrasts sharply with the white rump. A broad white bar on the upperwings is also obvious.

The Black-tailed Godwit feeds by probing mud with its long bill, often in deep water. It nests on the ground in a shallow, grass-lined scrape and forms flocks in winter, often mixing with other waders.

adult winter life-size

The upper visible section of the leg (tibia) is particularly long in this species, allowing it to navigate deeper water than many other waders.

juvenile

Juvenile plumage is variable but typically appears washed orange-buff, with pale fringes to the dark back feathers creating a scaly appearance.

Bar-tailed Godwit
Limosa Lapponica

The Bar-tailed Godwit is a large wader with a long, slender and subtly upturned bill. The sexes are separable in summer plumage. The summer adult male has upperparts of spangled grey, black and pale buff. The head, neck and underparts, including the undertail, are bright reddish-orange, the head having a darker crown. The bill is uniformly dark. The summer adult female has a greyish back, pale belly and a tinge of orange-buff to the head, neck and breast. The winter adult loses the bright summer colouration, becoming grey-brown on the head, neck and upperparts, and pale on the underparts. The bill is pink at the base. The juvenile is similar to the winter adult but displays a buffish tinge to the head, neck and upperparts. In all birds, the long delicate, dark-coloured legs are shorter than those of the similar Black-tailed Godwit. In flight, note the barred tail, whitish wedge-shaped rump patch and lack of an upperwing bar.

juvenile life-size
The bill is subtly upcurved when compared to the straighter bill of a Black-tailed Godwit; the pink base is typical in non-breeding birds.

adult summer
It breeds mainly north and east our region, but summer plumage birds are often seen in spring and autumn, before and after migration.

The Bar-tailed Godwit breeds in the Arctic, where it favours treeless tundra and nests in a shallow scrape in the ground. It migrates to the region during the early autumn, forming mixed flocks with other waders in suitable coastal habitats. Often favouring the edge of the tide to feed, it probes sand and mud energetically with its bill to locate suitable food items, often chasing quarry.

adult winter

In flight, note the uniform upperwings; the white rump extends as a wedge up the centre of the back.

Often feeds while running along the edge of breaking waves or rising tide.

adult winter

Factfile

LENGTH 33–42CM

WINGSPAN 70–80CM

HABITAT FAVOURS ESTUARIES, MUDFLATS, COASTAL LAGOONS AND SANDY SHORES.

FOOD FEEDS ON MUD-DWELLING INVERTEBRATES.

STATUS A WINTER VISITOR, PRESENT MAINLY SEPTEMBER TO APRIL, FAIRLY COMMON AND WIDESPREAD IN SUITABLE HABITATS. BREEDS IN THE HIGH ARCTIC.

VOICE UTTERS A SHARP *KVE-WEE* CALL WHEN IN FLIGHT.

Whimbrel
Numenius phaeopus

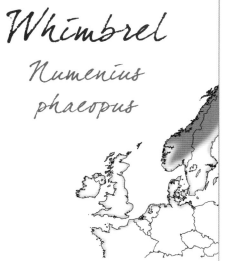

The Whimbrel recalls the larger Curlew, but has a proportionately shorter bill and distinctive head markings. The sexes are similar. The adult has grey-brown to buffish-brown plumage that is darkest on the upperparts, and paler below with fine dark streaking on the neck and breast. The head is diagnostically marked with a dark crown, a pale median stripe and pale supercilium. The long dark and slender bill is conspicuously downcurved, but shorter than that of the similar Curlew. The long legs are slender and light bluish-grey in colour. The juvenile recalls the adult, but has a warmer buff tinge to its plumage. In flight, note the dark upperwings and the barred tail contrasting with the white rump and lower back.

When on migration, Whimbrels tend to be solitary and are most frequently encountered in coastal locations. The species feeds by probing the mud and seaweed for invertebrates and readily takes to flight. Tundra and boggy moorland is favoured for breeding, and it nests on the ground in a shallow, sparsely lined depression. Most birds overwinter in southern Europe and north Africa, but a handful remain in the region for the duration of the winter.

Factfile

LENGTH **40–46CM**

WINGSPAN **75–85CM**

HABITAT **BOGGY MOORLAND AND TUNDRA DURING THE BREEDING SEASON, FAVOURING COASTAL LOCATIONS ON MIGRATION.**

FOOD **FEEDS ON A VARIETY OF INVERTEBRATES.**

STATUS **WIDESPREAD SUMMER BREEDING POPULATION IN NORTHERN SCOTLAND AND SCANDINAVIA, PRESENT MAINLY MAY TO AUGUST. MOST COMMONLY ENCOUNTERED AS A PASSAGE MIGRANT IN COASTAL REGIONS, WITH A HANDFUL OF BIRDS OVERWINTERING HERE.**

VOICE **UTTERS A BUBBLING CALL, COMMONLY DELIVERED IN SEVEN SWIFT DESCENDING NOTES.**

adult life-size

On migration, Whimbrels are often found on more rocky shores than those favoured by Curlews; they are appreciably smaller than that species when the two are seen side-by-side.

juvenile

In flight, a Whimbrel looks dainty by comparison with Curlew, the proportionately shorter bill being obvious.

juvenile

The central crown stripe is only really obvious when a bird is seen head-on; the crown itself can look reddish-brown, especially in juvenile birds.

Curlew
Numenius arquata

The Curlew is a large wading bird with a characteristic long downcurved bill and distinctive call. The sexes are similar but the female is slightly larger than the male and has a longer bill. The adult has primarily grey-brown plumage which is darker above than below. The feathers on the back are pale-fringed with darker centres and align to form a pattern of fine lines and scaling. The underside is lighter with streaked and spotted markings and a pale belly. During the summer months the plumage takes on a subtle warm yellowish tinge. The dark bill is the unmistakable feature of Curlew, being long, slender and noticeably downcurved. The juvenile recalls the adult but its plumage is more buffish-brown overall,

In flight, the uniform upperwings allow for easy separation from Black-tailed Godwit, with which it sometimes associates in winter.

adults

adult

Curlews sometimes form flocks outside the breeding season, especially at high-tide roosts, or when feeding on wetlands and coastal grassland.

Factfile

LENGTH 53–58CM WINGSPAN 80–100CM

HABITAT FAVOURS UPLAND AND MOORLAND GRASSLAND DURING THE BREEDING SEASON, PREFERRING COASTAL MUDFLATS, ESTUARIES AND ADJACENT GRASSLAND IN THE WINTER.

FOOD FEEDS ON MOLLUSCS, CRUSTACEANS, WORMS AND OTHER INVERTEBRATES.

STATUS PRESENT IN MOST SUITABLE HABITATS IN THE REGION THROUGHOUT THE YEAR. NUMBERS ARE BOOSTED IN WINTER IN MORE TEMPERATE REGIONS BY WINTER MOVEMENTS FROM NORTHERN SCANDINAVIA AND FURTHER EAST IN EUROPE. NUMBERS ARE IN DECLINE.

VOICE UTTERS A *CUR-LEW* CALL; ALSO A BUBBLING SONG DURING THE BREEDING SEASON.

with fine streaking on the neck and breast. The bill is noticeably shorter. In flight, the upperparts of all birds appear uniform in colour, but note the darker outer half of the wing, dark barring to the tail and the white rump and lower back.

The Curlew is a ground-nesting bird that breeds on upland grassland and moors in a grass-lined depression or on grassy tussocks. It moves to lowland coastal grassland, estuaries and mudflats in the winter months, where it is easy to observe, probing the mud with its long bill.

adult life-size

Even among adults, bill length varies considerably between individuals. However, in all birds, the bill is proportionately much longer than in a Whimbrel.

adult

No other wader has such a long downcurved bill. Seen well, the intricate markings on the back feathers can be appreciated.

Common Sandpiper
Actitis hypoleucos

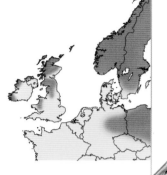

On migration, Common Sandpipers are seen feeding along the shallow margins of pools and other wetland habitats.

The Common Sandpiper is an active, plump-bodied little wader with a characteristic bobbing motion. The sexes are similar. The adult has buff-brown upperparts, the feathers on the back and flanks marked with a subtle pattern of faint bars and dark centres. The head, neck and breast are greyer, with an obvious demarcation at the breast from the white

juvenile

Factfile

LENGTH 19–21CM

WINGSPAN 35–40CM

HABITAT BREEDS ON STONY BANKS OF UPLAND STREAMS, RIVERS, LAKES AND LOCHS, MOVING TO SHELTERED COASTAL AREAS IN THE WINTER.

FOOD FEEDS ON A VARIETY OF INSECTS AND OTHER INVERTEBRATES.

STATUS WIDESPREAD AND LOCALLY COMMON IN SUITABLE HABITAT THROUGHOUT THE REGION IN THE BREEDING SEASON, PRESENT MAINLY MAY TO AUGUST. PASSAGE MIGRANT ELSEWHERE IN SPRING AND AUTUMN. MOST MIGRATE TO AFRICA FOR THE WINTER, BUT A FEW BIRDS OVERWINTER ALONG OUR COASTS.

VOICE UTTERS A *TSWEE-WEE-WEE* WHISTLING CALL IN FLIGHT.

adult life-size

Seen head-on, note the incomplete dark chest band that contrasts with the otherwise gleaming white underparts.

underparts. Note the extension of the white plumage to the shoulder, forming a 'tick'-like marking. The bill is dark with a lighter, yellowish base, and the legs are greenish-grey. The juvenile recalls the adult but the upperparts have a more pronounced pattern of scaling owing to the pale feather fringes. In flight, all birds display an obvious white wingbar; note also the barring to the white outer tail and lack of a white rump.

The Common Sandpiper flies on fluttering bowed wings, typically low over the water. It has a characteristic and busy 'bobbing' motion when standing or feeding, rarely keeping still. It breeds throughout the region in suitable habitat, nesting in a cup-shaped depression in the ground, lined with plant material and concealed in vegetation.

adult

In flight, birds are easy to overlook as they skim close to the water's surface, covering relatively short distances before they land again.

adult

Common Sandpipers typically nest beside streams and flowing water and territorial birds often call from a prominent mid-stream boulder.

Green Sandpiper
Tringa ochropus

The Green Sandpiper is a rather cautious, plump-bodied wader with a busy bobbing movement. The sexes are similar. The adult has dark greenish-brown upperparts, finely marked with a series of small pale spots; it can appear almost black from a distance or in poor light. The head and neck are similarly coloured, but marked with fine streaking. A pale supercilium can be determined on close inspection, boldest to the front of the eye. The bright white underparts show a clear separation from the darker breast. The slender bill is dark greenish-grey

adult life-size

Feeding birds are usually unobtrusive, wading along the shallow margins of streams and pools, often close to, or amongst, emergent vegetation.

adult

In flight, the striking white rump and dark-tipped white tail catch the eye; the upperwings appear uniformly dark brown at a distance.

adult

As the breeding season approaches, the upperparts become increasingly spangled with white. The call is loud and, once learned, is diagnostic.

Factfile

LENGTH 21–24CM

WINGSPAN 39–44CM

HABITAT BOGGY GROUND WITH OPEN WOODLAND IN SUMMER. AT OTHER TIMES FAVOURS A RANGE OF FRESHWATER HABITATS INCLUDING STREAMS, DITCHES, LAKES AND PONDS. PARTICULARLY ATTRACTED TO WATERCRESS BEDS.

FOOD FEEDS ON INVERTEBRATES AND FISH FRY.

STATUS SUMMER BREEDING SPECIES IN SCANDINAVIA AND EASTERN EUROPE, PRESENT THERE MAINLY MAY TO AUGUST. ELSEWHERE, A WIDESPREAD AND FAIRLY COMMON PASSAGE MIGRANT, WITH A FEW BIRDS WINTERING IN SUITABLE HABITATS.

VOICE WHEN IN FLIGHT, UTTERS A SHRILL TRISYLLABIC *CHLUEET-WIT-WIT* CALL.

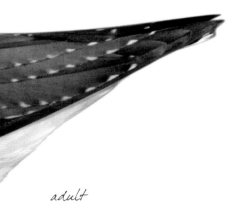

adult

The bill is noticeably longer and more slender than other sandpiper species, and subtly downcurved; the yellow legs are proportionately long.

and the delicate legs are greenish-yellow. In the winter, the white spotting on the upperparts of the adult is more subdued or absent altogether. The juvenile recalls the adult, but with more striking spotting to the upperparts. In flight, all birds appear mainly black and white, but note the extensive white to the tail and rump and the dark terminal banding on the tail.

The Green Sandpiper is a rather timid and agitated bird, commonly going unobserved until it is flushed and takes flight, uttering its characteristic yelping call. It is often found on relatively small ponds and ditches and most usually observed on migration. It nests in trees, often using old thrush nests.

Wood Sandpiper
Tringa glareola

The Wood Sandpiper is a slim-bodied, elegant-looking wader with proportionately longer legs than other similar sandpipers. The sexes are similar. The adult has upperparts of dark brownish plumage that are adorned with a spangling of pale spots, similar to Green Sandpiper but bolder and more obvious. The head and neck are marked with a dark streaking that fades gently into the pale underparts at the breast, lacking clear demarcation. A pale supercilium, extending in front of and behind the eye, is observed at close range. The dark bill is slender with a yellowish base, and the long legs are yellow. The juvenile

Factfile

LENGTH 19–21CM

WINGSPAN 35–39CM

HABITAT BREEDS IN BOGGY, OPEN WOODLAND, MARSHES AND RIVERSIDES. FAVOURS FRESHWATER POOLS ADJACENT TO THE COAST DURING MIGRATION, OCCASIONALLY OCCURRING INLAND.

FOOD FEEDS ON INVERTEBRATES, TADPOLES AND FISH FRY.

STATUS BREEDS IN SCANDINAVIA DURING THE SUMMER, PRESENT THERE MAINLY MAY TO AUGUST. BEST KNOWN IN OUR REGION AS A PASSAGE MIGRANT IN SPRING AND AUTUMN. IT OVERWINTERS IN AFRICA.

VOICE UTTERS A WHISTLING *CHIFF-IFF-IFF* IN FLIGHT.

adult

Long yellow legs allow Wood Sandpipers to wade in relatively deep water and the long toes provide support when walking on squelchy mud.

recalls the adult but the upperparts are darker and the pale spots more prominent. In flight, note the pale underwings; the upperwings are dark and lack a wingbar, but display spangling on the coverts. Note also the white rump, and dark barring on the tail that is more extensive than in the similar Green Sandpiper.

The Wood Sandpiper is most commonly encountered in our region during migration, favouring the margins of shallow freshwater, where it feeds in a confident and deliberate manner. It nests on the ground in dense vegetation and occasionally in trees, utilising abandoned nests of species such as Fieldfare.

adult

adult

Often calls as it takes off; in flight, note the uniform upperwings and strongly barred tail.

It feeds in a deliberate manner, picking invertebrates and other food items from the mud's surface or from shallow water.

adult life-size

Pale spangles on the upperparts are larger and more extensive than on a superficially similar Green Sandpiper.

Greenshank
Tringa nebularia

Juvenile
Seen from the rear in flight, the white rump extends as a narrow wedge up the centre of the back.

adult winter
Greenshanks are very active when feeding, sometimes running at speed to catch fast-moving prey.

juvenile life-size
A juvenile has neat back feathers that show little wear; in all birds the legs are yellow and proportionately long.

adult summer

In breeding plumage, the back is adorned with black and brown feathers, the margins of which have pale scalloping.

Factfile

LENGTH 30–35CM

WINGSPAN 60–70CM

HABITAT BREEDS ON BOGS AND MARSHES. DURING THE WINTER MONTHS FOUND PRIMARILY ON THE COAST, FAVOURING ESTUARIES AND SHELTERED LOCATIONS, BUT ALSO SOMETIMES ENCOUNTERED ON INLAND FRESHWATER.

FOOD FEEDS ON INVERTEBRATES, TADPOLES AND FISH FRY.

STATUS SUMMER BREEDING SPECIES TO THE NORTH OF THE REGION IN SCOTLAND AND SCANDINAVIA, PRESENT THERE MAINLY MAY TO AUGUST. MIGRATES SOUTH FOR WINTER, AND MOST COMMONLY ENCOUNTERED ACROSS OUR REGION AS A PASSAGE MIGRANT AND LOCAL WINTER VISITOR.

VOICE UTTERS A DIAGNOSTIC *TCHU-TCHU-TCHU* CALL.

The Greenshank is a light-coloured, handsome and long-legged wader. The sexes are similar but summer and winter plumages differ. The summer adult has grey-brown upperparts, the feathers along the back and flanks having dark centres. The head, neck and breast are marked with heavy streaking; the underparts are white. The winter adult is generally duller and less well marked, having uniformly pale grey upperparts and white underparts. The long slender legs are dull greenish-yellow and the bill is long and slightly upturned, greyish with a dark tip. The juvenile is similar to the winter adult but with browner plumage. In flight, all birds display uniform colouration to the upperwing and lack a wingbar; also note the white rump and 'wedge' on the lower back.

The Greenshank is an elegant wader that wades in shallow water and feeds with a deliberate, probing action, sometimes chasing fish and catching them in its long bill. It breeds on bogs and marshes in the north, nesting in a shallow scrape in the ground near a rock or tussock.

Spotted Redshank
Tringa erythropus

The Spotted Redshank is an attractive wader, superficially similar to a Redshank but with a longer bill and legs. The sexes are similar but often separable in summer; summer and winter plumages differ. The summer adult male has uniformly dark charcoal-grey, almost black, plumage. The pale fringes to the feathers of the upperparts give it a slight scaling, and a subtle white eye-ring surrounds the eye. More frequently encountered in the region are birds with incomplete summer plumage, having a more mottled appearance. The summer adult female is similar but displays more prominent white markings to the flanks. The winter adult is much lighter in colour, having pale grey upperparts and whitish underparts. The juvenile is similar to the winter adult but with darker plumage overall and barring to the underparts.

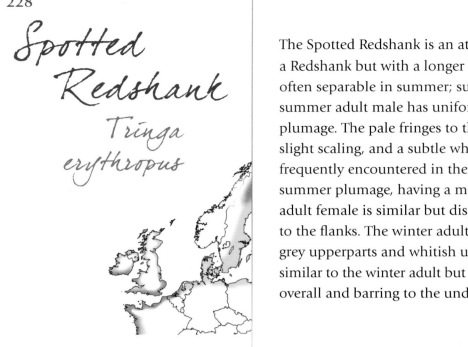

adult summer
Once learned, the shrill two-note call is easy to pick out and recognise, even if the bird in question is not in view.

adult winter

The flight is more rapid than that of a Redshank and the lack of any markings on the upperwings aids identification.

In all birds the bill is long and slender, and dark with an orange base to the lower mandible; the bill also has a subtle downward curve to the tip, aiding separation from Redshank. The reddish-orange legs are long and slender. In flight, note the uniform upperwings and lack of a white trailing edge.

The Spotted Redshank is an elegant wader that breeds in the Arctic and is most commonly seen in our region on migration. It is sometimes seen feeding in small groups, and wades in surprisingly deep water, repeatedly stabbing with its long bill and sometimes upending in a duck-like manner. When disturbed it quickly takes flight, rising almost vertically and uttering its characteristic call.

adult winter

The back feathers of winter birds show more pale scalloping than is apparent in most winter Redshanks.

adult winter life-size

The bill and legs are proportionately much longer than in Redshank.

Factfile

LENGTH 29–32CM

WINGSPAN 55–65CM

HABITAT BREEDS ON ARCTIC TUNDRA. IN WINTER, ALMOST EXCLUSIVELY COASTAL, FAVOURING ESTUARIES AND SHELTERED POOLS.

FOOD FEEDS ON MARINE INVERTEBRATES.

STATUS SUMMER BREEDING SPECIES OF ARCTIC TUNDRA. BEST KNOWN HERE AS A REGULAR PASSAGE MIGRANT IN AUTUMN AND SPRING, WITH A HANDFUL OF BIRDS OVERWINTERING IN THE SOUTH OF THE REGION.

VOICE IN FLIGHT, UTTERS A DIAGNOSTIC DISYLLABIC *TCHE-WIT* CALL.

Redshank
Tringa totanus

The Redshank is a nervous, medium-sized wader with bright orange or red legs. The sexes are similar but summer and winter plumages differ. The summer adult has dark grey-brown upperparts, heavily adorned with darker spots. The underparts are pale, the neck, breast and flanks marked with dark streaking. There is a faint pale supercilium, and a subtle pale eye-ring surrounds the eye. The base of the straight, slender bill is conspicuously reddish. The winter adult has more subdued plumage, being uniformly grey-brown on the upperparts, head, neck and breast; it is paler and mottled below. The bill and leg colours are similarly subdued. The juvenile recalls the winter adult but is browner overall and displays pale margins and notches to the feathers on the back. The bill base and the legs are dull yellow. A white trailing edge to the wings, white rump, white back 'wedge' and trailing red or yellow legs are features of all birds when observed in flight.

adult summer
Striking white markings on the back and wings are good identification features.

Factfile

LENGTH 27–29CM

WINGSPAN 55–65CM

HABITAT FAVOURS MOORLAND, MARSHES AND UNDISTURBED DAMP GRASSLAND HABITATS IN THE SUMMER MONTHS. MIGRATES TO COASTAL GRASSLAND, ESTUARIES AND MUDFLATS IN THE WINTER.

FOOD FEEDS ON A VARIETY OF TERRESTRIAL AND MARINE INVERTEBRATES.

STATUS COMMON AND WIDESPREAD SUMMER BREEDING SPECIES IN SUITABLE HABITATS. PRESENT YEAR-ROUND IN MORE TEMPERATE REGIONS, PARTICULARLY BRITAIN AND NORTHERN FRANCE, BUT A WINTER VISITOR TO ESTUARIES AND COASTAL WETLANDS ELSEWHERE, WITH BIRDS ARRIVING FROM THE NORTH AND EAST.

VOICE UTTERS A DISYLLABIC *TIU-UU* ALARM CALL.

adult summer life-size
In breeding plumage, the upperparts are spangled with black and the underparts are much more strongly marked than in winter.

A common sight in suitable habitats, the Redshank takes to the wing readily, accompanied by its distinctive alarm call. It feeds by busily probing the mud with its bill, often chasing prey items. Displays near the nest during the breeding season are common, the bird rising and falling in the air with rapid wingbeats. It nests in a lined depression in open ground.

adult winter
Although the leg colour is duller in winter than summer, it remains a very useful clue to identification.

adult summer
Territorial birds are constantly on the look-out for danger and when alarmed they utter their distinctive call; this is also a familiar sound on winter estuaries.

Turnstone
Arenaria interpres

Factfile

LENGTH 21–24CM

WINGSPAN 49–55CM

HABITAT **EXCLUSIVELY COASTAL OUTSIDE THE BREEDING SEASON, FAVOURING ROCKY SHORES AND BEACHES WITH EXTENSIVE STRANDLINES. TUNDRA IN THE BREEDING SEASON**

FOOD **FEEDS ON A VARIETY OF MARINE INVERTEBRATES.**

STATUS **BREEDS ON COASTAL TUNDRA IN SCANDINAVIA AND MIGRATES TO THE COASTS OF BRITAIN AND NORTHERN MAINLAND EUROPE FOR THE WINTER MONTHS.**

VOICE **UTTERS A REPETITIVE *TUK-UT-UT* IN FLIGHT.**

The Turnstone is robust-looking little wader with a short bill and short legs. The sexes are similar but summer and winter plumages differ. The summer adult has dark upperparts, with large patches of warm orange-red on the back and flanks. The underside is white, and the head, neck and breast are marked boldly with contrasting black-and-white plumage. The male displays brighter colouration than the female at this time. The winter adult is more subdued, having upperparts of uniform dark grey-brown, extending to the head and neck. The underparts are pure white and a bold black band at the breast forms a clear demarcation with the upperparts. The juvenile recalls the winter adult but with paler upperparts and pale fringes to

adult winter
Even in flight, birds look compact and plump; the striking white markings on the wings, back and rump assist with identification.

adult winter
A Turnstone's plumage is understated and a perfect match for seashore pebbles and washed-up seaweed.

adult summer moulting

Birds that are newly arrived on shores after the breeding season take a few weeks to moult into winter plumage, reddish feathers on the back being the last to be replaced.

the black feathers. In all birds, the dark bill is short and stout, and the short legs are bright orange. In flight, note the white wingbar, white rump-band and white linear patches on the back and inner wings.

The Turnstone is a busy little wader that feeds by turning stones and seaweed with its bill, searching for suitable food items. Its colouration often makes it easy to overlook at first glance, as it blends in with the seaweed and debris of the strandline. It nests in coastal tundra in a ground scrape or suitable rock crevice.

adult summer life-size

A Turnstone is extremely smart in breeding plumage, the male being particularly striking and colourful.

Red-necked Phalarope
Phalaropus lobatus

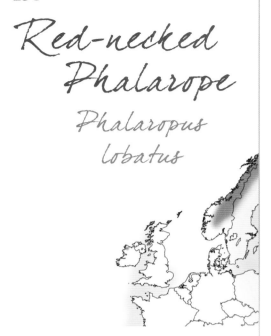

The Red-necked Phalarope is a mostly waterborne little wader, the males and females of which demonstrate role reversal during the breeding season. The sexes are separable in summer, and summer and winter plumages differ. The summer adult female has primarily brown upperparts marked with yellow and buff fringes to some of the back feathers. The bright orange neck and nape are obvious; the head is dark and marked with a white throat and cheeks. The breast is uniformly grey and the flanks mottled; both grade to the white of the underside. The summer adult male is similar but with more subdued colouration. The winter adult has predominantly grey upperparts, the feathers on the back having conspicuous white fringes. The head, throat and underparts are whitish with a darker hindcrown and nape, and black eye-patch. The juvenile is similar to the winter adult, but has brown upperparts with pale buff feather fringes. In all birds, the needle-like bill is dark and the toes are lobed to aid swimming.

The Red-necked Phalarope feeds busily on the water, spinning round swiftly in a diagnostic fashion, picking up invertebrates from the water's surface. The sexes reverse roles during the breeding season: the more colourful female initiates courtship while the duller male incubates the eggs. It nests on the ground in a shallow depression concealed among vegetation.

A Red-necked Phalarope is fast and agile in flight, the upperwings showing a bold white wingbar.

summer female

summer female life-size

The species spends most of its life on water and is buoyant when swimming.

Factfile

LENGTH 18–19CM

WINGSPAN 34–40CM

HABITAT FAVOURS SHALLOW FRESHWATER POOLS DURING THE BREEDING SEASON, SPENDING THE WINTER AT SEA; SOMETIMES ENCOUNTERED IN SHELTERED COASTAL POOLS ON MIGRATION AFTER SEVERE GALES.

FOOD FEEDS ON INVERTEBRATES.

STATUS ITS SOUTHERNMOST BREEDING RANGE ENCOMPASSES SCANDINAVIA AND THE NORTHERN TIP OF BRITAIN. IN OUR REGION IT IS PRIMARILY A PASSAGE MIGRANT SEEN ONLY OCCASIONALLY AFTER SEVERE WEATHER BRINGS IT CLOSE TO LAND.

VOICE UTTERS A SHARP *KIP* CALL.

The bill is noticeably more slender than in a superficially similar Grey Phalarope. Some of the buff and brown feathers on the back align to form lines; grey winter feathers gradually replace juvenile feathers.

juvenile

The male is much duller and less colourful than the female although the overall pattern of markings is similar.

summer male

Grey Phalarope
Phalaropus fulicarius

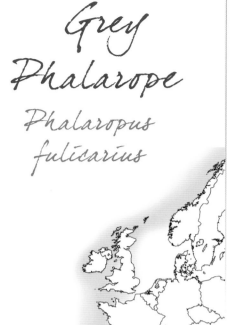

The Grey Phalarope is an endearing little wader that spends much of its time at sea. The sexes are separable in summer plumage (rarely seen in our region) and demonstrate role reversal at this time. The summer adult female has mainly striking orange-red plumage, the back having buff-fringed brown feathers. The head has a dark cap and white facial patch and the bill is yellow and dark-tipped. The summer

adult winter life-size
Grey Phalaropes swim buoyantly, the lobed feet allowing birds to paddle along at speed.

Factfile

LENGTH **20–22CM**

WINGSPAN **37–44CM**

HABITAT **HIGH ARCTIC TUNDRA DURING THE SUMMER MONTHS, OVERWINTERING AT SEA.**

FOOD **FEEDS ON INSECTS, CRUSTACEANS AND MOLLUSCS.**

STATUS **A SCARCE PASSAGE MIGRANT IN OUR REGION, USUALLY OBSERVED AFTER SEVERE WEATHER WHEN BIRDS CAN TURN UP ON SHELTERED COASTAL AREAS, SOMETIMES ON INLAND FRESHWATER LAKES AND RESERVOIRS.**

VOICE **IN FLIGHT, UTTERS A SHARP *PIT* CALL.**

adult male is similar but with subdued colouration. The species is most commonly seen here in non-breeding plumage: the adult has grey upperparts and white underparts, the head marked with a dark cap, nape and eye-patch. The yellow-based bill is dark and noticably stouter than that of Red-necked Phalarope. The juvenile is similar to the winter adult but with a buff tinge to the breast, neck and back; the dark back feathers are fringed buff.

The Grey Phalarope breeds on high Arctic tundra (north of our region) where it nests in a shallow, plant-lined cup in vegetation. It is mostly pelagic during the winter months. It is seen in our region only occasionally, mainly after strong gales blow small numbers close to land on migration or in early winter. At such times it favours sheltered coastal pools, and sometimes occurs on inland freshwater.

summer female

The breeding plumage is stunning. The pattern on the face is reversed when compared to winter plumage: the white patch around the eye is framed by black.

autumn

In flight, the dark wings show a striking white wingbar, and contrast with the pale grey back.

1st autumn

At home in the roughest of seas, Grey Phalaropes often feed on invertebrates along pelagic driftlines of seaweed.

Arctic Skua
Stercorarius parasiticus

Factfile

LENGTH 46–67CM

WINGSPAN 97–115CM

HABITAT BREEDS ON SUITABLE COASTS DURING THE SUMMER MONTHS. AT OTHER TIMES, SEEN AT SEA.

FOOD FEEDS ON FISH AND OTHER ITEMS THAT IT TYPICALLY STEALS FROM OTHER SEABIRDS, OFTEN FORCING THEM TO REGURGITATE.

STATUS SUMMER BREEDING SPECIES ON THE COASTS OF SCANDINAVIA AND NORTHERN BRITAIN, PRESENT MAINLY MAY TO AUGUST. PELAGIC AT OTHER TIMES. SEEN FROM BOATS AND FERRIES ON MIGRATION, SOMETIMES FROM COASTS AFTER SEVERE GALES. WINTERS IN SOUTHERN OCEANS.

VOICE UTTERS NASAL CALLS WHEN AROUND THE NEST.

The Arctic Skua is a large seabird and the most commonly encountered skua in the region. The sexes are similar but the adults have two colour phases. The light-phase adult has uniform grey-brown plumage, with the exception of a dark-capped pale head and white neck, breast and belly. The cheeks display a faint yellowish flush. The dark-phase adult is uniformly dark grey-brown. All adults in flight show a white patch near the wingtip on the underwing, and a more subtle white patch on the upperwing. Note also the pointed central tail streamers that extend beyond the wedge-shaped tail. The powerful bill is dark and hook-tipped. The juvenile has dark, variable rufous-brown plumage, and stubby tail streamers.

The Arctic Skua is an aggressive bird which, during the breeding season, is often seen squabbling over territories with neighbouring

adult life-size
The bill is hook-tipped and proportionately smaller than that of a Great Skua.

Light-phase birds are subtly variable: some have clean-looking white elements of plumage on the face and neck while in other birds these areas are suffused with yellow.

In flight, both light- and dark-phase birds show a pale patch at the base of the primaries. Flight is fast and agile; in direct flight birds fly low over the sea.

light phase

dark phase

birds, commonly raising its wings and attacking intruders, including people who stray into its territory. It nests in a shallow depression on open ground. It is a buoyant and aerobatic flier that displays masterful gliding and powerful wingbeats on rather narrow, pointed wings. It feeds by chasing and harassing other flying seabirds and forcing them to drop food or regurgitate their last meal.

dark phase

The underparts and nape are very subtly paler than the back and cap although in some lights the plumage appears uniformly brown.

On breeding grounds, off-duty birds often stand guard on the look-out for danger; they are fearless when it comes to attacking intruders.

light phase

Great Skua
Stercorarius skua

The Great Skua is a bulky gull-like seabird and the largest of its kind. The sexes are similar. The adult has chocolate-brown plumage marked with a series of streaks and spots, darkest on the back and tail. At close range a mane of golden brown feathers can be observed on the nape. The thickset, powerful bill is dark and hook-tipped. The dark legs are relatively short. The juvenile is similar to the adult but lacks the streaking and spotting. Its upperparts are uniformly dark brown, the neck and underparts reddish-brown. In flight, all birds show a conspicuous white patch on the outer wing, visible both from above and below.

adults displaying

Territorial birds often greet one another with wing-stretching displays, accompanied by loud calls.

Factfile

LENGTH 53–66CM

WINGSPAN 125–140CM

HABITAT NESTS ON SEA CLIFFS AND ADJACENT MOORLAND IN THE SUMMER; AT OTHER TIMES FOUND AT SEA.

FOOD FEEDS ON FISH, EGGS, CHICKS AND ADULT BIRDS. COMMONLY STEALS FISH FROM OTHER SEABIRDS.

STATUS SUMMER BREEDING VISITOR TO THE NORTH OF THE REGION; ENCOUNTERED AT SEA AND ON MIGRATION AT OTHER TIMES, SOMETIMES COMING CLOSE TO LAND IN SEVERE WEATHER.

VOICE MAINLY SILENT BUT CAN UTTER FIERCE ALARM CALLS.

adult

Flight is powerful and rapid, the stocky body borne on broad wings.

immature

A juvenile's pale streaking looks more uniform than in an adult; the head is rather uniformly dark, and lacks the somewhat 'moth-eaten' appearance seen in some autumn adults.

This is an aggressive bird that defends its nest and young vigorously and vocally when threatened. It breeds in loose colonies with the nest sited in a shallow scrape in the ground. Strong and direct in the air, it commonly feeds by harassing other seabirds in flight, stealing their catch from them or forcing them to regurgitate their last meal. Capable of catching fish for itself, it will also kill small seabirds such as Puffins and take eggs and chicks from nests.

juvenile

The uniformly brown plumage lacks any distinctive markings.

With its powerful bill, and attitude to match, very few birds will take on a Great Skua.

adult life-size

Kittiwake
Rissa tridactyla

At breeding colonies, birds are typically tolerant of human observers, allowing close-up views to be obtained. Sharp claws provide grip when birds are perched on slippery rock ledges.

adult

The Kittiwake is a dainty-looking little gull that spends the majority of its time outside the breeding season at sea. The sexes are similar but summer and winter plumages differ. The summer adult is predominantly pure white with a bluish-grey back and upperwings, not extending past the shoulders, giving the bird a very clean white head. The wings are tipped pure black, and classically described as looking as if they have been dipped in ink. The bill is yellow and the eye and legs are dark. The winter adult is similar but the pure white head plumage is marked with grubby-looking patches behind the eye. The juvenile has the bluish-grey and white plumage of the adult, but is marked with an obvious black 'V'-shaped wingbar, and a triangle of white on the flight feathers. There are also dark patches on the head, a dark half-collar on the neck and a dark terminal tail-band. The bill is dark. In first-winter birds, the dark tip to the tail and half collar are gradually lost.

Factfile

LENGTH 38–42CM   WINGSPAN 95–120CM

HABITAT BREEDS ON SHEER COASTAL CLIFFS AND INCREASINGLY ON MAN-MADE COASTAL STRUCTURES. OVERWINTERS AT SEA, WITH SMALL NUMBERS ENCOUNTERED AROUND HARBOURS ON OCCASION.

FOOD FEEDS ON FISH AND INVERTEBRATES.

STATUS BREEDS IN HUGE COLONIES IN SUITABLE HABITATS DURING THE SUMMER MONTHS, PARTICULARLY IN THE NORTH OF THE REGION. WIDESPREAD AT SEA DURING THE WINTER MONTHS, WITH A HANDFUL OF BIRDS ENCOUNTERED IN COASTAL AREAS. NUMBERS ARE IN DECLINE IN SOME AREAS, LINKED TO A DECREASE IN SUITABLE PREY FISH STOCKS.

VOICE AT BREEDING COLONIES, UTTERS A DISTINCTIVE *KITTEE-WAKE KITTEE-WAKE* CALL.

A Kittiwake spends much of its life at sea, making it a true 'seagull'.

Spending most of its life at sea, the Kittiwake is a buoyant and powerful flyer. It nests in large, noisy colonies on towering sea cliffs, constructing a cup-shaped nest of compacted mud and seaweed on cliff ledges. Birds disperse out to sea outside the breeding season and are only seen occasionally from land during severe weather at this time.

Kittiwakes are manoeuvrable in flight, birds wheeling and soaring along cliffs at breeding colonies, uttering their distinctive calls.

immature

Distinctive upperwing markings make for straightforward ageing and identification.

adult

adult life-size

The clean white head with its rounded outline give the Kittiwake a 'gentle' look compared to other gulls.

immature

Black-headed Gull

Chroicocephalus ridibundus

adult winter

The wing pattern is distinctive and, once learned, provides a reasonably foolproof means of identifying even distant birds.

adult summer life-size

Breeding plumage (the chocolate-brown head in particular) is acquired in late winter and by early spring most birds have settled on breeding grounds. Nesting colonies are typically beside those wetlands or on coastal habitats that are protected from human disturbance and land predators. Bill and leg colours are most intense during spring and summer.

1st winter

By November or December, most remnants of juvenile feathering have been replaced by 1st-winter plumage.

The Black-headed Gull is a commonly encountered medium-sized gull that occurs in a wide variety of habitats. The sexes are similar but summer and winter plumages differ. The summer adult has predominantly white plumage with a pale grey back and pale grey upperwings with black wingtips. The head is striking, being dark chocolate-brown, appearing almost black at distance or in poor light. Note the subtle and incomplete white eye-ring. In the winter adult the dark head is replaced with white, marked with dark smudges above and behind the eye. In flight, all adults show a white leading edge to the outer wings. The juvenile has brown upperparts with an orange flush; the underparts are pale. By late autumn, it has usually acquired first-winter plumage and displays a dark carpal bar, tail tip and trailing edge to the wings. Adult plumage is acquired by the following spring.

This is the most abundant and commonly seen gull in the region owing to its numbers and the wide variety of habitats it is found in. It favours freshwater habitats for breeding, nesting on the ground in a shallow scrape lined with leaves and feathers. Its numbers are boosted during the winter months by birds that have migrated from harsher climates to the east and north.

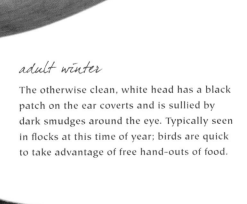

adult winter

The otherwise clean, white head has a black patch on the ear coverts and is sullied by dark smudges around the eye. Typically seen in flocks at this time of year; birds are quick to take advantage of free hand-outs of food.

Factfile

LENGTH 38–44CM

WINGSPAN 94–105CM

HABITAT FOUND IN A WIDE RANGE OF HABITATS, FROM SHELTERED COASTAL AREAS AND FRESHWATER LAKES, RIVERS AND RESERVOIRS TO FARMLAND AND EVEN URBAN LOCATIONS.

FOOD AN OPPORTUNIST, FEEDING ON A VARIED DIET OF INVERTEBRATES, PLANT MATERIAL AND HOUSEHOLD WASTE AND SCRAPS.

STATUS COMMON AND WIDESPREAD, PRESENT YEAR-ROUND THROUGHOUT THE REGION.

VOICE UTTERS VARIOUS RAUCOUS CALLS INCLUDING A NASAL *KAURRR*.

Little Gull
Hydrocoloeus minutus

This is a delicate-looking gull and the smallest of its kind in the region. The sexes are similar but summer and winter plumages differ. The summer adult has pale grey upperparts, the wings having distinctive rounded white wingtips and white margins to the trailing edges. The tail is also pure white. The head has a dark hood, sharply defined from the lighter plumage. The underparts are clean white, and the underside of the wings is sooty-grey. Note the dark bill and short reddish legs. The winter adult is similar but the dark hood is replaced by white and marked with dark patches on the crown and ear coverts. The juvenile has overall white plumage marked with an obvious dark bar to the upperwings and back, forming a 'W' shape. Dark markings adorn the mantle, nape and ear coverts, and the tail is marked with a dark terminal band. The first-winter bird is similar

adult winter life-size

Birds are buoyant when swimming. When seen alongside Black-headed Gulls they look noticeably smaller; the black (not reddish) bill aids identification.

adult winter

The underwings are diagnostically mostly dark except for a pale trailing margin. By late winter, some birds acquire a subtle pink flush to the underparts; the colour persists into the breeding season.

to the juvenile but has a grey back and upperwings; the dark 'W' mark is still present. Adult plumage is acquired over a series of moults by the third winter.

Its buoyant and agile flight gives the Little Gull a tern-like appearance in the air, and it often takes insects in flight close to the surface of the water. Generally it remains offshore during the winter months and is rarely seen in large numbers. Gales sometimes drive birds inshore.

adult summer

The wings have rather rounded tips, the effect enhanced by the pale trailing edge that broadens towards the tip.

immature

flight, the upperwing pattern gives an immature a passing resemblance to a miniature immature Kittiwake.

Factfile

LENGTH **25–28CM** WINGSPAN **70–77CM**

HABITAT **LAKE SHORES AND MARSHES DURING THE BREEDING SEASON. EXCLUSIVELY COASTAL DURING THE WINTER MONTHS.**

FOOD **FEEDS ON A VARIETY OF INSECTS AND MARINE INVERTEBRATES.**

STATUS **BREEDS MAINLY TO THE EAST OF OUR REGION DURING THE SUMMER MONTHS AND OCCURS AS A REGULAR PASSAGE MIGRANT AND WINTER VISITOR TO COASTAL REGIONS. OCCASIONALLY ENCOUNTERED ON INLAND FRESHWATER.**

VOICE **UTTERS A SHARP *KYECK* CALL.**

Mediterranean Gull
Larus melanocephalus

The Mediterranean Gull is a handsome bird, similar in appearance and size to a Black-headed Gull but separable with experience. The sexes are similar but summer and winter plumages differ. The summer adult has a pale grey back and upperwings; note the lack of black markings to the wingtips and the pure white of the underwing, allowing confident separation from Black-headed Gull. The head has a sharply contrasting black hood, and the eyes are marked with subtle white 'eyelids'. The red bill is stout with a black subterminal band and a yellow tip. The legs are also red. In the winter adult, the black hood is replaced by white and marked with dark smudges above and behind the eyes. In flight, the underside of the wings in all birds looks entirely white. The juvenile has grey-brown upperparts, the back feathers having pale

Factfile

LENGTH 36–38CM   WINGSPAN 98–105CM

HABITAT FAVOURS COASTAL AREAS PARTICULARLY IN THE WINTER MONTHS, SOMETIMES OCCURRING ON LAGOONS BUT OCCASIONALLY ALSO ON INLAND FRESHWATER. BREEDS ON SALT MARSHES AND COASTAL ISLANDS.

FOOD FEEDS ON A VARIETY OF INSECTS, FISH AND MARINE INVERTEBRATES.

STATUS SMALL NUMBERS BREED IN OUR REGION, GENERALLY ALONGSIDE COLONIES OF BLACK-HEADED GULLS. MOST COMMONLY SEEN OUTSIDE THE BREEDING SEASON ON SOUTHERN AND SOUTHWESTERN COASTS.

VOICE UTTERS A DISTINCTIVE *COW-COW* CALL.

adult summer

In breeding birds, the hood is noticeably black compared to the chocolate-brown head of a Black-headed Gull.

margins. The underparts are mainly pale with a darker flush to the breast. The tail has a dark terminal band, and the legs and bill are dark. The first-winter bird has a grey back and dark head smudges. Second-winter plumage birds resemble the adult but have black wingtips. The adult plumage is acquired by the third winter.

Outside the breeding season, the Mediterranean Gull favours coastal areas and rarely ventures far from land. It often associates with flocks of Black-headed Gulls and is sometimes tricky to pick out to the untrained eye. It breeds in salt marshes, nesting on the ground in a shallow depression lined with grass and feathers.

In flight, summer adults look almost pure white except for the dark head.

adult summer

adult summer life-size

The bill is relatively large and colourful and the white 'eyelids' show up well against the black hood.

adult winter

1st winter

Dark markings and smudges on the face give non-breeding adult birds a rather menacing appearance.

The upperwing pattern and extensive dark smudging around eye help with identification.

Common Gull
Larus canus

This is a medium-sized gull, recalling a Herring Gull but with a smaller bill. The sexes are similar but summer and winter plumages differ subtly. The summer adult has a grey back and upperwings, the wings displaying a white trailing edge and black wingtips adorned with white spots. The head, underparts and remaining plumage are pure white. The rather dainty bill is greenish-yellow and the legs are yellow-green. The winter adult is similar, but the head and neck are marked with dark streaking, and the bill is less colourful and has a dark subterminal band. In flight, all adults reveal a pure white tail. The juvenile has brown upperparts, the feathers on the back and upperwings having pale fringes; the underparts are pale and marked with dark streaking. The first-winter bird recalls the juvenile but with

adult winter life-size
In non-breeing birds, the head is marked with a variable extent of dark streaks and smudges; however, some birds can be very clean-looking.

1st summer

It takes two years for a young bird to acquire adult plumage. In their first summer (a year or so after hatching) birds have a mixture of immature and adult-like plumage characters.

1st winter

Factfile

LENGTH 38–44CM

WINGSPAN 110–125CM

HABITAT OCCURS IN A VARIETY OF WATERY HABITATS; FRESHWATER LAKES, RESERVOIRS, LARGE RIVERS, MARSHES AND COASTAL REGIONS. COMMONLY FOUND AWAY FROM WATER DURING THE WINTER MONTHS, TYPICALLY ON AGRICULTURAL LAND.

FOOD FEEDS ON A RANGE OF FISH AND INVERTEBRATES.

STATUS PRESENT YEAR-ROUND IN THE REGION. LOCALLY COMMON IN SUITABLE BREEDING HABITAT DURING THE SUMMER MONTHS. IT BECOMES MORE WIDESPREAD IN WINTER, ITS NUMBERS BOOSTED BY MIGRATING BIRDS AT THIS TIME.

VOICE UTTERS A MEWING *KEEOW*.

a grey back and a pink bill with a dark tip. The second-winter bird is similar to the adult but has more extensive black markings on the outer wing, and a broader band on the bill.

The Common Gull nests in colonies in marshes and beside freshwater lakes, constructing a shallow cup of vegetation on the ground or over marginal water. Birds disperse mainly to coastal regions during the winter months, and increasingly inland, where they are a common sight on refuse tips and ploughed arable fields.

adult summer

Yellow bill and legs are features in common with a Kittiwake; however, a Common Gull is appreciably larger with more complex wingtip markings.

adult summer

White spots on the otherwise black wingtips are striking in flight.

Compared to an immature Herring Gull a Common Gull always looks appreciably smaller with a much daintier bill.

Lesser Black-backed Gull

Larus fuscus

Similar to Herring Gull in size, its characteristic grey back and yellow legs allow straightforward identification. The sexes are similar but summer and winter plumages are subtly different. The summer adult has a dark grey back and upperwings, the wings having a white trailing edge and dark wingtips (often hard to distinguish in dark-coloured birds from the Baltic that sometimes occur in the region). Its head, underparts and remaining plumage are pure white. The large, powerful-looking bill is yellow with an orange-red patch towards the tip. The yellow iris in the eye is striking and surrounded by a red orbital ring. The winter adult is similar but with streaking to the head and neck; the bill and leg colour are more subdued. Acquiring adult plumage takes four years. Juvenile and first-winter birds have heavily streaked and mottled grey-brown plumage overall, with a paler head. The underwings appear uniformly dark brown, and the whitish tail has a dark terminal band. Both the eye and the bill are dark. The second-winter bird has a grey back; the underparts are paler with more subtle streaking. The legs and bill are pinkish, the latter having a dark tip. The third-winter bird recalls the adult, but has more extensive streaking on the head and neck, and a dark terminal band to the tail.

adult summer life-size

Head is clean and unmarked in the breeding season, and the bill and orbital ring colours are more intense.

Mainly a coastal species in the summer, the Lesser Black-backed Gull breeds in large colonies on sea cliffs. The winter months are traditionally spent out to sea, but in recent years large populations are increasingly overwintering inland, exploiting the food sources afforded by refuse tips and farmland. It often gathers in large roosts on reservoirs at this time.

Factfile

LENGTH 53–56CM

WINGSPAN 130–148CM

HABITAT BREEDS TRADITIONALLY ON SEA CLIFFS, BUT INCREASINGLY INLAND. OUTSIDE THE BREEDING SEASON IT OCCURS INLAND ON MARSHES, FARMLAND AND REFUSE TIPS AS WELL AS AT SEA.

FOOD FEEDS ON FISH, TERRESTRIAL AND MARINE INVERTEBRATES, CARRION AND REFUSE.

STATUS PRESENT YEAR-ROUND IN VARYING NUMBERS. LOCALLY COMMON BREEDING SPECIES. NUMBERS ARE BOOSTED IN WINTER BY MIGRANTS FROM THE NORTH AND EAST.

VOICE UTTERS A *KYAOO*, ALSO A *GA-KA-KA*, SIMILAR TO THAT OF HERRING GULL, BUT DEEPER AND LOUDER.

adult summer

In most birds seen in the region, the difference between the black wingtips and otherwise grey upperwing is striking.

2nd winter

By its 2nd winter, a grey back will have developed; more adult-like plumage is acquired over the next year or so.

adult summer displaying

Nests colonially and adjacent pairs often engage in noisy displays with their neighbours.

juvenile

Similar to other large gulls but the head usually appears relatively pale and the long primaries help create an elongated look.

Herring Gull

Larus argentatus

Factfile

LENGTH 56–62CM

WINGSPAN 130–158CM

HABITAT BREEDS ON COASTAL CLIFFS AND ISLANDS, BECOMING MORE WIDESPREAD BOTH ALONG THE COAST AND IN VARIOUS INLAND HABITATS DURING THE WINTER.

FOOD WIDE RANGING DIET AND IT WILL CONSUME VIRTUALLY ANYTHING EDIBLE.

STATUS LOCALLY COMMON RESIDENT BREEDING SPECIES BECOMING MORE WIDESPREAD AND ABUNDANT THROUGHOUT THE REGION IN WINTER, NUMBERS INCREASED BY MIGRATING BIRDS.

VOICE THE CLASSIC 'SEAGULL' CRY OF THE SEASIDE, AND A USEFUL YARDSTICK BY WHICH TO COMPARE SIMILAR SPECIES THAT CAN PROVE TRICKY TO SEPARATE. IT UTTERS A CHARACTERISTIC *KYAOO*, ALSO A *GA-KA-KA*.

juvenile
Remains in this plumage until early winter when subtle changes in appearance occur.

2nd winter
An adult's grey back has been acquired but juvenile-type plumage elements remain.

An opportunistic feeder that eats virtually anything; well known for scavenging bins and leftovers at popular seaside resorts.

adult summer
Breeds in colonies on sea cliffs and islands, and increasingly on rooftops in coastal towns.

2nd winter

adult summer

Silvery grey upperwing and back make identification straightforward in a bird of this size.

This is a noisy bird and our most familiar large gull species. The sexes are similar but summer and winter plumages differ subtly. The summer adult has a pale blue-grey back and upperwings, the wings showing black wingtips with white spots. The remaining plumage is pure white, including the head and neck. The large robust-looking bill is yellow with an orange-red spot near the tip, and the legs are pink. The eye is yellow and surrounded by an orange-yellow orbital ring. The winter adult is similar but has streaking on the head and nape. Full adult plumage takes four years to acquire. Juvenile and first-winter birds have mottled and streaked grey-brown plumage, paler on the head and with a dark-tipped pale tail. The bill is uniformly dark and the legs are dull pink. The second-winter bird has a grey back, the upperwing retaining the brown-grey mottling; the tail is white with a dark tip. The third-winter bird resembles the winter adult, but with more extensive black to the wingtips and a subtle dark tail-band.

adult winter life-size

The extent of streaking on the head and neck varies between individuals and throughout the winter months.

Iceland Gull

Larus glaucoides

Similar to Glaucous Gull, this species is smaller with proportionately longer wings and a rounded head. The sexes are similar but summer and winter plumages differ subtly. The summer adult has a pale grey back and upperwings, the latter having a white trailing edge and white primary feathers. The remaining plumage is white. The relatively small bill is yellow with an orange-red spot near the tip; the yellowish eye has a red orbital ring. The winter adult (most commonly encountered here) recalls the summer adult, but has subtle streaking on the head and neck. Full adult plumage takes four years to acquire. Juvenile and first-winter birds have grey-buff plumage and white primaries. The bill is dark with a faint pink base. The second-winter bird appears uniformly pale with subtle grey-buff marbling; the greyish-pink bill

1st winter

In flight, stands out as being extremely white, making it easy to pick out.

adult winter life-size

Bill is proportionately much smaller and more dainty than in other large gulls giving the species a rather 'gentle' appearance.

displays a narrow dark tip or submarginal band. The third-winter bird is similar but its plumage is paler still. All birds have pink legs.

The Iceland Gull is a rather graceful flier that breeds in the Arctic and is mainly pelagic during the winter months. It is sometimes encountered in the north of our region around docks and harbours, where it is attracted to returning fishing boats, scavenging for scraps with other gull species.

Factfile

LENGTH 52–60CM WINGSPAN 130–145CM

HABITAT A COASTAL SPECIES, FAVOURING DOCKS AND HARBOURS. OCCASIONALLY ENCOUNTERED INLAND ON LOCHS AND RESERVOIRS.

FOOD FEEDS PRIMARILY ON FISH, BUT ALSO PLANKTON AND THE EGGS AND CHICKS OF OTHER SPECIES.

STATUS SCARCE WINTER VISITOR RECORDED IN SMALL NUMBERS EACH YEAR, MAINLY ON THE COASTS OF SCANDINAVIA AND NORTHERN BRITAIN.

VOICE UTTERS A KYAOO, ALSO A GA-KA-KA, SIMILAR TO THAT OF HERRING GULL, BUT MORE SHRILL.

adult winter

Looks very pale in flight, with only a subtle difference evident between the pale grey upperwings and white trailing margin.

adult winter

Looks overall very pale, the long, white primaries adding to the relatively slender, elongated appearance.

1st winter

The plumage is overall very pale, adorned with extensive buff spots of varying intensity.

Glaucous Gull
Larus hyperboreus

Similar in appearance to Iceland Gull, the Glaucous Gull is bigger with a larger, more robust-looking bill and more angular head. The sexes are similar but summer and winter plumages differ subtly. The summer adult (rarely seen here) has a pale grey back and upperwings, the latter having white tips and a white trailing edge. The remaining plumage is white. The eye is pale with a yellow orbital ring. Compared to the similar Iceland Gull, note the much larger pale yellow bill marked with an orange-red spot towards the tip. The winter adult is similar but has variable dark streaking on the head and neck. Full adult plumage takes four years to acquire. Juvenile and first-winter birds have pale buffish plumage and pale primaries; the bill is pink with a small black tip. Second-winter birds are pale with dark marbling overall, the head and neck marked with darker streaks. Third-winter birds are pale overall with streaking on the head and neck. All birds have pinkish legs.

Factfile

LENGTH 62–68CM

WINGSPAN 150–165CM

HABITAT COASTAL HABITATS, BUT SEEN OCCASIONALLY ON INLAND RESERVOIRS AND LAKES.

FOOD STEALS FROM OTHER SEABIRDS, AND AN ACTIVE SCAVENGER WITH A VARIED DIET. WILL CONSUME MOST THINGS.

STATUS SCARCE WINTER VISITOR TO COASTAL REGIONS, NUMBERS VARYING ANNUALLY DEPENDENT ON WEATHER CONDITIONS FURTHER NORTH.

VOICE UTTERS A SHORT AND HIGH-PITCHED *KYAOO*, ALSO A YAPPING *GA-KA-KA*.

adult winter

Body plumage is overall white, but variably grubby-looking and streaked on the neck and upper breast in particular. Compared to an adult Iceland Gull, the body is appreciably more bulky and the bill is larger.

adult late winter

In flight, the upperwings are pale grey overall but with contrastingly white wingtips and a white trailing edge.

The Glaucous Gull breeds in the Arctic on coastal cliffs, alongside geese and auks, constructing a nest of seaweed and debris. It is generally encountered in our region in winter, usually in small numbers, although severe weather further north can result in large influxes at times.

1st winter

Looks pale in flight, but never quite as pale as a similar age Iceland Gull.

1st-winter life-size

The massive size and overall very pale plumage make identification relatively straightforward.

Great Black-backed Gull

Larus marinus

This is the largest gull encountered in the region and is similar in appearance to Lesser Black-backed Gull, but the upperparts are noticeably darker. The sexes are similar but summer and winter plumages differ subtly. The summer adult has uniformly dark plumage on its upperwings and back, the former being marked with a small white tip and white trailing edge that runs almost the entire length of the wing. The remaining plumage is white. The large bill is yellow with an orange-red spot towards the tip. The winter adult is similar to the summer adult but displays dark streaking to the neck and head. Full adult plumage takes four years to acquire. Juvenile and first-winter birds have mottled and streaked grey-brown plumage overall, paler on the head and neck. The bill is dark. In flight, note the pale panel on the upperwing coverts and inner primaries, and the dark terminal tail-band to the pale tail. By the third winter the back is dark and the dark-tipped bill is pink. All birds have pinkish legs.

The Great Black-backed Gull nests in small colonies in coastal areas, generally in the vicinity of other species. It constructs a nest of

adult winter life-size

The bill is massive by comparison with a Lesser Black-backed Gull. The extent of dark streaking on the head and neck varies between individuals and throughout the winter months.

Factfile

LENGTH 64–79CM

WINGSPAN 150–165CM

HABITAT PRIMARILY A COASTAL SPECIES DURING THE SUMMER MONTHS, BECOMING MORE WIDESPREAD INLAND DURING THE WINTER.

FOOD STEALS FROM OTHER SEABIRDS; ALSO AN ACTIVE PREDATOR AND SCAVENGER. IT HAS A VARIED DIET AND WILL CONSUME MOST THINGS, INCLUDING OTHER BIRDS.

STATUS FAIRLY COMMON AND WIDESPREAD BREEDING SPECIES, PRESENT YEAR-ROUND IN SUITABLE HABITATS THROUGHOUT THE REGION. BIRDS DISPERSE, AND NUMBERS ARE BOOSTED IN WINTER BY MIGRANT BIRDS FROM FURTHER AFIELD.

VOICE UTTERS A *KAA-GA-GA*, NOTICEABLY DEEPER IN TONE THAN LESSER BLACK-BACKED GULL.

seaweed and other vegetation on the ground or on cliffs. It disperses during the winter when numbers are boosted by migrant birds, especially in Britain, and is regularly encountered inland at this time.

adult winter
Upperwings appear almost uniformly black, except for the white trailing margin and markings at tip.

adult summer
A combination of large size, massive bill and pink legs ensure easy identification.

The large size and proportionately massive bill help with separation from other juvenile gulls.

juvenile

adult winter
Often aggressive and vocal towards other species, this is the 'bully boy' of the gull world.

Little Tern
Sternula albifrons

This is the smallest tern in the region. The sexes are similar but summer and winter plumages differ subtly. The summer adult has pale grey upperwings and back, the wings conspicuously dark-tipped when the bird is seen in flight. The remaining plumage is white, save for the contrasting black head which is adorned with a white forehead patch. The bill is long, yellow and black-tipped. The legs are orange-yellow. It begins to acquire winter plumage from the late summer onwards, the forehead becoming entirely white and the leg and bill colour more subdued. The juvenile is similar to the winter adult, but note the scaly appearance to the back, and the obvious dark leading edge to the wings when seen in flight.

adults

Extremely aerobatic; the flight pattern is changeable with birds sometimes flying on rapid clipped wingbeats, soaring or hovering before diving after fish.

adult life-size

A short-legged tern with a striking and diagnostic yellow bill and white forecrown.

adult

At the start of the
breeding season,
courting pairs chase
one another, the male
often carrying a fish
for presentation
to the female.

adult

adults

Nests colonially and, on arrival in spring,
flocks sometimes engage in aerial displays
before all landing whereupon disputes
about nest site location are settled.

Factfile

LENGTH 22–24CM

WINGSPAN 48–55CM

HABITAT PRIMARILY A COASTAL
SPECIES IN THE BRITISH ISLES,
FAVOURING SHINGLE AND SANDY
ISLANDS, AND BEACHES; ALSO OCCURS
ALONG RIVERS ON MAINLAND EUROPE
IN AREAS OFFERING SUITABLE
BREEDING HABITAT.

FOOD FEEDS ON SMALL FISH,
INSECTS AND CRUSTACEANS.

STATUS VERY LOCALLY COMMON
SUMMER BREEDING SPECIES, PRESENT
MAINLY MAY TO SEPTEMBER, IN
SUITABLE HABITATS THROUGHOUT
THE REGION EXCEPT THE NORTH.
OVERWINTERS IN AFRICA.

VOICE UTTERS A RAUCOUS
CREE-ICK CALL.

Appreciably smaller than other tern species encountered
in the region, the Little Tern is a buoyant and graceful flyer,
the wings slender and swept back. It is often observed hovering
over water before plunge-diving head-first after small fish and
invertebrates. It breeds colonially on undisturbed shingle and
sandy beaches, nesting in a shallow scrape.

Sandwich Tern *Sterna sandvicensis*

The Sandwich Tern is a handsome seabird with an elegant and buoyant flight. The sexes are similar but summer and winter plumages differ subtly. The summer adult has a pale grey back and upperwings, the latter being darker towards the wingtips. The remaining plumage is white, the head marked with a contrasting crested black cap that extends just below the eye. The black bill is long and slender with a yellow tip, and the legs are long and black. It begins to acquire winter plumage from the late summer onwards, the forehead becoming white. The juvenile recalls the winter adult, but displays a barred and scaled patterning on the back. In all birds, in flight the wings appear long and narrow, and note the short deeply forked white tail.

A summer breeding visitor, the Sandwich Tern is often one of the first migratory birds to arrive in the spring and the last to leave in the autumn. It breeds in colonies on suitable undisturbed beaches and islands, nesting in a shallow scrape on the ground. The loud raucous call is distinctive. It is often seen carrying fish back to the nest around breeding colonies and requires shallow water in which to feed. It frequently travels considerable distances from the nest to suitable feeding grounds.

adult winter

Towards the end of the breeding season, a proportion of adults will already have begun to moult, losing the intense black cap seen in spring birds.

adult summer life-size

Nests colonially on coastal shingle. The body plumage looks very pale, contrasting with the dark primary tips, black legs and cap. The bill is long, slender and black with a yellow tip.

adult summer

During the breeding season, adults are often seen returning to their nests carrying sand-eels and other small fish to feed their young.

adult summer

adult summer

Its direct flight is rapid, on deep, buoyant wingbeats; often veers and hovers if it spots potential food, before plunge-diving.

Factfile

LENGTH 36–41CM

WINGSPAN 95–105CM

HABITAT PREDOMINANTLY A COASTAL SPECIES, FAVOURING SHALLOW INSHORE SEAS.

FOOD FEEDS MAINLY ON SURFACE-DWELLING FISH SUCH AS SAND-EELS.

STATUS LOCALLY COMMON AND WIDESPREAD SUMMER BREEDING SPECIES, PRESENT MAINLY APRIL TO SEPTEMBER; OVERWINTERS IN VERY SMALL NUMBERS IN THE SOUTH OF THE REGION, WITH THE MAJORITY MIGRATING TO AFRICA.

VOICE UTTERS A LOUD AND DEEP DISYLLABIC *CHEE-URRICK* CALL.

Common Tern *Sterna hirundo*

A common and widespread tern, this species is similar to the Arctic Tern but separable with care. The sexes are similar but summer and winter plumages differ slightly. The summer adult has a pale grey back and upperwings; the remaining plumage is whitish, the head marked with a contrasting black cap that extends just below the eye. In flight and from below, note the slightly translucent look to the inner primaries and the subtle dark wingtips. From above, a subtly darker wedge is observed, formed from the dark shafts and tips of the outer primaries. Compared to an Arctic Tern, the large orange-red bill is black-tipped, and the reddish legs are slightly longer. The winter-plumage adult (sometimes observed in the late summer) is similar but develops white on the forehead and a dark carpal bar; the bill and legs are dark. The juvenile recalls the winter adult but has an incomplete dark cap; the upperparts appear 'scaly' and the back has a rufous tinge; in flight and from above, the leading and trailing edges of the inner wing appear dark. All birds have a long forked tail.

A Common Tern's flight is buoyant and effortless on long, slender wings. It feeds by plunge-diving for surface-feeding fish, which it can gather in large numbers in rich feeding areas. It nests on the ground in a shallow scrape.

summer adult life-size

Compared to an Arctic Tern, the bill colour is a subtly different shade of red and the tip is black; overall the body appears more compact perhaps due to the marginally shorter primary projection.

summer adult

Seen from below, the breast and belly appear appreciably darker than the neck and rear end.

Factfile

LENGTH 31–35CM

WINGSPAN 77–88CM

HABITAT FAVOURS COASTAL AREAS AND INLAND FRESHWATER SUCH AS GRAVEL PITS AND RESERVOIRS.

FOOD FEEDS PRIMARILY ON FISH AND CRUSTACEANS.

STATUS COMMON AND WIDESPREAD SUMMER BREEDING SPECIES, PRESENT MAINLY MAY TO SEPTEMBER IN SUITABLE HABITATS THROUGHOUT THE REGION. OVERWINTERS IN AFRICA.

VOICE UTTERS A VARIETY OF RAUCOUS CALLS INCLUDING *KREEEAR*.

Juvenile

The pattern of black on the outer primaries is similar to that seen in adult birds.

summer adult

In direct flight and in strong winds, wingbeats are rapid and scything.

Juvenile

Even after fledging, juveniles are often attended and fed by their parents, which helps with identification.

Roseate Tern
Sterna dougallii

This is the rarest of the region's terns and a globally threatened species. The sexes are similar but summer and winter plumages differ subtly. The summer adult has pale grey upperparts; the underside is whitish with a subtle pink tinge. The head has a contrasting dark cap that extends just below the eye. The long slender bill is black with a red base, the extent of which varies; the bill can appear all black. The legs are relatively long and bright red. When seen in flight, note the long tail streamers and the strikingly pale colouration. Sometimes occurring in the region in late summer, the winter adult loses its tail streamers and rosy flush, and acquires a white patch to the forehead. The juvenile displays a pattern of scaling to the upperparts; the underparts are white and the dark cap is incomplete. The upperwings display a dark leading edge to the inner wing.

The Roseate Tern is an elegant bird in flight, and its long tail streamers are obvious when it is in summer plumage. It breeds in a handful of colonies, mostly on undisturbed offshore islands close to shallow water suitable for feeding, which it does by plunge-diving for small surface-dwelling fish. It nests on the ground in a shallow scrape, typically under vegetation, and readily takes to specialist nest boxes in targeted conservation schemes.

summer adult
Overall, the body plumage looks very pale but a subtle pink flush is sometimes evident, especially in overcast conditions.

The back and innerwing appear scaly and brown and the upperwing pattern is subtly different from juveniles of similar-sized tern species.

juvenile

summer adult

In flight, very long tail streamers (outer tail feathers) are particularly obvious when birds hover and spread their tails for added lift.

summer adult life-size

The amount of black on the bill is always more extensive than in Common Tern; in some individuals, outside the breeding season, the red colour can be limited to just the base of the bill.

Factfile

LENGTH 33–38CM

WINGSPAN 72–80CM

HABITAT ENTIRELY COASTAL, FAVOURING SHELTERED SEAS AND SAND DUNES AND OFFSHORE ISLANDS FOR NESTING.

FOOD FEEDS PRIMARILY ON SMALL FISH.

STATUS RARE SUMMER BREEDING SPECIES (PRESENT MAINLY MAY TO AUGUST) THAT OCCURS MOSTLY IN BRITAIN AND IRELAND. OVERWINTERS IN TROPICAL AFRICA.

VOICE UTTERS A *CHEW-VIK* CALL.

Arctic Tern
Sterna paradisaea

The Arctic Tern is an elegant seabird, close in appearance to Common Tern but separable with experience. The sexes are similar but summer and winter plumages differ. The summer adult has a pale grey back and upperwings. The remaining plumage is whitish, being pale closest to the throat and cheeks, and greyish on the body. The head has a contrasting black cap that extends just below the eye. In flight, and from below, note the pale and slightly translucent look to the flight feathers and dark trailing edge to the primaries. From above, the wings appear uniformly grey. Compared to a Common Tern, the large bill is entirely

In some lights, the pale trailing edge to the innerwing can look striking.

summer adult
Looks long-tailed in flight, due to the impressive tail streamers.

juvenile

summer adult
When huddled against strong winds, the legs of standing birds can look amazingly short.

The whitish border below the eye and along the cheek is offset by a darker grey throat, breast and belly, and a black cap.

summer adult

red and the red legs are shorter. The juvenile has grey upperparts with a 'scaly' look, white underparts, and an incomplete dark cap. In flight and from above, the leading edges of the inner wings appear dark, while the trailing edges are white. All birds have a long forked tail.

The Arctic Tern is a powerful and buoyant flyer that undertakes the longest migration of any bird, breeding in the Arctic but wintering in the Antarctic. It nests in a shallow ground scrape in large colonies, sometimes mixing with other tern species, and defends its territory aggressively, particularly from human intruders. In common with other tern species, it feeds by plunge-diving for surface-dwelling fish.

summer adult life-size

Factfile

LENGTH 33–35CM

WINGSPAN 75–85CM

HABITAT NESTS ON UNDISTURBED DUNES AND IN FLAT COASTAL AREAS (TYPICALLY GRASS-COVERED ISLANDS), AND FEEDS IN ADJACENT SHALLOW SEAS.

FOOD FEEDS ON FISH, INSECTS AND CRUSTACEANS.

STATUS LOCALLY COMMON SUMMER BREEDING SPECIES, PRESENT MAINLY FROM MAY TO AUGUST IN SUITABLE HABITATS IN THE NORTH OF OUR REGION. OVERWINTERS IN THE ANTARCTIC.

VOICE UTTERS A SHRILL *KRT-KRT-KRT* NEAR THE NEST.

The bill is uniformly red, similar in colour to the legs. The long pale primaries and tail enhance a standing bird's slender, elongated appearance.

Black Tern
Chlidonias niger

The Black Tern is a handsome bird and an acrobatic flyer. The sexes are similar but summer and winter plumages differ. The summer adult has mainly dark grey upperparts; the head, neck, breast and belly are black. The long forked tail is grey with a contrastingly white undertail. The slender bill and short delicate legs are dark. The winter plumage

adults

At the start of the breeding season, pairs engage in courtship behaviour, which includes the male presenting the female with a food item such as a small fish or large insect.

adult

A combination of dark grey plumage and aerobatic flight make identification straightforward.

Factfile

LENGTH **22–24CM**

WINGSPAN **64–68CM**

HABITAT **FAVOURS FRESHWATER AND BRACKISH LAGOONS, AND WELL-VEGETATED WETLAND HABITATS INCLUDING MARSHES, LAKES AND GRAVEL PITS. SOMETIMES ENCOUNTERED ON THE COAST AND AT SEA DURING MIGRATION.**

FOOD **SMALL FISH, AMPHIBIANS AND AQUATIC AND TERRESTRIAL INVERTEBRATES.**

STATUS **SUMMER BREEDING BIRD OF EASTERN EUROPE (PRESENT MAINLY MAY TO AUGUST) WITH A FEW SCATTERED COLONIES TO THE WEST. PRIMARILY SEEN AS A SCARCE PASSAGE MIGRANT IN OUR REGION. OVERWINTERS IN TROPICAL WEST AFRICA.**

VOICE **MAINLY SILENT, BUT CAN UTTER A HARSH SQUEAK AND LOW GRUMBLING CALL WHEN AT THE NEST.**

is acquired between July and September, and moulting birds can look a little dishevelled. The upperparts are dark grey; the underparts are uniformly white. The black plumage on the head is less extensive, being restricted to the cap, nape and ear coverts. Note the black patches either side of the breast and the dull red legs. The juvenile recalls the winter adult, but the upperparts are grey-brown in colour and have a 'scaly' patterning.

The Black Tern breeds primarily in freshwater habitats in loose colonies, nesting on the ground in a scrape lined with vegetation, or on a floating mat of vegetation. A buoyant and consummate flyer, it catches invertebrate prey on the wing, frequently dipping close to the surface of the water. In northwest Europe it is seen primarily on migration, when small flocks are sometimes encountered.

Juvenile
The dark cap is defined by a white forecrown and collar; pale feather margins create a scaly appearance to the otherwise dark back.

adult life-size
The wings and back are subtly paler than the head and underparts; the bill is black and the legs are dull red.

Guillemot
Uria aalge

The Guillemot is a long-bodied seabird and the largest auk encountered in the region. The sexes are similar but summer and winter plumages differ, and regional plumage variation occurs. The summer adult is uniformly chocolate-brown on its head and upperparts; northern birds have darker plumage than those from the south. In all birds the underparts are pure white. Note the narrow white wingbar visible on the closed wings, formed by the white-tipped secondary feathers. On close inspection, a subtle furrow running from behind the eye can be discerned. The so-called 'bridled Guillemot' has a white eye-ring and line along the furrow, recalling a pair of spectacles. The winter adult is similar but has more extensive white on the head, cheeks and throat; the furrow behind the eye forms an obvious dark line. In all birds, the dark bill is large and dagger-like, the legs are dark and the feet are webbed. The juvenile is similar to the winter adult but with a stubbier bill.

adult summer

Only ever comes to land when nesting. Adopts an upright posture when standing on rocks in a breeding colony.

bridled adult summer life-size

The proportion of 'bridled' birds in a colony increases the further north you travel.

Factfile

LENGTH 38–41CM WINGSPAN 64–70CM

HABITAT **BREEDS ON ROCKY ISLANDS AND STEEP SEA CLIFFS IN SUMMER. AT OTHER TIMES, FOUND AT SEA.**

FOOD **FEEDS PRIMARILY ON FISH.**

STATUS **LOCALLY ABUNDANT SUMMER BREEDING SPECIES, PRESENT AT COLONIES MAINLY MAY TO AUGUST, MOST BEING FOUND IN THE NORTH AND WEST OF OUR REGION. DISPERSES OUT TO SEA DURING THE WINTER MONTHS.**

VOICE **UTTERS A NASAL GROWLING CALL AT THE BREEDING COLONY.**

bridled adult summer

Sometimes hangs on the wind at breeding colonies, riding updraughts rising off the cliffs.

The Guillemot is a familiar seabird that forms large, closely packed colonies on suitable nesting sites, generally seeking inaccessible precipitous cliffs and rocky islands, and nesting on bare rock. It is an expert swimmer that dives frequently and uses its narrow wings to propel itself underwater. It flies with rapid whirring wingbeats.

adult winter

Only occasionally seen in non-breeding plumage because winter months are usually spent out to sea, far from land.

adult summer

Swims buoyantly but rather low in the water.

Razorbill
Alca torda

The Razorbill is a familiar large and rather dumpy-looking black-and-white auk. The sexes are similar but summer and winter plumages differ. The summer adult has a black head, neck and upperparts (pure black, unlike a Guillemot); the underparts are white. Note the narrow white wingbar, visible on the back of a resting bird, formed by the white-tipped secondary feathers. The large black bill is deep and flattened laterally and, at close range, vertical ridges, a narrow white vertical band and a white horizontal line running from the eye to the base of the bill can be discerned. The winter adult is similar but with more extensive white plumage on the head and throat; the bill is more slender in appearance and the white bill-lines are less obvious. The juvenile is similar to a winter adult but smaller with a stubbier bill and dark brown upperparts.

The Razorbill forms large colonies on suitable nesting sites, favouring inaccessible precipitous cliffs and rocky islands and shores where it sometimes mixes with Guillemots. More at home in the water than on land, it is an expert swimmer that dives frequently and uses its wings to propel itself underwater. Flight is on rapid whirring wingbeats.

adult winter
Storm-driven birds in winter plumage are sometimes seen in harbours and sheltered bays.

summer adults
In flight, looks strikingly black-and-white.

adult summer
Swims low in the water and submerges smoothly and with ease.

adult summer

At breeding colonies, off-duty birds are often seen standing prominently on rocks in the vicinity of the nest crevice, adopting an upright posture.

Factfile

LENGTH 37–41CM   WINGSPAN 63–68CM

HABITAT IN THE BREEDING SEASON (MAY TO AUGUST), FAVOURS ROCKY ISLANDS AND COASTAL AREAS WITH STEEP CLIFFS AND BOULDER-STREWN UNDERCLIFFS. FOUND AT SEA AT OTHER TIMES.

FOOD FEEDS PRIMARILY ON FISH.

STATUS LOCALLY COMMON AND WIDESPREAD SUMMER BREEDING SPECIES, WITH MOST COLONIES IN THE NORTH AND WEST OF OUR REGION. DISPERSES OUT TO SEA DURING THE WINTER MONTHS.

VOICE MOSTLY SILENT BUT CAN UTTER A NASAL GROWLING CALL AT THE NEST.

adult summer life-size

Striking white lines on the otherwise black bill and head, combined with the bill shape, make identification easy.

Black Guillemot
Cepphus grylle

Factfile

LENGTH 30–34CM

WINGSPAN 52–58CM

HABITAT BREEDS ON SEA CLIFFS AND ROCKY COASTLINES. OVERWINTERS IN SHALLOW INSHORE WATERS.

FOOD FEEDS ON FISH AND CRUSTACEANS.

STATUS RESIDENT AND PRESENT YEAR-ROUND IN THE NORTH OF THE REGION, PRIMARILY SCANDINAVIA AND THE NORTHERN HALF OF THE BRITISH ISLES.

VOICE UTTERS SHRILL WHISTLING CALLS.

The Black Guillemot is a distinctive auk of coastal and inshore waters. The sexes are similar but summer and winter plumages differ. The summer adult has predominantly sooty-brown plumage that can appear black at distance or in poor light. A large pure white wing-patch is striking and diagnostic. The dark bill is rather slender compared to other auks, and note the red gape visible when the bird is calling. The short legs are bright red and the feet are webbed. The winter adult retains the dark colouration and contrasting white patch on its wings; the tail also remains dark. The remaining plumage on the upperparts acquires a mottled grey appearance; the underparts are white. First-winter birds are similar to the winter adult, but the white wing-patch contains dark markings.

The Black Guillemot generally nests in smaller groups than other auks, seeking cavities among boulder-strewn coasts and cliffs. It is an expert swimmer that dives frequently, feeding on bottom-dwelling fish and requiring shallow water for feeding. It remains in shallow inshore coastal regions during the winter months and is commonly seen around harbours at this time. It can occur south of its normal range during periods of extreme weather.

adult summer

Typically flies low over the water, when the white wing patches are striking and obvious.

adult summer

Nesting birds are very vocal, especially when returning to or leaving the colony; their high-pitched calls are surprisingly far-carrying.

adult summer life-size

In suitable habitats, nests in loose colonies and off-duty birds stand guard, perched on prominent rocks near their nest chamber.

adult winter

Swims low in the water; the white wing patch is a striking plumage feature at all times of year.

Little Auk
Alle alle

Breeds in large colonies inside the Arctic Circle; birds in breeding plumage are occasionally seen further south and are recognised by the uniformly dark head and neck.

The Little Auk is a dumpy little seabird and the smallest auk encountered in Europe. The sexes are similar but summer and winter plumages differ. The summer adult (rarely seen in our region) has a black head, neck and upperparts; the back is marked with a series of narrow white lines on the 'shoulder' of the wing, most obvious when the wings are folded. The underparts are white with an abrupt delineation from the black upperparts at the breast. A subtle white crescent marking above the eye can sometimes be discerned. The dark bill is short and stubby. The species is most commonly seen in the region in winter plumage, when the black of the breast, throat, cheeks and ear coverts is replaced with white. The juvenile is similar to the winter adult but with subtly browner plumage.

This is the most northerly breeding auk species, and it nests in huge colonies in the high Arctic in rock crevices on scree slopes. An accomplished and buoyant swimmer, it dives frequently, using its wings to propel itself through the water. A Little Auk's flight is rather Starling-like with rapid, whirring wingbeats.

Arctic breeding colony

adult summer

The all-dark head and neck highlight the white upper 'eyelid'.

adult winter life-size
Swimming birds look very compact and can
appear almost neck-less.

Factfile

LENGTH 18–20CM WINGSPAN 40–48CM

HABITAT **BREEDS NORTH OF OUR REGION, ON SCREE SLOPES OF
MOUNTAINS AND CLIFFS IN THE HIGH ARCTIC. OVERWINTERS AT SEA.**

FOOD **FEEDS MAINLY ON PLANKTONIC CRUSTACEANS.**

STATUS **SCARCE NON-BREEDING VISITOR FROM THE ARCTIC (SEEN HERE MAINLY NOVEMBER
TO FEBRUARY) THAT ONLY RARELY COMES CLOSE TO LAND. MOST COMMONLY SEEN FROM THE
COAST DURING PERIODS OF HARSH WEATHER, ALTHOUGH CAN OCCUR INLAND AFTER SEVERE STORMS.**

VOICE **MOSTLY SILENT WHEN ENCOUNTERED IN THE REGION. UTTERS SUBTLE TRILLING CALLS AT THE NEST.**

adult winter
In bright light, the gleaming white face and
flanks, and white 'braces' on the back, are
very striking.

Puffin
Fratercula arctica

Factfile

LENGTH 27–30CM

WINGSPAN 47–63CM

HABITAT FAVOURS UNDISTURBED SLOPING SEA CLIFFS AND ISLANDS DURING THE BREEDING SEASON. AT OTHER TIMES, FOUND FAR OUT TO SEA.

FOOD MAINLY MARINE FISH AND CRUSTACEANS.

STATUS LOCALLY COMMON BREEDING SPECIES, NESTING IN COLONIES IN SUITABLE HABITATS AROUND THE COASTS OF THE REGION. PRESENT AT COLONIES MAINLY APRIL TO AUGUST.

VOICE MOSTLY SILENT BUT UTTERS A CREAKING GROAN AT THE NEST.

The Puffin is arguably the most iconic and endearing seabird in the region. The sexes are similar but summer and winter plumages are subtly different. The summer adult (most commonly encountered) has mainly black upperparts, the head being marked with a bold teardrop-shaped, dusky-white face patch that extends from the base of the bill, encompasses the cheeks and surrounds the eye. The head has a clearly defined black cap. The underparts are white and neatly separated from the black neck. The huge, laterally flattened and wedge-shaped bill is unmistakable, being brightly marked with red, blue and yellow. The legs are bright orange-red and the feet are webbed. The winter adult is similar but the white face is grubby grey and the bill is much smaller and less colourful. The juvenile recalls the winter adult but with an even smaller, darker bill.

adult summer

As the breeding season progresses, adults bring increasingly large fish back to land to feed their chicks.

adult summer

Swimming birds are buoyant and sit high in the water.

At breeding colonies, off-duty birds often sit around in the vicinity of their burrows, adopting an upright posture.

adult summer life-size

summer adults
Wings are narrow and wingbeats are rapid; birds typically fly low over the water.

The Puffin breeds in large colonies, typically on islands and undisturbed coastal areas, nesting on sloping vegetated banks in burrows that they excavate themselves. Its nests are particularly vulnerable to predation from rodents, and most successful breeding colonies are established on islands where ground predators are absent. An accomplished and buoyant swimmer, it dives frequently after small fish such as sand-eels. It flies using rapid, whirring wingbeats.

adult summer
Bill-stretching behaviour reveals a surprisingly wide gape.

Rock Dove/ Feral Pigeon

Columba livia

Arrows indicate the haunts of wild Rock Doves in the region.

The wild Rock Dove is a shy bird of wild and inaccessible rocky coasts and cliffs. The sexes are similar. Much smaller than Woodpigeon, the adult Rock Dove has overall blue-grey plumage, palest on the upperwings and back, the breast flushed with pinkish-maroon. The upperwings are marked with two well-defined dark wingbars, obvious both in flight and in standing birds. In flight, note the small white rump patch, the dark trailing edge to the upperwings, dark terminal bar to the tail and white underwings. The juvenile is similar to the adult. The Feral Pigeon is the urbanised descendant of the Rock Dove. Its plumage is widely variable, from pure white to almost black, and many combinations between.

Arrows indicate the haunts of wild Rock Doves in the region.

adult

Typically seen in small flocks; all Rock Doves reveal a pale rump in flight.

adults

Flight is rapid when alarmed, but leisurely when relaxed and coming into land.

The species forms flocks and, in the case of Feral Pigeon, these can number many hundreds of birds. The Rock Dove is a fast-flying and rather timid bird which nests on rocky ledges and can be tricky to observe. The Feral Pigeon has adapted well to urban areas and is now abundant in many towns and cities, generally being extremely tame.

adult

In some lights, the sheen on the neck cannot be seen.

adult life-size

Many Feral Pigeons have identical plumage to their Rock Dove ancestors. As a rough guide, Rock Doves are shy so if you can get close to the bird in question it will almost certainly be one of their domesticated cousins.

Factfile

LENGTH 31–34CM WINGSPAN 63–70CM

HABITAT ROCKY COASTLINES AND COASTAL CLIFFS, OPEN COUNTRYSIDE, WITH FERAL POPULATIONS IN URBAN AREAS.

FOOD FEEDS ON A VARIETY OF PLANT SEEDS, GRAINS, OTHER VEGETATION AND INVERTEBRATES.

STATUS ROCK DOVE IS A LOCAL RESIDENT BREEDING SPECIES, RESTRICTED TO SUITABLE HABITAT IN COASTAL REGIONS TO THE NORTH AND WEST OF BRITAIN AND NORTHERN IRELAND. ITS TRUE STATUS IS HARD TO ASSESS BECAUSE OF THE LARGE POPULATIONS OF FERAL PIGEONS THROUGHOUT THE REGION, SOME OF WHICH RETURN TO THE WILD.

VOICE UTTERS A VARIETY OF COOING CALLS.

All manner of different colour forms can be found among flocks of Feral Pigeons, ranging from birds with white wing and nape feathers, to individuals that are dark lilac-maroon.

adult

Stock Dove
Columba oenas

The Stock Dove is similar to a Woodpigeon, but with a more slender body. The sexes are similar. The adult has uniform blue-grey upperparts; the underparts are paler grey with a pinkish-maroon tinge to the breast. Note the darker greenish half-collar patch to the sides and nape of the neck, which reveals a metallic sheen when seen in certain light. Note also the darker rear end in standing birds, formed by the dark flight feathers and terminal tail-band; both features are also obvious in flight. The upperwings are adorned with two narrow dark bars on the inner wing, also visible on the back of standing birds. The bill is grey-buff with an off-white patch at the base, and the legs are

adults

In flight, the grey-buff upperwings are marked with two dark bars (often very subtle) and contrast with the dark trailing margin and flight feathers.

An absence of white on the neck helps distinguish this species from the superficially similar Woodpigeon. Outside the breeding season, sometimes mixes with its cousin in feeding flocks.

Factfile

LENGTH 32–34CM

WINGSPAN 63–69CM

HABITAT WOODLAND ADJACENT TO OPEN COUNTRY AND ARABLE FARMLAND.

FOOD FEEDS ON SEEDS, FLOWERS, OTHER VEGETATION AND INVERTEBRATES.

STATUS RESIDENT YEAR-ROUND IN THE WEST OF OUR REGION; BIRDS THAT BREED FURTHER NORTH AND EAST MIGRATE DURING THE WINTER MONTHS TO SOUTHERN EUROPE. LARGELY ABSENT FROM NORTHERN SCANDINAVIA.

VOICE UTTERS A CHARACTERISTIC AND REPETITIVE OO-U-LOOK CALL DURING THE BREEDING SEASON.

bright pinkish-red. Note the uniformly dark eye, in contrast to the pale eye of Woodpigeon. The juvenile is similar to the adult, but is generally duller with fainter markings and lacks the sheen to the neck.

Primarily a bird of lowland areas, the Stock Dove nests in tree holes and is usually solitary during the breeding season. During the winter it forms large flocks, typically feeding on arable fields.

adult

adult life-size
The dark primaries and terminal band to the tail, and the dark wingbars, are good features for identification and separation from Woodpigeon.

Woodpigeon
Columba palumbus

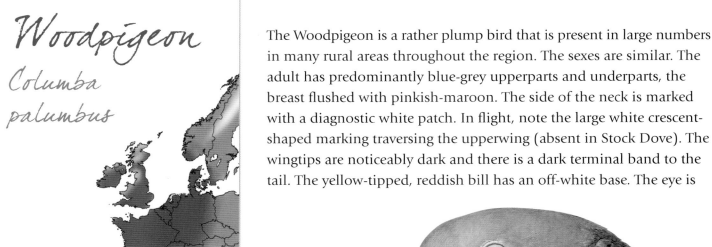

The Woodpigeon is a rather plump bird that is present in large numbers in many rural areas throughout the region. The sexes are similar. The adult has predominantly blue-grey upperparts and underparts, the breast flushed with pinkish-maroon. The side of the neck is marked with a diagnostic white patch. In flight, note the large white crescent-shaped marking traversing the upperwing (absent in Stock Dove). The wingtips are noticeably dark and there is a dark terminal band to the tail. The yellow-tipped, reddish bill has an off-white base. The eye is

adult life-size
Well-fed birds can look extremely plump; birds that are about to display often puff up their necks.

adult
Although primarily a farmland species, Woodpigeons are often found in rural gardens; clover leaves in lawns are a favourite food.

pale yellow and the legs are pinkish. The juvenile recalls the adult but has duller plumage overall and lacks the white neck-patch.

The Woodpigeon is a very successful species in many rural areas, and an increasingly common sight in urban locations. It has benefited directly from the increased production of oilseed rape. It nests in trees and tall bushes, constructing an untidy platform of twigs. A strong flier, it performs aerial displays during the spring, and the loud clattering of its wings as it takes flight is a familiar sound. Outside the breeding season it can form large flocks.

Factfile

LENGTH 40–42CM

WINGSPAN 75–80CM

HABITAT FAVOURS FARMLAND AND OPEN GRASSLAND ADJACENT TO HEDGEROWS AND WOODLANDS. IT IS BECOMING INCREASINGLY COMMON IN URBAN AREAS.

FOOD FEEDS PRIMARILY ON VEGETATION AND INVERTEBRATES.

STATUS COMMON AND WIDESPREAD RESIDENT BREEDING SPECIES THROUGHOUT MOST OF THE REGION. SOME SOUTHWARD MIGRATION OCCURS DURING THE WINTER FROM SCANDINAVIA.

VOICE UTTERS A SERIES OF SOFT, MONOTONE *oo-OO-oo-oo-oo* CALLS, THE EMPHASIS ON THE SECOND OF FIVE SYLLABLES.

Take-off is usually a noisy affair, with clattering wings; white markings on the neck and wings are certain identification features.

adults

Collared Dove
Streptopelia decaocto

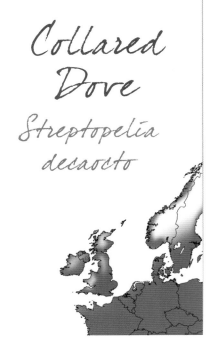

Factfile

LENGTH 31–33CM

WINGSPAN 47–55CM

HABITAT FOUND IN A VARIETY OF HABITATS INCLUDING GARDENS, ORCHARDS, FARMYARDS AND URBAN PARKS.

FOOD FEEDS PRIMARILY ON SEEDS AND CEREAL GRAINS.

STATUS WIDESPREAD RESIDENT BREEDING SPECIES FOUND YEAR-ROUND THROUGHOUT THE REGION IN SUITABLE HABITATS.

VOICE UTTERS A REPETITIVE TRISYLLABIC *OO-OO-oo* SONG, WITH THE EMPHASIS ON THE FIRST TWO SYLLABLES.

adult

Pale underwings are obvious in birds that hover as they come into land.

adult

Seen from below, the outer half of the tail is white and contrasts with the dark inner half.

adult life-size

In garden settings, often spends time just sitting on fence posts.

adult

The Collared Dove is a familiar small pigeon. The sexes are similar. The adult has mainly uniform sandy-grey plumage; the head, neck and breast are flushed pinkish. A conspicuous dark half-collar marks the nape. In flight, note the black tips to the wings, the pale-coloured underwings and the broad white terminal band on the undertail. The slender, rather dainty bill is black, and the legs are reddish. The eye is dark red with a pale orbital ring. The juvenile is similar to the adult but duller overall, with pale fringes to the back feathers and lacking the half-collar marking.

The Collared Dove is a recent addition to the region's fauna: the species' range expanded across the region during the early twentieth century, linked directly to the expansion of arable farmland and cereal production. It nests in trees, constructing a rough platform of twigs. Flight is assured and swift on a series of fast, clipped wingbeats and dipping glides on bowed wings.

Anxious birds tend to extend their necks, making the black-and-white neck patch more obvious and striking.

Upperparts are typically grey-buff but in some birds they are warmer buffish brown.

adult

Turtle Dove
Streptopelia turtur

The Turtle Dove is a beautifully marked, unmistakable little dove, often detected by its diagnostic song. The sexes are similar. The adult has a blue-grey head, neck and underparts; the breast displaying a slight pinkish-buff flush. The back and upperwings are a warm chestnut colour, the wing coverts having dark centres and pale margins creating a conspicuous scaling. A rounded patch of black-and-white barring on the side of the neck is obvious when seen at close range. The tail is mainly dark, but note the white corners that give it a wedge-shaped appearance when seen in flight. The dark bill is slender and pale-tipped, and the legs are reddish. The juvenile is similar to the adult, but the overall colouration is more subdued and it lacks the neck markings.

Compared to a similar sized Collared Dove, the neck markings and beautifully patterned back aid identification.

Looks scruffy overall when compared to an adult, and has less distinct markings.

juvenile

adult

Factfile

LENGTH 26–28CM

WINGSPAN 47–53CM

HABITAT FAVOURS ARABLE FARMLAND WITH ADJACENT WOODLAND, HEDGEROWS AND SCRUB COVER.

FOOD FEEDS ON SEEDS AND FRUITS OF ARABLE CEREALS AND WEEDS.

STATUS DECLINING MIGRANT SUMMER BREEDING SPECIES, RESTRICTED TO THE SOUTH OF THE REGION AND PRESENT MAINLY MAY TO AUGUST. WINTERS IN AFRICA.

VOICE UTTERS A DISTINCTIVE, PURRING *COO*.

The Turtle Dove is present as a summer migrant breeder only in the southern part of our region. It nests in trees and shrubs, constructing a rough platform of twigs, and is a difficult species to observe owing to its preference for the sanctuary of dense vegetation. Its numbers are in decline through a combination of the widespread use of agricultural herbicides and the shooting of migrating birds in the Mediterranean region.

adult

Flight is rapid, on 'flicked' wingbeats; the extensive white on the outer tail is striking.

adult life-size

Breeding birds tend to be unobtrusive in their nesting territories; were it not for the distinctive and diagnostic song, many would get overlooked.

Ring-necked Parakeet

Psittacula krameri

The Ring-necked Parakeet is an established alien species with colourful plumage and a distinctive long-tailed outline in flight. The sexes are similar but are separable with care. The adult male has primarily bright green plumage, but note the dark primary flight feathers, obvious both in flight and at rest. The tail is exceptionally long. The parrot-like red bill is powerful and heavily hook-tipped. The bird is also marked with a red eye-ring and a pinkish neck-ring, which is dark-bordered towards the lower half and merges with the black throat. The adult female is similar but lacks the throat and neck markings of the male. The juvenile recalls the adult female.

A rather bizarre addition to the European list, the Ring-necked Parakeet has established an extraordinarily successful feral population in localised areas. It nests in tree holes, often high above the ground. Outside the breeding season, it forms large flocks and is often seen roosting in trees. Its flight is strong and direct on rapid wingbeats.

In flight, the long slender tail gives the bird a very distinctive outline.

male

male

Also known as Rose-ringed Parakeet, the bright green plumage and unmistakable outline make for easy identification; only the male has the neck ring.

Factfile

LENGTH **40–42CM**

WINGSPAN **42–48CM**

HABITAT **URBAN PARKS, CITY SUBURBS AND OPEN WOODLAND.**

FOOD **VARIED DIET CONSISTING OF FRUITS, FLOWERS AND SEEDS, AND A REGULAR VISITOR TO BIRD TABLES IN THE AREAS IT INHABITS.**

STATUS **ITS NATURAL RANGE IS ASIA AND AFRICA, BUT ESCAPEE CAPTIVE BIRDS HAVE ESTABLISHED LARGE RESIDENT POPULATIONS IN CERTAIN AREAS. LONDON AND ITS SUBURBS ARE THE STRONGHOLD, AND LARGE NUMBERS ARE A REGULAR SIGHT IN ITS PARKS.**

VOICE **UTTERS LOUD SQUAWKING CALLS, ESPECIALLY IN FLIGHT.**

nesting pair life-size
(female above, male below)

All populations in Europe are alien, the result of escapes from captivity and deliberate releases. In most situations, which tend to be city outskirts and large towns, birds are confident and not particularly bothered by people. They announce their presence with noisy contact calls, and nest in tree holes. By doing so they pose a direct threat to native hole-nesting species that are unable to compete with this feisty bird.

Cuckoo
Cuculus canorus

The Cuckoo is a timid bird that is more often heard than seen. The sexes are generally similar, but some females are easily distinguished. The adult male, and the majority of females, have a mainly light blue-grey head, neck and upperparts; the upperwing is darker and tinged with brown. The underparts are white with a series of conspicuous narrow dark bars. The tail is rather long with dark feathers marked with white spots. The bill is dark with a yellow base; the iris of the eye and the legs are yellow. Some adult females have a barred brown head, neck and upperparts, with white underparts marked with a series of dark bars. The juvenile recalls a brown female but has a white patch on the nape. In flight, note the slender pointed wings and the long square-cut tail, somewhat resembling a falcon in outline.

The Cuckoo is an iconic bird, renowned for its practice of nest parasitism. It lays its eggs in the nests of other birds, leaving the surrogate parents to rear the single chick. Typical host species include Reed Warbler, Meadow Pipit and Dunnock;

adult

Often calls in flight; its raptor-like outline generally causes alarm among songbirds who are potential targets for nest parasitism.

juvenile

The shape is unmistakably that of a Cuckoo, and the barred brown plumage makes the ageing of juvenile birds easy.

the Cuckoo chick removes the legitimate eggs and chicks from the nest once it hatches. Adult Cuckoos return to Africa in early summer, and remarkably the chicks make the journey unaccompanied a few weeks later, relying purely on instinct.

adult life-size
Agitated, courting birds sometimes raise their tail and droop their wings while perched.

Factfile

Cuckoo chick
A young Cuckoo being fed by its surrogate parent, a Reed Warbler.

LENGTH 33–35CM

WINGSPAN 55–60CM

HABITAT VARIETY OF HABITATS, LINKED TO THE PRESENCE OF THE SONGBIRDS IT USES FOR NEST PARASITISM, INCLUDING REED BEDS, WOODLAND EDGES, SCRUB AND OPEN UPLANDS.

FOOD FEEDS ON INSECTS, ESPECIALLY BEETLES AND LARGE HAIRY CATERPILLARS.

STATUS SUMMER BREEDING MIGRANT (PRESENT MAINLY APRIL TO AUGUST) THAT BREEDS IN SUITABLE HABITAT THROUGHOUT THE REGION IN THE SUMMER MONTHS. OVERWINTERS IN AFRICA. NUMBERS HAVE DECLINED RAPIDLY OVER RECENT YEARS.

VOICE UTTERS AN ONOMATOPOEIC *CUCK-OO* DURING THE FIRST WEEKS OF ITS ARRIVAL. FEMALE HAS A BURBLING CALL.

Barn Owl
Tyto alba

This is a beautiful owl, its white plumage giving it a rather ghostly appearance. The sexes are similar but birds from Britain and mainland Europe differ slightly. The adult of the British race has soft orange-buff upperparts, attractively speckled with a series of small black-and-white spots. The underparts and feathery legs are white, as is the large heart-shaped facial disc. The eyes are dark and the rather dainty bill is pinkish. In flight, the underwings are pure white; the orange-buff flight feathers of the upperwing and tail are

adult life-size

Factfile

LENGTH **34–38CM**

WINGSPAN **85–93CM**

HABITAT **UNDISTURBED GRASSLAND, WETLAND MARGINS AND LOWLAND FIELDS WITH HEDGES AND ADJACENT WOODLAND.**

FOOD **FEEDS PRIMARILY ON VOLES AND OTHER SMALL MAMMALS.**

STATUS **A MAINLY RESIDENT BREEDING SPECIES, PRESENT YEAR-ROUND THROUGHOUT MOST OF THE REGION. ABSENT FROM MUCH OF SCANDINAVIA, AND NUMBERS ARE IN DECLINE ELSEWHERE.**

VOICE **UTTERS A BLOOD-CURDLING SCREECHING CALL AT NIGHT.**

The subtle flecking on the plumage can only really be appreciated with good views, but birds sometimes pose at close range on posts beside rural roads.

The broad wings and large wing area allow feeding birds to fly at surprisingly slow speeds, a great asset when looking out for potential prey.

adults

adult

marked with dark barring. Birds from mainland Europe are similar but have a dark orange-brown breast. Juveniles resemble their respective adults once the downy plumage is lost.

The Barn Owl is an endearing species that is active both at night and in the half-light of dawn and dusk. During the winter, or in the breeding season when it has young to feed, it can sometimes be encountered hunting during the day. The buoyant flight is slow and leisurely on well-rounded wings. It hunts by quartering the ground and dropping down suddenly, pouncing on unsuspecting prey. It nests in tree holes, barns and old rural buildings, and will also use purpose-built nest boxes.

The white facial disc, heart-shaped in outline, is unique among European owls; as with all owls, the feet have an extremely powerful grip and the talons are needle-sharp.

Little Owl
Athene noctua

This is an easily recognised, rather small and dumpy owl with a short tail and relatively large head. The sexes are similar. The adult has rich brown upperparts adorned with whitish spots; the underparts are pale and heavily marked with dark streaking. Note the large staring yellow eyes and the rather rectangular buffish-grey facial disc. Its bill is grey-brown, the feathered legs are buff-white and the feet are brown. The juvenile is similar to the adult but with more subdued spotting and streaking, particularly on the head. The flight is diagnostically undulating, typically close to the ground.

Habitually perching out in the open and often active during the hours of daylight, the Little Owl is one of the easiest of the owls to see. It often stands erect, bobbing its head up and down and making hissing calls when alarmed. It nests in tree holes, crevices and old buildings.

adult

The body is rounded in outline and the head is proportionately large, even by owl standards.

As with other owl species, a Little Owl is able to turn its head through almost 360 degrees, with the result that it misses very little of what goes on around it.

Factfile

LENGTH **21–23CM**   WINGSPAN **50–58CM**

HABITAT **FAVOURS OPEN COUNTRYSIDE, TYPICALLY FARMLAND WITH ADJACENT HEDGEROWS AND SCATTERED WOODLAND.**

FOOD **FEEDS PRIMARILY ON INSECTS, BUT ALSO CONSUMES SMALL MAMMALS, BIRDS AND EARTHWORMS.**

STATUS **AN INDIGENOUS RESIDENT BREEDING SPECIES OF MAINLAND EUROPE AND INTRODUCED TO BRITAIN DURING THE NINETEENTH CENTURY. ABSENT FROM SCANDINAVIA.**

VOICE **UTTERS A REPETITIVE AND AGITATED CAT-LIKE *KIU* IN THE EARLY EVENING.**

adult
The wings are broad and rounded, with strongly barred markings on the flight feathers.

adult life-size
The yellow, proportionately large eyes face forwards, as with other owls, giving it excellent binocular vision.

Tawny Owl
Strix aluco

Typically, it moves its head rather than its body when alerted to the presence of prey by sound or movement.

adult

adult

This is a medium-sized owl and the most commonly encountered of its kind throughout most of the region. The sexes are similar. The adult has beautifully marked variable plumage of chestnut-brown or grey-brown; the upperparts are darker, with dark streaks and pale spots. Its underparts can appear quite pale and are dark-streaked. Note the large rounded head and the dark eyes set in a well-defined facial disc. Grey patches mark the plumage surrounding the eyes. Note also the small yellowish bill and the lack of ear tufts. In flight, the broad, well-rounded wings appear quite pale on the underside and, on close inspection, are marked with brown barring on the primary feathers. The feathered legs and feet are buff. The juvenile is similar to the adult once the downy feathers have been lost.

More often heard than seen, the Tawny Owl is most vocal in the late winter and early spring when territorial boundaries are being disputed. It is a nocturnal owl that spends the day roosting in the trees, remaining well hidden with its superior camouflage; it is, however, regularly mobbed when discovered by small songbirds. The Tawny Owl nests in tree holes and cavities, and sometimes uses purpose-built nest boxes. Its flight is slow and leisurely. An adaptable species found in a variety of habitats, it is tolerant of close proximity to human habitation.

Factfile

LENGTH **38–40CM** WINGSPAN **82–96CM**

HABITAT **FAVOURS DECIDUOUS OR MIXED WOODLANDS, GARDENS AND SUBURBAN PARKS.**

FOOD **FEEDS ON A VARIETY OF SMALL MAMMALS, INSECTS, BIRDS, AMPHIBIANS AND EARTHWORMS.**

STATUS **A RESIDENT BREEDING SPECIES, PRESENT YEAR-ROUND AND COMMON AND WIDESPREAD IN SUITABLE HABITATS. ABSENT FROM THE EXTREME NORTH OF THE REGION.**

VOICE **UTTERS A SHARP *KEW-WICK*, TOGETHER WITH THE CLASSIC OWL HOOTING CALLS.**

adult life-size
The plumage is overall brown but subtly and beautifully patterned with dark streaks and white spots.

Like other owl species, its flight is virtually silent: the broad wings give it excellent 'lift'.

juvenile

Fluffy youngsters often leave the nest before they are fully fledged. This is normal and they are still attended by their parents.

Long-eared Owl
Asio otus

Factfile

LENGTH 32–35CM

WINGSPAN 90–100CM

HABITAT WOODLAND, CONIFER PLANTATIONS AND AREAS OF SCRUB ADJACENT TO OPEN COUNTRYSIDE.

FOOD FEEDS ON A VARIETY OF SMALL TO MEDIUM-SIZED MAMMALS AND BIRDS.

STATUS A RESIDENT BREEDING SPECIES THROUGHOUT MOST OF THE REGION. SOME SOUTHWARD MIGRATION OCCURS FROM THE EXTREME NORTH DURING THE WINTER MONTHS.

VOICE A MAINLY SILENT SPECIES THAT CAN UTTER SOFT, DEEP HOOTING CALLS DURING THE SPRING.

Compared to a Short-eared Owl note the much longer 'ear' tufts, more intensely streaked underparts and orange (not yellow) eyes.

adult life-size

adult

In flight, the flight feather undersides are strongly barred, particularly the outer primaries; compare this to a Short-eared Owl whose flight feathers show much less obvious markings.

This beautifully marked nocturnal owl raises two long 'ear' tufts when alarmed. The sexes are similar. The adult has dark brown upperparts, well marked with a pattern of darker streaking. The underparts are paler and also heavily adorned with dark streaking. The large round facial disc is orange-buff, with whitish-grey surrounding the grey bill and extending partly above the striking orange eyes. The ear tufts are appreciably longer than those of Short-eared Owl. In flight, note the contrasting orange-buff patch on the upperwing, the barred primaries on the underwing, and the lack of a white trailing edge, allowing certain separation from Short-eared Owl. The juvenile is similar to the adult.

The Long-eared Owl often stands tall with its ear tufts erect when alarmed, making it appear quite large. It is a strictly nocturnal owl that roosts in deep cover during daylight hours, making it hard to observe. It nests in trees, usually in an old nest of another species.

adult

'Ear' tufts are a striking feature. They are usually held flat but raised when a bird is alarmed, for example when it knows it is being watched. Typically, roosting birds are otherwise tolerant of people, more so than other owl species.

Short-eared Owl
Asio flammeus

This is an attractively marked owl that can often be seen hunting in the hours of daylight. The sexes are similar. The adult has buffish-brown upperparts and neck, heavily marked with a series of spots and streaks. The underparts are paler and similarly marked with dark streaking, particularly on the breast and throat. The tail displays heavy dark barring, most obvious when in flight. The large rounded facial disc is pale buff with dark areas surrounding the sunken yellow eyes; the bill is dark grey. Note the short 'ear' tufts. In flight and from below, its underparts appear rather plain, with the exception of the dark streaked throat and dark-tipped wings. The upperwings are marked with a light orange-buff patch and a subtle white trailing edge. The juvenile is similar to the adult.

adult

adult life-size
The eye's yellow iris changes size according to light levels and defines the dark central pupil.

This species' flight is slow and leisurely, and it is often seen gliding low, quartering the ground for prey. The Short-eared Owl frequently uses fence posts, tussocks and other low perches, and is often encountered during the day. It nests on upland moorland, constructing a shallow scrape on the ground, lined with vegetation. Displaying birds at this time can rise to great heights in the air.

The underwings look very pale except for the dark carpal patch and tips to the primary feathers. Its flight is silent and buoyant, on long broad wings.

adults

Its largely diurnal habits and preference for open country mean that, generally speaking, this is the easiest large owl to observe well and for extended periods.

Factfile

LENGTH 35–40CM

WINGSPAN 95–110CM

HABITAT NORTHERN AND UPLAND MOORLAND DURING THE BREEDING SEASON; HEATHLAND, COASTAL GRASSLAND AND LOWLAND MARSHES IN WINTER.

FOOD FEEDS ON VOLES AND OTHER SMALL MAMMALS, BUT WILL ALSO TAKE SMALL BIRDS.

STATUS A RESIDENT BREEDING SPECIES PRESENT YEAR-ROUND IN MUCH OF THE REGION, BUT SUMMER AND WINTER DISTRIBUTIONS DIFFER. PRESENT IN SCANDINAVIA ONLY DURING THE BREEDING SEASON, MOVING SOUTH IN WINTER.

VOICE MOSTLY SILENT, BUT DURING THE BREEDING SEASON DISPLAYING BIRDS MAY UTTER DEEP HOOTS.

Nightjar
Caprimulgus europaeus

The Nightjar is an enigmatic, long-tailed and rather hawk-like nocturnal bird. The sexes are similar but separation is possible with care. The adult male is uniformly marked with an intricate pattern of brown, grey and black markings, resembling tree bark. This cryptic plumage provides excellent camouflage when the bird is perched during the day. In flight, note the diagnostic and striking white patches near the wingtips and the corners of the tail. The eyes are large and dark, the bill is small and rather dainty. The adult female is similar to the adult male but lacks the obvious white markings on the wings and tail. The juvenile resembles the adult female.

male life-size

The male sings his unmistakable churring song at night, from a perch, which is usually a tree branch.

female
female
White markings are absent on the wings, and those on the tail are subdued when compared to the male.

A Nightjar's flight is buoyant, and generally silent save for the male's habit of clapping his wings snappily when patrolling his territory and displaying at rival males. It nests in a scrape on the ground and the incubating female is rarely flushed unless the approach is extremely close, relying on its effective camouflage and motionless posture for concealment. The male habitually perches low on tree branches during the day, taking flight at dusk to catch moths and beetles on the wing.

male

The white markings show up remarkably well in flying birds seen in twilight; when displaying, a male's flight is exaggeratedly slow and buoyant.

Factfile

LENGTH 24–27CM

WINGSPAN 57–64CM

HABITAT LOWLAND HEATHLAND, OPEN CONIFEROUS WOODLAND AND HEATHER MOORLAND.

FOOD FEEDS PRIMARILY ON MOTHS AND BEETLES CAUGHT ON THE WING.

STATUS A SUMMER MIGRANT SPECIES, PRESENT MAINLY MAY TO AUGUST, THAT BREEDS IN SUITABLE OPEN HABITAT. ABSENT FROM THE MORE NORTHERLY EXTREMES OF THE REGION. OVERWINTERS IN AFRICA.

VOICE MALE UTTERS A DISTINCTIVE AND CONSTANT CHURRING SONG.

female

Incubating birds rely on their camouflage amongst dead Bracken and leaf litter to avoid detection by predators.

Kingfisher

Alcedo atthis

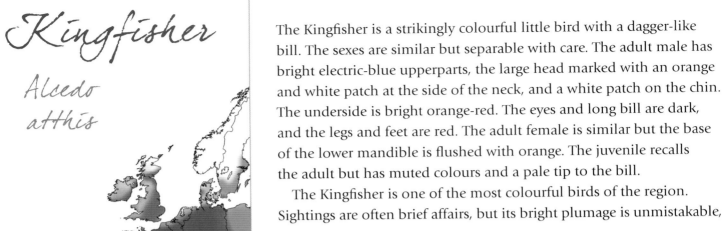

The Kingfisher is a strikingly colourful little bird with a dagger-like bill. The sexes are similar but separable with care. The adult male has bright electric-blue upperparts, the large head marked with an orange and white patch at the side of the neck, and a white patch on the chin. The underside is bright orange-red. The eyes and long bill are dark, and the legs and feet are red. The adult female is similar but the base of the lower mandible is flushed with orange. The juvenile recalls the adult but has muted colours and a pale tip to the bill.

The Kingfisher is one of the most colourful birds of the region. Sightings are often brief affairs, but its bright plumage is unmistakable,

adult

Seen in isolation and out in the open, the plumage is colourful and unmistakable. But in dappled light or shade, birds can be surprisingly hard to spot.

the bird commonly seen flying swiftly, close to the water's surface with rapid wingbeats. Flight is generally accompanied by its distinctive call. The Kingfisher requires clear water in which to feed, seeking perches directly above shallow water from which it plunge-dives for small fish. It nests in holes which it excavates in steep-sided waterside banks.

Factfile

LENGTH 16–17CM

WINGSPAN 24–26CM

HABITAT FRESHWATER HABITATS SUCH AS STREAMS, RIVERS, GRAVEL PITS, LAKES AND RESERVOIRS. OCCASIONALLY SEEN ON COASTS IN WINTER.

FOOD FEEDS PRIMARILY ON SMALL FISH.

STATUS MAINLY A SEDENTARY RESIDENT BREEDING SPECIES, PRESENT YEAR-ROUND THROUGHOUT MOST OF THE REGION, WITH THE EXCEPTION OF THE EXTREME NORTH.

VOICE IN FLIGHT, UTTERS A DIAGNOSTIC HIGH-PITCHED TIST-TSEEE.

adult

In flight, the bright sky-blue rump and centre to the back catch the eye; birds dive head-first into shallow water to catch small fish and large invertebrates such as dragonfly larvae.

adult life-size

Kingfishers are often easiest to see during the winter months, when the leaves are off the trees; the species' unmistakable outline and plumage colours make identification easy.

Swift
Apus apus

Factfile

LENGTH 16–17CM

WINGSPAN 42–48CM

HABITAT OCCURS AROUND MAN-MADE STRUCTURES, USING LOFT SPACES, CHURCH ROOFS AND FARM BUILDINGS IN WHICH TO NEST. OFTEN CONGREGATES IN AREAS WITH PROLIFIC INSECT LIFE, AND SEEN MAINLY IN THE AIR.

FOOD FEEDS ON INSECTS WHICH IT CATCHES ON THE WING.

STATUS A SUMMER BREEDING VISITOR, PRESENT MAINLY MAY TO AUGUST. WIDESPREAD THROUGHOUT MUCH OF THE REGION. OVERWINTERS IN AFRICA.

VOICE UTTERS A LOUD SCREAMING SHRILL CALL DURING THE BREEDING SEASON, TYPICALLY WITHIN GROUPS OF BIRDS IN FLIGHT.

The Swift is a common summer visitor and entirely airborne when not at the nest, eating, sleeping and even mating on the wing. The sexes are similar. The adult has uniform blackish-brown plumage. In good light, and at close range, a pale patch can be seen on the throat. In flight, the Swift has an anchor-like profile, with a streamlined, bullet-shaped body and long and slender curved wings. The tail is forked, but often held closed in active flight. The eye and small bill are dark. The juvenile is similar to the adult but with darker plumage, a lighter throat patch and pale forehead.

The Swift is mostly seen in small groups gliding on stiffly held wings; when required the wingbeats are rapid and whirring. A fast and aerobatic flyer, its large gape helps it catch flying insects on the wing. It nests in buildings, usually in roofs and loft spaces, constructing a shallow cup of plant material and feathers. The young develop quickly and migrate to the African wintering grounds with the adults.

adult

The outline in flight is distinctive with narrow swept-back wings and a forked tail that is fanned when birds are turning or banking.

Often seen in loose flocks near colonies and over areas where the feeding is good.

adults

Although sharp claws allow birds to cling onto vertical surfaces, the feet and legs are not designed for walking; consequently, nesting birds can only shuffle along at best.

adult life-size

Wryneck
Jynx torquilla

The Wryneck is a curious member of the woodpecker family, its plumage affording it superb camouflage. The sexes are similar. The adult has mainly grey-brown upperparts which, on close inspection, reveal a fine mosaic of grey, brown, black and buff, recalling tree bark. The underside is pale and marked with a pattern of fine dark spots and barring. Note the yellow flush to the throat and flanks, and the dark stripes running through the eye and down the crown, nape and centre of the back. The long tail is grey with a series of narrow dark bars. The eye is dark and the bill sharply pointed.

adult

Seen on migration, birds are typically unobtrusive and feed on the ground, and are often reasonably indifferent to human observers.

Factfile

LENGTH 16–17CM

WINGSPAN 25–27CM

HABITAT **FAVOURS OPEN WOODLAND, PARKS AND GARDENS IN WHICH TO BREED. SEEN ON MIGRATION AT OTHER TIMES, AND CLASSICALLY ENCOUNTERED IN COASTAL SCRUB.**

FOOD **FEEDS PRIMARILY ON ANTS, ALTHOUGH IT WILL CONSUME OTHER INSECTS.**

STATUS **A SUMMER BREEDING SPECIES IN MAINLAND EUROPE AND PARTS OF SCANDINAVIA, PRESENT MAINLY MAY TO AUGUST. A RARE PASSAGE MIGRANT IN COASTAL BRITAIN AND ELSEWHERE IN NORTHWEST EUROPE. OVERWINTERS MAINLY IN AFRICA.**

VOICE **MOSTLY SILENT. CAN UTTER A PIPING *PEE-PEE-PEE* IN DEFENCE OF TERRITORY.**

The juvenile is similar to the adult but the crown stripe is less well defined.

The Wryneck is a slim-bodied bird that is often seen on the ground hunting for ants and other insects. Alert birds adopt an upright posture and swivel their heads around. It nests in trees, in the old nest holes of other species, and also uses crevices in walls and banks.

adult life-size

Green Woodpecker
Picus viridis

female life-size

Before it commits to feeding on the ground, where it is potentially vulnerable to predators, a bird will often scan around from a perch, looking out for danger.

juvenile

The plumage is heavily streaked and spotted by comparison to an adult bird; all birds are extremely wary when feeding on the ground, lifting the head periodically to check for danger.

The Green Woodpecker is a rather timid and nervous bird that is often tricky to observe at close quarters. The sexes are similar but separation is possible with care. The adult male has bright olive-green upperparts, a bright yellow rump and dark primary feathers spotted with white (the latter two features are most obvious in flight); the underparts are whitish. The head is marked with a red crown, a bold black mask patch surrounding the eye, and a red-centred black moustachial stripe. The large dagger-like bill is grey with a yellowish flush to the lower mandible. The adult female is similar but lacks the red centre to the moustachial stripe. The juvenile is similar to the adult but heavily marked with dark streaks on the head and underside, and white spots on the back.

male

Factfile

LENGTH 32–34CM   WINGSPAN 40–50CM

HABITAT **WOODLANDS, PARKS, ORCHARDS AND GARDENS.**

FOOD FEEDS ALMOST EXCLUSIVELY ON ANTS AND THEIR LARVAE; SOME SEEDS AND FRUITS.

STATUS **WIDESPREAD RESIDENT BREEDING SPECIES PRESENT YEAR-ROUND THROUGHOUT THE REGION, WITH THE EXCEPTION OF NORTHERN SCANDINAVIA AND IRELAND.**

VOICE UTTERS A DISTINCTIVE LOUD AND YELPING SONG, COMPRISING A DOZEN OR MORE SHARP, RAPID NOTES, OFTEN REFERRED TO AS 'YAFFLING'.

Actively furtive when nesting, and birds are very reluctant to reveal the nest hole's location when they know observers are nearby. In poor light, the male's red centre to the 'moustache' is easily overlooked.

This is a shy bird that takes to the wing at the slightest sign of danger. Its flight is low and distinctively undulating, often accompanied by its yaffling call. The Green Woodpecker feeds almost exclusively on the ground, using its long tongue to extract ants from their nests. It nests in holes that it excavates in trees and can often be observed climbing up trunks using its long tail for support.

Grey-headed Woodpecker

Picus canus

Factfile

LENGTH 25–28CM

WINGSPAN 38–40CM

HABITAT OPEN DECIDUOUS WOODLAND AND MIXED WOODLANDS.

FOOD FEEDS PRIMARILY ON ANTS AND OTHER INSECTS; SOME FRUITS AND SEEDS.

STATUS RESIDENT BREEDING SPECIES, PRESENT YEAR-ROUND IN AREAS OF EXTENSIVE WOODLAND IN CENTRAL AND NORTHEAST EUROPE. ABSENT FROM BRITAIN AND IRELAND.

VOICE UTTERS A SERIES OF DESCENDING PIPING NOTES. HAS A SHORT DRUMMING PATTERN.

This is a brightly coloured woodpecker similar to, but smaller than, Green Woodpecker. The sexes are similar but separable with care. The adult male is bright green on the back and upperwings, the latter having dark brownish primaries marked with white barring. Note the bright yellow rump, which is most obvious in flight. The head and underparts are lightish grey, flushed yellow on the flanks and below. The underwing is dark grey and marked with white barring. The head is adorned with a bright red forecrown and a narrow black moustachial stripe. The bill is grey and dagger-like. The adult female is similar to the male but lacks the red forecrown and is duller overall. The juvenile has scruffy brown plumage.

female life-size

The absence of red on the crown allows separation from the male.

male

Compared to a Green Woodpecker, the head is rather plain and relatively unmarked except for the dark lores and 'moustache'.

The Grey-headed Woodpecker is found in similar habitat to Green Woodpecker but tolerates higher altitudes. It excavates holes in mature trees in which to nest.

Spends much of its time feeding on the ground, but also seeks out insects from the bark of trees and occasionally visits garden tables and feeders during the winter.

Middle Spotted Woodpecker

Leiopicus medius

This species is similar to a Great Spotted Woodpecker but appreciably smaller and with a more delicate bill. The sexes are similar but separable with care. The adult male has predominantly black upperparts and a black tail, marked with a large oblong white patch on the shoulder, and white barring on the primary feathers. The outer tail feathers are white. These markings are obvious in flight and at rest, and give the bird its pied appearance. The face and throat are white and gradually grade into light underparts, which are flushed with yellow from the breast and adorned with dark streaks. The nape is black. Note the black patch below the cheeks, which does not connect with the base of the grey bill, and the diagnostic bright red crown. The adult female is similar but the red crown is duller and less extensive. The juvenile recalls an adult female but is duller still with less well-defined markings.

The stronghold for this species is the mature deciduous forests of mid-central Europe. It excavates a hole in decaying wood in which to nest. It is rarely heard drumming, and this behaviour does not form part of its territorial display.

Often unobtrusive when feeding, shuffling behind a branch to avoid detection by an intruder into its territory.

male life-size

The red crown invites confusion with a juvenile Great Spotted (seen in this plumage mainly June–August) but note a Middle Spotted's appreciably smaller size, complete absence of black on the crown, and heavily streaked flanks.

Factfile

LENGTH 20–22CM

WINGSPAN 33–34CM

HABITAT **FAVOURS AREAS OF DECIDUOUS WOODLAND AND PARKLAND, PARTICULARLY MATURE OAK, HORNBEAM AND ELM.**

FOOD **FEEDS MAINLY ON INSECTS; OCCASIONALLY SEEDS.**

STATUS **SEDENTARY RESIDENT BREEDING SPECIES FOUND YEAR-ROUND IN SUITABLE HABITAT IN MAINLAND EUROPE. ABSENT FROM THE BRITISH ISLES AND SCANDINAVIA.**

VOICE **UTTERS A LOUD, HIGH-PITCHED SCREECHING CALL. DRUMMING IS RARE.**

male

Great Spotted Woodpecker

Dendrocopos major

Factfile

LENGTH 23–24CM WINGSPAN 34–39CM

HABITAT PREFERS MATURE DECIDUOUS WOODLAND, BUT A VERSATILE SPECIES THAT CAN BE FOUND IN A VARIETY OF HABITATS WITH TREES, INCLUDING PARKS AND GARDENS.

FOOD FEEDS PRIMARILY ON INSECTS BUT WILL ALSO TAKE EGGS AND NESTLINGS OF OTHER BIRDS. SOME SEEDS AND FRUITS. A COMMON VISITOR TO GARDEN TABLES AND FEEDERS.

STATUS WIDESPREAD RESIDENT BREEDING SPECIES, PRESENT YEAR-ROUND. THE COMMONEST WOODPECKER SPECIES ENCOUNTERED THROUGHOUT THE REGION IN SUITABLE HABITATS. OCCASIONAL VISITOR TO IRELAND.

VOICE UTTERS A LOUD, HIGH-PITCHED *TCHICK* ALARM CALL. MALES FREQUENTLY 'DRUM' DURING THE SPRING WHEN ESTABLISHING BREEDING TERRITORIES.

juvenile

Juveniles are often accompanied by their parents for the first few weeks after fledging.

The archetypal common pied woodpecker. The sexes are similar but separable with care. The adult male has mainly black upperparts and grubby white underparts. It has elongated white shoulder patches and narrow white barring towards the black tail. The head displays white cheeks and a white throat; the black cap and nape are connected to a black stripe that runs from the base of the bill. Note the small red nape patch and the bright red vent. The dagger-like bill, legs and feet are grey. In flight, the white barring on the wings and white shoulder patches are obvious. The adult female is similar, but lacks the red nape patch. The juvenile recalls the adult male but has a conspicuous red crown and the vent colouration is duller.

A Great Spotted Woodpecker's flight is characteristically undulating, rising on rapid wingbeats, followed by a closed-wing glide and dip. It excavates holes in rotten tree trunks and wood, both for food and to create chambers in which to nest. The territorial 'song' is produced by the bird 'drumming', hammering the tip of its bill rapidly and loudly on a tree trunk. This is the most likely woodpecker to visit garden tables and feeders.

The bold white shoulder patch and spots on the wings are striking in flight.

male

A female lacks the male's red nape but it can be surprisingly hard to determine the presence or absence of this feature, except at just the right angle.

female

male life-size
Decaying branches, rich in insect larvae, are ideal feeding locations. The claws and shape of the foot provide a good grip, and the tail is used as a support.

Lesser Spotted Woodpecker
Dendrocopos minor

The Lesser Spotted Woodpecker is a small and rather shy bird that is easy to overlook. The sexes are similar but separation is possible with care. The adult male has predominantly black upperparts, the upperwings marked with a series of white bars that align with barring on the back and create a ladder-back appearance when the bird is at rest. The underparts are grubby-white and marked with subtle dark streaking. The face and throat are white; the nape is black and a black stripe runs from the base of the bill, below the cheeks and towards the nape. Note the colourful white-flecked red crown, reminiscent of juvenile Great Spotted Woodpecker. The bill, legs and feet are grey. In flight, the bird appears overall black above, the series of bold white bars being contrasting and conspicuous. The adult female recalls the male but has a white crown. The juvenile is similar to the adult female.

This is the smallest pied woodpecker in the region, and its size and timid nature make it a difficult species to observe. It is often seen feeding on insects on the outermost branches of trees. It excavates a tree hole, commonly on the underside of a branch, in which to nest.

female

The plumage becomes increasingly grubby and worn as the breeding season progresses; the white (not red) crown distinguishes a female from a male.

male life-size

Absolutely tiny by woodpecker standards and people are often amazed at their small size when they see one for the first time.

Factfile

LENGTH 14–15CM

WINGSPAN 25–27CM

HABITAT **DECIDUOUS WOODLAND AND PARKLAND. SHOWS A PREFERENCE FOR COMMON ALDER.**

FOOD **FEEDS ALMOST EXCLUSIVELY ON INSECTS, BOTH ADULTS AND LARVAE. RARELY VISITS GARDEN FEEDERS.**

STATUS **RESIDENT BREEDING SPECIES, PRESENT YEAR-ROUND AND WIDESPREAD THROUGHOUT EUROPE IN SUITABLE HABITATS. NUMBERS IN BRITAIN ARE IN SHARP DECLINE, AND IT IS NOW THINLY DISTRIBUTED. ABSENT FROM IRELAND.**

VOICE **MALE UTTERS A RAPID SERIES OF HIGH-PITCHED PIPING WHISTLES, *KEE-KEE-KEE*, DURING THE SPRING. DRUMMING IS RAPID, HIGH-PITCHED AND RATHER FAINT WITH A LONG DURATION, AVERAGING 24 STRIKES PER BOUT.**

Golden Oriole
Oriolus oriolus

The Golden Oriole is an unmistakable, brightly coloured and handsome bird, more commonly heard than seen. The sexes are separable. The adult male has predominantly striking bright yellow plumage, with contrastingly black upperwings and a black tail. The face is marked with a small dark patch, running from the base of the bill and through the dark eye. The bill is reddish. The legs and feet are grey. The overall plumage pattern of the adult female is similar to the adult male, but the bright yellow plumage is replaced with a much more muted yellowish-green and the underparts are pale and marked with a subtle streaking. The juvenile is similar to the adult female, but the underparts are more heavily streaked.

Factfile

LENGTH 22–24CM   WINGSPAN 44–47CM

HABITAT OPEN WOODLAND, COPSES, PARKS AND GARDENS.

FOOD FEEDS ON INSECTS, LARVAE, BERRIES AND FRUITS.

STATUS MIGRANT SUMMER BREEDING SPECIES, PRESENT MAINLY MAY TO AUGUST, WITH A SCATTERED DISTRIBUTION THROUGHOUT MAINLAND EUROPE. LARGELY ABSENT FROM BRITAIN AND SCANDINAVIA AS A BREEDING SPECIES, BUT SEEN AS A RARE PASSAGE MIGRANT ON THE COAST. OVERWINTERS IN AFRICA.

VOICE SONG IS A VARIABLE, TROPICAL-SOUNDING, RICH AND FLUTY *WEE-LO-WEEOW*. ALSO UTTERS HARSH DISYLLABIC SCREECHING CALLS.

male life-size
A male's stunning yellow and black plumage is instantly recognisable. However, birds are surprisingly easy to overlook when perched amongst dappled foliage.

female
The Golden Oriole is a furtive woodland species that is tricky to observe.

Red-backed Shrike

Lanius collurio

Often perches prominently on the top of a bush.

juvenile

female

Plumage recalls that of a male but the colours are muted and the dark markings are less distinct.

The Red-backed Shrike is a predatory songbird with a powerful hook-tipped bill. The sexes are dissimilar. The adult male has a reddish-brown back; the underparts are whitish with a pinkish tinge to the breast and flanks. The nape and head cap are blue-grey, and a distinctive bold black mask-stripe runs from the base of the bill, through the eye to the ear coverts. The bill is black and the legs are dark grey. In flight, note the grey rump and striking white sides to the tail base. The adult female is similar, but with duller colouration; the dark eye-patch is less well defined and the underparts are marked with dark vermiculations. The juvenile has brown upperparts, the dark- and pale-edged feathers giving the back a scaly appearance. The underparts are pale, the feather fringes similarly dark-edged.

This is a predatory bird that spends lengthy periods perched on low vegetation on the look-out for suitable prey items. The Red-backed Shrike swoops low and rapidly, returning to the perch to either consume a prey item or create a food larder by impaling it on a thorn. It constructs a nest comprising a loose cup of vegetation in a low bush.

Striking markings and colourful plumage make for easy identification; for all its small size, this a bold and fearless predator.

male life-size

Factfile

LENGTH 16–18CM

WINGSPAN 24–27CM

HABITAT FAVOURS OPEN GROUND WITH BUSHY VEGETATION SUCH AS HEATHLAND, COMMONS AND SCRUB.

FOOD FEEDS PRIMARILY ON INSECTS BUT WILL ALSO TAKE SMALL BIRDS, REPTILES AND MAMMALS.

STATUS MIGRANT SUMMER BREEDING VISITOR TO MAINLAND EUROPE, PRESENT MAINLY MAY TO SEPTEMBER. NUMBERS HAVE DECLINED IN RECENT YEARS AND NOW LARGELY EXTINCT AS A BREEDING SPECIES IN NORTHWEST EUROPE, BUT STILL SEEN AS A SCARCE PASSAGE MIGRANT. OVERWINTERS IN AFRICA.

VOICE WHEN AGITATED, UTTERS A HARSH *TCHEK*.

Great Grey Shrike

Lanius excubitor

The Great Grey Shrike is a robust, predatory passerine with a hawk-like, hook-tipped bill. The sexes are similar. In harsh light, and at a distance, the adult can appear very black-and-white. When seen close up, note the grey cap and back, and pale underparts. It has a long black tail, marked with white on the outer edges. The face is adorned with a bold black mask-stripe running from the base of the bill and through the eye. The uppersides of the wings are primarily black and marked with a central white patch, most obvious in flight. The juvenile is similar to the adult, but the black plumage appears more 'washed-out' and the underparts display faint barring.

This is a rather elusive and strongly territorial bird that can spend long periods in deep cover. It is a predatory species that hunts by perching on a suitable vantage point, then pouncing on prey on the ground, or snatching small birds from the air. A Great Grey Shrike will impale prey on thorns or barbed wire to assist dissection or to store for future consumption.

Striking white patches on the otherwise black wings catch the eye, even in distant flying birds; note the proportionately long, white-sided black tail.

adult

adult life-size

In good light, birds look strikingly white at a distance; at close range the contrasting black elements of the plumage can be appreciated along with the powerful bill that is used to dismember prey.

Factfile

LENGTH 22–26CM

WINGSPAN 30–34CM

HABITAT HEATHLAND AND OTHER SIMILAR OPEN COUNTRYSIDE WITH SHRUB AND TREE COVER.

FOOD FEEDS PRIMARILY ON INSECTS BUT WILL ALSO TAKE SMALL BIRDS, REPTILES AND MAMMALS.

STATUS PRESENT YEAR-ROUND IN EASTERN MAINLAND EUROPE. MIGRANT BREEDING SPECIES TO MUCH OF SCANDINAVIA; BIRDS PRESENT MAINLY MAY TO SEPTEMBER. MOST MIGRATE SOUTH AND WEST IN AUTUMN; SOME REACH BRITAIN, WHERE IT IS A SCARCE WINTER VISITOR, PRESENT MAINLY OCTOBER TO MARCH.

VOICE UTTERS A HARSH TRILLING CALL.

Chough
Pyrrhocorax pyrrhocorax

The Chough is a uniformly dark, Jackdaw-sized corvid, instantly recognisable by its bright red downcurved bill. The sexes are similar. The adult has black plumage overall which, in good light, displays a conspicuous sheen. The bright red bill colour and reddish-pink legs are obvious and diagnostic. In flight, note the broad wings and long, finger-like primaries at the wingtips. The juvenile recalls the adult but the bill is dull yellow and the legs are more subdued in colour.

Extremely vocal in flight, with birds calling to one another in a sociable manner.

adult

adult

At certain angles, the feathers on the back and neck in particular have a subtle bluish-purple gloss.

The Chough's long bill is used to probe the ground for ants and other terrestrial invertebrates. An expert flyer, it can often be seen gliding, twisting and turning aerobatically on updrafts and thermals. Choughs are often seen in small family parties, with the birds almost always calling in flight. The species nests in rock crevices, constructing a lined platform of twigs. Its numbers have declined in recent years, most likely because of a reduction in traditional grazing practices on coastal grassland.

adult

Shows masterful control and manoeuvrability in the air, and able to soar effortlessly on its broad wings; splayed primaries facilitate fine control over lift and direction.

Factfile

LENGTH 38–40CM

WINGSPAN 73–90CM

HABITAT ASSOCIATED ALMOST EXCLUSIVELY WITH STEEP, GRASS-TOPPED COASTAL CLIFFS.

FOOD SOIL-DWELLING INVERTEBRATES, SEEDS, GRAIN AND FRUITS.

STATUS SCARCE RESIDENT BREEDING SPECIES, PRESENT YEAR-ROUND. RESTRICTED TO LOCALISED SUITABLE HABITAT, PRIMARILY ON THE WEST COASTS OF BRITAIN AND IRELAND, BUT ALSO NORTHWEST FRANCE. SOME SMALL AND LOCALISED INLAND POPULATIONS ALSO OCCUR.

VOICE UTTERS A DISTINCTIVE YELPING *CHYAH*, GENERALLY ACCOMPANIED BY AN AGITATED FLEXING AND FLICKING OF WINGS WHEN THE CALLER IS STANDING.

adult life-size
The bright red legs and downcurved bill are unique to the species and diagnostic features in field identification.

Magpie
Pica pica

The Magpie is a common bird, its distinctive long tail and black-and-white plumage making it instantly recognisable. The sexes are similar. The adult has mostly glossy black plumage with a contrasting white belly and patch of pure white on the shoulder of the closed wing. The bill is black and powerful, the culmen noticeably curved. The legs are dark. In flight, note the broad, short wings and the black-fringed pure white primaries. Also note the long black tail, which gives the bird a

adult

The striking plumage pattern and outline make it hard to confuse with any other species. Flight is often accompanied by its chattering call.

Factfile

LENGTH **45–50CM**

WINGSPAN **52–60CM**

HABITAT **FAVOURS LIGHTLY WOODED HABITATS INCLUDING OPEN WOODLAND, PARKS, GARDENS, FARMLAND AND URBAN AREAS.**

FOOD **A VERSATILE SPECIES THAT FEEDS ON A VARIETY OF CARRION, INVERTEBRATES, SEEDS AND FRUIT. ALSO A NOTORIOUS NEST RAIDER, TAKING THE EGGS AND YOUNG CHICKS OF SMALLER SONGBIRDS.**

STATUS **COMMON AND WIDESPREAD RESIDENT BREEDING SPECIES, PRESENT YEAR-ROUND THROUGHOUT THE REGION.**

VOICE **UTTERS A LOUD, RATTLING ALARM CALL.**

diagnostic outline. In good light, a beautiful bluish-green iridescent sheen is commonly visible. The juvenile is similar to the adult.

The Magpie is a widespread and familiar bird. An opportunistic feeder and an enthusiastic scavenger, it is often seen on roadsides taking advantage of roadkill and it possesses an amazingly well-developed road sense. It nests in trees, constructing a robust platform of twigs, often with a protective dome, which is frequently used year after year. It is commonly observed in small groups outside the breeding season.

Quick to take advantage of any new source of food such as discarded picnic scraps at roadside pull-offs and motorway service stations.

adult

adult life-size

Bold white markings contrast with the otherwise mainly black plumage; in good light, note the bluish sheen to the wings.

Jay

Garrulus glandarius

The Jay is a handsome and furtive woodland bird, commonly heard more often than seen. The sexes are similar. The adult has predominantly pinkish-buff plumage; the rump, undertail and lower belly are white. The longish tail is black, and the broad rounded wings display black-and-white on the primary flight feathers. A beautiful patch of blue, with black-and-white chequer-board markings is situated on the upperwing coverts. This feature is obvious both in flight and on the folded wings of standing birds. The head has a pale forecrown with dark streaks, and a black 'moustache'. The bill is dark and the legs are flesh coloured. In flight, note the conspicuous white rump and contrastingly dark tail.

The juvenile is similar to the adult, but the streaking on the crown and moustachial markings are less obvious.

The Jay is a wary bird that takes flight at the slightest hint of human presence, its disappearing white rump often accompanied by the raucous alarm

With even a partial or distant view, the white rump is the species' most striking feature in flight.

adult

adult life-size

Plumage colours are subtly understated except for the striking chequered blue patch on the wings.

Factfile

LENGTH 33–35CM

WINGSPAN 52–58CM

HABITAT ASSOCIATED WITH MATURE DECIDUOUS WOODLAND, PARTICULARLY WHERE OAKS PREDOMINATE. ALSO FOUND IN PARKS, AND AN OCCASIONAL GARDEN VISITOR.

FOOD ACORNS FORM AN IMPORTANT COMPONENT OF THE JAY'S DIET. ALSO FEEDS ON INVERTEBRATES, SEEDS, FRUITS AND THE EGGS AND CHICKS OF OTHER BIRDS.

STATUS WIDESPREAD RESIDENT BREEDING SPECIES, PRESENT YEAR-ROUND THROUGHOUT THE REGION IN SUITABLE HABITATS.

VOICE UTTERS A DIAGNOSTIC HARSH AND FAR-CARRYING RAUCOUS CALL.

call. An individual Jay may bury thousands of acorns during the autumn as a food larder for the winter months. It nests in trees, constructing a lined twig pile close to the trunk. It is a sedentary breeding species in the main, but some irruptive migration can occur when the crop of acorns is poor.

adult

Spends a lot of time sitting unobtrusively amongst foliage where it is easily overlooked.

adult

In the autumn months, strongly associated with oak trees and their fallen crop of acorns, which birds collect avidly.

Jackdaw
Corvus monedula

This the most common and widespread small corvid in the region. The sexes are similar. The adult at first glance appears to have uniformly dark charcoal-grey plumage. When seen in good light or under closer inspection, the plumage is darkest on the upperwings and crown, and the nape and throat are lighter silvery-grey. The eye is pale blue-grey, almost white, the robust bill is black and the legs are dark. The juvenile is similar to the adult, but the eye is darker and duller and the plumage displays a brown tinge.

The Jackdaw is a familiar and successful species that is capable of adapting to a range of environments and exploiting most food sources. It is often bold and approachable in urban environments. It nests colonially in a variety of locations including rock crevices, trees, old buildings and even chimney pots. It constructs an untidy, soft-lined platform of twigs.

adult life-size

This is the smallest of the dark corvid species with a relatively stubby bill and a diagnostic pale eye in adult birds.

Nordic race adult

Birds found from northern Scandinavia eastwards have paler heads than birds from elsewhere, and a variable pale half-collar.

Factfile

LENGTH 31–34CM

WINGSPAN 67–74CM

HABITAT A VERSATILE SPECIES, FOUND IN A VARIETY OF RURAL AND URBAN HABITATS, FROM COASTAL CLIFFS AND FARMLAND TO GARDENS AND URBAN PARKS.

FOOD OMNIVOROUS, AND CAN EXPLOIT MOST FOOD SOURCES.

STATUS COMMON AND WIDESPREAD RESIDENT BREEDING SPECIES, PRESENT YEAR-ROUND THROUGHOUT THE REGION, WITH THE EXCEPTION OF THE EXTREME NORTH.

VOICE UTTERS A SHARP AND OFTEN REPEATED *CHACK*.

adult

adult

Aerobatic and manoeuvrable in flight, and capable of soaring and hovering briefly too; often seen in flocks outside the breeding season.

Juveniles are rarely seen away from the company of adult birds and help swell the numbers in post-breeding flocks.

juvenile

Rook
Corvus frugilegus

The Rook is a common and gregarious farmland bird, often encountered in large flocks or at nesting colonies. The sexes are similar. The adult has uniformly black plumage that can display a purplish iridescence when seen at certain angles and in good light. The eye is dark and the large bill is dark grey, almost black. At the base of the bill, a diagnostic light-coloured bare skin patch allows certain separation from similar corvid species. The rather peaked crown is also a useful aid to accurate identification. In flight, note the broad wings, the long, finger-like primary feathers at the wingtips and the rounded tail. The juvenile is similar to the adult, but lacks the bare skin patch at the base of the bill and can be confused with Carrion Crow.

The bill is proportionately very long by the standards of other black corvids; bare skin at the base is an adaption to their ground-probing feeding habits.

adult

Factfile

LENGTH 43–48CM

WINGSPAN 81–99CM

HABITAT ASSOCIATED PRIMARILY WITH AGRICULTURAL LAND AND ADJACENT WOODLAND AREAS.

FOOD DIET TRADITIONALLY COMPRISES A MIXTURE OF SOIL-DWELLING INVERTEBRATES AND AGRICULTURAL SEED. LIKE MOST CORVIDS, IT IS AN OPPORTUNIST FEEDER AND OCCASIONALLY VISITS GARDEN TABLES AND SCAVENGES OPEN BINS.

STATUS WIDESPREAD RESIDENT BREEDING SPECIES, PRESENT YEAR-ROUND THROUGHOUT MOST OF THE REGION, EXCEPT THE FAR NORTH WHERE BIRDS MIGRATE TO AVOID EXTREME WEATHER.

VOICE UTTERS A REPETITIVE RAW KAW-KAW-KAW.

adult

The broad wings and splayed primaries give the Rook excellent control and manoeuvrability in flight.

Primarily a ground feeder, the Rook uses its long bill to probe the ground for beetle larvae, earthworms and seeds. It nests in large colonies in the tops of tall trees, constructing large and untidy twig platforms. These colonies are usually loud and raucous. Winter roosts can number many hundreds of birds, and populations are boosted in more temperate regions at this time by migrants from further afield.

juvenile

The bill size invites confusion with a Carrion Crow. Wing shape and association with adults offer clues to the identity of juvenile Rooks.

adult life-size

In spring, displaying birds are very vocal; when calling they typically stretch their necks out and raise their tails.

Carrion Crow
Corvus corone

The Carrion Crow is an iconic member of the crow family and the most likely corvid to be encountered either singly or in pairs. The sexes are similar. The adult has uniformly black plumage that displays a glossy sheen when seen in good light. The black bill is large, stout and powerful, and note the feathered base which allows separation from the adult Rook. The eyes and legs are also black. In flight, the wings are broad, with long, finger-like primary feathers at the wingtips. The tail is rather square-ended. The juvenile is similar to the adult.

Far less gregarious than the similar Rook or Jackdaw, the Carrion Crow is a rather wary bird that is widely persecuted. Flight is strong and direct. Pairs are typically faithful throughout the year, and the species generally only forms flocks at winter roosts and during springtime displays. It nests in trees, constructing a well-lined twig platform.

The wingbeats are powerful but fast level flight looks overall rather laboured.

adult
The uniform black plumage and bill size and shape offer clues to the identity of a Carrion Crow; the call is also distinctive and diagnostic although subtle regional variation exists.

adult

Carrion Crows are skilful fliers but lack the manoeuvrability of a Rook and soaring elegance of a Raven.

The feathers are subtly iridescent but lack the obvious oily sheen seen in both Rook and Raven.

adult

adult life-size

Factfile

LENGTH 43–50CM

WINGSPAN 90–100CM

HABITAT TRADITIONALLY ASSOCIATED WITH OPEN FARMLAND, BUT NOWADAYS ALSO FOUND IN A VARIETY OF RURAL AND EVEN URBAN HABITATS.

FOOD AN OMNIVOROUS AND OPPORTUNISTIC FEEDER, ITS DIET INCLUDES INVERTEBRATES, GRAINS, CARRION AND THE EGGS AND NESTLINGS OF OTHER BIRDS. A REGULAR VISITOR TO REFUSE TIPS AND A SKILLED BIN RAIDER.

STATUS COMMON AND WIDESPREAD RESIDENT BREEDING SPECIES, PRESENT YEAR-ROUND THROUGHOUT MUCH OF THE REGION. LARGELY ABSENT FROM IRELAND, NORTHERN SCOTLAND AND SCANDINAVIA WHERE ITS COUSIN THE HOODED CROW PREDOMINATES.

VOICE UTTERS A RAUCOUS *CREEAA-CREEAA-CREEAA* CALL.

Hooded Crow

Corvus cornix

adult

In the winter months, small groups congregate in areas of good feeding, such as seashores, and there is always a lot of vocal interaction between birds.

Depending on the light, the pale elements of the plumage can appear subtly suffused with lilac or even pink. In terms of size and overall outline, a Hooded Crow is the same as its Carrion cousin.

Factfile

LENGTH 43–50CM

WINGSPAN 90–100CM

HABITAT OCCURS IN A WIDE RANGE OF MAINLY RURAL HABITATS INCLUDING FARMLAND AND MOORLAND; COASTAL AREAS ARE A PARTICULAR FAVOURITE DURING THE WINTER MONTHS.

FOOD AN OMNIVOROUS AND OPPORTUNISTIC FEEDER, ITS DIET INCLUDES INVERTEBRATES, GRAINS, CARRION AND THE EGGS AND NESTLINGS OF OTHER BIRDS.

STATUS NORTHERN AND EASTERN COUNTERPART OF CARRION CROW AND A RESIDENT BREEDING SPECIES, PRESENT YEAR-ROUND. IT RANGES FROM IRELAND AND NORTHERN SCOTLAND TO SCANDINAVIA AND EASTERN EUROPE.

VOICE UTTERS A RAUCOUS *CREEAA-CREEAA-CREEAA* CALL.

Formerly treated as a geographically separated subspecies of Carrion Crow but now given full species status. The sexes are similar. Structurally similar to Carrion Crow, the adult has mainly grey body plumage, displaying a subtle lilac tinge in certain lights. The wings and tail are black, as are the head, the eye and the stout bill. The dark head plumage extends past the throat and forms an untidy bib. The legs are dark. In flight, note the sharp contrast between the grey body and the black wings, tail and head. The juvenile is similar to the adult.

The Hooded Crow is a wary species that is generally far less gregarious than other corvids. Interbreeding with Carrion Crow does occur where the ranges of the two species overlap. An opportunistic feeder, its varied diet allows it to take advantage of a number of food sources from carrion to live prey and scavenging refuse. It nests in trees, constructing a well-lined twig platform.

adult

Like their Carrion cousin, Hooded Crows are inventive feeders and some have learned to drop seashore molluscs from a height in order to smash their hard, protective shells.

adult life-size

adult

These hardy birds are adapted to harsh environments and can tolerate snow and ice during the winter months.

Raven
Corvus corax

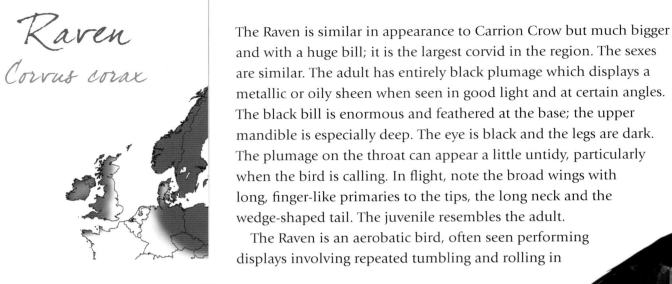

The Raven is similar in appearance to Carrion Crow but much bigger and with a huge bill; it is the largest corvid in the region. The sexes are similar. The adult has entirely black plumage which displays a metallic or oily sheen when seen in good light and at certain angles. The black bill is enormous and feathered at the base; the upper mandible is especially deep. The eye is black and the legs are dark. The plumage on the throat can appear a little untidy, particularly when the bird is calling. In flight, note the broad wings with long, finger-like primaries to the tips, the long neck and the wedge-shaped tail. The juvenile resembles the adult.

The Raven is an aerobatic bird, often seen performing displays involving repeated tumbling and rolling in

adult life-size

The massive bill is put to good use when scavenging at the carcasses of dead animals. Note the extensive bristly feathers that shroud the nostrils.

flight, particularly during the breeding season. It is an intelligent bird that is generally very wary and alert, and often seen in pairs and small family groups. The Raven pairs for life and seeks lofty nesting sites on a crag or in a tree, constructing large, multi-layered platforms of twigs and branches.

adult

Splayed primary feathers and a spread tail provide extra lift and manoeuvrability for soaring birds.

Birds are usually very vocal in flight; the long, wedge-shaped tail is diagnostic in an all-dark bird of this size.

adult

adult

On the ground a Raven stands head-and-shoulders above a Carrion Crow, with the proportionately thick neck and massive bill serving as additional clues to identity.

Factfile

LENGTH 55–65CM

WINGSPAN 115–130CM

HABITAT OCCURS IN A VARIETY OF HABITATS INCLUDING RUGGED COASTLINES, CRAGGY UPLAND AREAS AND ROLLING WOODED COUNTRYSIDE.

FOOD A LARGE PART OF ITS DIET CONSISTS OF CARRION, BUT IT ALSO PREYS ON SMALL BIRDS AND MAMMALS; SOME FRUITS AND SEEDS.

STATUS RESIDENT BREEDING SPECIES PRESENT YEAR-ROUND IN SUITABLE HABITATS THROUGHOUT THE REGION. STRONGHOLDS ARE SCANDINAVIA AND THE WEST OF BRITAIN AND IRELAND. NUMBERS ARE RECOVERING FROM RECENT DECLINES AND ITS RANGE IS EXPANDING BACK INTO PREVIOUSLY POPULATED AREAS.

VOICE UTTERS A DIAGNOSTIC LOUD AND GUTTERAL *CRONK*. ESPECIALLY VOCAL WHEN IN FLIGHT.

Blue Tit
Cyanistes caeruleus

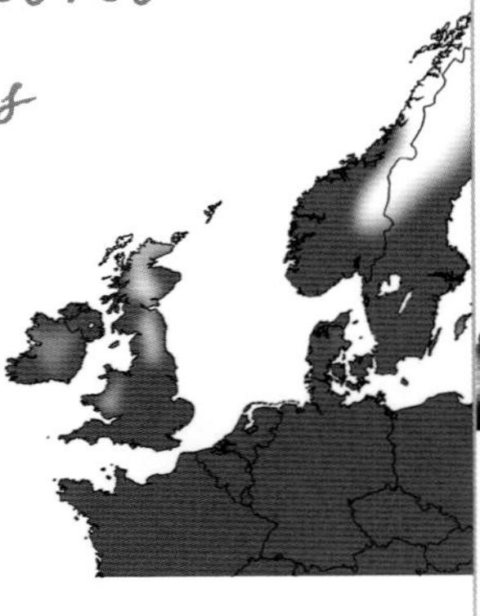

adult life-size

The white face and supercilium are neatly framed by black and blue, giving the bird a smart appearance.

The Blue Tit is a colourful little bird and a regular visitor to garden feeders. The sexes are similar, and separating them is tricky, but males are generally more brightly coloured than females. The adult has a compact body with a greenish back; the wings and tail are blue and the underparts are bright yellow. Note the subtle white wingbar,

A Blue Tit is most colourful during the winter months; the plumage becomes worn and faded as the breeding season progresses.

adult

Blue Tits are inquisitive birds, and are often seen searching for invertebrates in nooks and crannies around houses, and in tree bark crevices.

adult

Aerobatic and manoeuvrable in flight, birds are able to hover and land with precision on even the most awkward of perches.

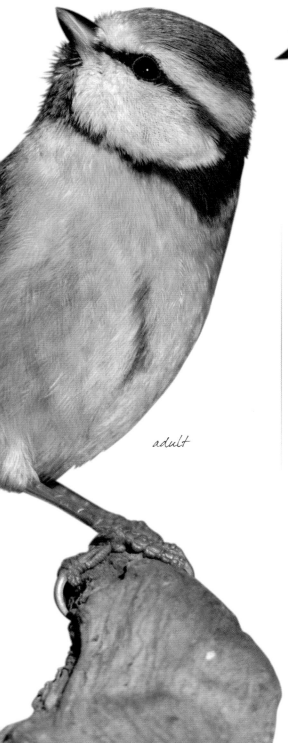

adult

Factfile

LENGTH 11–12CM

WINGSPAN 18–20CM

HABITAT FAVOURS AREAS OF DECIDUOUS WOODLAND, PARKS AND GARDENS. A COMMON VISITOR TO GARDEN TABLES AND FEEDERS.

FOOD FEEDS ON INVERTEBRATES, FRUITS AND SEEDS.

STATUS COMMON AND WIDESPREAD RESIDENT BREEDING SPECIES, PRESENT YEAR-ROUND THROUGHOUT THE REGION, BUT ABSENT FROM REMOTE OFFSHORE ISLANDS AND PARTS OF SCANDINAVIA.

VOICE CALL IS A CHATTERING *TSER ERR-ERR-ERR*. SONG INCLUDES WHISTLING AND TRILLING ELEMENTS.

and the central dark streak to the underparts. The head is mainly white, but boldly marked with a conspicuous bright blue cap and a dark blue (almost black) collar connected to a thin dark eye stripe and small bib. The dark bill is small and stubby, and the delicate legs are bluish. The juvenile is similar to the adult but with more subdued colours; it generally lacks any blue in its plumage.

The Blue Tit is an inquisitive and endearing little bird and a garden favourite. It naturally seeks tree holes in which to nest and readily uses purpose-built nest boxes, constructing a cup-shaped nest lined inside with hair and grasses. Rarely venturing far from the safety of cover, its flight is swift and agile on rapid wingbeats.

Great Tit
Parus major

adult life-size

The white cheek patch is a striking feature and one that allows easy identification, even with a partial view of a bird.

The Great Tit is a colourful woodland bird and a familiar garden visitor. The sexes are similar but separable with care. The adult male has a greenish back; the upperwings are blue with an obvious white wingbar. The underparts are yellow with a central bold black stripe that runs from between the legs across the belly and breast to connect with the black throat, collar and cap. A large white triangular cheek patch is framed by the black head markings. The black bill is small but robust-looking, and the legs are blue-grey. The adult female is similar, but the central black stripe is much narrower and more

adult

In the company of other tit species at feeders, a Great Tit is pugnacious and will stand its ground.

Factfile

LENGTH 14–15CM

WINGSPAN 22–25CM

HABITAT **FAVOURS AREAS OF DECIDUOUS WOODLAND, PARKS AND GARDENS. A COMMON VISITOR TO GARDEN TABLES AND FEEDERS.**

FOOD **FEEDS ON INVERTEBRATES, FRUITS AND SEEDS.**

STATUS **COMMON AND WIDESPREAD RESIDENT BREEDING SPECIES, PRESENT YEAR-ROUND THROUGHOUT THE REGION; ABSENT FROM REMOTE OFFSHORE ISLANDS.**

VOICE **UTTERS A SHARP *TCHE-TCHE-TCHE* CALL IN ALARM. SONG IS A DIAGNOSTIC *TEACHER-TEACHER-TEACHER*.**

adult

The bright yellow-green plumage and bold pale wingbar are striking features in flight.

adult

Compared to a male, the dark line down the centre of the breast is variably incomplete in a female Great Tit but to be sure of its gender the bird in question needs to be seen from below not sideways on.

broken, especially between the legs, and the head and throat are less glossy. The juvenile has much duller and less well-defined plumage, but with hints of adult colouration.

The Great Tit is a rather bold species and a common sight in rural and urban gardens, readily coming to feeders. It has the largest European distribution of any member of the tit family. It frequently forages on the ground or in low hanging branches, and its flight is fast and agile on rapid wingbeats. The Great Tit seeks tree holes or suitable gaps in walls and buildings in which to nest, and is an enthusiastic user of nest boxes. The nest is a cup lined with hair and feathers.

Crested Tit
Lophophanes cristatus

The Crested Tit is a handsome little bird, its distinctive crest making it unmistakable. The sexes are similar. The adult has predominantly brown upperparts; the underparts are buffish-white. The head is adorned with a conspicuous black-and-white barred crest. The head is otherwise whitish and marked with a thin black stripe that runs through the eye and around the ear coverts. Note the clearly defined bold black collar and throat. The black bill is narrow, pointed and relatively long for a tit. The legs are greenish-grey. The juvenile recalls the adult but its colouration is more subdued and less well defined.

The Crested Tit excavates a nest hole in a decaying tree stump, with the female undertaking most of the hard work. A new hole is prepared each year, the nest being constructed of moss and lined with hair and wool.

adult life-size

No other European bird of this size has a crest, making this feature diagnostic.

Crested Tits search for invertebrates among the epiphytic mosses and lichens that cloak the trees in their favoured habitats; they will occasionally visit feeders as well, particularly outside the breeding season.

adult

Factfile

LENGTH **11–12CM**

WINGSPAN **17–20CM**

HABITAT **FAVOURS MATURE CONIFER FOREST IN THE NORTH BUT MIXED WOODLAND FURTHER SOUTH; RESTRICTED TO ANCIENT CALEDONIAN PINE FORESTS IN SCOTLAND.**

FOOD **FEEDS PRIMARILY ON INSECTS AND SPIDERS; SOME SEEDS.**

STATUS **VERY SEDENTARY AND LOCALISED RESIDENT BREEDING SPECIES. PRESENT YEAR-ROUND THROUGHOUT MUCH OF THE REGION IN SUITABLE HABITATS BUT ABSENT FROM MOST OF THE BRITISH ISLES, EXCEPT THE HIGHLANDS OF SCOTLAND.**

VOICE **CALL IS A HIGH TRILLING. UTTERS A WARBLER-LIKE SONG COMPRISING A SERIES OF RAPID NOTES AND WHISTLES.**

Coal Tit
Periparus ater

Factfile

LENGTH 10–11CM

WINGSPAN 17–21CM

HABITAT FAVOURS CONIFEROUS FORESTS AND PLANTATIONS, BUT ALSO WIDESPREAD IN MIXED AND DECIDUOUS WOODLAND.

FOOD FEEDS ON INSECTS AND SPIDERS; ALSO SOME SEEDS. A REGULAR VISITOR TO GARDEN FEEDERS.

STATUS WIDESPREAD RESIDENT BREEDING SPECIES, PRESENT YEAR-ROUND AND COMMON THROUGHOUT THE REGION IN SUITABLE HABITAT.

VOICE CALL IS THIN AND PIPING. UTTERS A *TEECHU-TEECHU-TEECHU* SONG, REMINISCENT OF GREAT TIT, BUT WEAKER, HIGHER-PITCHED AND MORE RAPID.

adult

At bird feeders, Coal Tits typically collect an item of food and then quickly retreat to cover to eat it.

The Coal Tit is a tiny bird that is associated with coniferous woodland. The sexes are similar. The adult has bluish-grey to grey-brown upperparts, with two white wingbars; the underparts are pale pinkish-buff. Some subtle geographical plumage variation occurs, and birds from different areas of the region can display yellowish, green or brown tinges. The head and chin are black and marked with a triangular white cheek patch, running from the base of the bill and below the eye; note the diagnostic narrow white patch on the nape. The small bill and the delicate legs are black. The juvenile recalls the adult but with less well-defined markings and more subdued colouration. This is the species of tit most commonly associated with coniferous woodland. The Coal Tit feeds acrobatically, and is noticeably more agile than other tit species when foraging in the outer reaches of branches and treetops. It nests in tree holes or suitable crevices, and also uses nest boxes.

adult life-size

A Coal Tit is a compact little bird with the size and proportions of a warbler, but a proportionately large head and stubby bill.

Willow Tit
Poecile montana

346

adult
The thick neck and extensive black cap can be appreciated with a side-on view.

This species is very similar to Marsh Tit with subtle plumage differences; the two are tricky to separate except with experience. The sexes are similar. The adult has mainly grey-brown upperparts; the underparts are pale grey-buff. The head has a bold black cap that extends to the dark eye, the cheeks are whitish and the throat is marked with a black bib. The stubby bill is black and the legs are bluish. Compared to Marsh Tit, note the black cap which extends onto the upper mantle and lacks sheen, and the more extensive black bib. Note also the thicker-set neck and pale wing panel. The juvenile is similar to the adult.

The Willow Tit has quite precise habitat requirements that differ subtly from the similar Marsh Tit, although habitat preferences alter with range. The distinctive voice allows confident identification with experience. It excavates holes in rotting tree stumps in which to nest, constructing a cup of plant material lined with hair. The birds pair for life and inhabit the same territory throughout the year.

adult life-size
With a good view, the white panel on the wings is striking, along with the broad black 'bib'.

Factfile

LENGTH 12–13CM

WINGSPAN 17–21CM

HABITAT FAVOURS DAMP DECIDUOUS, MIXED AND CONIFEROUS WOODLAND; COMMON ALDER WOODLAND IS IDEAL.

FOOD FEEDS ON INVERTEBRATES, SEEDS AND BERRIES.

STATUS RESIDENT BREEDING SPECIES, PRESENT YEAR-ROUND BUT SCATTERED AND LOCAL IN SUITABLE HABITATS THROUGHOUT MOST OF THE REGION. NUMBERS ARE IN DECLINE IN BRITAIN; ABSENT FROM IRELAND.

VOICE UTTERS A NASAL *SI-SI TCHAY-TCHAY-TCHAY* CALL; SONG IS RATHER MUSICAL AND WARBLING.

Marsh Tit
Poecile palustris

Marsh Tits are much more familiar visitors to garden bird feeders than Willow Tits, although visits are typically brief.

The Marsh Tit is a feisty little woodland bird, very similar in appearance to Willow Tit and the more commonly encountered species of the two. The sexes are similar. The adult has uniform grey-brown upperparts; the underparts are grey-buff. The head is marked with a bold black cap that extends to the dark eye. The cheeks are whitish and the throat is marked with a small black bib patch. The black bill is stubby and a small white spot at the base is sometimes visible. The legs are delicate and bluish. Compared to the similar Willow Tit, note the glossy sheen to the black cap (discernible in good light), the smaller black bib and the lack of a pale wing panel. Note also the more slender-looking neck. The juvenile recalls the adult.

Extremely subtle differences in plumage make Marsh Tit difficult to separate from Willow Tit when encountered in most circumstances in the field. Habitat and voice allow confident separation with experience. It nests in existing holes in tree trunks and stumps, often enlarging them when necessary, and constructing a cup of plant material lined with hair. The species can pair for life and inhabits the same territory throughout the year. It occasionally visits bird tables and feeders, but less regularly than other species of tit.

adult

Factfile

In good light, a Marsh Tit has, on average, 'warmer' brown upperparts and buff underparts than a typical Willow Tit.

LENGTH 12–13CM   WINGSPAN 18–20CM

HABITAT **INHABITS DECIDUOUS WOODLAND, PARKS AND GARDENS.**

FOOD **FEEDS ON INVERTEBRATES, SEEDS, NUTS AND BERRIES.**

STATUS **A COMMON RESIDENT BREEDING SPECIES, PRESENT YEAR-ROUND THROUGHOUT MOST OF THE REGION, WITH THE EXCEPTION OF IRELAND AND THE EXTREME NORTH.**

VOICE **CALL IS A LOUD *PITCHOO* SNEEZE; UTTERS A LOUD AND REPETITIVE *CHIP-CHIP-CHIP* SONG.**

The narrow black 'bib' and glossy sheen to the cap are both good features for comparison with a Willow Tit.

adult

adult life-size

Bearded Tit
Panurus biarmicus

The Bearded Tit is an unmistakable, exquisite little bird with a plump body and long tail. The sexes are dissimilar. The adult male has mainly sandy-brown upperparts, underparts and tail. The wings are marked with conspicuous black-and-white markings, and the head and throat are contrastingly blue-grey. Note the bold black 'moustaches' that start at the eye and base of the bill and run either side of the throat. Also note the beady yellow eye and the stubby yellow bill. The vent area and the legs are black. The adult female is similar, but lacks the black moustache and has a pale vent and undertail. The juvenile recalls the adult female, but is generally darker and duller in colour overall. The upperparts are dark-streaked and the throat is pale. The juvenile male has a yellow bill, while the juvenile female has a dark bill.

male life-size

The combination of a compact body, long tail and bold facial pattern make a male Bearded Tit an unmistakable bird.

Seen facing an observer, a male's black 'moustache' is a striking and diagnostic feature. The species is very faithful to its favoured habitat and is seldom seen away from the cover of extensive reed beds.

Factfile

LENGTH 14–16CM

WINGSPAN 16–18CM

HABITAT FOUND EXCLUSIVELY IN AREAS OF EXTENSIVE REED BEDS, BORDERING COASTAL LAGOONS, SHALLOW LAKES AND MARSHES.

FOOD FEEDS PRIMARILY ON SEEDS AND INVERTEBRATES.

STATUS RESIDENT BREEDING SPECIES WITH LOCALISED POPULATIONS PRESENT YEAR-ROUND IN SUITABLE HABITATS.

VOICE CALL IS A CHARACTERISTIC, HIGH-PITCHED *PING*. THE SOFT AND RASPING SONG IS SELDOM HEARD.

Even though female Bearded Tits lack a male's bold facial markings, the combination of plumage colours, body shape and habitat make identification straightforward.

male

female

The Bearded Tit is an agile little bird that spends most of its time climbing and clinging to the stems of reeds, hidden deep within reed beds. Their characteristic pinging call is often the first sign of their presence. Outside the breeding season, they are usually encountered in small gregarious flocks. Flight is undulating on rapid, whirring wingbeats. It constructs a cup-shaped nest of dead reed leaves.

Long-tailed Tit
Aegithalos caudatus

The Long-tailed Tit is an endearing, fluffy-looking bird with a rounded head, plumpish body and long tail. The sexes are similar. At first glance, adults from most of the region appear to have mainly black upperparts and tail with white underparts. Closer inspection reveals a pinkish chestnut patch on the 'shoulder'; the underside and flanks are also flushed with pink. The head is predominantly white, with a bold black band running above the eye to the mantle. The eye is dark and the stubby little bill is black. The legs are delicate-looking and dark. Birds from Scandinavia have an entirely white head. Juveniles of all races lack the pinkish plumage elements, and have a dark wash across much of the face.

A Long-tailed Tit's flight is undulating and agile on rapid, whirring wingbeats. It is often seen in small agitated groups, particularly during the winter months, that never seem to remain in one place for long. It visits garden tables and feeders in rural areas, but is less regular in its appearance than other tit species. Its nest is an intricate ball, woven from moss, lichen, feathers and spiders' silk, and is commonly placed in a bush or hedgerow.

adult life-size
The rounded body shape and proportionately long tail mean that identification of the species is straightforward.

northern race adult
With their white heads and pale underparts, Scandinavian birds look unbelievably cute, especially when their feathers are fluffed up to keep them warm in cold weather.

northern race adult

Feeding groups are sometimes inquisitive about observers and will come and investigate them, perching briefly at close quarters.

Factfile

LENGTH 13–15CM

WINGSPAN 16–19CM

HABITAT FAVOURS DECIDUOUS WOODLAND, HEDGEROWS AND AREAS OF SCRUB.

FOOD FEEDS PRIMARILY ON INSECTS AND OTHER INVERTEBRATES; SOME SEEDS IN THE WINTER MONTHS.

STATUS WIDESPREAD AND FAIRLY COMMON RESIDENT BREEDING SPECIES, PRESENT YEAR-ROUND THROUGHOUT THE REGION IN SUITABLE HABITAT.

VOICE CONTACT CALL IS A RATTLING *TSRRR* AND THIN *TSEE-TSEE-TSEE*. THE SOFT SONG IS EASILY MISSED.

adult

Outside the breeding season, the species is usually seen in restless parties of a dozen or so birds.

Penduline Tit *Remiz pendulinus*

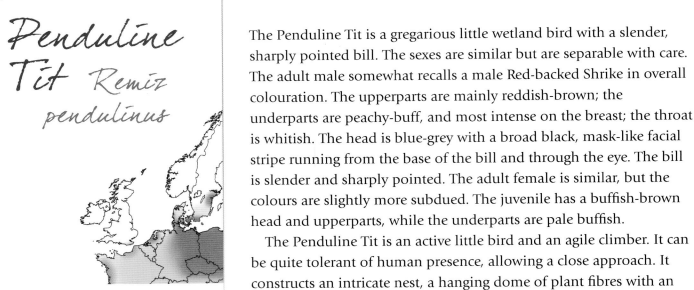

The Penduline Tit is a gregarious little wetland bird with a slender, sharply pointed bill. The sexes are similar but are separable with care. The adult male somewhat recalls a male Red-backed Shrike in overall colouration. The upperparts are mainly reddish-brown; the underparts are peachy-buff, and most intense on the breast; the throat is whitish. The head is blue-grey with a broad black, mask-like facial stripe running from the base of the bill and through the eye. The bill is slender and sharply pointed. The adult female is similar, but the colours are slightly more subdued. The juvenile has a buffish-brown head and upperparts, while the underparts are pale buffish.

The Penduline Tit is an active little bird and an agile climber. It can be quite tolerant of human presence, allowing a close approach. It constructs an intricate nest, a hanging dome of plant fibres with an entrance tunnel at the top, the whole structure suspended from the twigs of a tree.

male

Factfile

LENGTH 10–11CM   WINGSPAN 16–18CM

HABITAT FAVOURS WETLAND HABITATS OF FRESH OR BRACKISH WATER WITH PROLIFIC VEGETATION.

FOOD FEEDS PRIMARILY ON INVERTEBRATES AND LARVAE; SEEDS DURING THE WINTER.

STATUS LOCAL SUMMER BREEDING SPECIES IN THE EAST OF OUR REGION, PRESENT MAINLY APRIL TO SEPTEMBER; RARE PASSAGE MIGRANT AND WINTER VISITOR ELSEWHERE.

VOICE UTTERS A THIN, HIGH-PITCHED WHISTLE, *TSIUU.*

The pointed, needle-sharp bill is used to extract invertebrates from crevices and seeds from the tight seedheads of plants such as Reedmace.

Juveniles are invariably seen in the company of adults but their body- and bill-shape are good clues to the identity of solitary birds.

juvenile life-size

Woodlark
Lullula arborea

adults

In flight, note the compact shape and pale-framed dark patch on the leading edge of the wing.

Factfile

LENGTH 14–15CM

WINGSPAN 27–30CM

HABITAT FAVOURS HEATHLAND SITES ADJOINING WOODLAND THAT PROVIDE A MIXTURE OF LOW COVER AND GRASS.

FOOD FEEDS PRIMARILY ON INVERTEBRATES AND SEEDS.

STATUS PRESENT YEAR-ROUND AS A BREEDING SPECIES IN THE WEST OF ITS RANGE IN OUR REGION. BIRDS FROM THE EAST AND NORTHEAST ARE MIGRATORY, PRESENT DURING THE BREEDING SEASON FROM MAY TO AUGUST, THEREAFTER MIGRATING SOUTH AND WEST TO AVOID HARSH WINTER WEATHER.

VOICE SONG IS OFTEN DELIVERED IN FLIGHT, OR WHILE PERCHED IN A TREE, AND COMPRISES A SERIES OF FLUTY, YODELLING NOTES. CALL IS SIMILAR TO THE YODELLING PHRASE OF THE SONG, *DEET-LUEE*.

The Woodlark is a small lark with a rather short tail, its distinctive song commonly betraying its presence. The sexes are similar. The adult has upperparts that are predominantly sandy-brown and marked with dark streaking. The underparts are pale with a buff flush and dark streaking on the breast. The head has chestnut ear coverts and a pale supercilium that meets at the nape. The grey bill is slender and pale-based; the legs are pink. In flight, a white-edged black patch can be seen at the angle of the leading edge of the wing; on close inspection, it also visible as a black-and-white bar when the bird is perched. Note the relatively short tail when compared to the similar Skylark. The juvenile is similar to the adult, but the pale fringes to the feathers of the upperparts give it a scaly appearance.

The Woodlark is a rather unobtrusive bird that is often heard before it is seen. It requires specific habitat for breeding – short grass for feeding, long grass for nesting, trees for display – and is relatively scarce as a result. It is a ground-nesting bird that nests in a lined depression, sheltered by an adjacent bush. It can often be found in flocks of other songbirds during the winter months.

The beautiful yodelling song of the Woodlark carries quite a distance and is often heard at dawn and dusk. Silent birds are unobtrusive and easily overlooked but if seen well the chestnut ear coverts and pale supercilium give the face a distinctive appearance.

adult life-size

Skylark
Alauda arvensis

The Skylark is a rather plain bird, known for its fluty song delivered in flight. The sexes are similar. The adult has upperparts that are predominantly sandy-brown and marked with dark streaking. The underparts are pale, with a buff flush and dark streaking to the breast. The head is marked with buffish cheeks and a light buff supercilium, and a short crest is raised on occasion. In flight, note the subtle pale trailing edges to the wings and the white outer tail feathers. The bill is grey-brown and the legs are light brown. The juvenile is similar to the adult, but the pale fringes to the feathers of the upperparts give it a scaly appearance.

The Skylark's song is a familiar sound of open grassland habitats, typically delivered by birds fluttering and hovering at height for long periods. A ground-feeding species, it also nests on the ground in a shallow grass-lined depression. It often forms large flocks during the winter months. Its numbers are in decline as a result of intensive farming methods.

A Skylark's song is the best way of detecting the species' presence in an area of grassland; in many locations, birds sing for much of the year, albeit less enthusiastically in winter than in the breeding season.

adult

adult

Factfile

LENGTH 16–18CM

WINGSPAN 30–36CM

HABITAT FAVOURS NATURAL GRASSY HABITATS INCLUDING MEADOWS, MOORS, HEATHS AND COASTAL GRASSLAND.

FOOD FEEDS ON INVERTEBRATES, SEEDS, PLANTS AND ROOTS.

STATUS WIDESPREAD RESIDENT BREEDING SPECIES, PRESENT YEAR-ROUND ACROSS THE REGION IN SUITABLE HABITATS. BIRDS FROM SCANDINAVIA MIGRATE SOUTH DURING THE WINTER MONTHS. NUMBERS ARE IN DECLINE OVERALL.

VOICE SONG IS MOSTLY DELIVERED IN FLIGHT, AND COMPRISES A CONSTANT AND RAPID MIX OF TRILLING AND WHISTLING NOTES. CALL IS A ROLLING *CHRRRP*.

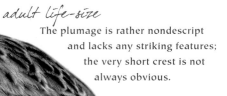

adult life-size
The plumage is rather nondescript and lacks any striking features; the very short crest is not always obvious.

Crested Lark
Galerida cristata

Factfile

LENGTH 17–19CM

WINGSPAN 29–38CM

HABITAT FAVOURS DRY OPEN GROUND WITH LOW VEGETATION, INCLUDING GRASSLAND, ROADSIDES, DISTURBED GROUND AND INDUSTRIAL SITES.

FOOD FEEDS ON SEEDS, OTHER PLANT MATERIAL AND INSECTS.

STATUS WIDESPREAD RESIDENT BREEDING SPECIES, PRESENT YEAR-ROUND ON MAINLAND EUROPE. ABSENT FROM SCANDINAVIA AND THE BRITISH ISLES, BUT VAGRANTS SOMETIMES TURN UP ON COASTS.

VOICE UTTERS A CALL COMPRISING A SERIES OF LONG WHISTLING *WEEEEELUU* NOTES.

The Crested Lark is similar to a Skylark but has a longer bill and a more pronounced crest. The sexes are similar. The adult has primarily greyish-brown upperparts, marked with a series of darker streaks that are particularly pronounced on the crown and back. The underparts are mainly whitish, with a slight orange-buff flush to the flanks and streaking on the breast and flanks. Facial markings are indistinct but, when seen at close range, darkish lores and a subtle pale supercilium behind the eye can be discerned. The spiky crest is more prominent than that of Skylark and can be seen even when flattened. The bill is grey-brown and conspicuously long; the legs are flesh-coloured. In flight, note the rufous tinge to the underwing coverts, the lack of pale trailing edges to the wings and the buff outer tail feathers. The juvenile recalls the adult.

In common with the Skylark, the Crested Lark's song is sometimes delivered by flying birds, fluttering and hovering at height for long periods. It both feeds and nests on the ground, and is commonly seen running along the ground in short bursts.

When raised, the species' crest is a diagnostic feature; note the proportionately large, stout bill.

adult

Compared to other lark species in the region, the body is more elongated and the tail proportionately longer.

adult life-size

adult

More usually associated with man-made sites and habitats modified by man than other lark species.

Shore Lark
Eremophila alpestris

This is a distinctive lark with striking black facial markings. The sexes are similar but summer and winter plumages differ slightly. The summer adult has sandy-brown upperparts, streaked on the back, but unmarked on the nape. The underparts are predominantly white with faint buff streaks on the flanks, and boldly marked with an obvious black band on the breast. The head is yellow and contrastingly marked with a bold black mask running from the base of the bill, underneath the eye and to the ear coverts. The black on the forecrown extends backwards to form two conspicuous 'horns'. The bill is dark grey and the legs are black. In flight, note the prominent central black marking on the undertail, and the black-and-white outer tail feathers of the upperside. The winter adult is similar, but the head colours are more subdued and the 'horns' are absent. The female generally has duller plumage than the male. The juvenile resembles the adult but with pale spots to the upperparts.

The Shore Lark is a rather unobtrusive bird than can be difficult to spot when foraging on the ground. In the winter it is generally found in small groups. Its flight is powerful with a bounding, undulating pattern. It nests on the ground in an unlined depression.

Factfile

LENGTH 16–18CM WINGSPAN 30–35CM

HABITAT BREEDS ON ARCTIC TUNDRA DURING THE SUMMER MONTHS AND ALMOST EXCLUSIVELY COASTAL DURING THE WINTER, TYPICALLY FAVOURING SALT MARSHES.

FOOD FEEDS ON INVERTEBRATES AND SEEDS.

STATUS A MIGRATORY SPECIES WHOSE BREEDING RANGE WITHIN THE REGION IS RESTRICTED PRIMARILY TO SCANDINAVIA; PRESENT THERE MAINLY MAY TO AUGUST. IT MOVES TO COASTAL AREAS IN THE WINTER, WHEN NUMBERS IN THE REGION ARE TYPICALLY SPARSE AND MAINLY RESTRICTED TO THE NORTH SEA COASTS.

VOICE UTTERS A THIN *SEE-SEER* IN FLIGHT.

The body plumage allows birds to blend in well with strandline debris and coastal habitats favoured in the winter months. By early spring, birds will have begun to acquire the striking facial colours and markings seen in breeding birds.

adult life-size

adult

As the winter progresses, the intensity of the facial colours increases but varies between individuals; some may even begin to acquire small 'horns' on the sides of the crown.

Sand Martin

Riparia riparia

The Sand Martin is the smallest hirundine species in the region and a summer visitor. The sexes are similar. The adult has mainly sandy-brown upperparts; the underparts are predominantly white with a bold brown band across the breast. The small bill and the legs are black. In flight, note the brown underwings, brown outer tail feathers on the underside, the rather triangular wing shape and the short forked tail. The juvenile is similar to the adult, but the pale margins to the feathers on the back give it a scaly appearance.

Fast and agile in the air, the Sand Martin flies with a series of glides on stiffly held wings, interspersed with regular bouts of rapid wingbeats. It tends to seek areas next to water for the abundance of insect life, which it snatches adeptly from the air when in flight. It excavates holes in sand cliffs and river banks, constructing a nest of feathers and vegetation. It is often one of the earliest migratory species to arrive in the spring.

adult life-size

The overall sandy brown and pale buff plumage make identification easy; the brown breast band is a diagnostic feature among hirundines.

adult

Factfile

LENGTH 12–13CM

WINGSPAN 27–29CM

HABITAT STEEP SANDBANKS ADJACENT TO WATER, TYPICALLY SAND PITS, GRAVEL PITS AND RIVERS.

FOOD FEEDS ON INSECTS AND AIRBORNE SPIDERS THAT IT CATCHES ON THE WING.

STATUS SUMMER BREEDING VISITOR FOUND THROUGHOUT THE REGION IN SUITABLE HABITAT; PRESENT MAINLY APRIL TO SEPTEMBER. OVERWINTERS IN AFRICA.

VOICE UTTERS VARIOUS RASPING JSEE-JSEE-JSEE CALLS IN FLIGHT.

Nesting birds often perch at the entrance to the burrow, and prolonged views can be had, especially when they are feeding young.

Swallow
Hirundo rustica

young
at nest

Prior to fledging, youngsters become very vocal at the arrival of a parent bird with food.

This iconic summer visitor is instantly recognisable by its pointed wings and long tail streamers. The sexes are similar, although the male generally has longer tail streamers than the female. The adult has a blue-black head and upperparts with a metallic sheen when seen in certain lights; the underparts are white, the dark breast forming a clear demarcation. The throat and forecrown are brick-red. The slender bill, legs and feet are black. In flight, and from below, note the dark primary flight feathers and the white subterminal band to the tail, made up of a series of adjacent white spots. The wings are slender and pointed, the tail deeply forked, and the long tail streamers are diagnostic. The juvenile resembles the adult but the tail streamers are shorter, the plumage lacks the glossy sheen and the throat is buffish-red.

Swallows are classic summer visitors in rural areas, their arrival traditionally used as a seasonal barometer. It is a fast and agile flyer, often seen gliding on stiffly held wings catching insects on the wing. It collects mud for nest building from puddles and pools. The nest is cup-shaped, lined with feathers, and built on top of a ledge or rafter, typically in a stable or rural outbuilding. The adults can often be observed feeding fledglings perched on overhead wires close to nesting sites.

In flight, the wing shape and long tail streamers make identification straightforward.

adult

In perched birds, note the rather short legs and elongated body shape.

adult
life-size

Factfile

LENGTH 17–19CM

WINGSPAN 32–35CM

HABITAT FAVOURS FARMLAND AND OPEN COUNTRYSIDE, OFTEN SEEKING FARM BUILDINGS, STABLES AND OTHER RURAL BUILDINGS IN WHICH TO NEST.

FOOD FEEDS ON INSECTS AND AIRBORNE SPIDERS, WHICH IT CATCHES ON THE WING.

STATUS WIDESPREAD SUMMER BREEDING VISITOR FOUND THROUGHOUT THE REGION IN SUITABLE HABITAT; PRESENT MAINLY APRIL TO SEPTEMBER. OVERWINTERS IN AFRICA.

VOICE CALL IS A SHARP *VIT* UTTERED IN FLIGHT. THE MALE PRODUCES A WARBLING SONG, OFTEN DELIVERED WHILE SITTING ON OVERHEAD WIRES.

House Martin

Delichon urbicum

The House Martin is a rather compact and stubby-looking summer visitor, instantly recognisable in flight by its white rump. The sexes are similar. The adult has a dark blue-black head and upperparts, with a strikingly white rump that is most obvious in flight. The underparts, including the chin and breast, are white; seen in flight, the undersides of the wings are grey. The small bill is black, the legs are feathered white and the feet are pink. In flight, note not only the white rump but also the triangular-shaped wings and the short forked tail. The juvenile is similar to the adult but with grubby white underparts and slightly duller plumage overall.

The House Martin's flight is swift and agile, a mixture of lengthy glides on stiffly held wings and bouts of rapid wingbeats. It is a familiar summer visitor that favours towns and rural villages, nesting either singly or in small colonies. It collects mud for nest building from puddles and pools. The nest itself is a half-cup of mud lined with feathers, which it attaches to a vertical surface under the eaves of a house or farm building, or beneath another overhanging feature.

adult

Seen from above in flight, note the striking white rump.

It takes several days for a House Martin to build its mud nest and repairs and additions are made throughout the breeding season.

adults

adult life-size

Seen from below in flight, note the absence of a dark breast band, seen in Sand Martin.

Factfile

LENGTH 13–15CM

WINGSPAN 26–29CM

HABITAT ASSOCIATED WITH AREAS OF HOUSING AND FARMYARDS, NESTING IN THE EAVES OF HOUSES AND OTHER BUILDINGS. OCCASIONALLY NESTS ON CLIFFS AND IN CAVE ENTRANCES.

FOOD FEEDS ON INSECTS AND AIRBORNE SPIDERS, CAUGHT ON THE WING.

STATUS WIDESPREAD SUMMER VISITOR FOUND THROUGHOUT THE REGION, PRESENT MAINLY APRIL TO SEPTEMBER. OVERWINTERS IN SOUTHERN AFRICA. NUMBERS HAVE DECLINED IN RECENT YEARS.

VOICE CALL IS A DISTINCTIVE *PRRRT*, UTTERED IN FLIGHT.

Goldcrest
Regulus regulus

Factfile

LENGTH 8–9CM

WINGSPAN 14–16CM

HABITAT A WOODLAND SPECIES THAT FAVOURS CONIFERS, BUT ALSO FOUND IN DECIDUOUS WOODLAND, AREAS OF SCRUB, PARKS AND RURAL GARDENS.

FOOD FEEDS PRIMARILY ON SMALL INSECTS AND THEIR LARVAE.

STATUS COMMON AND WIDESPREAD RESIDENT BREEDING SPECIES, PRESENT YEAR-ROUND THROUGHOUT MUCH OF THE REGION. NUMBERS ARE BOOSTED OUTSIDE THE BREEDING SEASON BY BIRDS MIGRATING FROM FURTHER NORTH AND EAST OF OUR REGION.

VOICE SONG IS A SERIES OF HIGH-PITCHED NOTES AND PHRASES, ENDING IN A FLOURISH. CALL IS A THIN *TSEE-TSEE-TSEE*.

The Goldcrest is a tiny warbler-like bird with a rather squat and rounded body; it is the region's smallest bird species. The sexes are often separable. The adult male has dull greenish upperparts; the underparts are uniformly yellow-buff. Note the two pale wingbars, the subtle light-coloured eye-ring and the striking black-bordered orange and yellow crown. The small, needle-like bill is black. The adult female is similar to the male, but the crown colour is pure yellow. The juvenile resembles the adult but lacks the distinctive crown markings and colours until the autumn.

The Goldcrest is a tricky bird to observe at times, owing to its size and habit of foraging for insects in the top of the tree canopy. Its distinctive call is often the first sign of its presence. Numbers are boosted in more temperate areas in the winter months by an influx of winter migrants. It constructs a nest of moss, lichens and cobwebs, generally in a coniferous tree.

adult

Although the crest on the crown is colourful, it can be hard to spot if the bird in question is feeding in the canopy, above the observer.

adult life-size

Feeds in the manner of a warbler, searching for invertebrates on twigs and among foliage.

Firecrest
Regulus ignicapilla

The Firecrest is a tiny bird with a rounded body, similar overall to a Goldcrest and only marginally larger. The sexes are separable. The adult male has yellowish-green upperparts with two pale wingbars. The underparts are buffish-white, and note the golden yellow flush to the sides of the neck. The head is adorned with a striking black-bordered orange crown, a dark eye stripe, and a white supercilium; the latter two features allow certain separation from the Goldcrest. Note also the small, needle-like black bill and the delicate brown legs. The adult female is similar to the male, but the crown colour is yellow. The juvenile resembles the adult but lacks the distinctive crown markings and colours until the autumn.

The Firecrest is less widespread than the similar Goldcrest. It is a woodland species that often favours mature coniferous woodland with a Holly understorey, although it is equally at home in deciduous and mixed woodland. It is an extremely active species that spends the majority of its time searching for food items in the tree canopy. It constructs a cup-shaped nest of moss, lichens and cobwebs, placed at the end of a tree branch.

male

The male's song is almost inaudibly high-pitched.

Firecrests have a dark eyestripe, a broad white supercilium and an orange-centred black crown stripe.

Factfile

LENGTH 9–10CM   WINGSPAN 13–16CM

HABITAT FAVOURS MATURE DECIDUOUS AND CONIFEROUS WOODLAND. PASSAGE MIGRANTS CAN ALSO OCCUR IN COASTAL WOODLAND AND SCRUB.

FOOD FEEDS ON INSECTS, SPIDERS AND OTHER INVERTEBRATES.

STATUS BREEDING SPECIES IN PARTS OF MAINLAND EUROPE AND SOUTHERN BRITAIN, PRESENT YEAR-ROUND BUT MOBILE IN WINTER. EASTERN POPULATIONS MIGRATE SOUTH AND WEST OUTSIDE THE BREEDING SEASON; IN COASTAL NORTHWEST EUROPE, BEST KNOWN AS A SCARCE PASSAGE MIGRANT AND WINTER VISITOR.

VOICE SONG IS A SERIES OF HIGH-PITCHED NOTES AND PHRASES, ENDING ABRUPTLY. CALL IS A THIN *TSUU-TSEE-TSEE*.

The upperparts are yellow-green and the wings have two obvious wingbars.

adult life-size

Cetti's Warbler

Cettia cetti

Its rather uniformly brown plumage is reminiscent of an *Acrocephalus* warbler.

adult life-size

adult

Often cocks its tail up when foraging.

adult

Most vocal in spring, but territorial males sing, off and on, throughout the year.

Factfile

LENGTH 13–14CM

WINGSPAN 15–19CM

HABITAT FAVOURS AREAS OF BUSH COVER ON THE MARGINS OF REED BEDS, MARSHES AND WETLAND SCRUB.

FOOD FEEDS ON INSECTS, SPIDERS AND OTHER INVERTEBRATES.

STATUS LOCAL RESIDENT BREEDING SPECIES, PRESENT YEAR-ROUND AND RESTRICTED TO THE SOUTHWEST OF OUR REGION. IN BRITAIN, IT ONLY OCCURS IN THE SOUTH, ALTHOUGH ITS RANGE IS EXTENDING NORTHWARDS.

VOICE UTTERS A LOUD AND EXPLOSIVE CHEE, CHIPPI-CHIPPI-CHIPPI SONG. CALL IS A LOUD PLUUT, ALSO RATTLING NOISES.

This is a stocky warbler with an unmistakable loud song that often betrays its presence. The sexes are similar. The adult has uniform reddish-brown upperparts and tail. In contrast, the underparts are pale, being grey-buff on the belly, grey on the breast and face, and whitish on the throat. The head is marked with a subtle light grey supercilium. The dark-tipped bill is slender and brown; the legs are light brown. Note the short, dark-tipped brown undertail coverts. The juvenile is similar to the adult.

The Cetti's Warbler is a rather unobtrusive species that spends much of its time hidden in deep cover, its presence most often betrayed by its explosive song. The males mate with a number of females and play little or no part in the rearing of young. The nest is cup-shaped, covered with an untidy outer layer of dead leaves and grass.

Wood Warbler
Phylloscopus sibilatrix

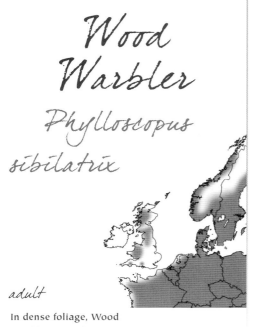

adult

In dense foliage, Wood Warblers are often easier to hear than to see.

This is a brightly coloured *Phylloscopus* warbler with specific habitat requirements. The sexes are similar. The adult has an olive-green head and upperparts; the underparts are primarily clean white, with a bright yellow flush to the throat and cheeks. The head is marked with a conspicuous bright yellow supercilium and a subtle dark eye stripe. Note the rather short tail and longish primary projection, the wingtips appearing to droop when the bird is at rest. The bill has a dark brown upper mandible, and a paler lower one. The legs are pale sandy-brown. The juvenile is similar to the adult.

adult life-size

The plumage is the most brightly marked of any *Phylloscopus* warbler in our region.

The Wood Warbler is a colourful songbird that spends most of its time foraging in the tree canopy, where it is difficult to spot among the leaves. It has a relatively short breeding season, arriving in the late spring and departing at the end of the summer. The nest is a dome of grass and leaves placed on the ground with little or no cover.

Plumage colours are most intense in spring, in newly arrived migrants.

adult

Factfile

LENGTH 11–12CM WINGSPAN 20–24CM

HABITAT PREFERS HILLY AREAS WITH TALL AND MATURE DECIDUOUS WOODLAND WITH A CLOSED CANOPY AND SPARSE GROUND COVER. HANGING SESSILE OAK WOODLANDS ARE A FAVOURITE.

FOOD FEEDS PRIMARILY ON INVERTEBRATES; SOME FRUIT.

STATUS LOCAL SUMMER VISITOR AND BREEDING SPECIES FOUND THROUGHOUT THE REGION IN SUITABLE HABITAT; PRESENT MAINLY MAY TO AUGUST. OVERWINTERS IN AFRICA.

VOICE SONG COMPRISES A SERIES OF RINGING NOTES ACCELERATING INTO A SILVERY TRILL, AND HAS BEEN LIKENED TO A COIN SPINNING ON A PLATE. CALL IS A SHARP *TSIP*.

Chiffchaff

Phylloscopus collybita

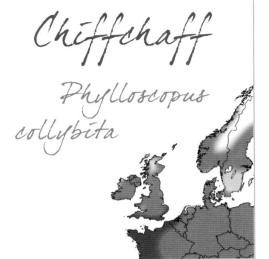

Factfile

LENGTH 10–11CM

WINGSPAN 15–21CM

HABITAT FAVOURS MATURE DECIDUOUS WOODLAND WITH A DENSE UNDERSTOREY OF SHRUBS.

FOOD FEEDS PRIMARILY ON INSECTS.

STATUS WIDESPREAD BREEDING SPECIES, COMMONEST FROM APRIL TO SEPTEMBER. MOST BIRDS MIGRATE TO SOUTHERN EUROPE FOR WINTER, BUT THE SPECIES IS PRESENT YEAR-ROUND IN SMALL NUMBERS IN THE SOUTHWEST OF OUR REGION.

VOICE UTTERS A DISTINCTIVE AND REPETITIVE *CHIFF-CHAFF* SONG THAT AFFORDS THE SPECIES ITS ENGLISH NAME. HEARD MOST FREQUENTLY DURING THE SPRING BUT CAN BE UTTERED THROUGHOUT THE SUMMER AND AUTUMN MONTHS. CALL IS A SOFT *HUITT*.

adult

Territorial birds sometimes display towards one another with fluttering wings.

The Chiffchaff is a small warbler with a distinctive song. The sexes are similar. The adult has a mainly grey-brown head and upperparts. The underparts are pale greyish and flushed with yellow-buff, particularly obvious on the throat and breast. The head is marked with a subtle pale yellow supercilium. The bill is slender. Note the comparatively short primary projection of the wings when at rest, and the dark legs, which allow separation from the similar Willow Warbler. The juvenile is similar to the adult.

Outside its resident range, the Chiffchaff is one of the first migrants to appear in the spring. A busy feeder, it is constantly on the move, foraging in the tree branches for invertebrates. During the breeding season, displaying birds can often be observed perched on branches and fluttering their wings rapidly. It nests in dense cover close to the ground, constructing a feather-lined grass dome.

Males are very vocal in spring, making identification straightforward.

In autumn, when birds are silent, look for dark legs to distinguish the species from a Willow Warbler.

adult

adult life-size

Willow Warbler

Phylloscopus trochilus

This is a small warbler, similar in appearance to Chiffchaff, but separable with care. The sexes are similar. The adult has mainly olive-green upperparts, and the head is marked with a pale yellow supercilium. The underparts are mainly grubby-white with a yellow flush to the throat. The slender bill is brown and the legs are orange-brown. Compared to a Chiffchaff, note the overall brighter colouration, the more obvious supercilium, the lighter-coloured legs and the longer projection of the primary feathers. The juvenile recalls the adult but is paler and more yellow overall, particularly on the underparts.

adult

Has proportionately longer wings than a Chiffchaff; in folded wings, the primary feathers project further.

adult life-size

The pinkish-brown legs as well as the song help with identification.

The Willow Warbler is a common warbler, and a relatively short-staying breeding visitor. The male defends its territory aggressively, chasing off rivals and other songbirds. It performs an elaborate, fluttering courtship display and nests on the ground in thick cover, constructing a grass dome.

Favours a wide range of habitats, including heathland, and not just willow scrub.

adult

Factfile

LENGTH 11–12CM WINGSPAN 17–22CM

HABITAT INHABITS AREAS OF WOODLAND INCLUDING COPPICES AND SCRUB. PARTICULARLY FAVOURS BIRCH WOODLAND AND WILLOW SCRUB.

FOOD FEEDS ON INSECTS AND OTHER INVERTEBRATES.

STATUS SUMMER MIGRANT BREEDING SPECIES, COMMON AND WIDESPREAD THROUGHOUT THE REGION IN SUITABLE HABITAT; PRESENT MAINLY APRIL TO AUGUST. OVERWINTERS IN AFRICA.

VOICE UTTERS A REPETITIVE, DESCENDING TINKLING PHRASE THAT ENDS IN A FLOURISH. CALL IS A DISYLLABIC *HUEET*, SIMILAR TO THAT OF CHIFFCHAFF.

Blackcap
Sylvia atricapilla

The male's black cap is diagnostic among warblers in our region.

Factfile

LENGTH 14–15CM

WINGSPAN 20–23CM

HABITAT FAVOURS A RANGE OF HABITATS INCLUDING DECIDUOUS WOODLAND WITH AN UNDERSTOREY OF DENSE SCRUB, MATURE GARDENS, PARKS, HEDGEROWS AND SCRUB.

FOOD FEEDS ON INSECTS AND BERRIES.

STATUS COMMON AND WIDESPREAD SUMMER BREEDING SPECIES, PRESENT MAINLY APRIL TO SEPTEMBER. MOST MIGRATE TO AFRICA IN AUTUMN, BUT SOUTHWESTERN PARTS OF OUR REGION HOST AN INCREASING NUMBER OF OVERWINTERING BIRDS.

VOICE SONG IS A DELIGHTFUL, RICH MUSICAL WARBLE, SIMILAR TO THAT OF GARDEN WARBLER BUT LACKING THE THRUSH-LIKE TONES. UTTERS A *TCHEK* CALL IN ALARM.

The Blackcap is a distinctive and handsome warbler with a beautiful melodic song. The sexes are separable. The adult male has primarily grey-brown upperparts with a lighter grey face and nape. The underparts are light silvery-grey, palest on the throat and undertail. The head is adorned with a bold and obvious black cap, and a subtle pale ring surrounds the eye. The bill is dull black and the legs are grey. The adult female is similar but has a richer brown flush to the upperparts, and the cap is reddish-chestnut. The juvenile resembles the adult female.

The Blackcap is a relatively common and widespread species, and an occasional garden visitor that can often be observed singing from an exposed perch. It seeks wooded areas with plenty of low undergrowth in which to nest, constructing a thin cup of vegetation within a metre or two of the ground.

male life-size

A bold songster whose song is more lively and agitated, and less fluty, than that of a Garden Warbler.

Overwintering birds in particular will often feed on garden berries, and visit bird feeders.

female

Garden Warbler

Sylvia borin

This is a thick-set warbler with rather plain plumage, but with one of the most musical songs of all the songbirds. The sexes are similar. The adult has a mainly uniform grey-brown head and upperparts, darkest on the wings. The underparts are pale with a buffish flush, most obvious on the breast and flanks. Note the subtle grey patch on the side of the neck (not always easy to discern), the stubby grey bill, grey legs, pale eye-ring and rather rounded head, all of which aid identification. The juvenile is similar to the adult.

The Garden Warbler is a rather shy and unobtrusive species that seeks the cover of woodland and undergrowth in which to forage. Its musical song is often the first indication of its presence. It nests in low-lying scrub, constructing a loose cup of dry grass.

adult

The proportionately stout bill and large head give the Garden Warbler a chunky appearance; note the distinctive grey patch on the side of the neck.

adult life-size

Often sings from deep cover and views of singing birds are typically partial.

Factfile

LENGTH **14–15CM** WINGSPAN **20–24CM**

HABITAT **FAVOURS DECIDUOUS OR MIXED WOODLAND WITH AN UNDERSTORY OF DENSE SCRUB.**

FOOD **FEEDS PRIMARILY ON INSECTS, SPIDERS AND FRUITS.**

STATUS **SUMMER MIGRANT BREEDING SPECIES, COMMON AND WIDESPREAD THROUGHOUT THE REGION IN SUITABLE HABITAT; PRESENT MAINLY MAY TO AUGUST. OVERWINTERS IN AFRICA.**

VOICE **SONG IS BEAUTIFULLY MUSICAL, SIMILAR TO THAT OF BLACKCAP, BUT LOWER-PITCHED WITH THRUSH-LIKE NOTES AND OFTEN WITH LONG, UNINTERRUPTED PERIODS OF BUBBLING. UTTERS A SHARP *CHEK-CHEK* CALL IN ALARM.**

Lesser Whitethroat

Sylvia curruca

The Lesser Whitethroat is a small, short-tailed and rather furtive warbler with a characteristic song. The sexes are similar. The adult has primarily grey-brown upperparts and tail, darkest on the wing. The underparts are mainly pale and flushed with buff on the flanks, and white on the throat. The head has a blue-grey crown and nape, and is marked with a subtle dark mask, formed by black feathering on the lores and ear coverts. The slender bill is grey and dark-tipped, the legs are dark; note the pale iris to the eye, which is sometimes hard to discern. The juvenile is similar to the adult.

The Lesser Whitethroat is an active bird that tends to skulk in dense cover, making it tricky to observe clearly. It has a distinctive song that often betrays its presence. It nests in dense low cover, constructing a loose cup of grass and twigs.

Factfile

LENGTH 12–13CM   WINGSPAN 16–20CM

HABITAT FAVOURS MATURE SCRUB, HEDGEROWS AND WOODLAND EDGES; RARELY FOUND IN DENSE WOODLAND.

FOOD FEEDS PRIMARILY ON INSECTS AND SPIDERS, WITH SOME WORMS AND FRUITS.

STATUS MIGRANT SUMMER BREEDING SPECIES, WIDESPREAD IN SUITABLE HABITAT THROUGHOUT MOST OF THE REGION, WITH THE EXCEPTION OF THE EXTREME NORTH. PRESENT MAINLY MAY TO AUGUST.

VOICE SONG IS A DIAGNOSTIC, RATHER MONOSYLLABIC TUNELESS RATTLE, PRECEDED BY A WARBLING PHRASE. UTTERS A SHARP *CHEK* CALL IN ALARM.

adult

adult life-size

The rattling song of a Lesser Whitethroat could only really be confused with a distant Cirl Bunting, a much rarer species that has different habitat requirements.

Compared to a Whitethroat, the plumage looks overall 'colder' and lacks the buff and brown hues seen on that species' wings and underparts in particular.

Whitethroat
Sylvia communis

Often associated with Bramble patches which provide both cover for nesting and a good supply of invertebrate food.

The Whitethroat is the most widespread *Sylvia* warbler in the region, and commonly seen perched in the open, allowing easy observation. The sexes are similar but separable with care. The adult male has grey-brown upperparts with conspicuous rufous-brown edges to the wing feathers; the head has a blue-grey cap and face, with a bold white eye-ring. The underparts are pale with a pinkish-buff flush, most obvious on the breast. Note the striking white throat and the white outer tail feathers. The slender bill is sandy-brown and dark-tipped, and the legs are pale pinkish-brown. The adult female is similar to the male but the cap and face are tinged with brown, while the underparts are flushed with pale buff. The juvenile recalls the adult female.

adult

adult

Territorial males are very vocal and often deliver their song in flight, particularly at the start of the breeding season.

The Whitethroat is one of the easiest warblers to observe owing to its bold nature and habit of perching out in the open, often on the highest point of a scrub patch. Its song is characteristic. The male initiates the construction of several nests, the female choosing one and completing the work. The nest is a grass cup in low-lying scrub.

Factfile

LENGTH 13–15CM

WINGSPAN 19–23CM

HABITAT **FAVOURS OPEN HABITATS WITH AREAS OF LOW SCRUB COVER SUCH AS HEDGEROWS, HEATHLAND, FARMLAND AND COASTAL GRASSLAND.**

FOOD **FEEDS PRIMARILY ON INSECTS; ALSO FRUITS AND BERRIES.**

STATUS **COMMON AND WIDESPREAD SUMMER BREEDING VISITOR FOUND IN SUITABLE HABITATS THROUGHOUT MOST OF THE REGION; PRESENT MAINLY APRIL TO AUGUST. OVERWINTERS IN AFRICA.**

VOICE **THE SONG IS A CHARACTERISTIC RAPID COARSE WARBLE, OFTEN DELIVERED WHEN IN FLIGHT OR PERCHED IN THE OPEN. CALL IS A HARSH *CHECK* ISSUED IN ALARM.**

adult life-size

Whitethroats keep to cover for much of the time but once in a while a bird will pop up and perch on a prominent twig.

Dartford Warbler
Sylvia undata

Factfile

LENGTH 12–13CM

WINGSPAN 13–18CM

HABITAT **FAVOURS HEATHLAND WITH TALL MATURE GORSE BUSHES, ALSO FOUND ON THE COAST DURING THE WINTER MONTHS.**

FOOD **FEEDS ALMOST EXCLUSIVELY ON INVERTEBRATES; OCCASIONALLY FRUITS AND BERRIES.**

STATUS **LOCAL RESIDENT BREEDING SPECIES FOUND IN THE EXTREME SOUTH OF BRITAIN AND WESTERN MAINLAND EUROPE.**

VOICE **SONG IS A RAPID, SCRATCHY WARBLE. UTTERS A DISTINCTIVE *TCHRR-TCHE* CALL, OFTEN BETRAYING ITS PRESENCE.**

This is a handsome little warbler with a rounded head; characteristically perches with its tail cocked upwards. The sexes are separable. The adult male in spring and summer has mainly darkish blue-grey upperparts, and a slate-grey head. The underparts are a rich chestnut-red with a contrasting white belly. The throat is marked with a series of white spots, and the beady red eye is surrounded by an obvious red eye-ring. The dark brown bill is rather needle-like, and the legs are pinkish-yellow. Plumage colours are subtly subdued in the winter months. The adult female is similar to the male but the colours are more subdued, and note the uniformly pale throat. The juvenile recalls the adult female, but colours are more muted still.

The Dartford Warbler is a distinctive little songbird that is rather furtive, spending much of its time skulking in deep cover. It is occasionally observed perched on the top of a gorse bush, typically on clear sunny mornings, cocking its tail characteristically. It nests in low scrub, constructing a cup-shaped nest of grass lined with wool and plant down.

male summer

A Dartford Warbler's colourful plumage, compact body size and long tail make identification straightforward.

male life-size

Spring is the best time to look for Dartford Warblers, when males occasionally emerge from cover and sing from an exposed perch.

Outside the breeding season, and in cold spells in particular, birds are sometimes completely indifferent to the presence of human observers.

adult winter

Grasshopper Warbler

Locustella naevia

adult

Singing birds are most easily observed at dusk, and will continue singing off-and-on throughout the night.

adult life-size

Moves with surprising agility and ease through dense vegetation in search of invertebrates.

Factfile

LENGTH 12–13.5CM

WINGSPAN 15–19CM

HABITAT **FAVOURS DAMP GRASSLAND AND MARSHES WITH RUSHES AND PATCHES OF BRAMBLE.**

FOOD **FEEDS ALMOST EXCLUSIVELY ON INSECTS.**

STATUS **SUMMER BREEDING VISITOR THAT IS WIDESPREAD BUT LOCAL IN SUITABLE HABITATS THROUGHOUT THE REGION, EXCEPT THE EXTREME NORTH; PRESENT MAINLY MAY TO AUGUST. OVERWINTERS IN AFRICA.**

VOICE **SONG COMPRISES A RAPID, RATHER MECHANICAL TRILLING, OFTEN LIKENED TO THAT OF A BUSH CRICKET. GENERALLY SUNG CONTINUOUSLY, MOST OFTEN AT NIGHT. UTTERS A SHARP *TSSVET* CALL IN ALARM.**

This is a rather furtive warbler that spends most of its time skulking in deep cover, making observation tricky. The sexes are similar. The adult has olive-brown upperparts, the dark feather centres giving it a streaked appearance. The underparts are pale buff, and the breast suffused with buffish-brown. Note the characteristic long undertail coverts that are dark-streaked and extend well beyond the primary feathers on the folded wing. The slender bill is dark brown with a yellow base and the legs are pale pinkish-brown. The juvenile resembles the adult but the underparts have a more intense flush of yellow-buff.

The Grasshopper Warbler is the only common and widespread *Locustella* warbler in the region. It often creeps through low vegetation like a small rodent. It nests in low vegetation, constructing a nest from leaves and grass; it is often approached via a short tunnel.

Icterine Warbler

Hippolais icterina

Plumage is brightest and most colourful in newly arrived birds seen in spring.

adult

The pale wing panel helps with separation from a superficially similar Melodious Warbler.

adult life-size

Factfile

LENGTH 12–13.5CM

WINGSPAN 21–24CM

HABITAT BREEDING HABITATS INCLUDE LOWLAND WOODLANDS, FARMLAND AND MATURE GARDENS. COASTAL SCRUB ON MIGRATION.

FOOD FEEDS PRIMARILY ON INSECTS AND OTHER INVERTEBRATES; SOME FRUITS AND BERRIES.

STATUS SUMMER BREEDING SPECIES THROUGHOUT MUCH OF MAINLAND EUROPE, INCLUDING SCANDINAVIA; PRESENT MAINLY MAY TO AUGUST. ABSENT FROM THE BRITISH ISLES AS A BREEDING SPECIES BUT SEEN AS A SCARCE PASSAGE MIGRANT IN SPRING AND AUTUMN. OVERWINTERS IN AFRICA.

VOICE SONG COMPRISES A RAPID AND RATHER NASAL FLUTY WARBLE THAT CAN INCLUDE ELEMENTS OF MIMICRY. THE CALL IS A SHARP *TCHET* OR RATTLING NOISE.

This is a proportionately large and robust-looking warbler, and the northeastern counterpart of the superficially similar Melodious Warbler. The sexes are similar. The adult has rather uniform plumage, with greyish-green upperparts and pale yellow underparts. Note the pale wing panel which comprises pale feather fringes (this feature is absent in Melodious Warbler), the pale yellow lores and the rather plain-faced appearance. Note also the blue-grey legs and the longer primary projection, compared to Melodious Warbler. Juvenile and first-autumn birds are similar to the adult but the colours are subdued overall, and the underparts are noticeably paler.

The Icterine Warbler spends the majority of its time foraging among the treetops, making observation tricky. The male is fiercely territorial during the spring and will defend his territory with song, bill snapping and even physical altercation. The nest is a softly lined deep cup of plant materials placed in the fork of a bush or tree.

Melodious Warbler

Hippolais polyglotta

1st autumn

Noticeably larger than a *Phylloscopus* warbler with bluish legs, and a proportionately larger bill and longer tail.

Factfile

LENGTH 12–13CM

WINGSPAN 17–20CM

HABITAT FAVOURS LOWLAND WOODLANDS ADJACENT TO WATER. COASTAL SCRUB ON MIGRATION.

FOOD FEEDS ON INSECTS AND OTHER INVERTEBRATES, AND FRUIT.

STATUS SUMMER BREEDING VISITOR TO WESTERN MAINLAND EUROPE, PRESENT MAINLY MAY TO AUGUST; ABSENT FROM THE BRITISH ISLES AS A BREEDING SPECIES BUT SEEN THERE AS A SCARCE PASSAGE MIGRANT. OVERWINTERS IN AFRICA.

VOICE SONG IS A PROLONGED SERIES OF RAPID WARBLING PHRASES AND NOTES. UTTERS A HARSH *TCHET* CALL.

This is a medium-sized warbler with a long bill; it is similar to the Icterine Warbler and that species' western counterpart. The sexes are similar. The adult has rather uniform plumage, the upperparts olive-green and the wings displaying a brownish tinge. Note that the wings generally lack the pale panel seen in Icterine Warbler. The underparts are pale and flushed with yellow, which is most intense on the throat and breast. The large bill is brown and broad at the base; the legs are blue-grey. Other features to note are the proportionately large head, pale lores and the shorter primary projection compared to Icterine Warbler. Juvenile and first-autumn birds are similar to the adult but with much paler underparts, and with a hint of yellow only on the throat and breast.

The Melodious Warbler is a busy bird that spends most of its time feeding in the cover of dense shrubs and trees. Its nest is a softly lined deep cup of plant materials, placed in the fork of a bush or tree, and generally within a metre or two of the ground.

adult life-size

Overall the plumage usually looks a shade browner than in otherwise similar Icterine Warbler.

Marsh Warbler

Acrocephalus palustris

Factfile

LENGTH 13–14CM

WINGSPAN 18–21CM

HABITAT FAVOURS DENSE, RANK WATERSIDE VEGETATION.

FOOD FEEDS PRIMARILY ON INSECTS AND SPIDERS, WITH SOME SNAILS AND BERRIES.

STATUS SUMMER BREEDING SPECIES RESTRICTED MAINLY TO MAINLAND EUROPE, INCLUDING SOUTHERN SCANDINAVIA; PRESENT MAINLY MAY TO AUGUST. EXTREMELY RARE IN BRITAIN WHERE IT IS A VERY RARE BREEDER AND SCARCE PASSAGE MIGRANT. OVERWINTERS IN AFRICA.

VOICE THE RICH AND VARIED MUSICAL SONG MIMICS SONGBIRDS FROM EUROPE AND THOSE FROM ITS WINTERING GROUNDS IN AFRICA. THE CALL IS A SHARP *TCHE*.

This is rather plainly marked warbler, superficially similar to a Reed Warbler but separable with care. The sexes are similar. The adult has grey-brown upperparts, subtly 'cooler' in tone than those of Reed Warbler. The underparts are whitish and have a pale yellow flush to the breast and flanks. The head is rather rounded and marked with a faint pale supercilium. The dark bill is straight and appreciably shorter than that of a Reed Warbler. The legs are pinkish. Note the long primary projection (equal to, or longer than, the exposed tertials in Marsh but less than or equal to the tertials in Reed Warbler). Juvenile and first-autumn birds recall the adult but have warmer upperparts, a faint reddish-brown rump and pale underparts with a buffish tinge.

The Marsh Warbler is a less agile bird than the Reed Warbler and occurs in subtly different habitats, seeking low-lying lush waterside vegetation as opposed to dense reed beds. It is an extremely vocal bird, and its song mostly mimics those of other songbirds. It constructs an untidy nest of plant material attached to plant stems.

adult

adult life-size

Look and listen for Marsh Warblers in rank vegetation along the margins of reed beds, rivers and other wetland habitats.

Territorial birds sometimes perch and stay still long enough for an observer to appreciate the longer wings compared to a Reed Warbler.

Reed Warbler

Acrocephalus scirpaceus

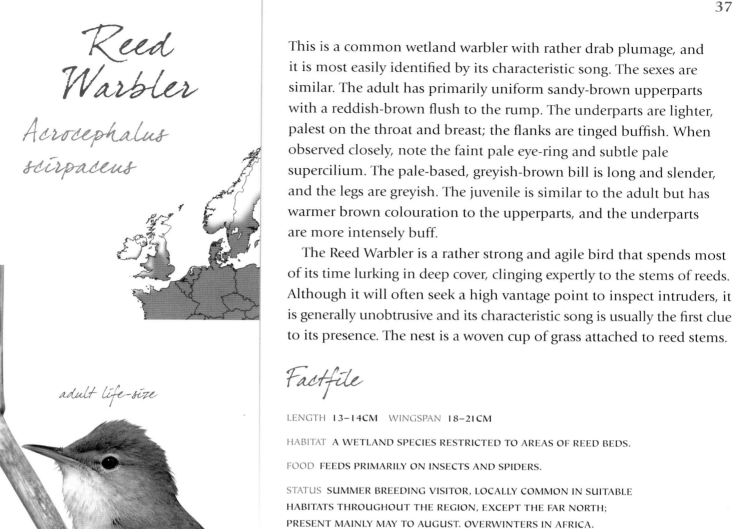

This is a common wetland warbler with rather drab plumage, and it is most easily identified by its characteristic song. The sexes are similar. The adult has primarily uniform sandy-brown upperparts with a reddish-brown flush to the rump. The underparts are lighter, palest on the throat and breast; the flanks are tinged buffish. When observed closely, note the faint pale eye-ring and subtle pale supercilium. The pale-based, greyish-brown bill is long and slender, and the legs are greyish. The juvenile is similar to the adult but has warmer brown colouration to the upperparts, and the underparts are more intensely buff.

The Reed Warbler is a rather strong and agile bird that spends most of its time lurking in deep cover, clinging expertly to the stems of reeds. Although it will often seek a high vantage point to inspect intruders, it is generally unobtrusive and its characteristic song is usually the first clue to its presence. The nest is a woven cup of grass attached to reed stems.

Factfile

LENGTH 13–14CM WINGSPAN 18–21CM

HABITAT A WETLAND SPECIES RESTRICTED TO AREAS OF REED BEDS.

FOOD FEEDS PRIMARILY ON INSECTS AND SPIDERS.

STATUS SUMMER BREEDING VISITOR, LOCALLY COMMON IN SUITABLE HABITATS THROUGHOUT THE REGION, EXCEPT THE FAR NORTH; PRESENT MAINLY MAY TO AUGUST. OVERWINTERS IN AFRICA.

VOICE SONG COMPRISES A MIXTURE OF LOW GRATING AND CHATTERING NOISES, PHRASES OFTEN REPEATED RHYTHMICALLY TWO OR THREE TIMES. UTTERS A SHARP *TCHE* CALL IN ALARM.

adult life-size

Reed Warblers can be hard to see among swaying reeds but once in a while a bird will clamber up a stem to scan its territory.

adult

Birds usually sing from deep within a reed bed, so patient observation is needed to view the songster.

Sedge Warbler
Acrocephalus schoenobaenus

Dense Bramble patches around the margins of wetlands are ideal for breeding Sedge Warblers.

adult

adult life-size

This is a distinctively marked wetland warbler with a lively diagnostic song. The sexes are similar. The adult has primarily sandy-brown upperparts which are boldly marked with dark streaking. The underparts are whitish and tinged with orange-buff on the breast and flanks. Note the unstreaked warm brown rump. The head has a dark-streaked crown, dark eye stripe and an obvious pale supercilium. The slender, pale-based bill is blackish and the legs are grey-brown. The juvenile is similar to the adult but can show pale streaking on the breast and a more obvious yellow flush to the underparts.

The Sedge Warbler is the most common and widespread *Acrocephalus* warbler in Europe. Although associated with relatively dense pockets of vegetation, it betrays its presence with its characteristic song, often delivered from an exposed perch or when in flight. It nests in low vegetation, constructing a soft-lined nest of grasses.

The strongly patterned head and streaked back allow separation from a Reed Warbler; the two species often occur within earshot of one another.

adult

Newly arrived territorial males often display and sing in flight.

Factfile

LENGTH 12–13CM

WINGSPAN 17–21CM

HABITAT FAVOURS SCRUB PATCHES AND THICK VEGETATION ON THE EDGE OF REED BEDS AND ADJACENT TO WATER, SUCH AS MARSHES AND OVERGROWN DITCHES.

FOOD FEEDS PRIMARILY ON INSECTS AND SPIDERS.

STATUS SUMMER BREEDING VISITOR, COMMON AND WIDESPREAD IN SUITABLE LOWLAND HABITATS; PRESENT MAINLY MAY TO AUGUST. OVERWINTERS IN AFRICA.

VOICE SONG IS A LOUD SERIES OF HARSH GRATING NOISES AND MUSICAL TRILLS AND WHISTLES. UTTERS A *CHEK* CALL IN ALARM.

Waxwing
Bombycilla garrulus

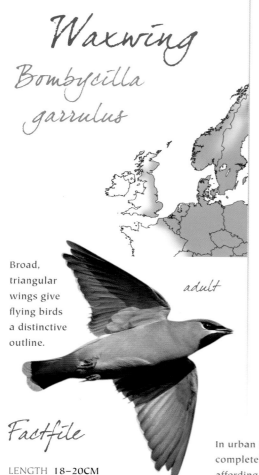

Broad, triangular wings give flying birds a distinctive outline.

adult

Factfile

LENGTH 18–20CM

WINGSPAN 32–38CM

HABITAT FAVOURS CONIFEROUS PINE FORESTS DURING THE SUMMER MONTHS. DISPERSES TO OTHER HABITATS IN WINTER IN SEARCH OF FOOD, AND OFTEN FREQUENTS PARKS AND GARDENS CONTAINING TREES AND SHRUBS WITH PLENTIFUL WINTER BERRIES.

FOOD FEEDS PRIMARILY ON INSECTS DURING THE SUMMERS MONTHS, FRUITS AND BERRIES DURING THE WINTER.

STATUS BREEDING RANGE EXTENDS EASTWARDS FROM NORTHERN SCANDINAVIA. BEST KNOWN IN OUR REGION AS A MIGRANT WINTER VISITOR, PRESENT MAINLY NOVEMBER TO MARCH; NUMBERS AND RANGE DEPEND ON THE SEVERITY OF THE WEATHER AND FOOD AVAILABILITY. COMMONEST IN WINTER IN EASTERN MAINLAND EUROPE, BUT RANGE EXTENDS TO EASTERN BRITAIN.

VOICE UTTERS A TRILLING WHISTLE.

The Waxwing is a colourful songbird, the sexes of which are similar but separable with care. The adult male has primarily pinkish-buff plumage, darkest on the back and nape, and palest on the belly. The rump is light grey and the undertail is chestnut. A number of distinctive and colourful markings adorn the bird, the most distinctive being the obvious long crest feathers. Note the black throat and face mask, and the bright yellow-tipped dark tail. Also note the conspicuous black-and-white barring, yellow markings and red wax-like projections to the wings. The adult female is similar to the adult male but has a narrower yellow tip to the tail. First-winter birds recall the adult but lack the white feather margins and red projections to the wings. In flight, the outline recalls that of a Starling, with rather short triangular-shaped wings.

Revered by many, this colourful species is most commonly seen during the winter months when it migrates in search of winter fruits and berries; numbers vary from year to year. Flocks frequently turn up in urban parks, gardens and even supermarket car parks when natural resources in the countryside become depleted.

In urban settings, birds are often completely indifferent to people, affording excellent views.

Berry-laden trees and bushes act like magnets for hungry Waxwings in winter.

adult

adult life-size

Treecreeper
Certhia familiaris

The Treecreeper is a furtive little woodland bird with a downcurved bill and long brown tail. The sexes are similar. The adult has mainly brown upperparts, marked with lighter blotches and darker streaks; this provides superb camouflage against tree bark. Note the broad zigzag markings on the wings. The underparts are silvery-white with a subtle buff tinge towards the rear end of the flanks. The head has a grubby-white supercilium. The dark brown bill is long, thin and conspicuously downcurved. The legs are light brown; note the long toes and extended hind claw. The juvenile is similar to the adult but has subtle spotting on the underparts.

The Treecreeper is an unobtrusive bird that feeds by spiralling around tree trunks, starting at the base and working its way up before flying to the next tree when it reaches the top. It keeps its body held close to the trunk and creeps on its short legs, using its long tail for support. It is a rather sedentary bird that roosts (sometimes communally) in bark crevices. It nests in crevices and behind tree bark.

The plumage is overall cleaner-looking than a Short-toed Treecreeper and the bill is proportionately shorter.

adult life-size

adult

Stiff, bristly tips to the tail feathers provide rigid support for climbing birds.

Factfile

LENGTH 12–13CM

WINGSPAN 18–21CM

HABITAT MATURE DECIDUOUS AND MIXED WOODLAND HABITATS.

FOOD FEEDS PRIMARILY ON INSECTS AND SPIDERS, OCCASIONALLY SEEDS.

STATUS RESIDENT BREEDING SPECIES, PRESENT YEAR-ROUND. COMMON AND WIDESPREAD IN SUITABLE HABITATS THROUGHOUT MOST OF THE REGION.

VOICE SONG COMPRISES A SHORT SERIES OF HIGH-PITCHED NOTES TERMINATING IN A TRILL. UTTERS A SHALLOW, HIGH-PITCHED *TSEERT* CALL.

Short-toed Treecreeper
Certhia brachydactyla

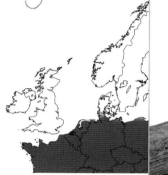

adult life-size

The bill is proportionately longer than in Treecreeper but the most reliable way of separating the species is by listening to the calls and song.

Although the hind claw is noticeably shorter than in Treecreeper, this feature can be hard to see and is of little use in the field.

adult

Factfile

LENGTH 12–13CM

WINGSPAN 17–20CM

HABITAT FAVOURS TALL, MATURE TREES IN PARKS, GARDENS, ORCHARDS, AND FORESTS AND WOODLAND EDGES.

FOOD FEEDS ON INSECTS, SPIDERS AND OTHER INVERTEBRATES.

STATUS WIDESPREAD RESIDENT BREEDING SPECIES, PRESENT YEAR-ROUND ACROSS MUCH OF CENTRAL AND SOUTHERN MAINLAND EUROPE. ABSENT FROM BRITAIN, IRELAND AND SCANDINAVIA, ALTHOUGH THE ODD VAGRANT APPEARS THERE FROM TIME TO TIME.

VOICE SONG IS SHORTER AND MORE PENETRATING THAN THAT OF TREECREEPER. UTTERS A SHRILL *ZEEHT*, STRIKINGLY UNLIKE THE TREECREEPER'S CALL.

The Short-toed Treecreeper is a small woodland bird, virtually identical in appearance to Treecreeper, but with subtle differences that allow separation with care. The sexes are similar. The adult has streaked brown upperparts, the folded wing marked with an even-sided pale wingbar (Treecreeper has a jagged margin). The underparts are grubby-white with a conspicuous buff suffusion to the flanks. Compared to Treecreeper, note the appreciably longer downcurved, needle-like bill. Note also the shorter hind claw. Overall the plumage appears duller than that of Treecreeper. The juvenile is similar to the adult.

The most reliable aid to separating this species from Treecreeper is its significantly louder and more piercing voice. It feeds in a similar manner to Treecreeper, probing crevices in tree bark for insects and other invertebrates. It nests in crevices and behind tree bark.

Nuthatch
Sitta europaea

Factfile

LENGTH 12–14CM

WINGSPAN 23–27CM

HABITAT ASSOCIATED WITH DECIDUOUS AND MIXED WOODLAND HABITATS, PARKS, GARDENS AND OTHER AREAS WITH MATURE TREES.

FOOD FEEDS ON INSECTS, SEEDS AND FRUITS.

STATUS COMMON AND WIDESPREAD RESIDENT BREEDING SPECIES, PRESENT YEAR-ROUND ACROSS MUCH OF THE REGION, WITH THE EXCEPTION OF IRELAND, THE EXTREME NORTH OF SCOTLAND AND NORTHERN SCANDINAVIA.

VOICE SONG COMMONLY COMPRISES A LOUD SERIES OF *PEE-PEE-PEE* NOTES. UTTERS A LOUD AND INSISTENT *ZWITT* CALL IN ALARM.

The Nuthatch is a rather stout-bodied and short-tailed woodland bird. The sexes are similar but can be separated with care. The adult has primarily blue-grey upperparts, including the nape and crown; the underparts are mainly orange-buff. The head is marked with white cheeks and a bold black eye stripe which runs from the base of the bill, through the dark eye and past the ear coverts. The robust dark bill is rather long and sharply pointed, and the legs are sandy-brown. The male can sometimes be separated by the more intense reddish-buff tinge to the rear of the flanks. The juvenile is similar to the adult female but with more muted colours and a less well-defined eye stripe.

The Nuthatch is a familiar bird of woodland habitats. It is commonly seen descending the trunks of trees head-first, and the only species in the region to do so. It feeds by using its chisel-like bill to dig insects out of tree bark and to split open acorns and other seeds it wedges into bark crevices, storing food for the winter months. A very sedentary bird that pairs for life, it nests in tree holes and typically lines the entrance with mud to reduce the size of the hole.

Powerful feet and claws provide a confident grip when climbing up and down tree trunks.

adult

adult life-size
On average males tend to have more richly colourful underparts than females. British race birds are more colourful than their mainland European cousins.

Wren
Troglodytes troglodytes

Factfile

LENGTH 9–10CM   WINGSPAN 13–17CM

HABITAT FAVOURS AREAS OF THICK UNDERGROWTH AND CAN BE FOUND IN A VARIETY OF HABITATS INCLUDING WOODLANDS, PARKS, SCRUB AND COASTAL CLIFFS. A FAMILIAR GARDEN SPECIES.

FOOD FEEDS PRIMARILY ON INSECTS AND SPIDERS, OCCASIONALLY SEEDS.

STATUS COMMON AND WIDESPREAD RESIDENT BREEDING SPECIES, PRESENT YEAR-ROUND IN MUCH OF THE REGION. BIRDS IN THE EXTREME NORTH AND EAST MIGRATE SOUTH FOR THE WINTER.

VOICE A VOCAL BIRD WHOSE SONG IS LOUD AND WARBLING, ENDING IN A TRILL. UTTERS A LOUD RATTLING CALL IN ALARM.

The Wren is a tiny, round-bodied bird with a short tail and dark brown plumage. The sexes are similar. The adult has mainly dark reddish-brown upperparts, the wings and tail displaying subtle barring. The underparts are greyish-white, lightest on the throat and breast, and with a buff flush to the flanks. The head is marked with a conspicuous pale supercilium. The long, thin bill is grey-brown and slightly downcurved, and the legs are reddish-brown. The juvenile is similar to the adult. Isolated populations on remote islands to the north of the British Isles are typically darker and more rufous than birds that occur further south.

The Wren is a busy little bird that spends most of its time skulking in low vegetation in search of insects. Typically, it holds its short tail erect when perched in the open. The male constructs a number of dome-shaped nests of grass and leaves to attract the female, one being chosen and the rest discarded. Its numbers suffer badly in severe winters, and birds sometimes roost communally in tight groups during harsh winter nights.

Although the species is common across much its range from year to year, its numbers crash in particularly cold winters and it can take several seasons for the population to recover.

adult

adult life-size

The vibrant song is extraordinarily loud for such a small bird.

Starling
Sturnus vulgaris

The Starling is a common sight in rural and urban areas and an extremely vocal bird, uttering a range of sounds. The sexes are similar but usually separable with care during the summer. The summer adult has entirely dark plumage with an obvious oily sheen and an iridescence that includes green, bronze and blue tones when seen in good light. The bill is yellow and the legs are reddish. The bill of the male has a blue base to the lower mandible, and the female generally displays some spotting on the underside. The winter adult is beautifully adorned with strikingly contrasting pale feather tips. These take the form of white 'V'-shaped marks on the breast, bronze spots on the

adult summer

adult winter life-size

Although the species is still common and widespread, numbers of breeding and wintering birds have declined significantly in Britain in particular.

Song and calls vary between birds and some individuals are extraordinary mimics of neighbouring sounds, whose repertoire can include everything from car alarms to wolf-whistles.

head and back, and bronze edges to the wing feathers. The bill is dark. The juvenile has uniformly grey-brown plumage with a dark bill, acquiring adult plumage in the main by the autumn, but often retaining the grey-brown to the head and neck. By the first winter the plumage is indistinguishable from the adult. In flight, note the diagnostic short triangular-shaped wings seen in all birds.

The Starling typically forms large flocks outside the breeding season. Numbers in western Europe are boosted in autumn by birds that have migrated from further east and north to avoid harsh winter weather. Hundreds of thousands of birds congregate at popular roosting sites such as lowland marshes, the flying flocks forming huge clouds in the sky at dusk; this display can be spectacular. Its nest is a grass platform in a tree hole, nest box or building.

In winter, noisy groups of Starlings descend upon garden bird tables in towns and cities.

adult winter

adult winter

A solitary Starling is an unusual sight and most are found sizeable flocks.

Factfile

LENGTH 20–22CM

WINGSPAN 37–42CM

HABITAT AN ADAPTABLE SPECIES THAT OCCURS IN A VARIETY OF HABITATS FROM LOWLAND FARMLAND, MARSHLANDS AND OPEN COUNTRYSIDE TO COASTAL REGIONS AND URBAN AREAS.

FOOD FEEDS ON INSECTS AND OTHER INVERTEBRATES, SEEDS AND FRUITS.

STATUS WIDESPREAD AND ABUNDANT RESIDENT BREEDING SPECIES, PRESENT YEAR-ROUND IN MOST OF THE REGION. NUMBERS ARE BOOSTED IN THE WINTER MONTHS BY BIRDS MIGRATING HERE FROM FURTHER EAST AND NORTH.

VOICE AN ENTHUSIASTIC MIMIC AND LIVELY SONGSTER. SONG INCLUDES MIMICRY OF OTHER BIRD SONG AND MAN-MADE SOUNDS. ALSO UTTERS VARIOUS CLICKS AND DESCENDING WHISTLES.

Dipper
Cinclus cinclus

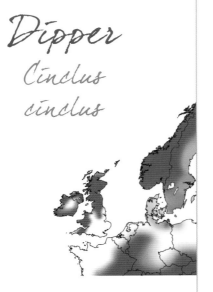

Factfile

LENGTH 18–20CM

WINGSPAN 26–30CM

HABITAT ASSOCIATED WITH SWIFTLY FLOWING UPLAND RIVERS AND STREAMS WITH ROCKS AND BOULDERS.

FOOD FEEDS MAINLY ON AQUATIC INVERTEBRATES, NOTABLY INSECTS AND WORMS; SOME SMALL FISH.

STATUS RESIDENT BREEDING SPECIES THAT CAN BE FOUND YEAR-ROUND IN SUITABLE HABITAT THROUGHOUT THE REGION. SOME ALTITUDINAL MIGRATION TO LOWER-LYING HABITATS TAKES PLACE IN WINTER, INVOLVING BIRDS FROM HIGHER ALTITUDES.

VOICE UTTERS A HARSH *STRIITZ* CALL.

The Dipper is a rather rotund little bird with a short tail. The sexes are similar but plumage differences exist between birds found in Britain and those on mainland Europe. The adult bird in Britain has dark grey-brown upperparts and tail; the head is reddish-brown. There is a strikingly white throat and bib, sharply divided from a reddish-chestnut belly that grades to blackish-brown at the rear. Both the legs and the bill are stout and robust-looking, and black-brown. Birds from mainland Europe are similar but have a uniformly dark belly and rear. The juvenile is like the adult in shape but has greyish upperparts; the underparts are pale and heavily barred but with a clean throat.

The Dipper is associated with upland streams and rivers. It is most commonly observed perched on boulders in fast-flowing water, or flying low over the river on rapid whirring wingbeats. It dives frequently, swimming and walking along the bottom against the current in search of aquatic invertebrates. It nests in a hole or crevice in the river bank, constructing a dome of moss and grass.

British race adult

Typically, perched birds bob up and down and sometimes raise their tails if agitated.

Sometimes forced to move to lowland
waterways in winter if freezing
conditions prevail; mainland
European birds occasionally turn
up in Britain at this time.

*Scandinavian race
adult life-size*

Shares the same dumpy body form
as an adult but has grey, rather
scaly-looking upperparts.

juvenile

Ring Ouzel
Turdus torquatus

Factfile

LENGTH 24–26CM

WINGSPAN 38–42CM

HABITAT FAVOURS RUGGED UPLAND MOORLANDS AND LOWER MOUNTAIN SLOPES DURING THE BREEDING SEASON.

FOOD FEEDS ON INVERTEBRATES, BERRIES AND FRUITS.

STATUS SUMMER BREEDING SPECIES RESTRICTED TO AREAS OF SUITABLE HABITAT, AND PRESENT THERE MAINLY APRIL TO SEPTEMBER. ALSO SEEN ON MIGRATION. OVERWINTERS IN THE MEDITERRANEAN REGION.

VOICE HAS A RATHER FLUTY SONG, DELIVERED IN SHORT BURSTS. CALL IS A HARSH *TCHUCK* UTTERED IN ALARM.

The best chances of getting a good look at a Ring Ouzel come at migration times; on their breeding grounds, they are extremely shy and secretive.

The Ring Ouzel is the upland cousin of Blackbird and a distinctive-looking thrush. The sexes differ. The adult male has primarily dull black plumage, but note the subtle pale edges to the feathers on the underside that give a slightly scaly appearance when seen in good light. The breast is diagnostically marked with a striking large white crescent-shaped patch. The bill is yellowish and the legs are dark. The adult female is similar, but browner overall and the white crescent is grubby-white. The first-winter bird is more uniformly dark and it displays pale fringes to the feathers all over; the crescent breast marking is very subtle. All birds appear rather silvery-winged when seen in flight, owing to the pale feather margins.

The Ring Ouzel breeds on remote upland moorland and mountain slopes. It is a very alert and wary bird at this time, making close observation a challenge. It migrates to the Mediterranean for the winter months, seeking rugged upland slopes, similar to the breeding grounds. Birds on migration often provide the best opportunity for good views, with large groups sometimes encountered. It weaves a nest of grass among boulders.

male life-size

The prominent white chest band allows easy separation from a male Blackbird.

female

Blackbird
Turdus merula

The Blackbird is a common ground-dwelling thrush and a familiar garden visitor. The sexes differ. The adult male has uniformly black plumage with a subtle glossy sheen when seen in good light. Note the bright yellow bill and the yellow eye-ring surrounding the dark eye. The legs are dark. The first-winter male is similar but has a dark bill and a less well-defined eye-ring. Adult and first-winter females have dark brown upperparts and tail; the underparts are paler with a reddish suffusion, subtly spotted and marked with streaking on the breast. The bill is dark, but marked with yellow at the base of the lower mandible. The juvenile resembles the female but with pale yellow spots adorning the back and underparts.

The Blackbird is an abundant and relatively easy species to observe, particularly in urban environments, where it becomes quite tolerant of human presence. It is a regular garden visitor. Its nest is a robust cup of mud, grass and leaves, generally located in a dense shrub or hedgerow.

Factfile

LENGTH **25–28CM**   WINGSPAN **34–39CM**   HABITAT WIDE RANGE OF HABITATS INCLUDING WOODLANDS, FARMLAND, SCRUB, HEATHS AND COASTS. A REGULAR GARDEN VISITOR IN BOTH RURAL AND URBAN AREAS.   FOOD FEEDS ON A VARIETY OF INSECTS, WORMS AND OTHER INVERTEBRATES; ALSO FRUITS AND BERRIES.   STATUS WIDESPREAD RESIDENT BREEDER, PRESENT YEAR-ROUND THROUGHOUT MOST OF THE REGION. BREEDING POPULATIONS FROM THE EXTREME NORTH AND EAST MIGRATE TO THE MORE TEMPERATE ZONES IN THE SOUTH AND WEST, SWELLING POPULATIONS IN THESE AREAS IN WINTER.   VOICE MALE IS A CONSUMMATE SONGSTER, HAVING A VARIED REPERTOIRE OF FLUTY AND MUSICAL PHRASES. UTTERS A HARSH, REPETITIVE *TCHAK* AT DUSK OR IN ALARM.

male life-size

Males are conspicuous in the garden, feeding on lawns and alarm-calling loudly if danger threatens.

male

Searches through leaf matter, throwing leaves aside with sharp flicks of its head, in search of worms and other invertebrates.

female

Song Thrush

Turdus philomelos

Factfile

LENGTH **20–23CM** WINGSPAN **33–36CM**

HABITAT **FAVOURS HABITATS OFFERING A MIXTURE OF OPEN GROUND AND DENSE VEGETATION, TREES AND SHRUBS, SUCH AS WOODLAND, PARKS AND MATURE GARDENS.**

FOOD **FEEDS ON INSECTS, SNAILS, WORMS AND OTHER INVERTEBRATES; FRUITS AND BERRIES IN THE AUTUMN AND WINTER MONTHS.**

STATUS **COMMON AND WIDESPREAD RESIDENT BREEDING SPECIES, PRESENT YEAR-ROUND THROUGHOUT MUCH OF THE REGION. NORTHERN AND EASTERN BREEDING BIRDS MIGRATE SOUTH FOR THE WINTER, THE GEOGRAPHICAL RANGE AND NUMBERS DEPENDENT UPON THE SEVERITY OF THE WINTER.**

VOICE **A RENOWNED SONGSTER, WITH A LOUD AND MUSICAL SONG OF SHORT PHRASES EACH OF WHICH IS REPEATED THREE OR MORE TIMES. CALL IS A THIN *TIK*, MOST COMMONLY DELIVERED IN FLIGHT.**

Compared to a Mistle Thrush, a Song Thrush is a smaller and altogether more dainty bird.

The Song Thrush is a familiar and handsomely marked songbird best known for its beautiful song. The sexes are similar. The adult has primarily warm brown upperparts, the wing showing a faint orange-buff bar. The head is subtly marked with a pale eye-ring, pale throat and thin, dark moustachial stripe. The underparts are pale with a yellowish-buff tinge to the breast, and are marked with a series of bold, dark arrowhead-shaped spots (unlike the rounded spots in the similar Mistle Thrush). The bill is dark and the legs are flesh-coloured. In flight, note the obvious and diagnostic orange-buff underwing coverts. The juvenile is similar but the markings and colouration lack the definition of the adult.

The Song Thrush is a familiar garden visitor, well known for its liking of snails. It often uses favoured rocks and stones as 'anvils' on which to smash the shells, holding the shell in its beak and delivering a swift hammering blow. It constructs a cup-shaped nest of grass, lined with mud or wood pulp.

adult

The underwing coverts are buffish-orange while those of a Mistle Thrush are white.

adult life-size

adult Mistle Thrush

Mistle Thrush

Turdus viscivorus

Superficially similar to Song Thrush, the Mistle Thrush is appreciably larger with a plumper appearance. The sexes are similar. The adult has primarily grey-brown upperparts with a subtle white wingbar. The underparts are pale, flushed with orange-buff on the flanks and heavily marked with rounded bold black spots (arrowhead-shaped in Song Thrush). The bill is blackish-brown and the legs are yellowish-brown. In flight, note the diagnostic white underwings and white tips to the outer tail feathers. The juvenile is similar to the adult, but the back and head are marked with white spots.

A Mistle Thrush's flight is powerful and direct, with a series of rapid wingbeats followed by a brief closing of the wings. It habitually sings in early spring and in dull and rainy weather. The resident population is boosted during the winter months by birds that have migrated from further north and east. Its nest is a large cup of vegetation, typically constructed in the fork of a tree or similar visible location.

Factfile

LENGTH 27–29CM   WINGSPAN 42–48CM

HABITAT FAVOURS OPEN WOODLAND, PARKS, ORCHARDS AND MATURE GARDENS.

FOOD FEEDS ON A VARIETY OF INVERTEBRATES, BERRIES AND FRUITS.

STATUS RESIDENT BREEDING SPECIES FOUND YEAR-ROUND IN THE WEST OF THE REGION. NORTHERN AND EASTERN POPULATIONS MIGRATE SOUTH FOR THE WINTER MONTHS.

VOICE SONG COMPRISES LOUD AND FLUTY NOTES, DELIVERED IN SHORT PHRASES AND LONG PAUSES. UTTERS A LOUD RATTLING CALL IN ALARM.

adult life-size

Note the striking white underwing coverts.

The body looks stocky and plump, and the spots on the underparts are bold and distinct.

Redwing
Turdus iliacus

The Redwing is a small, well-marked thrush that is particularly vulnerable to harsh weather. The sexes are similar. The adult has mainly grey-brown upperparts. The underparts are pale with a conspicuous orange-red flush to the flanks and underwing, and are neatly marked with numerous bold dark spots. The head has bold facial markings that include a conspicuous pale supercilium, dark eye stripe and pale patch below the cheek. The bill is blackish-brown with a yellow base, and legs are yellowish-brown. The juvenile is similar to the adult, but with more subdued colouration on the flanks and pale spotting on the upperparts.

The Redwing is best known in the region as a winter visitor; it forms large nomadic flocks at this time, often mixed with Fieldfares. It feeds largely on berries and fallen fruits and is vulnerable to harsh weather; mortality rates can be high during severe winters. The nest is a mud-lined cup of grass and moss.

Usually seen in restless flocks during the winter months; flying birds call to one another and reveal their orange-red underwing coverts.

adult

Factfile

LENGTH **20–22CM**

WINGSPAN **33–35CM**

HABITAT **FAVOURS OPEN COUNTRYSIDE, OPEN WOODLAND, FARMLAND, PARKS AND MATURE GARDENS.**

FOOD **FEEDS ON INSECTS, WORMS AND OTHER INVERTEBRATES; FRUITS AND BERRIES IN THE AUTUMN AND WINTER MONTHS.**

STATUS **COMMON AND WIDESPREAD WINTER VISITOR ACROSS MUCH OF THE REGION, MAINLY OCTOBER TO MARCH. BREEDS IN ICELAND, SCANDINAVIA AND FURTHER NORTH AND EAST.**

VOICE **SONG COMPRISES WHISTLING AND FLUTY PHRASES DELIVERED IN SHORT BURSTS. CALL IS A HIGH-PITCHED *TSEEP*, COMMONLY UTTERED FROM MIGRATING BIRDS IN FLIGHT.**

The bold pattern on the head and colourful orange-red flanks make identification easy.

adult life-size

Berry-laden Hawthorn bushes are a magnet for nomadic Redwing flocks in autumn and early winter; typically a bush will be stripped bare within a day or so, forcing the flock to move on in search of alternative food.

adult

During snowy periods, Redwings sometimes feed on garden lawns and can be attracted with windfall apples.

adult

Fieldfare
Turdus pilaris

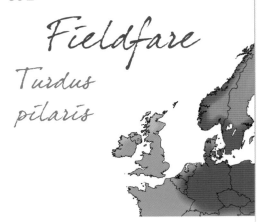

The Fieldfare is a large, colourful thrush that forms sizeable flocks during the winter months. The sexes are similar. The adult has a chestnut-brown back and a grey rump. The tail is black and the head is blue-grey and marked with a pale supercilium and dark lores. The underparts are flushed with orange yellow, grading to whitish on the belly and adorned with conspicuous dark spots on the breast and flanks. The bill is yellow with a variable amount of brown at the tip, and breeding males may develop an all-yellow bill. In flight, the grey

The white underwing is a character shared with the Mistle Thrush, but the colourful plumage allows easy separation.

adult

A covering of snow makes feeding difficult and birds often seek out disturbed or sheltered areas where they can forage on bare ground or leaf litter.

adult life-size

Factfile

LENGTH 24–26CM

WINGSPAN 39–42CM

HABITAT **FAVOURS OPEN WOODLAND AND ADJACENT FARMLAND, PARKS AND GARDENS.**

FOOD **FEEDS ON A VARIETY OF INSECTS, WORMS AND OTHER INVERTEBRATES; ALSO FRUITS AND BERRIES.**

STATUS **RESIDENT BREEDING SPECIES THROUGHOUT MUCH OF NORTHERN EUROPE. BIRDS FROM THE NORTH AND EAST MIGRATE SOUTH AND WEST DURING THE WINTER MONTHS. PRIMARILY A WINTER VISITOR TO THE BRITISH ISLES AND WESTERN FRANCE, MAINLY FROM OCTOBER TO MARCH.**

VOICE **THE FLUTY MUSICAL SONG IS GENERALLY DELIVERED IN SHORT BURSTS. CALL IS A HARSH *CHACK-CHACK-CHACK*, SOMETIMES UTTERED AT NIGHT WHEN ON MIGRATION.**

rump and white underwings are diagnostic. The juvenile is similar to the adult but with noticeable pale spots on the wing coverts.

The Fieldfare is a common breeding species in central Europe and Scandinavia. Birds from the north migrate south and west in autumn; winter numbers and range depend on weather severity and the availability of food. Typically they form large flocks that feed on the fruit and berry crops in hedgerows and trees. The nest is a robust mud-lined cup of grass and leaves.

During the winter months, Fieldfares often form mixed flocks with Redwings, and these nomadic groups both feed and roost together.

adult

adult

Often feeds on the ground in the manner of other thrushes, searching in particular for earthworms in areas of short grassland.

Spotted Flycatcher
Muscicapa striata

The plumage is rather plain overall but note the streaked crown and subtle pale wingbar.

adult

Factfile

LENGTH 14–15CM

WINGSPAN 23–25CM

HABITAT FAVOURS OPEN WOODLAND, PARKS AND GARDENS; COMMONLY NESTS IN RESIDENTIAL GARDENS AND ADJACENT TO HABITATION.

FOOD FEEDS PRIMARILY ON FLYING INSECTS, WHICH IT CATCHES ON THE WING.

STATUS SUMMER BREEDING VISITOR, WIDESPREAD THROUGHOUT THE REGION IN SUITABLE HABITATS; PRESENT MAINLY MAY TO AUGUST. ALSO SEEN ON MIGRATION. OVERWINTERS IN AFRICA. NUMBERS HAVE DECLINED IN RECENT YEARS.

VOICE SONG IS RATHER QUIET AND COMPRISES SIMPLE HIGH-PITCHED CALL-LIKE NOTES. UTTERS A BUZZING *TSEE* CALL.

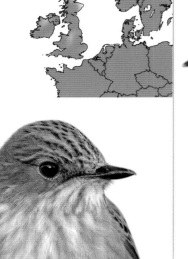

adult life-size

Uses regular perches from which fly-catching aerial sorties are made.

Sometimes hovers momentarily while in pursuit of an insect.

adult

The Spotted Flycatcher is a lively but rather elusive, drab-coloured bird, and the larger of the two flycatcher species commonly seen in the region. The sexes are similar. The adult has rather nondescript grey-brown upperparts, the crown marked with dark streaks. The underparts are pale greyish-white and flushed brown on the flanks, the breast adorned with subtle dark streaking. The fine bill, eyes and legs are dark. The juvenile is similar to the adult but has light spots on the back and dark spots on the throat and breast.

The Spotted Flycatcher feeds by making frequent sorties for flying insects from favoured perches, which it sits on in a characteristic upright posture. It is a rather secretive bird during the breeding season; combined with its rather drab appearance this makes it easily overlooked. It constructs a finely woven, cup-shaped nest from grasses and plant material, typically in a tree fork, wall creeper or suitable crevice in a building.

Pied Flycatcher
Ficedula hypoleuca

This is a distinctively marked flycatcher, with rather specific habitat requirements. The sexes are separable and some seasonal plumage variation occurs. The summer adult male is boldly marked with dull black upperparts adorned with a contrasting bold white band on the wings and a small white patch at the base of the bill. The underparts are white and unmarked. The stout bill, eyes and legs are black. The adult female has a plumage pattern similar to that of the adult male, but brown plumage replaces the black plumage elements. In the autumn, the adult male resembles the female. The first-winter bird recalls the adult female.

The Pied Flycatcher feeds by catching insects on the wing from among the tree canopy. Although the species can occur in a variety of wooded habitats, it is most closely associated with Sessile Oak woodlands in the west of the region, and open park woodland elsewhere. Some males pair with several females in the same season, establishing separate territories. It nests in tree holes, constructing a loose cup of bark, leaves and grass, and readily takes to using nest boxes.

male life-size

The bold black-and-white plumage means that males are unmistakable.

female

The striking white wingbar is obvious in hovering birds.

female

Uses regular perches from where it watches for passing insects.

Factfile

LENGTH 12–13CM

WINGSPAN 21–24CM

HABITAT DECIDUOUS OR MIXED OPEN WOODLAND, ORCHARDS AND OCCASIONALLY GARDENS. MATURE HANGING SESSILE OAK WOODLAND IS PARTICULARLY FAVOURED.

FOOD FEEDS ON A VARIETY OF INVERTEBRATES AND LARVAE.

STATUS SUMMER BREEDING VISITOR, WIDESPREAD BUT LOCAL IN SUITABLE HABITATS; PRESENT MAINLY MAY TO AUGUST. OVERWINTERS IN AFRICA.

VOICE RAPIDLY DELIVERED, SWEET AND RINGING SONG. UTTERS A REPETITIVE SHARP PLIT CALL IN ALARM.

Robin
Erithacus rubecula

The Robin is instantly recognisable and one of the region's best-loved birds; in Britain in particular it is a familiar and surprisingly tame garden regular. The sexes are similar. The adult has a rotund body with reddish-brown upperparts, and a faint buff wingbar. The face, throat and breast are conspicuously bright orange-red, separated from the upperparts by a subtle band of blue-grey. The remaining underparts are pale buff and clearly separated from the brightly coloured breast. The eyes and small bill are dark, and the legs are dark brown. The juvenile lacks the bright orange-red colour of the adult, having brown upperparts marked with a series of pale buff spots and teardrop-shaped streaks. The underparts are pale buff with darker spots and crescent-shaped markings.

The Robin is a perky little bird that likes the damp and shady areas of woodland and garden habitats. It can be particularly bold, especially in the winter months, becoming very tolerant of people and even hand-tame at times. It is a highly territorial species, particularly in the spring, fighting off intruders and rivals aggressively. It constructs a cup-shaped nest of grass, moss and leaves in a suitable hollow or crevice.

adult

Sometimes hovers if it spots a potential meal, such as an insect moving on the foliage of a bush.

adult
life-size

In parts of its range, notably Britain, Robins take an active interest in gardening activities, and are quick to spot a wriggling worm revealed by digging.

adult

Often uses perches to scan the ground for the movement of an unsuspecting invertebrate.

adult

Robins are extremely territorial during the breeding season and puff themselves up if they spot a rival.

Factfile

LENGTH 13–14CM   WINGSPAN 20–22CM

HABITAT FAVOURS DECIDUOUS AND MIXED WOODLAND, PARKS AND GARDENS IN RURAL AND SUBURBAN AREAS.

FOOD FEEDS ON A VARIETY OF INVERTEBRATES, LARVAE, FRUITS AND SEEDS.

STATUS COMMON AND WIDESPREAD RESIDENT BREEDING SPECIES, PRESENT YEAR-ROUND THROUGHOUT MOST OF THE REGION. BIRDS BREEDING IN THE EXTREME NORTH AND EAST MIGRATE TO MORE TEMPERATE AREAS OF THE REGION FOR THE WINTER MONTHS.

VOICE SONG COMPRISES A RATHER MELANCHOLY SERIES OF WHISTLES AND WARBLES, DELIVERED BY BOTH SEXES DURING THE WINTER. UTTERS A SHARP *TIC* IN ALARM.

Nightingale
Luscinia megarhynchos

Factfile

LENGTH 16–17CM

WINGSPAN 23–26CM

HABITAT FAVOURS MATURE HEDGEROWS, AREAS OF SCRUB AND COPPICED WOODLAND WITH DENSE UNDERGROWTH.

FOOD FEEDS ON A VARIETY OF INVERTEBRATES AND THEIR LARVAE; SOME FRUITS AND BERRIES IN AUTUMN.

STATUS DECLINING SUMMER BREEDING VISITOR RESTRICTED TO THE CENTRAL AND SOUTHERN PARTS OF THE REGION, INCLUDING SOUTHERN BRITAIN; PRESENT MAINLY MAY TO AUGUST. OVERWINTERS IN AFRICA.

VOICE BEST KNOWN FOR ITS VARIED SONG OF RICH, FLUTY WHISTLES AND CLICKING SOUNDS, CHARACTERISTICALLY PRECEDED BY A WHISTLING *TU-TU-TU-TU*; DELIVERED AT NIGHT AS WELL AS DURING DAYLIGHT HOURS. UTTERS A FROG-LIKE CROAKING CALL.

The Nightingale is a rather secretive and drab-looking bird that tends to remain in deep cover. The sexes are similar. The adult has uniformly brown upperparts, with a warm reddish-chestnut tinge to the tail and rump; the face and sides of the neck display a hint of grey. The underparts are greyish-white and flushed with pale buffish-brown on

On still nights, a Nightingale's song can be heard over a considerable distance – a hundred metres or more in some situations.

adult

adult

Nightingales feed mainly on the ground, foraging for invertebrates among leaf litter and soil debris.

the breast. The grey-brown bill is longish and pale-based, and the legs are pinkish-brown. The juvenile is similar to the adult.

The Nightingale is an unobtrusive bird, and its beautiful and iconic song is often the first indication of its presence. Numbers have declined significantly in recent years, linked to the loss of traditional habitat. The nest is a bulky cup of loose material situated on or close to the ground.

adult

In good quality habitat, a lucky observer standing in one spot may be able to hear the songs of two or three adjacent territorial males.

Although many woodland birds are vocal in the twilight of dawn and dusk, the Nightingale is one of the few to sing in the dead of night.

adult life-size

Black Redstart

Phoenicurus ochruros

The Black Redstart is an active little bird with a striking orange-red tail, which it often quivers. The sexes are dissimilar. The adult male has mainly charcoal-grey plumage, but note the striking red-orange tail and vent, the white wing patch, and the whitish area to the lower belly. During the breeding season, the face and breast darken and appear almost black. The eyes, bill and legs are black. The adult female is similar to the adult male, but the dark grey elements of the plumage are replaced with grey-brown, darkest on the wings and palest on the belly; the white wing patch is absent, and note the obvious pale eye-ring. Immature birds recall the adult female.

Naturally a bird of rocky upland areas, the Black Redstart has adapted well to urban environments within its main breeding range, and is often found nesting in the cracks and crevices of buildings. A bold and often confiding species, it commonly perches out in the open, allowing easy observation. Its nest is a loose cup of plant matter lined with feathers and hair.

Factfile

LENGTH 14–15CM   WINGSPAN 23–26CM

HABITAT FAVOURS A VARIETY OF HABITATS IN THE BREEDING SEASON INCLUDING ROCKY UPLAND, WASTE GROUND AND URBAN AREAS. SEEN IN COASTAL AREAS ON MIGRATION AND DURING THE WINTER MONTHS.

FOOD FEEDS PRIMARILY ON INVERTEBRATES, BERRIES AND FRUITS.

STATUS LOCALLY COMMON SUMMER BREEDING SPECIES THROUGHOUT MUCH OF THE CENTRAL BELT OF EUROPE; PRESENT THERE MAINLY APRIL TO AUGUST. LARGELY ABSENT FROM THE NORTH AND A SCARCE BREEDER AND PASSAGE MIGRANT IN BRITAIN AND IRELAND. OVERWINTERS IN SOUTHERN EUROPE, ALTHOUGH SOME REMAIN ON THE SOUTH COASTS OF THE BRITISH ISLES AND THE NORTH COAST OF FRANCE.

VOICE SONG COMPRISES A MIXTURE OF STATIC-LIKE CRACKLING AND WHISTLING NOTES. UTTERS A *SVIT* OR *SVIT-IT-IT* CALL.

The red tail is most obvious in flight.

juvenile

male life-size

Pale feather tips mask the black on the face and underparts but wear away with time.

Outside the breeding season, most encounters with the species are of birds with female or juvenile-type plumage.

juvenile

Redstart
Phoenicurus phoenicurus

Compared to a male, a female's plumage is understated, except for the trademark red tail.

female

The Redstart is a Robin-sized bird with a distinctive dark-centred red tail. The sexes are dissimilar. The adult male has primarily dark grey upperparts. The face and throat are black; the head is marked with a white forehead patch and subtle white supercilium. The underparts are bright orange-red, most striking on the breast; note the obvious colourful red tail, which it quivers. The eyes, bill and legs are black. The adult female has grey-brown upperparts; the underparts are pale with an orange tinge. First-winter birds display gender-specific plumage that recalls the respective adult, but colours are muted and markings less distinct; the underparts appear scaly and barred.

The Redstart is an active bird that uses favoured perches from which to launch feeding sorties, preying on flying and ground-dwelling invertebrates. Perched birds habitually pump their tails up and down continuously. It shows a preference for wooded habitats with a mixture of mature trees to provide suitable nesting sites, and constructs a cup of grass and moss in tree holes.

Factfile

LENGTH 14–15CM   WINGSPAN 20–24CM

HABITAT FAVOURS OPEN DECIDUOUS WOODLAND WITH LOW GROUND COVER, WOODED FARMLAND, HEATHS AND PARKLAND.

FOOD FEEDS PRIMARILY ON INSECTS, BUT OCCASIONALLY TAKES FRUITS AND BERRIES.

STATUS SUMMER BREEDING VISITOR, WIDESPREAD BUT LOCAL ACROSS MOST OF THE REGION IN SUITABLE HABITATS; PRESENT MAINLY MAY TO AUGUST. OVERWINTERS IN TROPICAL AFRICA.

VOICE UTTERS A RATHER MELANCHOLY, TUNEFUL SONG. CALL IS A SOFT *HUIIT-TUT-TUT*.

The male is colourful and unmistakable with his black mask and orange-red underparts.

male life-size

Whinchat
Saxicola rubetra

male

Superficially similar to the Stonechat, the Whinchat is a small bird of open country. The sexes are separable. The adult male has primarily streaked dark brown upperparts, the head strikingly marked with a bold white supercilium. The underparts are whitish and conspicuously flushed with orange on the throat and breast. A pale stripe cleanly separates the orange of the throat from the brown of the head and face. Note the short dark tail. The eyes, bill and legs are black. The adult female is similar, but with muted colours and definition to the markings; note particularly the washed-out orange of the throat and breast, lighter face and grubby supercilium. The first-winter bird is similar to the adult female.

The Whinchat favours open country and is often found in dry, scrubby grassland habitats; it commonly occurs on the coast during migration. It is often seen perched out in the open, fence posts and fence wire being a popular choice. It nests on the ground, constructing a lined cup of leaves and grass.

The striking facial pattern and peachy chest mean that the male is unmistakable.

Factfile

LENGTH 12–14CM   WINGSPAN 21–24CM

HABITAT FAVOURS ROUGH GRASSLAND SLOPES WITH SCATTERED SCRUB.

FOOD FEEDS PRIMARILY ON INVERTEBRATES; SOME SEEDS.

STATUS BREEDING SUMMER VISITOR, WIDESPREAD BUT LOCAL ACROSS THE REGION IN SUITABLE HABITAT; PRESENT MAINLY MAY TO SEPTEMBER. OVERWINTERS IN AFRICA.

VOICE SONG COMPRISES A LONG SERIES OF RAPIDLY DELIVERED, WARBLING NOTES. UTTERS A SHARP *WHI-TUC* CALL IN ALARM.

female life-size

male

The pale, clean-looking underparts and undertail coverts contrast with the dark tail.

The facial pattern is reminiscent of that seen in a male.

Stonechat
Saxicola rubicola

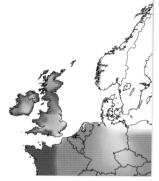

The Stonechat is a small round-bodied bird with a short tail; it is often observed conspicuously perched in the open. The sexes are separable. The adult male has primarily dark brown upperparts; the head and throat are black with a well-defined, and sharply contrasting, white collar-like patch to each side of the neck. The underparts are pale with an orange flush, most intense on the breast. Note the spotted and streaked appearance of the brown rump. The eyes, bill and legs are black. The adult female is similar to the male, but with muted colours and less well-defined markings overall; the head and back are uniformly brown and streaked, the white neck patch grubby. The juvenile is similar to the adult female, but with more uniform and brighter brown plumage overall.

The Stonechat is often seen perched in the open on a spray of gorse or along a fence wire. Perched birds habitually flick their tails repeatedly while uttering their alarm call. The cup-shaped nest is constructed using dead leaves and vegetation in dense low-lying scrub.

Territorial males use prominent perches as look-outs; the uniform black cap is diagnostic in a bird of the size and proportions of a Stonechat.

male

Factfile

LENGTH 12–13CM   WINGSPAN 18–21CM

HABITAT DRY OPEN COUNTRYSIDE, PARTICULARLY HEATHLAND, COMMONS AND COASTAL SCRUB.

FOOD FEEDS PRIMARILY ON INVERTEBRATES; SOME SEEDS.

STATUS LOCALLY COMMON RESIDENT BREEDING SPECIES IN THE WEST OF THE REGION. RANGE IS PATCHY FURTHER EAST AND IT IS LARGELY ABSENT FROM THE NORTH. SOME MIGRATION DOES OCCUR, WITH BIRDS MOVING SOUTH AND WEST TO ESCAPE SEVERE WINTER WEATHER.

VOICE UTTERS A RAPID, WARBLER-LIKE SONG, RECALLING WHITETHROAT. CALL IS A DISTINCTIVE *TCHAK*, SIMILAR TO TWO STONES BEING KNOCKED TOGETHER.

The plumage is rather uniform, and face lacks any obvious pattern.

female life-size

Wheatear
Oenanthe oenanthe

The Wheatear is a widespread bird of open country, renowned for its diagnostic white rump. The sexes are dissimilar. The adult male has a blue-grey crown and back; the wings and tail are black. The head is adorned with a bold black mask running from the base of the bill and through the eye, with a contrasting white supercilium above. The underparts are pale, the breast displaying an orange-buff flush. The rump and uppertail coverts are white overall but marked with a dark upside-down 'T' which is obvious in flight. The eyes, bill and legs are dark. The adult female has mainly grey-brown upperparts, darkest on the wings. The underparts are pale, the face, throat and breast are flushed with orange-buff, and the head is adorned with a pale supercilium. The first-winter bird is similar to the adult female, but the upperparts are generally a warmer buffish-brown. The Greenland race is sometimes encountered on migration (ssp. *leucorhoa*); it is larger and displays a more intense orange-buff flush to the underparts.

The Wheatear usually chooses conspicuous perches such as fence wire and boulders, and adopts an upright posture, bobbing up and

With strongly contrasting plumage, the male is a striking bird.

1st autumn

Overall the plumage is warm buffish-brown but note the diagnostic black-and-white pattern on the tail.

male life-size

down when agitated. Its flight is generally low and undulating, with the white rump obvious and diagnostic. It nests in a hole or crevice in a rock or wall, and will also use old Rabbit burrows; the nest itself is a loose cup of grass and moss.

juvenile

Seen from below in flight, the white inner half of the tail contrasts markedly with the black outer half.

female

Wheatears are usually easy to observe: they hop around on the ground in open areas, and often perch prominently.

Factfile

LENGTH 14–16CM WINGSPAN 26–32CM

HABITAT FAVOURS OPEN COUNTRY AND TYPICALLY ASSOCIATED WITH AREAS OF SHORT GRASSLAND INCLUDING OPEN MOORLAND, UPLANDS, TUNDRA AND COASTAL CLIFFTOPS.

FOOD FEEDS PRIMARILY ON INSECTS, SPIDERS AND OTHER INVERTEBRATES; SOME FRUITS AND BERRIES.

STATUS SUMMER BREEDING VISITOR, WIDESPREAD BUT LOCAL THROUGHOUT THE REGION IN SUITABLE HABITATS; PRESENT MAINLY APRIL TO SEPTEMBER. ALSO SEEN ON MIGRATION. OVERWINTERS IN AFRICA.

VOICE SONG IS A RAPID WARBLE. UTTERS A SHARP *CHAK* CALL, SIMILAR TO TWO PEBBLES BEING KNOCKED TOGETHER.

Dunnock
Prunella
modularis

adult

Often feeds on the ground, usually beneath a bush or on the edge of cover into which it retreats at the first sign of disturbance.

adult

The song is vaguely reminiscent of a *Sylvia* warbler but the delivery is more rapid and the tone lacks any rich or fluty notes. And birds begin singing in early March, well before any migratory warblers have arrived back.

In March and April, territorial birds abandon their normally shy and retiring habits and become bold.

The Dunnock is a common sparrow-like bird with a plump body. The sexes are similar. The adult has chestnut-brown upperparts with a pattern of darker streaking; note the faint pale wingbar. The underparts are primarily bluish-grey, the flanks displaying bold brown and chestnut streaks. The head is marked with bluish-grey on the face and throat; the crown and ear coverts are streaked with brown. The warbler-like bill is slender and dark, and the legs are reddish-pink. The juvenile is similar to the adult, but is more boldly streaked.

The Dunnock is a rather furtive bird that tends to spend most of its time skulking in deep cover, and is mainly seen on, or close to, the ground. During the breeding season males become much bolder and highly territorial, often singing from a conspicuous perch in the top of a bush or bramble patch. Their courtship and reproductive behaviour is surprisingly complex, with both sexes often engaging with multiple partners. The nest is a sturdy cup of woven plant material in a low bush or hedge.

Factfile

LENGTH 13–14CM   WINGSPAN 19–21CM   HABITAT FAVOURS WOODLANDS, HEDGEROWS, SCRUB AND MATURE GARDENS.   FOOD FEEDS ON INVERTEBRATES AND SEEDS.   STATUS COMMON AND WIDESPREAD RESIDENT BREEDING SPECIES, PRESENT YEAR-ROUND AND FOUND IN SUITABLE HABITAT ACROSS MOST OF THE REGION. BIRDS IN THE EXTREME NORTH MIGRATE SOUTH DURING THE WINTER MONTHS.   VOICE UTTERS A LIVELY WARBLER-LIKE SONG, DELIVERED IN SHORT BURSTS. CALL IS A RATHER WEAK *TSEER*.

adult

adult life-size

Sometimes visits bird tables in the winter, especially during cold snaps; it also forages on the ground beneath for fallen scraps.

House Sparrow

Passer domesticus

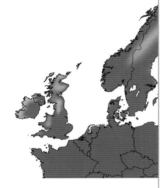

Factfile

LENGTH 14–15CM WINGSPAN 24CM

HABITAT FAVOURS AREAS OF HUMAN HABITATION AND OCCURS IN VILLAGES, TOWNS AND AROUND FARMS.

FOOD FEEDS ON A VARIETY OF ITEMS INCLUDING SEEDS, KITCHEN SCRAPS AND INVERTEBRATES. REGULAR VISITOR TO GARDEN BIRD TABLES AND FEEDERS IN MANY AREAS.

STATUS WIDESPREAD RESIDENT BREEDING SPECIES, PRESENT YEAR-ROUND AND COMMON THROUGHOUT MOST OF THE REGION IN SUITABLE HABITATS. ITS NUMBERS HAVE DECLINED SEVERELY IN RECENT YEARS.

VOICE UTTERS A VARIETY OF SHARP CHIRPING CALLS.

The House Sparrow is a familiar species that shows a distinct affinity with human habitation. The sexes are dissimilar. The adult male has mainly chestnut-brown upperparts, marked with a series of dark streaks; note the bold white wingbar. The head is distinctively marked with a grey crown and cheeks, with chestnut brown beneath the crown and on the nape. The underparts are primarily pale grey with a large and contrasting black patch on the throat and breast. The bill is short, robust and varies seasonally in colour from black to brown; the legs are reddish. The adult female is more plainly marked: the upperparts and the head are mainly brown, the back is marked with buff streaks. Note the pale buff supercilium behind the eye. The underparts are uniformly pale grey. Juvenile plumage is similar to the adult female but has less well-defined patterning; it becomes indistinguishable from the adult by the first autumn.

The House Sparrow is often seen in small groups around bird tables and feeders, perched on roofs and wires, or taking dust baths. It can become surprisingly bold in some urban areas, and often hand-tame in locations such as urban parks and outdoor restaurant seating areas. The species usually pairs for life and will use favoured nesting sites several years running. It constructs a loose nest of grass in a building crevice or hole.

male

The pale wingbar is striking in flight.

male life-size

At the height of the breeding season, a male's bill is black. Bib size and intensity determines dominance in a flock.

female

The plumage is buffish-brown and rather nondescript.

Tree Sparrow
Passer montanus

Factfile

LENGTH 13–14CM   WINGSPAN 20–22CM

HABITAT VARIETY OF HABITATS INCLUDING OPEN WOODLAND, PARKS AND WOODED SUBURBS. PARTICULARLY ATTRACTED TO ARABLE FARMS AND GRAIN SPILLS.

FOOD FEEDS PRIMARILY ON SEEDS AND INVERTEBRATES.

STATUS LOCAL RESIDENT BREEDING SPECIES, PRESENT YEAR-ROUND THROUGHOUT THE REGION EXCEPT IN THE EXTREME NORTH. ITS NUMBERS HAVE DECLINED SEVERELY IN RECENT YEARS.

VOICE IT UTTERS A CHIRP SIMILAR TO THAT OF HOUSE SPARROW. IN FLIGHT, IT ALSO COMMONLY DELIVERS A SHARP *TIK-TIK*.

This is the rural counterpart of House Sparrow and broadly similar in appearance. The sexes are similar. The adult has primarily streaked brown upperparts, with two obvious white wingbars. The underparts are pale greyish-white, the flanks showing a buffish tinge. The head is boldly marked with a chestnut cap, a small black bib and white cheeks with a central black patch. The black bill is rather stubby and stout-looking; the legs are pale brown. The juvenile is similar to the adult but displays more subdued and less well-defined facial markings.

The Tree Sparrow is rather timid compared to its cousin the House Sparrow, and less tolerant of human habitation. It favours more rural environments and can be found in flocks with finches and buntings during the winter months, typically feeding on the ground. A sociable species, it breeds in small, loose colonies and readily takes advantage of nest boxes.

Hovering birds reveal obvious pale wingbars.

adult

adult life-size

adult

Males and females share the same bold facial pattern.

The chestnut crown and white-framed black check patch allow easy separation from a male House Sparrow.

Yellow Wagtail

Motacilla flava

The Yellow Wagtail is a rather dainty species with a distinctive long tail. The sexes are dissimilar. It is represented by a number of distinct races across Europe, mainly separable by differing male plumage. Yellow Wagtail ssp. *flavissima* occurs in Britain. The adult male has greenish-yellow upperparts, the darker wings marked with pale wingbars. The underparts are bright yellow, including the throat, face and supercilium. The eyes, slender bill and legs are dark. The adult female is similar, but is less well marked, the plumage colouration being subdued. The juvenile has olive-buff upperparts and pale underparts. The Blue-headed Wagtail (ssp. *flava*) occurs on mainland Europe. The male is similar to a ssp. *flavissima* adult male, but the head has a bluish cap and ear coverts, and a white supercilium. The Grey-headed Wagtail (ssp. *thunbergi*) breeds in Scandinavia; it is similar to ssp. *flava* but has a grey cap, black ear coverts and no supercilium. Note the white outer tail feathers in all birds, most obvious in flight.

This is an endearing little bird that is often observed feeding in short grassland, typically around the feet of grazing cattle, or perched on wire fences. Its long tail is characteristically pumped swiftly up and down when the bird is perched or on the ground. It nests in a cup of leaves and grass, constructed in a shallow scrape on the ground.

ssp. *thunbergi* male

Note the absence of a supercilium or obvious 'moustachial' stripe.

ssp. *flavissima* male

The beautiful yellow colouration of a male Yellow Wagtail (ssp. *flavissima*) means that individuals are unmistakable. The population of this British subspecies has declined in recent years, and it has disappeared completely from many of its former haunts in the south.

ssp. flava male

Represented across its vast European and Asian breeding range by a number of subspecies, males of which have different facial patterns; three ssp. breed regularly in our region. Ssp. *flava* males have a bluish head, white supercilium and white 'moustachial' stripe separating the dark blue-grey cheek from the yellow throat.

Factfile

LENGTH 16–17CM

WINGSPAN 23–27CM

HABITAT FAVOURS LOWLAND WETLANDS SUCH AS WATER MEADOWS, DAMP GRASSLAND AND SALT MARSHES.

FOOD FEEDS SOLELY ON SMALL INVERTEBRATES.

STATUS SUMMER BREEDING SPECIES, LOCAL THROUGHOUT THE REGION IN SUITABLE HABITATS AND PRESENT MAINLY APRIL TO SEPTEMBER. COMMONLY SEEN IN AREAS OF SHORT GRASSLAND ON MIGRATION.

VOICE UTTERS A DISTINCTIVE SHRILL *TSREE-EE* CALL.

female

Females are hard to assign to subspecies and typically have rather pale yellowish-grey upperparts and an obvious pale supercilium.

Grey Wagtail

Motacilla cinerea

Factfile

LENGTH 18–19CM   WINGSPAN 25–27CM

HABITAT FAVOURS RUNNING FRESHWATER AND PARTICULARLY FOND OF STONY, FAST-FLOWING STREAMS.

FOOD FEEDS PRIMARILY ON INVERTEBRATES, WITH SOME SMALL FISH AND TADPOLES.

STATUS WIDESPREAD RESIDENT BREEDING SPECIES IN SUITABLE HABITAT, FOUND YEAR-ROUND THROUGHOUT THE REGION, EXCEPT THE FAR NORTH. SOME WINTER MOVEMENT OCCURS, BIRDS FROM UPLAND AND NORTHERLY LOCATIONS MIGRATING TO LOWLANDS AND MORE SOUTHERLY AREAS.

VOICE IT UTTERS A SHARP *TIP-TIP* CALL IN FLIGHT.

The Grey Wagtail is a beautifully coloured bird with a diagnostically long tail. The sexes differ, and some seasonal plumage variation occurs. The summer adult male has primarily blue-grey upperparts, the wing displaying dark grey primary feathers. The underparts are lemon-yellow, most intense on the breast and vent area; the flanks have a

male

female

Looks long-tailed even by wagtail standards, the white outer feathers contrasting with the dark central ones.

The underparts look strikingly pale with a bright yellow flush on the undertail coverts.

Territorial males often perch in bushes overhanging the water in the vicinity of the nest.

male

subtle grey wash. The head is boldly marked with a white supercilium and submoustachial stripe, with a contrasting black bib. The slender bill is black and the legs are reddish. In flight, note the obvious white wingbar and white outer tail feathers. The summer adult female is similar but with more subdued colouration, particularly on the underside. The bib is whitish and commonly marked with grey. Winter adults recall their summer plumages, but have white throats. Juvenile and first-winter birds are similar to the adult female.

The Grey Wagtail is an elegant bird that is typically seen perched on rocks by fast flowing streams, its tail pumped up and down swiftly. It constructs a cup-shaped nest of grass in a bankside hole or crevice.

male life-size

If seen well, a male is unmistakable with his yellow underparts and mainly grey upperparts; the facial pattern is striking.

Pied Wagtail/ White Wagtail

Motacilla alba

The Pied Wagtail is an attractive little black, grey and white bird with a very long tail. The sexes differ, and some seasonal plumage variation exists. The summer adult male has overall black upperparts and white underparts, with a black throat and breast and a smoky tinge to the flanks. The head is black and marked with a large and contrasting, white facial mask. Note the white wingbars and the white outer tail feathers, most obvious when the bird is in flight. The winter adult male develops a white throat, and the black on the breast is less intense. The adult female is seasonally similar to the adult male, but the upperparts are grey. The juvenile and first-winter are similar to the female but with more subdued markings, a black rump, white barring to the wings and a yellowish flush to the face. The White Wagtail (ssp. *alba*) is similar to the Pied Wagtail in its seasonal variations, but has a grey (not black) back and rump; the underparts are cleaner white.

This is the most familiar member of the wagtail family, owing to its ability to adapt to human habitation. Its flight is generally undulating and low to the ground. The nest is a cup of grass and twigs, placed in a hole or crevice.

White Wagtail
adult winter

Markings on the head are indistinct compared with the breeding season.

The black markings on the head contrast markedly with the grey back.

White Wagtail
summer male

Factfile

LENGTH 17–19CM

WINGSPAN 25–30CM

HABITAT GENERALLY FOUND ON OPEN GROUND, PREFERRING AREAS OF SHORT GRASS SUCH AS PARKS, FARMLAND, COASTAL GRASSLAND AND CAR PARKS.

FOOD FEEDS PRIMARILY ON SMALL INVERTEBRATES.

STATUS WIDESPREAD AND COMMON RESIDENT BREEDING SPECIES, PRESENT YEAR-ROUND THROUGHOUT MOST OF THE REGION. PIED WAGTAIL (SSP. *YARRELLII*) IS MAINLY RESTRICTED TO BRITAIN AND IRELAND; WHITE WAGTAIL (SSP. *ALBA*) OCCURS IN MAINLAND EUROPE. NORTHERLY POPULATIONS MIGRATE SOUTH FOR THE WINTER, AND SOME GEOGRAPHICAL OVERLAP OCCURS AT THIS TIME.

VOICE THE CALL IS A LOUD *CHISSICK*.

White Wagtail summer male

The long tail and white outer feathers are striking in flight.

Ssp. *alba* breeds occasionally in Britain but is more typically encountered there as a passage migrant along coasts.

White Wagtail summer male

There is little distinction between the black cap and the dark blackish grey colour on the back. Note also the flanks, which are much darker than in ssp. *alba*.

Pied Wagtail summer male life-size

Meadow Pipit
Anthus pratensis

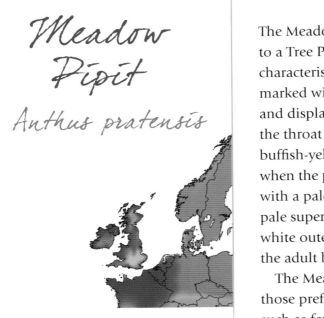

The Meadow Pipit is a rather plain brown bird, similar in appearance to a Tree Pipit, but separable by habitat preferences and song characteristics. The sexes are similar. The adult has brown upperparts, marked with dark streaks and pale wingbars. The underparts are pale and display thrush-like dark spots and streaks to the breast and flanks; the throat and belly are unmarked. The breast and flanks also have a buffish-yellow tinge that is particularly conspicuous in the autumn, when the plumage is overall warmer brown. The head is subtly marked with a pale eye-ring, pale lores, buff submoustachial stripe and faint pale supercilium. Note the dark eyes, grey-buff bill, pinkish legs, white outer tail feathers and long hind claw. The juvenile is similar to the adult but the markings on the underside are typically subdued.

The Meadow Pipit generally occurs in more open habitats than those preferred by the similar Tree Pipit, and uses low, open perches such as fence posts and wires. It often forms loose flocks outside the breeding season and on migration. The Meadow Pipit nests on the ground, constructing a grass cup hidden in vegetation.

Migrant birds in autumn are often seen near the coast and will even feed on the seashore strandline alongside Rock Pipits.

adult autumn

adult autumn
Meadow Pipits are active feeders that even chase flying insects.

adult spring

The plumage has a rather grey tone to it during the breeding season.

Factfile

LENGTH 14–15CM

WINGSPAN 22–25CM

HABITAT ROUGH GRASSLAND HABITATS DURING THE BREEDING SEASON, INCLUDING HEATHS, COASTAL GRASSLAND, DOWNLAND AND MOORLAND. DURING THE WINTER IT MOVES TO LOWLAND GRASSLAND AND COASTAL AREAS.

FOOD FEEDS PRIMARILY ON INVERTEBRATES, WITH SOME SEEDS AND PLANT MATERIAL DURING THE WINTER.

STATUS WIDESPREAD RESIDENT BREEDING SPECIES, PRESENT YEAR-ROUND ACROSS MUCH OF THE REGION. BIRDS FROM THE EXTREME NORTH MIGRATE SOUTH AND WEST FOR THE WINTER MONTHS.

VOICE SONG IS GENERALLY UTTERED ON THE WING AND COMPRISES A SERIES OF DESCENDING NOTES, DELIVERED IN A RISING AND FALLING FLIGHT, AND USUALLY INITIATED AND CULMINATING ON THE GROUND. IT UTTERS A *PSEET-PSEET-PSEET* CALL.

adult spring life-size

During the breeding season, territorial birds will often use a perch to scan for danger and rivals.

Rock Pipit
Anthus petrosus

The Rock Pipit is a bulky and darkly coloured pipit. The sexes are similar. The adult has grey-brown upperparts marked with dark streaks and indistinct pale wingbars. The underparts are pale and grubby-looking, and are marked with a pattern of heavy dark streaking on the breast and flanks. The throat and vent area are unmarked. The markings on the head are rather indistinct and include a pale eye-ring, pale supercilium, dark submoustachial stripe and dark malar stripe. The eyes are dark, the bill and legs are dark grey-brown. Note the greyish-white outer tail feathers and long hind claw. Generally, the plumage markings are more distinct and colourful during the breeding season. The juvenile is similar to the adult.

The Rock Pipit is a rather bold bird, and a familiar sight around much of the coastline despite its rather unremarkable plumage. It seeks cliffs and rocky areas for breeding, constructing a nest of seaweed hidden in vegetation in rock crevices and overhanging banks. During the winter it can form loose flocks that congregate in areas rich in food.

The Rock Pipit typically lives within sight of the sea and only very rarely is it seen inland.

adult spring life-size

adult spring

Often perches on boulders and rocks, particularly during the breeding season.

Factfile

LENGTH 16–17CM   WINGSPAN 22–27CM

HABITAT ALMOST EXCLUSIVELY COASTAL, PREFERRING ROCKY COASTS AND CLIFFS DURING THE BREEDING SEASON, BECOMING MORE WIDESPREAD IN THE WINTER AND OFTEN SEEN FORAGING ALONG THE BEACH STRANDLINE.

FOOD FEEDS PRIMARILY ON INVERTEBRATES.

STATUS LOCALLY COMMON RESIDENT BREEDING SPECIES, OCCURRING ALONG MUCH OF THE REGION'S COASTLINE; IN SCANDINAVIA IT IS A SUMMER BREEDING SPECIES THAT MOVES SOUTH FOR THE WINTER.

VOICE ITS SONG RECALLS THAT OF MEADOW PIPIT, DELIVERED IN FLIGHT, BUT GENERALLY STARTING AND ENDING ON A ROCK PERCH. THE CALL IS A SINGLE *PSEET*.

adult spring

The markings on the underparts are more striking in the spring than they are outside the breeding season.

adult autumn

Searches for flies and sandhoppers along the strandline and actively chases flying insects.

Tree Pipit
Anthus trivialis

Factfile

LENGTH 14–16CM WINGSPAN 25–27CM

HABITAT FAVOURS OPEN WOODLAND WITH GRASSY CLEARINGS, HEATHLAND WITH TREE POCKETS, AND WOODLAND FRINGES.

FOOD FEEDS PRIMARILY ON INVERTEBRATES.

STATUS SUMMER BREEDING SPECIES THAT IS WIDESPREAD IN SUITABLE HABITATS THROUGHOUT THE REGION; PRESENT MAINLY APRIL TO AUGUST. OVERWINTERS IN AFRICA.

VOICE SONG CONSISTS OF AN ACCELERATING TRILL, STARTING WHEN THE BIRD IS PERCHED AND CONTINUING IN FLIGHT, CULMINATING IN LONGER, THIN NOTES ISSUED AS THE BIRD FLOATS DOWN TO SETTLE ON ANOTHER PERCH. THE CALL IS A BUZZING *SPZZZT*, ISSUED IN FLIGHT.

The song is delivered mainly in flight.

adult

The Tree Pipit is a rather nondescript bird, similar in appearance to a Meadow Pipit. The sexes are similar. The adult has sandy-brown upperparts, marked with darker streaks and pale wingbars. The pale underparts are whitish, boldly streaked and flushed with yellow-buff on the breast and flanks. The belly and throat are unmarked. The head is adorned with a conspicuous pale supercilium, a dark submoustachial stripe and a pale spot to the rear edge of the ear coverts. The eyes are dark, the bill is dark grey-brown and the legs are pinkish. Note the white outer tail feathers and the rather short hind claw. The juvenile is similar to the adult.

This species is superficially similar to other pipits and tricky to separate on plumage details alone. The precise habitat requirements and its fondness for perching in trees is generally a good indication of its identification. Its trilling song and accompanying flight habits are diagnostic. A ground-nesting species, it constructs a shallow cup of grass and leaves.

This seasonal visitor is very vocal after its arrival with its call, song and mode of song delivery being distinctly different from a Meadow Pipit.

adult life-size

The plumage shows more contrast on the underparts than in a Meadow Pipit.

adult

Water Pipit
Anthus spinoletta

A similar size and shape to a Rock Pipit (to which it is closely related) but overall it has much paler and cleaner-looking plumage.

adult autumn

Factfile

LENGTH 16–17CM

WINGSPAN 23–28CM

HABITAT BREEDS ON HIGH MOUNTAIN SLOPES. IN WINTER, MOVES TO LOWER ALTITUDES AND TO COASTS, ESTUARIES AND FRESHWATER MARSHES.

FOOD FEEDS PRIMARILY ON INVERTEBRATES, BUT ALSO EATS SEEDS AND SOME ALGAE AND PLANTS.

STATUS BREEDS IN MOUNTAINS OF CENTRAL, SOUTHERN AND EASTERN EUROPE. SOME EASTERN BIRDS OVERWINTER ON COASTS AND WETLANDS OF NORTHWEST EUROPE; PRESENT THERE MAINLY OCTOBER TO MARCH.

VOICE THE CALL IS A SINGLE *PSEET*.

The Water Pipit is a rather bulky pipit, formerly considered to be a race of Rock Pipit but now granted full species status. The sexes are similar but subtle seasonal plumage variation occurs. The winter adult has streaked buffish-brown upperparts with subtle white wingbars. The underparts are pale and streaked, the breast and flanks being tinged with buffish-brown. The throat is pale and unmarked. The head markings are subtle and indistinct and comprise a whitish supercilium and contrasting dark eye stripe. Note the dark grey-brown bill, dark legs and white outer tail feathers. The adult in summer plumage is sometimes encountered in the region in late winter. It is similar but has almost unmarked underparts, which display a pinkish flush on the breast. The upperparts are brown; the neck and head are grey and marked with a pale throat and pale supercilium. The first-winter bird is similar to the winter adult.

This species occurs in our region only as a passage migrant or winter visitor in low numbers, and is generally solitary at this time. It can be encountered in a number of sheltered coastal areas, but is also seen in freshwater environments on occasion, showing a distinct liking for Watercress beds and the flooded margins of marshes.

adult spring life-size
The peachy flush to the underparts varies in intensity but always contrasts with the 'cold' grey look of the upperparts.

Chaffinch
Fringilla coelebs

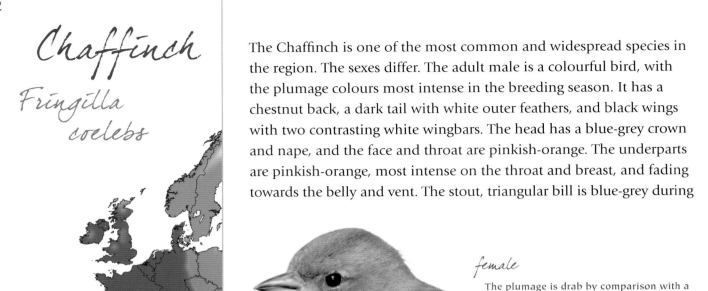

The Chaffinch is one of the most common and widespread species in the region. The sexes differ. The adult male is a colourful bird, with the plumage colours most intense in the breeding season. It has a chestnut back, a dark tail with white outer feathers, and black wings with two contrasting white wingbars. The head has a blue-grey crown and nape, and the face and throat are pinkish-orange. The underparts are pinkish-orange, most intense on the throat and breast, and fading towards the belly and vent. The stout, triangular bill is blue-grey during

female

The plumage is drab by comparison with a male but shows the same striking white markings on the wings.

During the breeding season male Chaffinches use a prominent perch from which to sing and watch for danger; if a threat is identified, an insistent and persistent alarm call is uttered.

male life-size

the breeding season and grey-brown at other times. In flight, the extensive white on the wings and tail is striking. The adult female has mainly buffish-brown plumage overall, darkest on the upperparts; note the two pale wingbars. The juvenile is similar to the adult female.

During the winter months the Chaffinch forages for seeds on the ground; it is also a familiar garden bird that is readily attracted to feeders. Outside the breeding season it forms loose flocks, and numbers in western Europe are boosted by migrant birds from further north and east. It nests in a beautifully constructed cup of lichen and moss, placed in the fork of a tree or bush.

Factfile

LENGTH 14–15CM

WINGSPAN 25–28CM

HABITAT **VARIETY OF HABITATS INCLUDING WOODLANDS, FARMLAND AND PARKS; A FAMILIAR GARDEN VISITOR.**

FOOD **FEEDS ON SEEDS AND INVERTEBRATES.**

STATUS **COMMON AND WIDESPREAD THROUGHOUT. PRESENT YEAR-ROUND IN MUCH OF THE REGION BUT SCANDINAVIAN POPULATIONS MIGRATE SOUTH AND WEST FOR THE WINTER MONTHS.**

VOICE **SONG IS A DESCENDING TRILL THAT FINISHES WITH A FLOURISH. THE CALL IS A DISTINCTIVE** *PINK PINK*.

male

In flight, a considerable extent of white on the wings and outer tail is revealed.

male

The plumage colours intensify as the breeding season approaches, with pale feather tips being worn away to reveal the bird's true splendour.

Brambling
Fringilla montifringilla

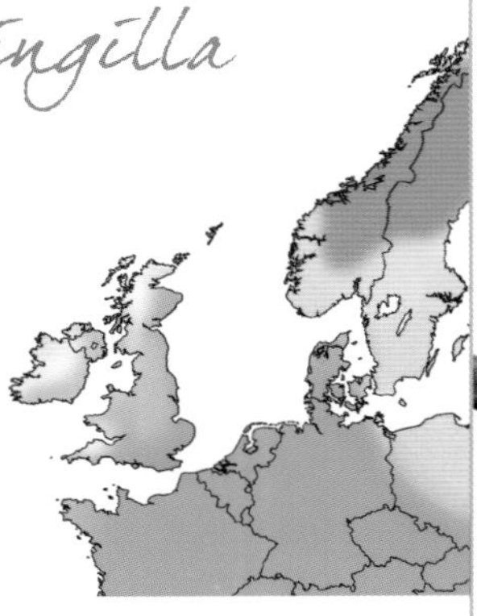

In winter, males have more strikingly marked and richly colourful plumage than females.

male

As winter progresses, pale feather tips wear away and the male's cap becomes dark, eventually appearing all-black.

male life-size

adults

Winter Brambling flocks are usually faithful to areas of good feeding as long as supplies last. When they take to the wing, note that birds have pale underparts and a white rump.

Factfile

LENGTH 14–15CM

WINGSPAN 25–26CM

HABITAT VARIETY OF OPEN AND WOODED HABITATS, SHOWING A PREFERENCE FOR LOCATIONS WHERE BEECH PROLIFERATES.

FOOD IN WINTER, FEEDS ON SEEDS, PARTICULARLY THOSE OF BEECH. DIET INCLUDES INVERTEBRATES DURING THE SUMMER MONTHS.

STATUS SUMMER BREEDING VISITOR TO SCANDINAVIA, PRESENT MAINLY MAY TO SEPTEMBER. ELSEWHERE, BEST KNOWN AS A WINTER VISITOR, MAINLY OCTOBER TO MARCH. NUMBERS VARY EACH YEAR DEPENDING ON WEATHER AND FOOD AVAILABILITY ELSEWHERE.

VOICE SONG IS SELDOM HEARD IN THE REGION, BUT COMPRISES A SERIES OF BUZZING NOTES. CALL INCLUDES A HARSH, WHEEZING *JSEEERRP*.

The Brambling is a handsome finch. The sexes differ and seasonal plumage variation occurs. The winter adult male has a dark head and back, the feathers displaying grey-buff fringes which gradually wear off. The wings are dark with pale feather margins, and whitish-orange wingbars. The lesser wing coverts are orange, the colour extending to the throat and breast, and grading to white on the belly and vent. Note the dark spots on the flanks and the triangular, dark-tipped yellow bill. The summer adult male is similar but the hood, back and bill are black or blackish. The adult female is similar to the adult winter male but with muted colouration overall; the pale fringes on the back feathers are more obvious. The head is grey-brown and marked with dark lines to the nape and sides of the crown. The immature is similar to the winter adult but with subdued colouration, although the sex cannot always be reliably determined. In flight, the obvious white rump is a good aid to identification of all birds.

Best known as a winter visitor, the Brambling's numbers and distribution at this time are affected by the food supply in its summer range. With a particular liking for Beech seeds, it will linger until supplies dwindle, forcing it to move south and west. Outside the breeding season, it can form large flocks.

female

Even though female Bramblings are less colourful than males, they share the same orange colour on the wings and flanks; the precise hue is subtly unique to the species.

Greenfinch
Chloris chloris

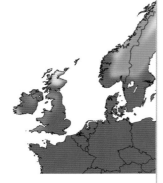

The Greenfinch is a brightly coloured finch with a large conical bill. The sexes differ. The adult male has intense yellowish-green plumage overall, darkest on the upperparts. Grey patches adorn the sides of the face, neck and wings; note the striking bright yellow patch to the edge of the wings, and the yellow sides to the base of the tail (most obvious in flight). The intensity of the plumage colour increases as winter progresses, as pale feather tips wear away. Note the pale stout-looking bill and the pale legs. The adult female is similar to the adult male, but the plumage is muted, with less yellow on the wings and tail; there is usually faint streaking on the back, although this is variable. The juvenile is similar to the adult female, but with more conspicuous streaking all over.

male

Factfile

LENGTH 14–15CM

WINGSPAN 25–27CM

HABITAT FAVOURS LOWLAND HABITATS, INCLUDING WOODLAND EDGES, HEDGEROWS, PARKS AND GARDENS.

FOOD FEEDS ON SEEDS, BERRIES AND FRUITS, WITH INVERTEBRATES IN THE BREEDING SEASON.

STATUS RESIDENT BREEDING SPECIES, COMMON, WIDESPREAD AND PRESENT YEAR-ROUND ACROSS MUCH OF REGION EXCEPT NORTHERN SCANDINAVIA; HERE IT IS A SUMMER VISITOR.

VOICE SONG IS RATHER VARIED, RANGING FROM RAPID, TRILLING WHISTLES TO WELL-SPACED, WHEEZING *WEEEISH* PHRASES, SOMETIMES DELIVERED IN FLIGHT. CALL IS A HARSH *JRRRUP* UTTERED IN FLIGHT.

male life-size
Even at his most colourful, the male retains a grey patch on the cheeks.

In flight, note the pale underside to the flight feathers and the yellow-green sides to the base of the tail.

All birds show a striking yellow bar along the edge of the folded wing.

The Greenfinch is a widespread species and a familiar garden resident. It is an enthusiastic visitor to garden bird tables and feeders, and pecking-order quarrels often break out. The nest is a cup of grass and twigs placed in the fork of a tree or bush.

female

Goldfinch
Carduelis carduelis

Factfile

LENGTH 12–13CM

WINGSPAN 21–25CM

HABITAT LOWLAND AREAS, FAVOURING SCRUB, HEDGEROWS, WOODLAND MARGINS AND MATURE GARDENS.

FOOD FEEDS ON SEEDS AND PARTICULARLY FOND OF TEASEL, THISTLES AND DAISIES.

STATUS COMMON AND WIDESPREAD BREEDING SPECIES FOUND THROUGHOUT THE REGION, EXCEPT FOR THE NORTH. PRESENT YEAR-ROUND IN MOST AREAS, ALTHOUGH LOCAL DISPERSAL AND GENERAL SOUTHERLY MIGRATION DOES OCCUR IN AUTUMN.

VOICE SONG IS A RAPID, CHEERFUL TWITTERING. UTTERS A TINKLING, TRISYLLABIC CALL.

adult life-size

The white-framed red face and yellow on the wings make for a colourful appearance.

This is a colourful finch with unmistakable markings. The sexes are similar. The adult has upperparts that comprise a buffish-brown back and black wings and tail, marked with a series of white patches and a striking yellow wingbar. The head has a bold black-and-white pattern and a large red facial patch. The underparts are whitish and display a pale buff flush to the flanks and breast. The pale bill is relatively long and conical, and the legs are flesh-coloured. In flight, note the broad yellow wingbar, the white feather tips to the black upperwings, and the white tips to the tail feathers. The juvenile is buffish overall with an unmarked head and an obvious yellow wingbar.

The Goldfinch is an acrobatic bird that generally feeds by extracting seeds with its bill directly from the heads of favoured plants such as Wild Teasel and thistles. It is readily attracted to garden feeders and tables and forms large flocks outside the breeding season. The nest is a cup of grass and moss hidden among the outer twigs of a tree.

adult

In flight, the yellow wingbars are a striking feature.

adult

The slender bill is ideally adapted to extracting seeds from dense seedheads.

Siskin
Spinus spinus

The Siskin is a brightly coloured little finch, easily recognised by the yellow elements of its plumage; the colours are most intense during the breeding season. The sexes are similar but separable with care. The adult male has streaked bright yellowish-green upperparts, with dark wings and yellow wingbars. The head is adorned with a contrasting black cap and bib. The underparts are pale whitish and boldy marked with dark streaking on the flanks and an intense yellowish-green flush on the breast. Note the bright yellow rump and yellow triangular patches on the base of the tail. The bill is conical and finely pointed. The adult female is similar but the colouration is subdued overall and it lacks the black cap and bib markings. The juvenile displays the wing and tail patterns of the adult, but has mainly streaked, grey-brown plumage overall, paler on the head and underparts.

The Siskin feeds primarily on the seeds of trees such as spruce, alder and birch. It extracts them directly with its tweezer-like bill, hanging acrobatically from the cones and twigs. It occasionally visits garden feeders where it shows a fondness for peanuts, but generally it is a more reluctant visitor than many of its counterparts. It nests high up in the outer twigs of conifers, constructing a moss-lined cup of twigs and grass.

Colourful and unmistakable during the breeding season, with a dark cap and broad wingbars.

male

1st-winter life-size

The yellow wingbars and rump are obvious in flight.

male

Plumage is overall pale, with streaked underparts and the species' trademark yellow wingbars.

Factfile

LENGTH 11–12CM   WINGSPAN 20–23CM

HABITAT FAVOURS CONIFEROUS FORESTS IN THE BREEDING SEASON, BUT MORE WIDESPREAD IN THE WINTER, WITH A PREFERENCE FOR ALDER AND BIRCH WOODLANDS, AND MATURE GARDENS.

FOOD FEEDS PRIMARILY ON THE SEEDS OF SPRUCE, ALDER AND BIRCH.

STATUS LOCALLY COMMON BREEDING SPECIES IN THE NORTH AND EAST OF THE REGION, AND PRESENT YEAR-ROUND EXCEPT IN THE EXTREME NORTH WHERE IT IS A SUMMER VISITOR. IN ITS RESIDENT RANGE, AND IN WESTERN EUROPE, NUMBERS ARE BOOSTED IN WINTER BY BIRDS MIGRATING FROM FURTHER NORTH AND EAST.

VOICE SONG COMPRISES A SERIES OF WARBLING, TWITTERING PHRASES. UTTERS A DISYLLABIC *SPEEOO* WHISTLING CALL.

Linnet

Linaria cannabina

Plumage is rather nondescript and grey-brown with spot-like streaks on the underparts.

female

Factfile

LENGTH 13–14CM

WINGSPAN 21–25CM

HABITAT FAVOURS AREAS OF OPEN GROUND WITH LOW COVER, CLASSICALLY HEDGEROWS, SCRUB AND MATURE GORSE PATCHES IN HEATHLAND AND COASTAL GRASSLAND. IT CAN OCCASIONALLY ALSO BE ENCOUNTERED ON PLOUGHED OR STUBBLE FIELDS AND WAYSIDE GROUND.

FOOD FEEDS ALMOST EXCLUSIVELY ON SEEDS, WITH SOME INVERTEBRATES IN THE BREEDING SEASON.

STATUS WIDESPREAD AND LOCALLY COMMON BREEDING SPECIES, PRESENT YEAR-ROUND ACROSS MOST OF THE REGION, EXCEPT SCANDINAVIA WHERE IT IS A SUMMER VISITOR.

VOICE MALE DELIVERS A TWITTERING, WARBLING SONG, COMMONLY FROM A PROMINENT PERCH. CALL IS A DISTINCTIVE *TETTER-TETT*.

The Linnet is an endearing little finch that is often easily overlooked. The sexes differ, and seasonal plumage variations occur. The summer adult male has a chestnut back, darker wings with a whitish patch, and a grey head with a rosy-pink forecrown. The underparts are pale, the throat is streaked and the breast has a distinctive rosy-pink flush. The adult male in the winter is similar, but the rosy flush is lost and replaced by dull brown, or is obscured by pale feather tips. The adult female has grey-brown upperparts; the underparts are pale with a grey-buff flush to the breast, and a pattern of streaks and spots. The juvenile is similar to the adult female, but is more heavily streaked and has duller colouration overall. In flight, note the lightly forked tail and the whitish patch on the wings in all birds.

During the winter months, the Linnet is often observed in large flocks that feed, roost and migrate together. In the breeding season, the male often uses a conspicuous perch from which to sing, and breeding pairs commonly associate in small, loose colonial groups. The nest is a cup of grass and twigs which is placed in low, thick cover.

male life-size

The male's lively song can be heard in April and May.

Winter flocks favour overgrown grassy habitats with plenty of dead seedheads.

winter flock

Twite *Linaria flavirostris*

Factfile

LENGTH 13–14CM

WINGSPAN 22–24CM

HABITAT FAVOURS OPEN COUNTRYSIDE, TYPICALLY HEATHER MOORLAND AND COASTAL GRASSLAND IN THE BREEDING SEASON, MOVING TO SALT MARSHES AND FIELDS ADJACENT TO THE COAST FOR THE WINTER MONTHS.

FOOD FEEDS EXCLUSIVELY ON SEEDS.

STATUS BREEDS IN SUITABLE HABITATS IN THE NORTH OF THE REGION, WHERE IT IS PRESENT MAINLY MAY TO SEPTEMBER. IT MIGRATES TO MORE SOUTHERLY AND TEMPERATE LOCATIONS FOR THE WINTER. THE BIRDS THAT OCCUR IN BRITAIN ARE A SEPARATE SUBSPECIES FROM SCANDINAVIAN BREEDERS, AND ITS DECLINING NUMBERS MERIT SPECIAL CONSERVATION MEASURES.

VOICE SONG COMPRISES A SERIES OF TRILLING AND RATTLING NOTES. CALL IS A CHARACTERISTIC SHARP AND TWANGING *TVEEHT*.

Outside the breeding season, the yellowish bill is a reliable way of separating the species from a Linnet, which has a grey bill.

winter flock

The male's pink rump is most obvious in flight.

The Twite is a dumpy little finch, and in many ways it is the northern counterpart of the Linnet. The sexes are similar but are separable in some instances, and some seasonal plumage variation occurs. The summer adult male has streaked dark brown upperparts. The flight and tail feathers have contrasting white margins, and the face and throat are buffish-brown. The underparts are pale and heavily streaked, particularly on the breast and flanks. The rump is pinkish, but this feature is not always easy to see. The conical bill is grey. The adult winter male is similar but with subdued markings, the head and breast being warm buffish-brown; the bill is yellow. The adult female and the juvenile are similar to the adult male, but note the brown (not pink) rump. A reliable tip to allow certain separation from the Linnet is to look at the buff throat which lacks any spotting or streaking.

The Twite is a gregarious species that forms large flocks outside the breeding season, when it is usually found in salt marshes and coastal grassland. It breeds on upland moorland and constructs a cup-shaped nest of twigs and bracken in low vegetation.

juvenile life-size

summer male

Breeding birds are extremely secretive and if you encounter a male the chances are he will be nowhere near his nest.

Lesser Redpoll
Acanthis cabaret

The Lesser Redpoll is a compact little finch with a small yellow bill. The sexes are similar but are sometimes separable. The adult male has heavily streaked grey-brown upperparts, darkest on the back, and with pale wingbars. The underparts and rump are pale, heavily streaked, with a pinkish-red flush usually discernible on the breast. The head has a red forecrown, black lores and black bib. The short, triangular bill is yellow. The adult female and immature birds are similar to the adult male but lack the pinkish-red flush to the breast. In flight, note the forked tail and pale wingbars in all birds.

Outside the breeding season, the Lesser Redpoll forms large gregarious flocks, often mixing with Siskins. It is an acrobatic feeder, dangling from thin twigs and plucking seeds from treetop cones with its small bill. It builds a nest of twigs and grass, usually positioned high up in a tree.

The lively song has elements in common with the call.

male

male

The extent and intensity of red in a male's plumage varies between individuals and increases throughout spring.

female life-size
The plumage is streaked brown, with pale wingbars and a yellowish bill.

Factfile

LENGTH 12–14CM

WINGSPAN 20–25CM

HABITAT DURING THE BREEDING SEASON FAVOURS BIRCH WOODLAND, BUT OCCURS IN AREAS OF BOTH BIRCH AND ALDER AT OTHER TIMES.

FOOD FEEDS PRIMARILY ON THE SEEDS OF ALDER AND BIRCHES.

STATUS RESIDENT BREEDING SPECIES PRESENT YEAR-ROUND IN SUITABLE HABITAT THROUGHOUT THE REGION, EXCEPT THE FAR NORTH. SOME SOUTHWARD MIGRATION OCCURS IN AREAS THAT EXPERIENCE HARSH WINTERS.

VOICE SONG COMPRISES A SERIES OF WHEEZING AND RATTLING NOTES. CALL IS A RATTLING *CHEK-CHEK-CHEK* UTTERED IN FLIGHT.

Common Redpoll
Acanthis flammea

On average, all birds are slightly larger than a typical Lesser Redpoll with noticeably paler, 'colder'-looking plumage.

adult

Factfile

LENGTH 12–14CM   WINGSPAN 23CM

HABITAT DURING THE BREEDING SEASON FAVOURS BIRCH WOODLAND, BUT OCCURS IN AREAS OF BOTH BIRCH AND COMMON ALDER AT OTHER TIMES.

FOOD FEEDS PRIMARILY ON THE SEEDS OF ALDER AND BIRCHES.

STATUS BREEDS IN THE NORTH OF THE REGION IN BIRCH WOODLAND, AND PRESENT THERE MAINLY MAY TO SEPTEMBER. MIGRATES SOUTHWARDS IN AUTUMN; IN WINTER, FOUND IN VARYING NUMBERS THROUGHOUT THE REGION IN SUITABLE HABITATS.

VOICE SONG COMPRISES A SERIES OF WHEEZING AND RATTLING NOTES. CALL IS A RATTLING *CHEK-CHEK-CHEK* UTTERED IN FLIGHT.

Very similar to, but larger than, Lesser Redpoll, the Common Redpoll's plumage is overall much paler. The sexes are similar but sometimes separable. The adult male has heavily streaked pale grey-buff upperparts, darkest on the back, and with pale wingbars. The underparts are pale and heavily streaked, the rump is pale and subtly streaked, and a red flush is sometimes present on the breast. The head has a red forecrown, black lores and black bib. The short, triangular bill is yellow. The adult female and immature birds are similar to the adult male but lack the red flush to the breast. In flight, note the forked tail and the pale wingbars in all birds.

The Common Redpoll is very similar to its cousin the Lesser Redpoll, but the two do not interbreed where their breeding ranges overlap. It breeds in the birch woodlands of Scandinavia and northern Europe, building a nest of twigs and grass that is usually positioned high up in a tree. During the winter, harsh weather and lack of food in its summer range force a southward migration and dispersal; at this time it often mixes with flocks of Lesser Redpoll.

The extent of red on the face and underparts varies considerably but all adult birds have a red forecrown.

adult life-size

Crossbill
Loxia curvirostra

Factfile

LENGTH 15–17CM

WINGSPAN 27–30CM

HABITAT **FOUND ALMOST EXCLUSIVELY IN MATURE CONIFEROUS WOODLANDS.**

FOOD **FEEDS ON THE SEEDS OF CONIFEROUS TREES, PARTICULARLY SPRUCE.**

STATUS **GENERALLY A SEDENTARY RESIDENT BREEDING SPECIES THAT OCCURS YEAR-ROUND THROUGHOUT THE REGION IN SUITABLE HABITATS. HOWEVER, A LACK OF FOOD IN WINTER MONTHS, CAUSED BY A SEED CROP FAILURE, CAN CAUSE LONG IRRUPTIVE JOURNEYS IN SEARCH OF FOOD.**

VOICE **UTTERS A HARSH *KIP-KIP-KIP* CALL DELIVERED IN FLIGHT. SONG COMPRISES CALL-LIKE NOTES.**

male life-size

Looks plump-bodied with a proportionately large head.

The Crossbill has precise habitat requirements, with its feeding habits reflected in its distinctive bill with cross-tipped mandibles. The sexes differ. The adult male has mainly red plumage overall, which is darker above than below, and brownish on the wings. The large bill is dark and robust-looking; the tips of the mandibles are crossed. The adult female has mainly yellowish-green plumage overall, with brownish wings. Immature birds are similar to adults of the respective sexes, but have muted colouration. The juvenile has heavily streaked grey-brown plumage overall.

The Common Crossbill's bill shape has evolved to extract seeds from conifer cones. Although typically sedentary, food shortages can result in nomadic behaviour. Two closely related species also occur in our region. The Scottish Crossbill *L. scotica* has a larger bill than the Common Crossbill and is confined to ancient Scots Pine forests in the Scottish Highlands. The Parrot Crossbill *L. pytyopsittacus* has an even larger bill; it is resident in Scandinavia and sometimes irrupts if cone crops fail.

A dextrous feeder that sometimes uses its feet to help manipulate cones for the extraction of seeds by the bill.

male

The fact that the bill tips overlap is not always obvious in side view.

female

Bullfinch

Pyrrhula pyrrhula

The white rump is an obvious feature in flight, contrasting with the dark tail.

male

Usually seen in the company of a male and the pair is often site-faithful throughout the year.

female

Factfile

LENGTH 16–17CM WINGSPAN 25CM

HABITAT A SPECIES OF MAINLY RURAL AREAS, FOUND IN DECIDUOUS WOODLAND, HEDGEROWS AND MATURE GARDENS.

FOOD FEEDS PRIMARILY ON BUDS, SEEDS, BERRIES AND FRUITS.

STATUS A COMMON AND WIDESPREAD RESIDENT BREEDING SPECIES, PRESENT YEAR-ROUND THROUGHOUT THE REGION IN SUITABLE HABITATS.

VOICE THE SONG IS RATHER QUIET AND SELDOM HEARD, CONSISTING OF SLOW, FLUTY NOTES. THE CALL IS DISTINCTIVE, A SOFT, MONOSYLLABIC PIPING *PEW*, SOMETIMES DELIVERED BY A PAIR IN DUET.

The Bullfinch has a plump body and distinctive plumage. The sexes differ. The adult male has a blue-grey back and nape; the tail is black and the black wings display a broad white wingbar. The head has a bold black cap and bib, contrasting with the rosy-pink face, breast and belly. The vent and rump are white and the stubby bill is dark. The adult female is similar to the adult male, but the rosy-pink elements of the plumage are replaced with dull pinkish-buff. The juvenile is similar to the adult female but lacks the black cap and is generally buffish-brown. In flight, the white rump is obvious and diagnostic in all birds.

The Bullfinch is a rather timid species that seeks the sanctuary of deep cover, and is heard more frequently than it is seen. When encountered it is commonly seen in pairs. It feeds on the buds, seeds and fruits of trees and is an occasional visitor to garden feeders in rural areas. It nests in deep cover, constructing a platform of twigs.

The precise hue of a male's rosy pink underparts is subtly unique to the species.

male life-size

Hawfinch
Coccothraustes coccothraustes

Factfile

LENGTH 17–18CM

WINGSPAN 29–33CM

HABITAT MAINLY ASSOCIATED WITH MATURE DECIDUOUS AND MIXED WOODLAND, PARKS, ORCHARDS AND LARGE MATURE GARDENS.

FOOD FEEDS ON SEEDS, FRUIT STONES AND SOME INVERTEBRATES.

STATUS RESIDENT BREEDING SPECIES PRESENT YEAR-ROUND AND WIDESPREAD ACROSS MUCH OF EUROPE; DISTRIBUTION IS RATHER PATCHY AND LOCAL IN BRITAIN AND SCANDINAVIA. SOME WESTWARD MIGRATION OF BIRDS FROM THE EAST OF THE REGION OCCURS IN AUTUMN.

VOICE SONG IS SELDOM HEARD, BEING RATHER QUIET AND SUBDUED. CALL IS A SHARP ROBIN-LIKE *TSIC*.

The Hawfinch is a large and stout-looking finch with a large head, thickset neck and proportionately massive bill. The sexes are similar but separable with care. The adult male has overall pinkish-buff plumage, with a brown back, broad whitish wingbar and blue-black primary flight feathers. The short tail is marked with a white tip. The head is marked with a grey neck, black lores, black bib and black to the bill base. The triangular bill is unmistakable, looking too large for its head; it is dark metallic grey in summer and buffish-brown in winter. The adult female is similar to the adult male but the colours are more subdued and it sometimes displays an additional wing panel. The juvenile is similar to the adult female but the markings are less distinct and the colours are more muted. In flight, note the short tail and the extensive white patches on the wings and the tail in all birds.

The Hawfinch is a rather shy and unobtrusive bird that seeks the sanctuary of deep cover, particularly during the breeding season, when it nests in a tree, constructing a twig platform. Its large bill is used great effect cracking hard-cased seeds of the to of Hornbeam (*Carpinus betulus*) and likes Wild Cherry (*Prunus avium*). It forms small flocks around plentiful food sources outside the breeding season.

male

Reveals a large extent of white on the wings and tail in flight.

The large head and proportionately massive bill are unique and diagnostic.

Plumage colours and markings are subtly understated when compared to a male.

male life-size

female

Snow Bunting

Plectrophenax nivalis

The Snow Bunting is a delightful songbird with extensive areas of white plumage. The sexes differ, and some seasonal plumage variation occurs. The summer adult male is mainly white with a blackish back, and wings marked with black-and-white. Some birds have a subtle orange-buff tinge to the white elements of their plumage. The stubby, triangular bill and the legs are black. The summer adult female is similar to the male but the back is brownish and the head, neck and the sides of the breast

1st winter

Immature birds have clean white underparts but a strong orange-buff wash to the back and face.

winter male

As winter progresses, the plumage of adult males becomes increasingly black-and-white.

1st winter

In flight, all birds reveal a considerable extent of white in the wings and tail.

Factfile

LENGTH 16–17CM   WINGSPAN 32–38CM

HABITAT BREEDS ON MOUNTAIN TOPS, TUNDRA AND REMOTE UPLAND AREAS. IN WINTER, USUALLY ASSOCIATED WITH LOWLAND AND COASTAL GRASSLAND.

FOOD FEEDS ON SEEDS AND INVERTEBRATES.

STATUS BREEDS IN SCANDINAVIA, WITH A FEW PAIRS NESTING IN SCOTLAND; PRESENT THERE MAINLY MAY TO SEPTEMBER. OUTSIDE THE BREEDING SEASON, SEEN ON MIGRATION ACROSS THE CENTRAL BELT OF EUROPE BUT WINTERS MAINLY ON THE COASTS OF NORTHWEST EUROPE.

VOICE SONG COMPRISES TWITTERING PHRASES. UTTERS A TINKLING, ROLLING *PRRRT* CALL IN FLIGHT.

are streaked with varying amounts of brown and buff. The winter adults of both sexes and first-winter birds have buffish-orange upperparts and white underparts. The winter adult male can be distinguished by the greater amount of white in its wings, face and underparts. The bill is yellowish in all birds at this time.

Outside the breeding season the Snow Bunting forms flocks; these can be a surprising sight when they take to the air, flashing their white wings. It can be quite a confiding bird, particularly when encountered on migration, when close views are sometimes possible. It seeks rock crevices in which to nest.

summer male life-size

Summer males are unmistakable; at the height of the breeding season the bill and the legs are black.

Lapland Bunting

Calcarius lapponicus

This is a well-marked bunting. The sexes differ, and seasonal plumage variation occurs. The summer adult male has primarily streaked brown upperparts and white underparts. The head has a chestnut patch on the nape, a black crown, a bold black facial mask and a black bib, all of which are sharply defined by a broad white dividing line. The stubby triangular bill is yellow. The summer adult female also has a chestnut nape, but the head markings comprise less well-defined black and brown streaks than those of the male; the pale underside is marked with streaking on the flanks. The sexes of the winter adults are hard to determine, all birds having streaked brown upperparts with a chestnut wing panel bordered by two pale wingbars. The head has a rather open-faced look, being reddish-brown in colour with a dark line defining the ear coverts, pale and unmarked lores, and a dark crown with a subtle pale median stripe. The bill is pinkish. The juvenile is similar to the winter adult.

The Lapland Bunting is generally a wary species, most commonly encountered on the coast during migration or in winter. At this time of the year it can form small flocks with other ground-feeding songbirds and is difficult to approach, taking flight readily. It breeds on Arctic tundra, nesting among grassy tussocks; the colourful breeding plumage and its open habitat make it rather conspicuous at this time.

autumn

Feeding birds tend to creep along the ground and can be unobtrusive.

summer male life-size

In breeding plumage, the male is a stunning bird with a striking pattern on the head.

Factfile

LENGTH 14–16CM

WINGSPAN 26–28CM

HABITAT DURING THE BREEDING SEASON, FAVOURS ARCTIC TUNDRA, MOVING TO OPEN FARMLAND AND COASTAL REGIONS DURING THE WINTER MONTHS.

FOOD FEEDS ON SEEDS AND INVERTEBRATES.

STATUS SUMMER BREEDING SPECIES, PASSAGE MIGRANT AND WINTER VISITOR. IN OUR REGION RESTRICTED TO SCANDINAVIAN ARCTIC TUNDRA IN THE BREEDING SEASON, MIGRATING SOUTH IN THE AUTUMN AND WINTERING ON THE NORTH SEA COASTS OF NORTHWEST EUROPE.

VOICE UTTERS A DISTINCTIVE RATTLING *TIDDLIP-TEW* CALL, DELIVERED IN FLIGHT. SONG COMPRISES JINGLING PHRASES.

autumn

autumn

Lapland Bunting non-breeding plumage varies with age and between the sexes, but all birds show a chestnut patch on the nape and a broad chestnut panel on the wings.

Outside the breeding season, all birds typically have a pinkish bill.

Yellowhammer
Emberiza citrinella

The Yellowhammer is a colourful bunting, the summer male being particularly eye-catching. The sexes are separable, and some seasonal plumage variation occurs. The adult male in summer has a reddish-brown back, the dark feather centres giving it a rather streaked appearance; the rump is reddish-brown. The underparts and the head are bright yellow, the head being marked with faint dark lines. The flanks are adorned with streaking, and the breast has a chestnut flush. The stubby triangular bill is greyish. The adult male in winter has subdued yellow elements to its plumage and the dark streaking on the head and upperparts is more intense. The adult female has brown upperparts, with a reddish-brown rump. The underparts are

Factfile

LENGTH 15–17CM   WINGSPAN 23–29CM

HABITAT OPEN GRASSLAND AND FARMLAND WITH SCATTERED SCRUB AND HEDGEROWS.

FOOD FEEDS PRIMARILY ON SEEDS AND INVERTEBRATES.

STATUS RATHER SEDENTARY RESIDENT BREEDING SPECIES, PRESENT YEAR-ROUND ACROSS MOST OF THE REGION IN SUITABLE HABITATS. BIRDS FROM UPLAND REGIONS AND FROM MORE NORTHERLY AND EASTERLY EXTREMES MOVE SOUTH AND WEST IN THE AUTUMN.

VOICE SONG COMPRISES A SERIES OF CHIRPING AND WHEEZING PHRASES. CALL IS A SHARP *STTUT*.

Bright and colourful in flight, and usually seen in flocks outside the breeding season.

male

male life-size

The male's bright yellow head and classic plump-bodied bunting shape make for easy identification.

pale yellow and streaked, and the head and breast are greenish-grey, and are also streaked. The immature is similar to the adult female but the streaking is more intense.

The Yellowhammer is a classic bunting of farmland and open countryside, its distinctive song and bright colouration make identification simple. Outside the breeding season it often forms flocks and mixes with other buntings and finches, typically around grain spills and other concentrations of food. It nests in low scrub or on the ground, constructing a bulky platform of grass and straw.

A particularly colourful female can look confusingly similar to a male with dull plumage.

female

male

The intensity of the colour on the head, and markings on the flanks, varies between individuals and throughout the year; birds are most striking at the start of the breeding season.

Cirl Bunting
Emberiza cirlus

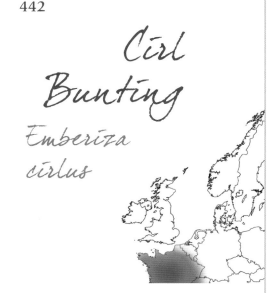

Factfile

LENGTH 16–17CM

WINGSPAN 22–25CM

HABITAT FAVOURS A MIXTURE OF OPEN COUNTRYSIDE AND WOODED COVER SUCH AS OPEN WOODLANDS, SCRUB AND FARMLAND WITH EXTENSIVE HEDGEROWS.

FOOD FEEDS PRIMARILY ON SEEDS AND INVERTEBRATES.

STATUS A MAINLY SOUTHERN SPECIES IN EUROPE, ITS RANGE EXTENDS TO THE NORTHWEST AND INCLUDES SOUTHWEST BRITAIN. IT IS A RESIDENT BREEDING SPECIES IN ITS RANGE, PRESENT YEAR-ROUND.

VOICE SONG IS A TUNELESS RATTLE, SIMILAR TO THAT OF LESSER WHITETHROAT. UTTERS A SHARP *TZIIP* CALL.

The Cirl Bunting is superficially similar to a Yellowhammer but separable on plumage details. The sexes differ, and some slight seasonal plumage variation occurs. The summer adult male has reddish-brown upperparts, the dark feather centres giving it a conspicuously streaked appearance. The underparts are yellow with chestnut streaks and a chestnut flush on the flanks. The head has a distinctive pattern consisting of a bold black eye stripe and throat, separated and defined by yellow. The crown, nape and breast are greenish-grey, and the stout triangular bill is greyish. The adult male in winter is similar but with muted colours. The adult female has streaked reddish-brown upperparts; the underparts are yellowish and streaked. The head displays a pattern of dark and yellow stripes, and streaking on the greenish-grey crown, neck and breast. The juvenile is similar to the adult female but the yellow elements of its plumage are paler. When compared to the similar Yellowhammer, note the olive rump in all birds (reddish-brown in Yellowhammer) which is particularly obvious when in flight.

female

A female's plumage is rather drab by comparison with a male, and heavily streaked; it lacks the yellow tone seen in a female Yellowhammer.

The Cirl Bunting is a rather timid bird that forms small single-species flocks in the winter. It breeds in cover on, or close to, the ground in a nest of moss and grass.

The striking pattern on the head allows easy separation from a male Yellowhammer.

male

In flight, note that the rump is olive-buff not chestnut.

male life-size

Reed Bunting
Emberiza schoeniclus

male

Whitish underparts and underwings are striking in flight.

Factfile

LENGTH 14–15CM

WINGSPAN 21–27CM

HABITAT FAVOURS REED-BED MARGINS AND SCRUBBY WETLANDS, PARTICULARLY DURING THE BREEDING SEASON. ALSO FOUND ON FARMLAND, ESPECIALLY IN WINTER.

FOOD FEEDS PRIMARILY ON SEEDS AND INVERTEBRATES.

STATUS WIDESPREAD AND LOCALLY COMMON BREEDING SPECIES. PRESENT YEAR-ROUND IN MUCH OF THE REGION, BUT BIRDS FROM THE NORTH AND EAST MIGRATE SOUTH AND WEST IN THE AUTUMN, RETURNING IN THE SPRING.

VOICE UTTERS A DISTINCTIVE AND REPETITIVE CHINKING SONG. CALL IS A THIN *SEEU*.

The Reed Bunting is a distinctive bird of wetland margins. Seasonal plumage variation occurs, and the sexes can be separated in the summer. The summer adult male has mainly reddish-brown upperparts marked with dark streaking. The underparts are mostly white with faint streaking. The head, throat and bib are black with a white submoustachial stripe and collar. The stubby triangular bill is dark. The winter male and adult female recall the summer male, but the distinctive black-and-white head and throat markings are replaced with a pattern of dark brown and buffish-brown stripes. The bill is greyish in colour. The male can display a suggestion of summer plumage, with spotting to the throat and bib. The juvenile is similar to the female but with even more subdued markings on the head. In all birds, note the white outer tail feathers, which are most obvious in flight.

In the breeding season, the male Reed Bunting uses exposed, elevated perches or fences from which to sing, making observation easy. At other times it is unobtrusive and the species favours the cover of reed beds and field furrows; in winter it sometimes forms small flocks.

female

Note the streaked brown plumage and white in the outer tail feathers.

The black cap and contrasting white collar and underparts are good identification features and stand out even at a distance.

male life-size

444

Corn Bunting

Emberiza calandra

Factfile

LENGTH 16–18CM

WINGSPAN 26–32CM

HABITAT FARMLAND HABITATS, FAVOURING MEADOWS AND ARABLE FIELDS WITH EXTENSIVE HEDGEROWS.

FOOD FEEDS PRIMARILY ON SEEDS AND INVERTEBRATES.

STATUS LOCALLY COMMON RESIDENT BREEDING SPECIES, PRESENT YEAR-ROUND IN MOST OF THE REGION. ABSENT FROM THE EXTREME NORTH, BIRDS ON THE NORTHERN EDGE OF ITS RANGE MIGRATING SOUTH FOR THE WINTER. ITS NUMBERS ARE IN DECLINE THROUGHOUT THE REGION, LINKED TO MODERN INTENSIVE FARMING PRACTICES.

VOICE HAS A RATHER JINGLING SONG THAT HAS BEEN LIKENED TO THE SOUND OF JANGLING KEYS. CALL IS A SHARP *TSIT*.

The Corn Bunting is a rather plain bird which is readily identified by its distinctive song. The sexes are similar. The adult has brown upperparts marked with dark streaking. The underparts are whitish with a buffish flush, and dark streaks on the breast and flanks. The stubby triangular bill is yellowish. The juvenile is similar to the adult. It generally flies in rather short, fluttering bursts, the legs dangling beneath its body.

The Corn Bunting is most commonly observed during the breeding season, when males perch conspicuously in the open, frequently using fence posts and wires to deliver their characteristic song. Its rather nondescript plumage makes it a tricky species to identify with certainty at other times. Outside the breeding season it forms flocks and often mixes with other ground-feeding songbirds. It constructs a loose nest of grasses placed in a scrape on the ground.

adult

The appearance in flight, particularly the dangling legs, is characteristic of the species.

adult

adult life-size

The Corn Bunting's song is evocative of traditional farmland; sadly it is no longer heard in large parts of its former range.

Note the proportionately large and stubby yellow bill.

Index

A

Acanthis cabaret 431
Acanthis flammea 432
Accipiter gentilis 142
Accipiter nisus 144
Acrocephalus palustris 374
Acrocephalus schoenobaenus 376
Acrocephalus scirpaceus 375
Actitis hypoleucos 220
Aegithalos caudatus 350
Aix galericulata 36
Alauda arvensis 354
Alca torda 276
Alcedo atthis 310
Alectoris rufa 86
Alle alle 280
Alopochen aegyptiaca 32
Anas acuta 48
Anas clypeata 50
Anas crecca 44
Anas penelope 42
Anas platyrhynchos 40
Anas querquedula 46
Anas strepera 38
Anser albifrons 22
Anser anser 24
Anser brachyrhynchus 20
Anser fabalis 18
Anthus petrosus 418
Anthus pratensis 416
Anthus spinoletta 421
Anthus trivialis 420
Apus apus 312
Aquila chrysaetos 134
Ardea cinerea 112
Arenaria interpres 232
Asio flammeus 306
Asio otus 304
Athene noctua 300
Auk, Little 280
Avocet 176
Aythya ferina 52
Aythya fuligula 56
Aythya marila 58

B

Bittern 108

Blackbird 387
Blackcap 366
Bombycilla garrulus 377
Botaurus stellaris 108
Brambling 424
Branta bernicla 30
Branta canadensis 26
Branta leucopsis 28
Bucephala clangula 68
Bullfinch 434
Bunting, Cirl 442
    Corn 444
    Lapland 438
    Reed 443
    Snow 436
Burhinus oedicnemus 178
Buteo buteo 148
Buteo lapogus 150
Buzzard 148
    Rough-legged 150

C

Calcarius lapponicus 438
Calidris alba 194
Calidris alpina 202
Calidris canutus 192
Calidris ferruginea 200
Calidris maritima 196
Calidris minuta 198
Calidris pugnax 204
Calidris temminckii 199
Capercaillie 82
Caprimulgus europaeus 308
Carduelis carduelis 427
Cepphus grylle 278
Certhia brachydactyla 379
Certhia familiaris 378
Cettia cetti 362
Chaffinch 422
Charadrius dubius 180
Charadrius hiaticula 182
Charadrius morinellus 184
Chiffchaff 364
Chlidonias niger 272
Chloris chloris 426
Chough 324
Chroicocephalus ridibundus 244
Ciconia ciconia 114
Cinclus cinclus 384

Circus aeruginosus 136
Circus cyaneus 138
Circus pygargus 140
Clangula hyemalis 62
Coccothraustes coccothraustes 435
Columba livia 284
Columba oenas 286
Columba palumbus 288
Coot 170
Cormorant 104
Corncrake 166
Corvus corax 338
Corvus cornix 336
Corvus corone 334
Corvus frugilegus 332
Corvus monedula 330
Coturnix coturnix 87
Crake, Spotted 164
Crane 172
Crex crex 166
Crossbill 433
    Parrot 433
    Scottish 433
Crow, Carrion 334
    Hooded 336
Cuckoo 296
Cuculus canorus 296
Curlew 218
Cyanistes caeruleus 340
Cygnus columbianus 14
Cygnus cygnus 16
Cygnus olor 12

D

Delichon urbicum 359
Dendrocopos major 318
Dendrocopos minor 320
Dipper 384
Diver, Black-throated 92
    Great Northern 94
    Red-throated 90
Dotterel 184
Dove, Collared 290
    Rock 284
    Stock 286
    Turtle 292
Duck, Long-tailed 62
    Mandarin 36
    Tufted 56

Dunlin 202
Dunnock 406

E

Eagle, Golden 134
    White-tailed 132
Egret, Little 110
Egretta garzetta 110
Eider 60
Emberiza calandra 444
Emberiza cirlus 442
Emberiza citrinella 440
Emberiza schoeniclus 443
Eremophila alpestris 356
Erithacus rubecula 396

F

Falco columbarius 156
Falco peregrinus 160
Falco subbuteo 158
Falco tinnunculus 154
Ficedula hypoleuca 395
Fieldfare 392
Firecrest 361
Flycatcher, Pied 395
    Spotted 394
Fratercula arctica 282
Fringilla coelebs 422
Fringilla montifringilla 424
Fulica atra 170
Fulmar 96
Fulmarus glacialis 96

G

Gadwall 38
Galerida cristata 355
Gallinago gallinago 208
Gallinula chloropus 168
Gannet 102
Garganey 46
Garrulus glandarius 328
Gavia arctica 92
Gavia immer 94
Gavia stellata 90
Godwit, Bar-tailed 214
    Black-tailed 212

Goldcrest 360
Goldeneye 68
Goldfinch 427
Goosander 74
Goose, Barnacle 28
  Bean 18
  Brent 30
  Canada 26
  Egyptian 32
  Greylag 24
  Pink-footed 20
  White-fronted 22
Goshawk 142
Grebe, Black-necked 126
  Great Crested 120
  Little 128
  Red-necked 122
  Slavonian 124
Greenfinch 426
Greenshank 226
Grouse, Black 80
  Red 76
Grus grus 172
Guillemot 274
  Black 278
Gull, Black-headed 244
  Common 250
  Glaucous 258
  Great Black-backed 260
  Herring 254
  Iceland 256
  Lesser Black-backed 252
  Little 246
  Mediterranean 248

Haematopus ostralegus 174
Haliaeetus albicilla 132
Harrier, Hen 138
  Marsh 136
  Montagu's 140
Hawfinch 435
Heron, Grey 112
Hippolais icterina 372
Hippolais polyglotta 373
Hirundo rustica 358
Hobby 158
Honey-buzzard 146
Hydrobates pelagicus 100
Hydrocoloeus minutus 246

Ibis, Glossy 116

Jackdaw 330
Jay 328
Jynx torquilla 313

Kestrel 154
Kingfisher 310
Kite, Red 130
Kittiwake 242
Knot 192

L

Lagopus lagopus 76
Lagopus muta 78
Lanius collurio 322
Lanius excubitor 323
Lapwing 190
Lark, Crested 355
  Shore 356
Larus argentatus 254
Larus canus 250
Larus fuscus 252
Larus glaucoides 256
Larus hyperboreus 258
Larus marinus 260
Larus melanocephalus 248
Leiopicus medius 317
Limosa lapponica 214
Limosa limosa 212
Linaria cannabina 429
Linaria flavirostris 430
Linnet 429
Locustella naevia 371
Lophophanes cristatus 344
Loxia curvirostra 433
Loxia pytyopsittacus 433
Loxia scotica 433
Lullula arborea 353
Luscinia megarhynchos 398

Lymnocryptes minimus 206
Lyrurus tetrix 80

M

Magpie 326
Mallard 40
Martin, House 359
  Sand 357
Melanitta fusca 66
Melanitta nigra 64
Merganser, Red-breasted 72
Mergellus albellus 70
Mergus merganser 74
Mergus serrator 72
Merlin 156
Milvus milvus 130
Moorhen 168
Morus bassanus 102
Motacilla alba 414
Motacilla cinerea 412
Motacilla flava 410
Muscicapa striata 394

N

Netta rufina 54
Nightingale 398
Nightjar 308
Numenius arquata 218
Numenius phaeopus 216
Nuthatch 380

O

Oceanodroma leucorhoa 101
Oenanthe oenanthe 404
Oriole, Golden 321
Oriolus oriolus 321
Osprey 152
Ouzel, Ring 386
Owl, Barn 298
  Little 300
  Long-eared 304
  Short-eared 306
  Tawny 302
Oystercatcher 174

P

Pandion haliaetus 152
Panurus biarmicus 348
Parakeet, Ring-necked 294
Partridge, Grey 84
  Red-legged 86
Parus major 342
Passer domesticus 408
Passer montanus 409
Perdix perdix 84
Peregrine 160
Periparus ater 345
Pernis apivorus 146
Petrel, Leach's 101
  Storm 100
Phalacrocorax aristotelis 106
Phalacrocorax carbo 104
Phalarope, Grey 236
  Red-necked 234
Phalaropus fulicarius 236
Phalaropus lobatus 234
Phasianus colchicus 88
Pheasant 88
Phoenicurus ochruros 400
Phoenicurus phoenicurus 401
Phylloscopus collybita 364
Phylloscopus sibilatrix 363
Phylloscopus trochilus 365
Pica pica 326
Picus canus 316
Picus viridis 314
Pigeon, Feral 284
Pintail 48
Pipit, Meadow 416
  Rock 418
  Tree 420
  Water 421
Platalea leucorodia 118
Plectrophenax nivalis 436
Plegadis falcinellus 116
Plover, Golden 186
  Grey 188
  Little Ringed 180
  Ringed 182
Pluvialis apricaria 186
Pluvialis squatarola 188
Pochard 52
  Red-crested 54
Podiceps auritus 124
Podiceps cristatus 120

Podiceps grisegena 122
Podiceps nigricollis 126
Poecile montana 346
Poecile palustris 347
Porzana porzana 164
Prunella modularis 406
Psittacula krameri 294
Ptarmigan 78
   Willow 76
Puffin 282
Puffinus puffinus 98
Pyrrhocorax pyrrhocorax 324
Pyrrhula pyrrhula 434

Q

Quail 87

R

Rail, Water 162
Rallus aquaticus 162
Raven 338
Razorbill 276
Recurvirostra avosetta 176
Redpoll, Common 432
   Lesser 431
Redshank 230
   Spotted 228
Redstart 401
   Black 400
Redwing 390
Regulus ignicapilla 361
Regulus regulus 360
Remiz pendulinus 352
Riparia riparia 357
Rissa tridactyla 242
Robin 396
Rook 332
Ruff 204

S

Sanderling 194
Sandpiper, Common 220
   Curlew 200
   Green 222

   Purple 196
   Wood 224
Saxicola rubetra 402
Saxicola rubicola 403
Scaup 58
Scolopax rusticola 210
Scoter, Common 64
   Velvet 66
Shag 106
Shearwater, Manx 98
Shelduck 34
Shoveler 50
Shrike, Great Grey 323
   Red-backed 322
Siskin 428
Sitta europaea 380
Skua, Arctic 238
   Great 240
Skylark 354
Smew 70
Snipe 208
   Jack 206
Somateria mollissima 60
Sparrow, House 408
   Tree 409
Sparrowhawk 144
Spinus spinus 428
Spoonbill 118
Starling 382
Stercorarius parasiticus 238
Stercorarius skua 240
Sterna dougallii 268
Sterna hirundo 266
Sterna paradisaea 270
Sterna sandvicensis 264
Sternula albifrons 262
Stint, Little 198
   Temminck's 199
Stone-curlew 178
Stonechat 403
Stork, White 114
Streptopelia decaocto 290
Streptopelia turtur 292
Strix aluco 302
Sturnus vulgaris 382
Swallow 358
Swan, Bewick's 14
   Mute 12
   Whooper 16
Swift 312
Sylvia atricapilla 366

Sylvia borin 367
Sylvia communis 369
Sylvia curruca 368
Sylvia undata 370

T

Tachybaptus ruficollis 128
Tadorna tadorna 34
Teal 44
Tern, Arctic 270
   Black 272
   Common 266
   Little 262
   Roseate 268
   Sandwich 264
Tetrao urogallus 82
Thrush, Mistle 389
   Song 388
Tit, Bearded 348
   Blue 340
   Coal 345
   Crested 344
   Great 342
   Long-tailed 350
   Marsh 347
   Penduline 352
   Willow 346
Treecreeper 378
   Short-toed 379
Tringa erythropus 228
Tringa glareola 224
Tringa nebularia 226
Tringa ochropus 222
Tringa totanus 230
Troglodytes troglodytes 381
Turdus iliacus 390
Turdus merula 387
Turdus philomelos 388
Turdus pilaris 392
Turdus torquatus 386
Turdus viscivorus 389
Turnstone 232
Twite 430
Tyto alba 298

U

Uria aalge 274

V

Vanellus vanellus 190

W

Wagtail, Grey 412
   Pied 414
   White 414
   Yellow 410
Warbler, Cetti's 362
   Dartford 370
   Garden 367
   Grasshopper 371
   Icterine 372
   Marsh 374
   Melodious 373
   Reed 375
   Sedge 376
   Willow 365
   Wood 363
Waxwing 377
Wheatear 404
Whimbrel 216
Whinchat 402
Whitethroat 369
   Lesser 368
Wigeon 42
Woodcock 210
Woodlark 353
Woodpecker, Great Spotted 318
   Green 314
   Grey-headed 316
   Lesser Spotted 320
   Middle Spotted 317
Woodpigeon 288
Wren 381
Wryneck 313

Y

Yellowhammer 440

Photo credits and useful resources

Photo credits

All the photographs used in this book were taken by either **Paul Sterry** or **Rob Read** of **Nature Photographers Ltd** with the exception of those listed below. These can be identified using a combination of subject and page number.

From **Nature Photographers Ltd**:
Klaus Bjerre: Purple Sandpiper, flock 196; Little Gull, immature 247; Little Tern, flying (left) 262; Black Tern, flying 272; Black Tern, pair 272; Black Tern, life-size 273; Great Grey Shrike, flying 323; Shore Lark, life-size 356; Stonechat, female 403. **Frank Blackburn**: Green Woodpecker, male 315; Willow Tit, life-size 346 (bottom). **Mark Bolton**: Roseate Tern, flying 268; Roseate Tern, adult flying 269. **Laurie Campbell**: Scaup, male flying 59; Ptarmigan, winter male 79; Black-throated Diver, life-size 93; Fulmar, life-size 96; Fulmar, flying (left) 97; Gannet, life-size 102; Gannet, standing 103; Grey Heron, life-size 112; White-tailed Eagle, life-size 132; Golden Eagle, life-size 134; Hen Harrier, life-size 138; Hen Harrier, female flying 138; Hen Harrier, male flying 139; Kestrel, life-size 154; Common Sandpiper, calling 221; Guillemot, life-size 274; Black Guillemot, calling 279; Puffin, calling 283; Fieldfare (top) 393. **Colin Carver**: Stock Dove, life-size 287 (right). **Hugh Clark**: Snipe, standing 209; Great Skua, adult flying 241; Short-eared Owl, flying (left) 307; Kingfisher 310; Grey Wagtail, flying 412. **Andrew Cleave**: Shag, adults 107; Black-necked Grebe, both birds 126; Little Auk, colony 280; Little Auk, summer 280; Turtle Dove, juvenile 292; Ring Ouzel, male 386; Cirl Bunting, female 442; Cirl Bunting, flying 442. **Michael Foord**: Puffin, life-size 283; Goldfinch (bottom left) 427; Siskin, flying 428; Lesser Redpoll, female 431. **Martin Goodey**: Little Egret, life-size 111. **Ernie Janes**: Long-eared Owl 304; Red Grouse, female 77; Sparrowhawk, male 144; Woodcock, standing 210; Woodcock, life-size 211; Woodcock 211; Turnstone, flying 232. **Philip Newman**: Red Grouse, male 76; Black Grouse, female 81; Hen Harrier, male 139; Hen Harrier, female 139; Ring Ouzel, female 386; Mistle Thrush, wings raised 389. **David Osborn**: Osprey, standing 152; Osprey, flying 153; Merlin, life-size 156; Grey Plover, life-size 189; Grey Plover, summer 189. **Joe Pender**: Long-tailed Duck, female flying 63; Common Scoter, flock flying 65; Slavonian Grebe, flying 124; Grey Phalarope, flying 237; Arctic Skua, flying dark phase 239; Arctic Skua, flying light phase 239; Arctic Tern, juvenile flying 270; Little Auk, winter (bottom) 281. **Richard Revels**: Capercaillie, male 83; Grey Heron, flying 113; Great Crested Grebe, adult with chick 120; White-tailed Eagle, flying 133; Guillemot, flying 275; Puffin, flying 282; Fieldfare, flying 392. **Brian Small**: Scaup life-size male 59; Red-breasted Merganser, female 73; Willow Ptarmigan 77; Ptarmigan, winter 78; Red-necked Grebe, life-size 122; Osprey, flying 153; Knot, summer 192; Turnstone, life-size 233; Red-necked Phalarope, male 235; Red-necked Phalarope, juvenile 235; Arctic Tern, adult flying 270; Arctic Tern, adult standing 270; Long-eared Owl, flying 305; Short-eared Owl, adult (right) 306; Pied/White Wagtail, winter 414; Common Redpoll 432; Snow Bunting, summer male 437; Lapland Bunting, summer male 439. **Don Smith**: Tawny Owl, flying 302. **Roger Tidman**: Pink-footed Goose, flying birds 21; Shelduck, adult standing 34; Gadwall, flying birds 39; Wigeon, male flying 42; Wigeon, female 43; Garganey, male flying 47; Shoveler, flying birds 51; Pochard, male flying 52; Red-crested Pochard, flying 54; Goldeneye, flying birds 68; Red-breasted Merganser, male flying 72; Red-breasted Merganser, female flying 72; Capercaillie, life-size 82; Red-legged Partridge, life-size 86; Pheasant, male and female flying 89; Gannet, juvenile 103; Bittern, both birds 108; Spoonbill 118; Spoonbill, adult feeding and standing 119; Little Grebe, top image 128; Red Kite, perched 130; White-tailed Eagle, adult 133; Golden Eagle, immature 135; Golden Eagle, adult 135; Marsh Harrier, immature male 136; Marsh Harrier, male and female flying 137; Sparrowhawk, flying 144; Rough-legged Buzzard, male 151; Coot, flying 170; Oystercatcher, winter 174; Stone-curlew,

standing and flying birds 178; Little Ringed Plover, flying 181; Ringed Plover, flying 183; Ringed Plover, adult 183; Temminck's Stint, flying 199; Ruff, male summer 204; Black-tailed Godwit, flying 213; Bar-tailed Godwit, summer 214; Bar-tailed Godwit, flying 215; Green Sandpiper, flying 222; Spotted Redshank, flying 229; Red-necked Phalarope, flying 234; Stock Dove, flying 286; Stock Dove, adult (left) 287; Ring-necked Parakeet, flying 294; Wryneck (bottom) 313; Sand Martin, flying 357; Swallow, young 358; Blackcap, female 366; Melodious Warbler (bottom) 373; Sedge Warbler, flying 376; Sedge Warbler, flying 376; Waxwing, flying 377; Short-toed Treecreeper (top) 379; Mistle Thrush, life-size 389; Redwing, flying 390; Redwing (top) 391; Spotted Flycatcher, flying 394; Pied Flycatcher, flying 395; Nightingale (top and bottom) 398; Linnet, female 429; Twite, flock 430; Hawfinch, male standing and flying 435; Reed Bunting, female 443; Corn Bunting, life-size and flying 444. **Derek Washington**: Common Tern, life-size 266. **Steve Young**: Pochard, female flying 53; Scaup, female flying 59; Leach's Petrel, flying birds 101; Lesser Black-backed Gull, juvenile 253; Roseate Tern, life-size 268; Black Tern, juvenile 273; Grey Wagtail, female 412.

From other sources:
Ian Andrews: Velvet Scoter, flying 67. **Richard Brooks**: Bittern, life-size 109; Spotted Crake, adult 165; Yellow Wagtail, female 411. **Nick Clayton**: Temminck's Stint, juvenile 199. **Rudi Debrunye**: Quail, life-size 87. **Richard Greenwood** Black Guillemot, flying 279. **Stephen Hiscock**: Rough-legged Buzzard, juvenile perched and flying 151. **Jamie MacArthur**: Little Owl (all pictures) 300 & 301. **Chas Moonie**: Red Grouse, flying 76. **Chris Upson**: Roseate Tern, juvenile flying 269.

From **Alamy**:
David Tipling Photo Library/Alamy Stock Photo: Eider, male flying 61. **Bill Coster**/Alamy Stock Photo: Common Scoter, male flying 65. **FLPA**/Alamy Stock Photo: Velvet Scoter, female 67. **Arndt Sven-Erik**/Arterra Picture Library/Alamy Stock Photo: Smew, flying 71. **Arndt Sven-Erik**/Arterra Picture Library/Alamy Stock Photo: Goosander, male flying 75. **Wayne Hutchinson**/Alamy Stock Photo: Red Grouse, life-size 77. **Peter Cairns**/Nature Picture Library/Alamy Stock Photo: Ptarmigan, flying 79. **Blickwinkel**/Alamy Stock Photo: Black Grouse, life-size 81. **Christoph Bosch**/Alamy Stock Photo: Capercaillie, female 82. **Christian Hütter**/imageBROKER/Alamy Stock Photo: Cormorant, life-size 105. **Ann and Steve Toon**/Alamy Stock Photo: Shag, life-size 106. **Glenn Bartley**/All Canada Photos/Alamy Stock Photo: Black-necked Grebe, life-size 127. **Arndt Sven-Erik**/Arterra Picture Library/Alamy Stock Photo: White-tailed Eagle, immature 132. **WILDLIFE GmbH**/Alamy Stock Photo: Golden Eagle, flying 135. **James Hager**/robertharding/Alamy Stock Photo: Rough-legged Buzzard, life-size 150. **Michele and Tom Grimm**/Alamy Stock Photo: Osprey, life-size 152. **Robert Bannister**/Alamy Stock Photo: Kestrel, male 154. **FLPA**/Alamy Stock Photo: Merlin, female flying 157. **Nature Picture Library**/Alamy Stock Photo: Arctic Skua, life-size 238. **Bill Coster**/Alamy Stock Photo: Great Skua, life-size 241. **Nature Picture Library**/Alamy Stock Photo: Turtle Dove, flying 293. **Mike Lane**/Alamy Stock Photo: Cuckoo, life-size 296. **pronature**/Alamy Stock Photo: Kingfisher, diving 311. **Sally Andrews**/Alamy Stock Photo: Green Woodpecker, female 314. **Erich Thielscher**/Alamy Stock Photo: Grey-headed Woodpecker, female 316. **Friedhelm Adam**/imageBROKER/Alamy Stock Photo: Grey-headed Woodpecker, male 316. **Dave Watts**/Alamy Stock Photo: Middle Spotted Woodpecker (left) 317. **tbkmedia.de**/Alamy Stock Photo: Middle Spotted Woodpecker (right) 317. **Duncan Usher**/Alamy Stock Photo: Great Spotted Woodpecker, flight 318. **FLPA**/Alamy Stock Photo: Lesser Spotted Woodpecker, male 320. **Horst Jegen**/imageBROKER/Alamy Stock Photo: Lesser Spotted Woodpecker, female 320. **FLPA**/Alamy Stock Photo: Red-backed Shrike, female 322. **INSADCO Photography**/Alamy Stock Photo: Penduline Tit, juvenile 352.

Useful websites

Birdlife International www.birdlife.org
British Ornithologists' Union (BOU) www.bou.org.uk
British Trust for Ornithology (BTO) www.bto.org
Dansk Ornitologisk Forening (DOF) (Denmark) www.dof.dk
Ligue pour la Protection des Oiseaux (LPO) (France) www.lpo.fr
Nature and Biodiversity Conservation Union (NABU) (Germany) www.nabu.de
Norwegian Ornithological Society (NOF) (Norway) www.birdlife.no
Royal Society for the Protection of Birds (RSPB) www.rspb.org.uk
Society for the Protection of Birds (VBN) (Netherlands) www.vogelbescherming.nl
Swedish Ornithological Society (SOF) (Sweden) www.sofnet.org
Wildfowl and Wetlands Trust www.wwt.org.uk
The Wildlife Trusts www.wildlifetrusts.org

Recommended reading

Mullarney, K., Svennson, L. and Zetterstrom, D. (2009). *Collins Bird Guide*. HarperCollins.
Sterry, P. and Stancliffe, P. (2015). *Collins BTO Guide to British Birds*. HarperCollins.